THE GUINNESS BOOK OF

HUMOROUS ANECDOTES

THE GUINNESS BOOK OF

HUMOROUS ANECDOTES

NIGEL REES

GUINNESS PUBLISHING

This Publication copyright © Guinness Publishing Ltd., 1994
33 London Road, Enfield, Middlesex.

'Guinness' is a registered trade mark of Guinness
Publishing Ltd.

Designed by Stonecastle Graphics Ltd

Typeset by Ace Filmsetting Ltd., Frome, Somerset.
Printed and bound in Great Britain by The Bath Press.

A catalogue record for this book is available from the British
Library.

ISBN 0–85112–792–4

INTRODUCTION

We all know what an anecdote is when we hear one but defining what we mean by the word is not so easy. And I am not going to strain myself trying. Safe to say, an anecdote is a story – purporting to be a factual account – of some incident or situation which is revelatory (to some degree) about the person or persons about whom it is told. Indeed, it is possible that in an anecdote about a named person we get nearer to the real man or woman than we do in pages of biography or autobiography. Yes, even if the anecdote does not have a word of literal truth in it.

So, an anecdote does not have to be true? No, I don't think it does. An anecdote, probably, contains – more often than not – considerable exaggeration, if not plain falsehood. But the mere fact of its telling is significant. By its very existence, the anecdote is apparently answering a need in people, who know or observe the subject of the story, to make a telling point about him or her. So if, at times, my choice of stories shades into gossip and trivia, then so be it.

Does an anecdote have to be humorous? Well, it all depends what you mean by the word 'humorous'. There are a few anecdotes in this book which, I guarantee, will *not* produce thigh-slapping merriment. They may not even provoke the flicker of a hint of a smile. But they are 'humorous' in the sense that they tell us something of the disposition and character of the people involved.

In that case, is it possible to distinguish between an anecdote and a joke? Yes, it is. The only thing is, I am not inclined to do so very often. Broadly speaking, however, I could say that an anecdote concerns a specific, named person. But as I have chosen to include similar material about unnamed groups of people, should I not more properly refer to these anecdotes as jokes? Perhaps. Yet whereas a joke does not have to be revelatory or descriptive – it may simply be funny or silly – some jokes which *are* interesting or entertaining about people deserve to be called anecdotes. And so they are included.

The anecdotes in this book are presented in alphabetical order according to subject. Interleaved are special sections devoted to the following groups of people:

ACCOUNTANTS
ACTORS
ADVERTISERS
AIRLINE OPERATORS
AIRLINE PILOTS
ANTI-ENGLISH PEOPLE
ARISTOCRATS
ARTISTIC TYPES
BEREAVED PEOPLE
BIBLIOPHILES
BISHOPS
BLURB WRITERS
BORES
BOX-OFFICE PERSONNEL
BROADCASTERS
BUILDERS
BUS PASSENGERS
CHILDREN
CINEMA-GOERS
CIVIL SERVANTS
CLERGY
COMEDIANS
COMMENTATORS
CRITICS
DEAD PEOPLE
DEBATERS
DIPLOMATS
EDUCATIONISTS
ELDERLY PEOPLE
EMBARRASSED PEOPLE

ENGLISH PEOPLE
ENVIRONMENTALISTS
EXCUSE-MAKERS
FILM PEOPLE
GENTLEMEN
HONEYMOONERS
HOSTS AND HOSTESSES
HYGIENISTS
HYMNOLOGISTS
INDEXERS
IRISH PEOPLE
JEWISH PEOPLE
JOURNALISTS
JUDGES
LANDLADIES (THEATRICAL)
LAPLANDERS
LAWYERS
LINGUISTS
LIVERPUDLIANS
LOVERS
MALAPROPS
MOTHERS-IN-LAW
NAME-DROPPERS
NEIGHBOURS
NEWSREADERS
NUNS
OPERA SINGERS
OVERHEARERS
OXFORD PEOPLE
PARENTS

POLICE PERSONS
POLITICIANS
PROFESSORS
PUBLIC-RELATIONS
    PRACTITIONERS
PUBLISHERS
PUNSTERS
QUOTERS
RADIO LISTENERS
RUMOURISTS
SAILORS
SCOTS
SEX OBJECTS
SHOPPERS
SPEECH-MAKERS
STUTTERERS
TEACHERS
TELEVISION VIEWERS
THEATRE-GOERS
TOURISTS
TRANSCRIBERS
TRANSLATORS
TRAVELLERS
VICTIMS
WAITERS
WEATHER FORECASTERS
WELL-MANNERED PEOPLE
THE WELSH
WRITERS

There is also a thorough index at the end of the book. This is designed to show where named people appear in other people's anecdotes. It is especially designed, however, to help readers find suitable anecdotes for their own purposes. Hence, keyword entries guide the story-hunter towards specific subjects and themes.

The mother of all anecdote books (or perhaps I should say the mother-in-law of all joke books) is *Joe Miller's Jests*, first published in 1739, the year after the famous comedian died. It was compiled by a man called John Mottley and included the kind of jokes that the eponymous Miller had liked to tell. Things being the way they often are, it turned into something of a back-handed compliment, as a 'Joe Miller' became the nickname for a joke that has so many whiskers on it that it must be old enough to have appeared in the jest book.

I think the first time I registered that people kept joke books for their own use and amusement (let alone the type intended for publication) was when I was reading the diaries of Nicholas Blundell (1669–1737), a village squire from my native heath near Liverpool. Published by the Record Society of Lancashire and Cheshire in three volumes (1968–72), these were the rather factual listings of a most meticulous man. I was intrigued by the sheer volume of his record-keeping. In addition to his day-to-day diaries, Blundell kept half-a-dozen different record books. He had a disbursement book to keep track of his spending ('one penny for a mousetrap', and that sort of thing), a letter book full of drafts and copies, a prescription book recording remedies and medicines, and especially an anecdotes and jokes book (though he did not call it that).

This recorded over five hundred stories which Blundell had heard related at inns, on the bowling green, or at after-dinner gatherings. It also contained instructions for performing a number of tricks and card games. I have never actually seen this book, as it was not published with the other papers, but Frank Tyrer, who edited the diaries, told me that quite a few of the stories were bawdy, though the only one he could remember off hand was not:

In some village, they wanted a new priest. The old one had died and they wanted a new one, so two men were called up to be interviewed. One of them was named 'Adam' and the other was named 'Lowe'. Now, Mr Lowe was called upon to preach his trial sermon in the morning and he took for his text, 'Adam, where art thou?' Mr

Adam preached in the evening, but for his text he chose, 'Lo, I am with you always' . . .

It was shortly after this (in the early 1970s) – and possibly inspired by what I had been told of Nicholas Blundell's little jottings – that I, too, began to write down jokes and anecdotes as and when I heard them. This means that I now have a pretty good idea of when I first encountered a humorous story. But, in a sense, these dates are only of academic interest. It is a truism that there are no new jokes – or that there are only, say, two hundred basic jokes which get endlessly rejigged and recycled – but, particularly with the anecdotal type of joke, there is a certain fascination in attempting to pin down a first appearance or occurrence.

When my BBC Radio programme *Quote...Unquote* began in 1976, I had an additional need to keep track of the humorous material that was contributed by my guests and sent in by listeners. The dividing line between joke and anecdote and quotation was often blurred. Tellers of anecdotes were – and still are – famously loose with the facts and often shamelessly promiscuous with regard to attribution. But, what the hell? A story is a story is a story.

Still, my records have proved invaluable in compiling this book, in that it is sometimes possible to trace the way a story has developed in the telling over the years, to point to possible origins, and to pin down, at least for a moment, a subject that otherwise flaps about like a tent in a hurricane.

I have to admit that it is a pretty pointless form of scholarship but it is curiously interesting to come across early examples and old forms of jokes and anecdotes which people tend to relate as though they have just been minted recently.

When little books of humour come to be catalogued at the British Library or at the Library of Congress in America – the data is usually on the page following the title page – they often end up described as containing 'English wit and humour' or 'bulls, colloquial' or 'anecdotes, facetiae, etc.'

'Facetiae', curious word, means 'pleasantries, witticisms' – which is descriptive enough, although there is a secondary meaning, in bookselling, which is 'pornography'. Which is by the by, as what I am going to examine next is the question 'Where *do* jokes and anecdotes come from?'

Normally, I would say that such a question was impossible to answer. An anecdote about a famous person may begin life in gossip and tales told by acquaintances, colleagues or mere observers. Pure jokes, on the other hand, seem to arise spontaneously in more than one place at a time. Those places and the moment of birth are usually impossible to pinpoint. It is as if jokes are embedded in the language waiting for the right circumstances – the context, the arrangement of the words in a sentence – for them to burst forth in a form of spontaneous combustion.

Oddly, however, what happens to jokes and anecdotes *after* their conception follows more of a pattern. The anecdote may become detached from its original inspiration and be applied to someone completely new. Rather as with quotations, there is a tendency for an anecdote to become attached to a more famous person, simply because the person is more famous. And so anecdotes become subjected to the same pressures as pure jokes. They get distorted in the retelling. They are fathered upon unlikely subjects. They get worn out.

Especially if they are useful. Anecdotes or jokes which can be used to make a point, if not also to adorn a passage of spoken or written prose, are always in demand. That is why the present collection sets out to be a really useful anecdote book. It may be read simply for enjoyment but it can also be set to many a task.

There is a sense in which we are now living in the Age of the Anecdote. The rise of the 'professional personality', who is 'famous for being famous' and who may only exist when sprawling on the sofas of TV chat shows, has created a requirement for the tasty, bite-sized chunk of biography or autobiography. All human life has to be boiled down to a pithy parable that can be communicated by researcher to host and extracted from guest before studio audience, followed by a laugh and a round of applause.

That is the down side of anecdotalia, but it is not the end of the world. It is also not particularly new, though an odd modern phenomenon is the person – I am thinking of a former TV chat-show host here – who is unable to talk in any other form except the anecdote, even off-screen. Telling tales are trotted out in an apparently inexhaustible stream.

But compulsive anecdote-telling was noticed long ago when Isaac Disraeli remarked in his *Curiosities of Literature* (1839):

> Among my earliest literary friends, two distinguished themselves by their anecdotical literature: James Petit Andrews, by his 'Anecdotes, Ancient and Modern', and William Seward, by his 'Anecdotes of Distinguished Persons'. These volumes were favourably received, and to such a degree that a wit of that day, and who is still a wit as well as poet, considered that we were far gone in our 'Anecdotage'.

Isaac Disraeli's son Benjamin made use of this term in his novel *Lothair* (1870): 'When a man fell into his anecdotage it was a sign for him to retire from the world.' (The word 'anecdotage' in a less critical sense had been used by De Quincey in 1823 simply to describe anecdotes collectively.)

Suffice it to say that there is a long – I won't say 'honourable' – tradition of anecdote-collecting and retelling. In the 16th century, John Aubrey the 'antiquary' was little more than an anecdotalist. In the 19th century, the industry began. At the end of the 20th century, there is no sign of any diminution in people's enthusiasm for the form.

Because I was keen to produce a book that was not too heavy to handle, **The Guinness Book of Humorous Anecdotes** restricts itself, with a very few exceptions, to anecdotes of the 20th century (in so far as it is possible to date the origins of some of them). On the other hand, the amount of information about sources and the general 'foot-notoriety' is unusual in a work of this type.

The anecdote book compiler is under two foolish pressures. He will be criticized if he includes too many old chestnuts. Just as surely, he will be criticized for his omissions. Undaunted, I have pursued a policy of only including an old favourite if I felt I had something useful or interesting to say about it. At the same time, I have tried to concentrate on introducing less familiar examples of anecdotes involving the old war-horses of such collections (Dorothy Parker, Sir Thomas Beecham, and so on). Having said that, I have also reserved the right not to abide by these conditions as and when the mood takes me . . .

I am most grateful to the hundreds of people who have told me these stories in one form or another over the years. Their names are attached to the individual entries. Donald Hickling has again proved a stalwart provider of information, especially about some of the more marginal names mentioned in the course of the book. My thanks as always to him.

So many anecdotes have arisen from discussions before, during and after BBC Radio *Quote...Unquote* programmes – though not always actually broadcast on them – that I have decided not to mention this provenance every single time. Rather to my surprise, I now appreciate that my programme is not just about quotations. Its near twenty-year-old archive is equally a national treasury of anecdote. It is time now to open the doors and make the riches more generally available . . .

A

George ABBOTT

(1887–) American playwright, producer and director. He was still at work on Broadway in his hundredth year.

—— 1 ——

When an actor, no doubt under the influence of The Method, was agonizing over his 'motivation' and asked this director, 'Just *why* do I cross the stage? Why, why?', Abbott told him: 'To pick up your pay check'.

Retold by Mark Steyn on BBC Radio *Quote... Unquote* (1990). *The Faber Book of Anecdotes* (1985) ascribes it to Noël Coward, without offering a source.

ACCOUNTANTS

—— 2 ——

In about 1979, I received a letter from an aspiring anthologist who had been commissioned to write a book on the subject of the humour of accountancy – a potentially slim volume, if ever there was one. I replied that the only two accountancy jokes I knew were a secret between me and the Inland Revenue. I don't think the book was ever published. However . . .

—— 3 ——

When accountants are asked for the result of adding one and two, the following may occur. A newly qualified accountant may need to refer to senior partners to see if there is a previous ruling on what the answer might be. A long-established accountant may take a year to arrive at an answer and will be unable to explain how it was derived. A professional accountant may respond with a question: 'What sort of figure did you have in mind, sir?'

This story was told in a letter to *The Times* (19 September 1990) from L. Dorman.

—— 4 ——

According to a writer in *Time* Magazine, accountancy is 'a profession whose idea of excitement is sharpening a bundle of No. 2 pencils . . .'

From *Time* Magazine (19 April 1993).

—— 5 ——

A wealthy Wall Street financier was famous for his numerical skills – he could take in the most complicated balance sheet at one glance. Trained as an accountant, he would come to his office every day, open a wall safe behind his desk, take out a small piece of tightly rolled paper, look at it, then place it back in the safe.

When the financier died, his executive assistant was naturally very interested to know what was written on that slip of paper. He gained access to the safe, took out the paper, and unrolled it. Written in the financier's own handwriting were these words: 'Debit is on the left, Credit is on the right.'

Told to me by Charles G. Francis (1993).

—— 6 ——

Did you hear about the accountant who went in for his annual medical check-up and took his wife along with him? While he was getting dressed afterwards, the doctor said to the wife, 'I don't like the look of him.'

She said, 'No, I don't either. But he's good to the kids.'

Told to me by Charles G. Francis (1993).

ACTORS

—— 7 ——

A certain actor was not going to be put out when he heard someone state that 'actors have to be *born*'. He said, 'I looked up my birth certificate and I found I was all right.'

Told by Gemma O'Connor on BBC Radio *Quote...Unquote* (1988).

—— 1 ——

Then there was the actor who put in his will that he wanted to be cremated and ten per cent of his ashes thrown in his agent's face.

Told by Larry Adler (1976).

—— 2 ——

It was said of an actor much given to self-aggrandisement and who 'looked the part' – whatever that was: 'He's like an explorer who has never been anywhere.'

Source unknown.

—— 3 ——

In answer to the question much puzzled over by Shakespearean scholars, 'Did Hamlet actually sleep with Ophelia?', an old actor-manager is said to have replied, 'In our company – *always!*'

Related by Sir Cedric Hardwicke in *A Victorian in Orbit* (1961). Peter Hay in *Broadway Anecdotes* (1989) identifies the actor specifically as John Barrymore.

—— 4 ——

One Saturday night, the actor playing the lead in Shakespeare's *Richard III* had taken rather too much drink with a fellow cast member prior to the evening performance. This fact communicated itself to the audience when he came on swaying like a ship at sea. Someone shouted, 'Get off – you're drunk!' At which the actor, steadying himself, replied: 'Who, me? Drunk? Just wait till you see Buckingham!'

Related by Sir Cedric Hardwicke in *A Victorian in Orbit* (1961). Sometimes told as though involving Wilfred Lawson, a noted tippler, though he does not appear to have played either part.

—— 5 ——

When the actor playing Jeff Arnold in Charles Chilton's BBC radio serial *Riders of the Range* warned his companions that they were in danger of being trampled underfoot by a 'horde of wild hearses', he was apparently the only actor who didn't crack up. He had to carry the show (live) for the next few minutes while the others collected themselves.

Letter from F. H. Little, Swansea (22 August 1990). The series was broadcast from 1949 to 1953.

—— 6 ——

Two actors met in the Haymarket, London, and one said to the other, 'Where have you been?' 'I've been away . . . but I've been away so long some people think I'm dead.' 'Oh, surely not,' said the first, 'not if they look closely enough.'

Told by Sir Anthony Quayle on BBC Radio *Quote ... Unquote* (1985).

—— 7 ——

Osgood Perkins, the American character actor, was appearing in a long-running melodrama during which he had to stab another in the last act with a stiletto-type letter opener. One day, the props man forgot to put the knife on the table and there was no other murder implement to hand. Instead of throttling his victim, Perkins apparently kicked him up the backside. The man fell down dead. Perkins turned to the audience and said: 'Fortunately, the toe of my boot was poisoned!'

Told to Richard Burton by Stanley Donen and recorded by Burton in his diary for 16 October 1968 (and printed in Melvyn Bragg, *Rich: The Life of Richard Burton*, 1988). But compare the story about Donald Wolfit 198:5.

ADVERTISERS

—— 8 ——

One of the great pioneers and practitioners of advertising was J. Walter Thompson (born 1847). Travelling one blustery day on 'the El' (the elevated railway in Chicago), Commodore Thompson found himself next to a shabby, grubby, burly fellow, carrying a large sandwich board. The sandwich board touted a local restaurant on the front and on the back, a good place to get a haircut. Finally, the man spoke to Thompson: 'Hi, I'm just going to work. I'm in advertising, you know. What do you do?'

Shifting in his seat, the Commodore replied that he, too, was in advertising. With a conspiratorial smile, the board-man leaned toward the Commodore, nudged him with his elbow, and said, 'Ain't it hell when the wind blows?'

Told to me by Charles G. Francis (1993).

——— 1 ———

Jerry Della Femina, an American advertising executive, likes to tell the story about the time he was working on the Panasonic account. Everybody was sitting around thinking about the Japanese electronics giant and trying to come up with a worthy slogan. Finally, he decided: 'What the hell, I'll throw a line to loosen them up . . . "The headline is: From Those Wonderful Folks Who Gave You Pearl Harbor."' This was followed by complete silence on the part of the client.

> In fact, Della Femina (born 1936) entitled a book *From Those Wonderful Folks Who Gave You Pearl Harbor* (1970).

——— 2 ———

Peter Marsh was a flamboyant presence on the British advertising scene in the early 1980s, appearing to win for the agency Allen, Brady and Marsh some of the most high-profile accounts. When the agency was pitching for the British Rail account, representatives of the client were summoned to Marsh's office for a meeting. They were appalled at what they found. The reception area had paper peeling off its walls, there were broken springs sticking out of the seats, and none of the ashtrays had been emptied. When the BR people approached the receptionist, she did not remove the cigarette from her mouth and continued to hold an involved personal conversation over the phone. After about twenty minutes of this – and amid mounting exasperation – the BR executives were just preparing to walk out, when in walked Peter Marsh. Gesturing about the reception area, he beamed: 'There you are, you see. You think we've got an image problem? Don't you see this is just how people see British Rail?'

The agency won the account.

> Told to me in March 1981 by a Guinness PR. (Marsh's agency also had the Guinness account for a while.)

——— 3 ———

The following advertisement is said to have appeared in a South African newspaper: 'Man of 38 wishes to meet woman of 30 owning a tractor. Please enclose picture of tractor . . .'

> According to *The Mail on Sunday* of 4 January 1987, this was an advertisement in *The Mountain Echo* of Himeville 'in Drakesburg Mountain', South Africa. (They probably meant 'Drakensberg mountains'.) But if it did ever appear in that newspaper, it was by no means original. Compare the slightly

earlier citation in a book called *Glad to Be Grey* by Peter Freedman, published in 1985: 'Young farmer with 100 acres would be pleased to hear from young lady with tractor. Please send photograph of tractor.' The source given for this was 'the personal columns of the *Evesham Admag*, 1977'.

In 1983, Ronnie Corbett or Ronnie Barker had used the same gag in one of their BBC comedy programmes (an edition featured on the video *The Best of The Two Ronnies*) – though here the context was that of a man visiting a psychiatrist and the prize was not a tractor but tickets for the Cup Final.

How far back can we take the matter beyond this? Well, Roger S. Windsor, writing to me from Arequipa, Peru, in 1988, made a confident bid for January 1963: 'I was in my final year of veterinary studies at the Royal Veterinary College in Edinburgh and we organized the Annual Conference of the Association of Veterinary Students of Great Britain and Ireland. At one of the formal lunches organized for the delegates, Arthur Smith was the after-lunch speaker. He was at the time captain of Scotland's rugby team and had recently returned from South Africa where he had captained the Lions. At the lunch he told the story of an advertisement in *The Rand Daily Mail* in which a man has advertised for a wife who had to be in possession of two tickets for the test. The advertisement ran, "Please send a photograph . . . of the tickets" . . .'

If nothing else, Mr Windsor's recollection takes the joke back to South Africa. Is that where it really started? And did such an ad ever appear in a paper there – or anywhere?

A curious parallel joke appeared in the obituary of Brigadier John Reed, founder of the Aldershot Military Museum, in *The Daily Telegraph* (12 March 1992). Apparently, the section of the museum devoted to the Canadian Army's connection with Aldershot displays a letter written to Vincent Massey, the Canadian High Commissioner in London (1935–46). It was from a woman who lived in the town. She wrote: 'A Canadian soldier on leave has stayed at my house and as a result both my daughter and myself are pregnant. Not that we hold that against your soldier, but the last time we saw him he took away my daughter's bicycle which she needs to go to work. Can you get him to return it?'

——— 4 ———

The man sitting next to Philip K. Wrigley on a flight to Chicago asked the multi-millionaire why he continued to advertise his chewing gum when it was far and away the most successful product in the field. Wrigley replied: 'For the same reason that the pilot keeps this plane's engines running even though we're already 30,000 feet in the air.'

> Told to me by Charles G. Francis (1993).

—— 1 ——

Between the wars, a type of fuel was on the market known as 'ethyl' (because it was derived from tetraethyl lead). For example, 'Esso Ethyl' was for sale in 1935. Despite, or because of, the less-than-exciting name, advertising copywriters were drafted in to come up with a slogan that was as dashing as the current rival, 'That's Shell – That Was!' All they could manage was, 'Flat Out – On Ethyl!' – which had to be rejected for reasons of decorum.

> This was told me by Malcolm Ross-Macdonald in a letter dated 5 October 1979. Subsequently I was told by another correspondent that it had never really reached the slogan stage: it was no more than the answer to the joke question, 'What's better than 50 mph on Shell?'
>
> A similar joke: in the 1960 US presidential election, John F. Kennedy quoted 'Stand Pat with McKinley' as an example of Republican reaction. So Richard Nixon countered with 'America Cannot Stand Pat' – until it was politely pointed out that he was married to a woman with that name. 'America Cannot Stand Still' was rapidly substituted. (The last is apocryphal but quoted in William Safire, *Before the Fall*, 1975.)

—— 2 ——

The following conversation was overheard in a northern supermarket: *He:* 'I say, what was the name of the teabags them monkeys talked about on the telly?' *She:* 'PG Tips.' *He:* 'I think we should get some – they spoke very highly of them.'

> I included this remark (sent to me by Mrs Joan Scott of Burton) in my book *Eavesdroppings* (1981), following its broadcast on BBC Radio *Quote... Unquote* (1980). It has become an oft-quoted example of advertising influence, or whatever. John A. Thornton of London SW11 sent me another version in 1992: 'I overheard a very English old lady in a smart chemist's shop in St James's, when offered the choice of two toothbrushes, say, "I will take that one; they speak very well of them in the advertisements."'
>
> And then I noticed in David Ogilvy's introduction to *Confessions of an Advertising Man* (1963): 'My father used to say of a product that it was "very well spoken of in the advertisements". I spend my life speaking well of products in advertisements.' So there.

—— 3 ——

Because the Scottish *Sunday Mail* was just about the only Sunday newspaper that was not imported from England, the Mirror Group's advertising agents came up with a slogan which, they felt, demonstrated the *Mail*'s ability to carry all the very latest news on its pages. The slogan was 'If it's going on, it's going in.' This served well for some months (in about 1983) but was quietly withdrawn when it was discovered that some local wits had been going round public houses applying the promotional stickers with the message 'If it's going on, it's going in' to contraceptive vending machines.

> Told to me by Ken Bruce in a letter (14 March 1985).

—— 4 ——

The Mercedes-Benz company once used an interesting but ambiguous slogan to promote its cars in Britain: 'Once you've driven one, you're unlikely to drive another.' One could think of other brands that might well use the same slogan, though not in that sense.

> Reported in *The Times* (June 1980).

—— 5 ——

When Margaret Thatcher became Leader of the Conservative Party in 1975, it wasn't long before the Young Conservatives organization came up with a slogan drawing attention to her sex. It was 'Put a woman on top for a change.' Originally 'Have a Woman on Top' (or 'F*** me, I'm a Tory'), it was distributed as a sticker at the Tory Party Conference in 1976. In 1979, it seems to have had some circulation as an official party slogan in the General Election that took Mrs Thatcher to Downing Street.

> Information (1984) from Rob Hayward MP who had been National Vice-Chairman of the YCs at the time. A much later re-write was: 'Get her off, she's hurting.'

—— 6 ——

The most famous unfortunate advertising juxtaposition appears to have occurred in about 1952–3 at Charing Cross Station, London. A billposter had obviously had great fun putting alongside each other one advert which had the headline 'VD' in very large letters and another advert with the slogan 'I got it at the Co-Op.'

> Letter from Brian Blackwood of Stevenage (23 February 1981). Others remember the second slogan as, 'You can always get it at the Co-Op'.

See also OGILVY 145:2–3.

James AGATE

(1877–1947) English dramatic critic who wrote a
nine-part diary/autobiography called *Ego*.

—— 1 ——

Agate considered that Lilian Braithwaite was 'the
wittiest woman in London' but, rather curiously, decided to say to her (when he found her
sitting alone in the Savoy Grill), 'My dear Lilian, I
have long wanted to tell you that in my opinion you
are the second most beautiful woman in London.' If
she was curious to know the identity of her superior,
he was going to award the first place to 'a beauty of
antique and challengeless fame'. But she was not
curious and replied: 'Thank you so much. I shall
cherish that, coming from our second-best dramatic
critic.'

Recounted by Agate in *Ego* (1935).

See also under TYNAN 185:3.

AIRLINE OPERATORS

—— 2 ——

The name of the German airline Lufthansa is not
an acronym. As Luftwaffe means 'air force', so
Lufthansa means 'air association'. This has not
prevented the invention of a sentence that could
give rise to such an acronym, viz.: 'Let Us F*** The
Hostesses And Not Say Anything.'

**I obtained this from a book that had been alluded
to by Godfrey Smith in his *Sunday Times* column
some time prior to 1983. Alas, I have quite forgotten what the book was. The acronym was broadcast
on BBC Radio *Quote...Unquote* (1983), using the
word 'fondle'.**

AIRLINE PILOTS

—— 3 ——

A failed Trappist monk attempted to hijack an
Aer Lingus flight to Heathrow. The plane's cap-
tain, Eddie Foley, calmly announced to passengers:
'I'm sorry, ladies and gentlemen, I would like to land

but there's a gentleman here who would prefer to go
to Le Touquet in France.'

From a report in *The Daily Mail* (4 May 1981).

—— 4 ——

Captain Moody of British Airways had to deal
with an unusual problem as his 747 ran into a
volcanic storm over southern Sumatra and plunged
25,000 feet. Said he, 'Ladies and gentlemen, this is
your captain speaking. We have a small problem. All
four engines have stopped. We are doing our
damnedest to get them working again. I trust you are
not in too much distress . . .'

**The crew managed to restart the engines. Quoted
in *The Sunday Express* (4 July 1982).**

Martin AMIS

(1949–) English author whose early success
tempted people to believe that his being the son of
another novelist, Kingsley Amis, had probably
been no hindrance.

—— 5 ——

In the late 1970s, there was a *New Statesman* competition in which readers were asked to provide
improbable titles for new books by famous authors.
One suggestion was '*My Struggle* by Martin Amis.'

Recalled in *The Observer* (4 July 1993).

Eamonn ANDREWS

(1922–87) Irish broadcaster. Originally a radio
boxing commentator, Andrews sweatily hosted
many editions of the British TV version of *This is
Your Life* and presided uneasily over *The Eamonn
Andrews Show*, an early chat show in the 1960s.

—— 6 ——

In the 1950s, Andrews was best known as the
chairman of the archetypal TV panel game *What's
My Line?* in which the panel had to guess contestants' jobs. In the British version of what was originally
an American show, the job still most remembered is
that of Mr R. Adams who appeared on 14 January
1952. He beat the panel before revealing that he was

a 'saggermakers' bottom knocker'. (A 'sagger' is a receptacle in which china is baked.)

Source: *The Television Annual* (c. 1954).

—— 1 ——

A journalist was writing a profile of the great broadcaster but encountered a dearth of anecdotal material. Accordingly, he phoned up a researcher on *This Is Your Life* and asked if there were any nice anecdotes about Eamonn.

'Er, no,' replied the researcher. 'You see, I don't think Eamonn would want to be involved in anything as risqué as an anecdote.'

A version of this story appears in Ned Sherrin, *Theatrical Anecdotes* (1991).

Julie ANDREWS

(1935–) English singer and actress.

—— 2 ——

After her great stage success as Eliza Doolittle in *My Fair Lady*, Julie Andrews was rejected in favour of Audrey Hepburn in the Warner Bros. film version of the musical. And this despite the fact that Hepburn's singing voice had to be dubbed. Andrews was thus available to go on and star in *Mary Poppins* for which she duly won an Academy Award. Collecting her Oscar she said, 'I'd like to thank all those who made this possible – especially Jack L. Warner.'

Recounted in Leslie Halliwell, *The Filmgoer's Book of Quotes* (1973).

Princess ANNE

(1950–) British Royal and sportswoman. Latterly known as the Princess Royal, though she probably still remains Princess Anne deep down inside.

—— 3 ——

So closely did the Princess become identified with horses that she was quoted on one occasion as having said, 'When I appear in public people expect me to neigh, grind my teeth, paw the ground and swish my tail.'

Quoted in Noël St George, *Royal Quotes* (1981).

Walter ANNENBERG

(1908–) US businessman (owner of *TV Guide*) and, briefly, diplomat. Awarded an honorary knighthood in 1976.

—— 4 ——

As the newly arrived US Ambassador to the Court of St James, Annenberg went to present his credentials to the Queen in 1969. Unfortunately for him, a film crew was hovering at his elbow making the TV film *Royal Family*, so millions were able to hear the peculiarly orotund remarks he thought appropriate for the occasion. When asked by the Queen how he was enjoying his official residence, he admitted to feeling: 'Some of the discomfiture as a result of a need for, uh, elements of refurbishment and rehabilitation.'

Source: the first *Quote...Unquote* book (1978).

ANTI-ENGLISH PEOPLE

—— 5 ——

At the Commonwealth Parliamentary Conference in 1986, a Mr Hall representing the Turks and Caicos Islands had the delegates applauding and banging on the tables by saying, 'There was an Englishman and an Indian . . . And the Englishman was boasting that the sun really never did set on the British Empire. At which the Indian replied, "No, because God would never trust an Englishman in the dark."'

The *Guardian* (2 October 1986) correctly identified this an an 'old chestnut'. The original description of the British empire as one 'upon which the sun never sets' – i.e. one that, at its apogee, was so widespread that the sun was always shining on some part of it – was coined by 'John Wilson' (Christopher North) who wrote in *Noctes Ambrosianae*, No. 20 (April 1829) of: 'His Majesty's dominions, on which the sun never sets.'

The earliest appearance of the joke rejoinder I have come across is ascribed to 'Duncan Spaeth' (is this John Duncan Spaeth, the US educator?) in Nancy McPhee, *The Book of Insults* (1978) in the form: 'I know why the sun never sets on the British Empire: God wouldn't trust an Englishman in the dark.' During a visit to New York City by Prince Charles in June 1981, an Irish Republican placard was photographed bearing the words, 'The Sun Never Sets on the British Empire Because God Doesn't Trust the British in the Dark.'

—— 1 ——

An American visitor to England was driving through London with his English host. The host said, 'I must stop and clean the *windscreen*.' The American replied, 'You mean the *windshield*. We Americans invented the automobile, and we call it a wind*shield*.'

To which the Englishman said, 'That's quite true. But just remember who invented the *language*.'

Told by Edward E. Whitacre Jr in a speech at the University of Missouri, St Louis (April 1992).

ARISTOCRATS

—— 2 ——

The Tory Party is the cream of society – thick and rich and full of clots.

This comment appeared in my *Graffiti 4* as from Cambridge, and is not entirely original. Samuel Beckett, the playwright, once taught briefly at Campbell College in Belfast. When told he was teaching the cream of Ulster, he replied, 'Yes, rich and thick.' (*The Times* diary, 21 February 1948.)

—— 3 ——

Definition of 'upper crust': 'a lot of crumbs held together with dough'.

This appeared in *Pass the Port Again* (1980), having previously appeared as a graffito from the University of Newcastle in my *Graffiti Lives OK* (1979).

—— 4 ——

In the course of a routine house-to-house inquiry in Belgravia, a highly-placed old lady was told of the murder of Sandra Rivett, the nanny it is believed Lord Lucan mistakenly killed instead of his wife. 'Oh dear, what a pity,' the old lady said, 'Nannies are so hard to come by these days.'

Report in *The Sunday Times* Magazine (8 June 1975).

—— 5 ——

A patrician lady in her country house invited an extremely boring and loquacious gentleman to come and pay her a visit. He ended up trapping her in a corner and talking and talking and talking to her.

After a while, she said, 'How very interesting, my dear. Why don't you go away and *write it all down*?'

Told by Dr John Rae on BBC Radio *Quote... Unquote* (1983).

George ARLISS

(1868–1946) English stage actor who became immensely successful on the screen, becoming known as 'King of Hollywood'.

—— 6 ——

Having become involved in some court case, Arliss was in the witness box and was asked by counsel, 'Would it be true to say, Mr Arliss, that you are the world's greatest actor?' Arliss replied, 'Yes', and then turned, with a smile of apology to the judge, and added: 'Forgive me, my Lord, but I *am* on oath.'

Told by Basil Boothroyd (1984).

John ARLOTT

(1914–91) English journalist and radio cricket commentator.

—— 7 ——

At Lord's, a South African googly bowler named 'Tufty' Mann was tying a Middlesex tail-end batsman named George Mann into such knots that the crowd was reduced to laughter. When it occurred for the fourth time in a single over, Arlott, apparently without a moment's thought, reported, 'So what we are watching here is a clear case of Mann's inhumanity to Mann.'

Reported in *The Daily Mail* (3 September 1980). The phrase 'Man's inhumanity to man' appears in a poem by Robert Burns called 'Man was made to mourn', though the thought that lies behind it is, of course, a very old one.

ARTISTIC TYPES

—— 1 ——

Two London taxi drivers were having a heated dispute. Said one, 'You know what you are, don't you? – pretentious!' And the other adopted a tone of hurt pride. *'Pretentious?'* he replied. *'Moi?'*

> Told by Anna Ford on BBC Radio *Quote ... Unquote* (1979).

Herbert Henry ASQUITH

> (1852–1928) (later 1st Earl of Oxford and Asquith) British Liberal Prime Minister and noted tippler. His nicknames included 'Squiffy' and 'P. J.' (for Perrier-Jouët).

—— 2 ——

At a public meeting, a heckler demanded of Asquith, 'Why did you murder those workmen at Featherstone in 1893?' He replied calmly, 'It was not 1893, it was '92.'

> Quoted in *Geoffrey Madan's Notebooks* (ed. Gere & Sparrow, 1981). A slightly different version is given in Kenneth Rose, *Superior Person* (1969).

Margot ASQUITH

> (1865–1945) (later Countess of Oxford and Asquith) English second wife of H. H. Asquith and noted for her curious, occasionally inspired, way with words. Her *Autobiography* (1922) embarrassed almost everybody.

—— 3 ——

In the 1930s, Lady Asquith was still delivering her opinions on all and sundry and at full volume. Her wrath fell upon Lord Dawson, King George V's doctor. Said she: 'My dear old friend King George V always told me he would never have died but for that vile doctor, Lord Dawson of Penn.'

> This remark was made by Lady Asquith several times in her old age, but especially to Lord David Cecil (and recorded first by Mark Bonham-Carter in his introduction to *The Autobiography of Margot Asquith*, 1962 edition). It turns out to be not so preposterous as might first have been thought. In

December 1986, Dawson's biographer suggested in *History Today* that the doctor had in fact hastened the King's departure with lethal injections of morphine and cocaine at the request of the Queen and the future Edward VIII. Dawson's notes revealed that the death was induced at 11 p.m. not only to ease his pain but also to enable the news to make the morning papers, 'rather than the less appropriate evening journals'. *The Times* was advised that important news was coming and to hold back publication. So Dawson of Penn *might* have had a hand in the King's death, though quite how George V communicated his view of the matter to Margot Asquith is not known.

—— 4 ——

On a visit to the United States, Lady Asquith met Jean Harlow. The film actress inquired whether the name of the Countess was pronounced 'Margo' or 'Margott'. '"Margo",' replied the Countess, 'the "T" is silent – as in "Harlow".'

> I have always had a lingering doubt about this story as I have never come across a reputable source. I heard it first in about 1968. It did not appear in print until T. S. Matthews's *Great Tom* in 1973. Then, in about 1983, I was given a much more convincing version of its origin. Margot *Grahame* (1911–82) was an English actress who, after stage appearances in Johannesburg and London, went to Hollywood in 1934. Her comparatively brief career as a film star included appearances in *The Informer*, *The Buccaneer* and *The Three Musketeers*, in the mid-1930s.
>
> It was when she was being built up as a rival to the likes of Harlow (who died in 1937) that Grahame herself apparently later claimed the celebrated exchange had occurred. She added that it was not intended as a put-down. She did not realize what she had said till afterwards.
>
> Grahame seems a convincing candidate for speaker of the famous line. I believe she *did* say it and, when her star waned, people attributed the remark to the other, better-known and more quotable source.

Violet ASQUITH

> (1887–1969) (later Lady Violet Bonham Carter, later Baroness Asquith of Yarnbury) Daughter of H. H. Asquith by his first wife. English Liberal politician and publicist.

—— 5 ——

Her father's great predecessor as a Liberal Prime Minister was W. E. Gladstone who, most famously, was held up as an example to countless generations of children as the man who chewed each mouthful of food *32 times* before swallowing it. Lady Asquith recalled having had a meal with Gladstone when she was a little girl, at which she remembered he did no such thing. Quite the reverse, in fact: he *bolted* his food.

In the BBC TV programme *As I Remember* **(30 April 1967).**

—— 1 ——

Lady Asquith liked to tell a story about an Indian called Sir Beneval Rao who was in the jungle on a hunting expedition. After they had been out a few days, the Indian bearers laid down their burdens and refused to go a step further. Sir Beneval asked if they were tired. No, they replied, they were not in the least tired. 'But we must wait here at least twenty-four hours until our souls catch up with our bodies.'

Told on BBC TV, *As I Remember* **(30 April 1967). Lady Asquith added: 'You know, I sometimes wonder whether we ought not perhaps to do the same.'**

—— 2 ——

On her deathbed, Lady Asquith's last words were, 'I feel amphibious'.

'Isn't that wonderful – conveying that feeling of floating off,' commented Lord St John of Fawsley in *The Observer* **Magazine (24 January 1988). 'She never reached out lazily for the nearest words to hand but always perfectly judged them, even on her deathbed.'**

Fred ASTAIRE

(1899–1987) American dancer of genius; actor and singer, less so.

—— 3 ——

On arriving in Hollywood, Astaire had to undergo the usual screen test. The verdict? 'Can't act. Slightly bald. Can dance a little.'

Quoted by David Niven, *Bring On the Empty Horses* **(1975). Ned Sherrin's** *Theatrical Anecdotes* **(1991) has the additional information that the test was for RKO in 1933 and that the test report also stated: 'Enormous ears and bad chin-line [but] his charm is tremendous.'**

Nancy (Lady) ASTOR

(1879–1964) Garrulous American-born British politician, outspoken by few. The first woman to take her seat in the House of Commons.

—— 4 ——

Lady Astor, who was always preaching against the evils of drink, was doing this in the House of Commons one day when she said to the crowded chamber, 'Well, there's nothing I wouldn't do rather than let a glass of beer cross my lips. I'd do anything. Why, I'd even commit adultery.' A voice from the back benches said, 'And so would I!'

Quoted by Ludovic Kennedy on BBC Radio *Quote...Unquote* **(1983). Walter H. Brown of Weston-super-Mare wrote to me subsequently: 'I was of the opinion that her comment of "I would rather commit adultery" was made at a public political meeting at Plymouth and immediately a reply came from the back of the hall, "Who wouldn't?"'**
**   *Pass the Port Again* (1980) has the exchange involving a Cambridge academic called E. E. Genner rather than Lady Astor. In** *The Lyttelton Hart-Davis Letters* **(Vol. 3, 1981) in a letter dated 9 July 1958, George Lyttelton has: 'I prefer the perfectly true comment of – who was it? – who, when some teetotal ass said he would rather commit adultery than drink a glass of port, said, "So would we all, my dear L., so would we all."'**

—— 5 ——

At Ascot one year, Lady Astor told the Duke of Roxburghe, 'You are really becoming too grand for words . . . never leaving the royal stand. You might just as well be the court dentist.' To which Roxburghe retorted, 'If ever I do have to pull out the King's teeth, I shall certainly come to you for the gas.'

Told by Kenneth Rose in *King George V* **(1984).**

—— 6 ——

Canvassing for her first parliamentary seat in Plymouth, Lady Astor was allotted a senior naval officer as a minder, and together they went round knocking on doors. When they approached one house, the door was opened by a small girl.
'Is your mother in, dear?' Lady Astor demanded, grandly. 'No,' the girl replied, 'but she said if a lady came with a sailor, you was to use the upstairs room and leave half a crown on the table.'

Told to me by an anonymous correspondent (*c.* **1980).**

—— 1 ——

Sir John J. (Jakie) Astor described his last visit to his mother before she died. 'I sat beside her for a bit and then she opened her eyes and saw I was there. She looked me straight in the face and said, "Jakie, is it my birthday or am I dying?" – which was quite difficult to answer. So I said, "A bit of both, Mum".'

In John Grigg, *Nancy Astor: Portrait of a Pioneer* (1980). Her last word was 'Waldorf', uttered the day before she died.

Robert ATKINS

(1886–1972) English actor-manager

—— 2 ——

When Atkins founded the Regent's Park Open Air Theatre in 1933, with Sydney Carroll, the acting arena was made of lush turf imported from south London. On one occasion, Carroll stepped forward during the curtain calls – with the cast ranged behind him – and proudly informed the audience, 'Every sod on this stage comes from Richmond.'

Told by Michael Coveney in *The Observer* (21 July 1991).

—— 3 ——

Atkins's production of *Hamlet* was, on one occasion, notable for his loudly whispered stage directions to the cast. It was also clear when he himself had forgotten his lines. He would say, 'Couch me awhile and mark', shuffle down to the prompt corner for enlightenment, and carry on until the next uncertainty brought him back there again.

Recalled by Michael York in *Travelling Player* (1991). The line does actually occur in *Hamlet*, spoken by the Prince (V.i.222).

—— 4 ——

Atkins was rehearsing one of his open-air productions in Regent's Park with the cast all seated round him on the ground. When one young actress failed to pick up her cue, Atkins noted that she was sitting disconsolately with her head in her lap, and said: 'It's no good looking up your entrance, dear – you've missed it.'

Recounted by Ian McKellen on BBC Radio *Quote...Unquote* (1979).

—— 5 ——

Michael Bentine was playing Lorenzo in an Atkins production of *The Merchant of Venice* but Atkins decided that he looked too small. 'You've got to wear lifts,' Bentine was told, and accordingly wedges of cork, 2½-in thick, were put in his boots. The result was that he came on stage with his body thrown forward as though walking in a high wind. Said Atkins, 'Michael, you're supposed to come from Venice, not from bloody Pisa!'

Told by Michael Bentine on BBC Radio *Quote... Unquote* (1989). Oddly, Kitty Black in *Upper Circle* (1984), telling the same story, casts Bentine as Demetrius – in *A Midsummer Night's Dream* – and has Atkins say, 'You're supposed to come from Verona, my boy. Not bloody Pisa.' Meanwhile Ned Sherrin, *Theatrical Anecdotes* (1991), has it involving the *Dream*, Athens and Pisa. I'll stick to Bentine's own version.

—— 6 ——

Atkins once employed a young Canadian (or American) actor at the Open Air Theatre. The young actor went to Brighton for the day and forgot there was a matinée. When he got back to London for the evening performance, the other actors said, 'My goodness, are you for it!'

So, in fear and trembling, he presented himself in front of Atkins who had been walking up and down a lot between the matinée and the evening performance composing this speech. He looked at the young man and said: 'You come here from a foreign shore. We instruct you in the tongue that was Shakespeare's and Milton's. We give you God's green sward to walk upon. You treat me with base ingratitude, your fellow actors with grave discourtesy, your profession with something approaching contempt. There's only one word for you, laddie – you're a shit. Those are the gates!'

Told by Siân Phillips (1993).

Sir David ATTENBOROUGH

(1926–) English natural history broadcaster and TV executive.

—— 1 ——

When filming in Paraguay for *Zoo Quest*, Attenborough was told that it would be cheaper to *buy* a couple of horses rather than *hire* them. Besides, they were inexpensive, and could be set free when they were no longer required. On his return to London, Attenborough was faced with a formidable, desk-bound BBC administrator who had discovered the purchase among all the paperwork. 'The horses are clearly BBC property,' she insisted. In best army fashion, they therefore had to be 'accounted for', so where were they? Attenborough forestalled much further paperwork by saying conclusively, 'Madam, we ate them.'

Source: Leonard Miall, broadcast talk 'In at the Start', 1982. Also told in Paul Ferris, *Sir Huge*, 1990.

—— 2 ——

In 1976, the Queen decided to reward Attenborough for his many years of service producing Her Majesty's Christmas broadcasts. 'We must give a knighthood to that nice Mr Attenborough,' she told one of her flunkeys. Accordingly, in the next Honours List there duly appeared a knighthood for . . . David's brother, Richard.

This is a story 'which is sometimes told at Buckingham Palace', according to 'The Weasel' in *The Independent* Magazine (24 July 1993). True or not, there is one small error of detail in this version: David Attenborough did not start producing the Christmas broadcasts until much later. He was knighted – at last – in 1985.

A similar tale of confusion – at Downing Street rather than Buckingham Palace – is sometimes told concerning the award of honours to Harry H. Corbett, the actor in *Steptoe and Son*, and Harry Corbett of Sooty fame. It is suggested that the wrong one was given the award. However, as they were both awarded the OBE in the same New Year's Honours List in 1976, this is clearly not the case.

That this is not a recent problem is shown by the story of a supplier of fishing tackle called Thomas Hardy who was reputedly awarded the Order of Merit in advance of the distinguished novelist who received his OM in 1910.

Sir Richard ATTENBOROUGH

(1923–) English film actor and director and busy bee in most areas of popular culture. Often referred to as 'Dicky Darling'. Lord Attenborough from 1993.

—— 3 ——

When the film *Brighton Rock* was being launched in America, the New York distributor wired: 'ATTENBOROUGH'S NAME TOO BIG FOR BANNERS'. The producers of the film – the Boulting Brothers – wired back: 'GET BIGGER BANNERS'.

Reported in *The Sunday Telegraph* (22 August 1965).

—— 4 ——

In 1987, during the filming of *Cry Freedom*, Attenborough stood up before a crowd of 5,000 Zimbabwean extras and called them by a term of endearment they had seldom heard outside their homes: 'Darlings!' he cried, 'Look at *me*, darlings!'

Recounted in *The Independent* (14 November 1992)

—— 5 ——

Dicky Darling's propensity for blubbing – particularly when collecting awards – was parodied by the Monty Python team as early as 1972: '*[Dickie] gets out an onion and holds it to his eyes; tears pour out . . . Attenborough weeps profusely.*' *Spitting Image* later continued the lampooning, except that co-creator Roger Law stated in 1992 that Attenborough's puppet had hardly appeared at all in the previous two years. 'He stopped being a regular character,' Law explained, 'because the overuse of his tear mechanism began rotting the puppet.'

Reported in *The Independent* (14 November 1992).

Clement ATTLEE

(1883–1967) (later 1st Earl Attlee) British Labour prime minister. Bald, with a rarish prime ministerial moustache.

—— 1 ——

As Kenneth Harris has observed, Attlee's use of language was very much 'prep school'. He called people by their nicknames and used words like 'Rotten', 'Piffle' and 'Tripe'. He referred to one person as 'a good egg'.

Recounted by Harris in *The Times* (15 October 1967) and also in his biography of Attlee (1982).

—— 2 ——

Few thought he was even a starter
There were many who thought themselves smarter
But he ended PM, CH and OM
An Earl and a Knight of the Garter.

Attlee composed this little rhyme himself. Quoted in Kenneth Harris, *Attlee* (1982).

—— 3 ——

Shirley Williams was conscripted to pass a vote of thanks to Attlee – 'many, many years ago' – which was difficult because, 'He used to make very long and dull speeches – but he was a very fine man.' She said that when she had been working in the House of Commons as an assistant secretary, she had 'found this in a wastepaper basket'. It was a genuine poem written by Attlee when he was working in Limehouse in 1906:
In Limehouse, in Limehouse, before the break of
   day,
I hear the feet of many men that go upon their way.
That wander through the city,
The grey and cruel city,
Through streets that have no pity,
Through streets where men decay.

Quoted by Shirley Williams on BBC Radio *Quote...Unquote* (1982).

Winifred ATWELL

(1914–83) West Indies-born honky-tonk pianist.

—— 4 ——

Fred Russell, ventriloquist father of Val Parnell, when very old and almost blind liked to attend the rehearsal of his son's *Sunday Night at the London Palladium*. On one occasion after he had watched Winifred Atwell rehearsing her performance, Russell exclaimed about his son: 'He gets some extraordinary acts, he does. I've just seen a gorilla playing the piano.' Indeed, he could be forgiven for thinking so. The artistes used to rehearse in their street coats and Atwell had been wearing a big hairy overcoat.

Told to me by Roy Hudd (June 1984).

—— 5 ——

Atwell was one of the investors in the original production of Samuel Beckett's play *Waiting for Godot*.

Not a lot of people know that.

W. H. AUDEN

(1907–73) British-born American poet and writer.

—— 6 ——

Someone said of Auden, 'He didn't love God, he just fancied him.'

Anon., by 1983.

—— 7 ——

During his summer holidays in the 1930s, Auden liked to have a fire blazing in the sitting room if at all possible. On his bed, he would like to have two thick blankets and an eiderdown, with both his and Christopher Isherwood's overcoats on the top.

If the bedclothes were too light, Auden would use anything he could lay his hands on to provide sufficient weight for his slumbers. Staying with one family, he put the bedroom carpet on his bed. Staying with another, he took down the bedroom curtains and used these as extra blankets. Another time it was the stair carpet. Once he was discovered in the morning sleeping beneath (among other things) a larged framed painting.

Recalled in Charles Osborne, *W. H. Auden* (1980), and Humphrey Carpenter, *W. H. Auden* (1981).

AUDIENCES

See CINEMA-GOERS and THEATRE-GOERS.

Warren AUSTIN

(1877–1962) American diplomat.

—— 1 ——

In a debate on the Middle East question, as US delegate to the United Nations, Austin exhorted warring Jews and Arabs to 'sit down and settle their differences like Christians'.

From Fadiman & Van Doren, *The American Treasury* (1955).

Alan AYCKBOURN

(1939–) Prolific English playwright. Spends much of his time in Scarborough.

—— 2 ——

Talking of the odd things that bereaved people do and say (*à propos* his play *Absent Friends*), Ayckbourn recalled what one member of the audience had said coming out of a play of his at Scarborough: 'Oh, Mr Ayckbourn, I haven't laughed so much since my father died!'

Told to me by Ayckbourn, 17 May 1974. This was the occasion – an interview for the BBC Radio programme *Kaleidoscope* – when proceedings were interrupted by heavy banging noises from outside the studio in Broadcasting House, London. The builders making the noise were asked to desist. We were told they could not do so unless we obtained the required 'knocking chit' from the clerk of the works.
Incidentally, 'I haven't laughed so much since my husband died' is also said to have been 'a compliment from a woman to Victor Borge' – according to Frank S. Pepper, *Handbook of 20th Century Quotations*, 1984.

B

Francis BACON

(1909–92) Irish artist noted for producing distinctive paintings of a butcher's-shop tendency.

—— 1 ——

Bacon delighted in anonymity – though his face was as recognizable as his painting style – and was happy to mingle with those who hadn't a clue who he was or of his eminence. In a Soho pub, he was offered work doing up an old house by someone who had heard he was a painter.

From *The Independent* (29 April 1992).

—— 2 ——

Before Bacon became rich, he was taken out to lunch by the composer Lionel Bart who, at that particular time, was still in the money. During the meal, Bacon was aware (as who wouldn't be?) of Bart's diving under the table every so often and emerging after a while with a white powdery substance adhering to his upper lip.

At the end of the meal, Bacon saw that Bart had left behind a small bag of this white substance and decided to pick it up, reasoning that it was probably worth a good deal of money. Bacon told his friend John Edwards that this would get them into any nightclub in London. So indeed it did. But the doorman who had accepted the gift and had wafted them into one club soon came hurtling over to their table and ejected them.

The doorman's face, like Bart's, showed traces of white powder but his nostrils also had the appearance of being glued together. It transpired that Bacon had given him the dental fixative that Bart had been using following an operation.

A version of this story was told by Stan Gebler Davies in *The Independent* (8 May 1993).

Bill BAILEY

—— 3 ——

Who was the person of whom it was sung, 'Bill Bailey, Won't You Please Come Home?' Well, the song was written by Hughie Cannon in 1902 and one version is that it was about a wandering eccentric called Bill Bailey of the Coconut Grove, Singapore, whose refusal to leave his celebrated bar led to his immortalization in the popular song.

Source: James Morris, *Farewell the Trumpets* (1978). The song is already being referred to familiarly in a *Punch* cartoon caption in the edition of 12 October 1904.

Arthur BALFOUR

(1848–1930) (later 1st Earl Balfour) British Conservative prime minister. A rare bachelor PM, he occasionally arrived at Cabinet meetings on a bicycle.

—— 4 ——

In a routine letter to the Foreign Office, the British Minister in Athens reported that the monks in some of the monasteries in northern Greece had allegedly violated their monastic vows. Unfortunately, due to a typing error, 'cows' appeared in the letter instead of 'vows'. On receiving this report, Balfour, then Foreign Secretary, pencilled a note in the margin, 'Appears to be a case for a Papal Bull.'

Source: letter from Mr L. Road of Bromley, Kent, in BBC Radio *Quote...Unquote* (1979). In Lewis Broad, *Sir Anthony Eden* (1955), the marginal comment is said to have been written by Lord Curzon.

Tallulah BANKHEAD

(1903–68) American actress with a manly voice.

—— 1 ——

Tallulah's manner was rather overwhelming, and she could wear one out, to say the least. Howard Dietz commented: 'A day away from Tallulah is like a month in the country.'

Recalled by Dietz in his book *Dancing in the Dark* (1974).

—— 2 ——

She is said to have declared to a lover, 'I'll come and make love to you at five o'clock. If I'm late, start without me.'

Quoted in Ted Morgan, *Somerset Maugham* (1980).

—— 3 ——

A man came up to her at a party and exclaimed, effusively, 'Tallulah! I haven't seen you for 41 years!' She replied, deadpan, 'I thought I told you to wait in the car.'

Told by Kenneth Williams on BBC Radio *Quote... Unquote* (1979).

—— 4 ——

Of Bankhead as Shakespeare's Cleopatra in 1937, critic John Mason Brown wrote, 'She barged down the Nile last night and sank . . . As the serpent of the Nile she proves to be no more dangerous than a garter snake.'

Quoted in *Current Biography* (1941).

—— 5 ——

When Bankhead played Shakespeare's Cleopatra in a lavish New York production, Orson Welles was appearing in a much simpler version of *Julius Caesar* elsewhere in the city. When told that the Welles production had cost only $6,000, Bankhead exclaimed, 'Six thousand dollars! That's less than one of my f****** breast-plates!'

Told by Frank Brady in *Citizen Welles* (1989).

—— 6 ——

Apparently cut by a man she knew – in the foyer of the Savoy Hotel, London – Bankhead called outto him in a loud voice, 'Don't you recognize me with my clothes on?'

Told by Glenda Jackson (1983). Brendan Gill in *Tallulah* (1973) has it said to a peer.

—— 7 ——

Outside the theatre one night she encountered a group from the Salvation Army, tambourines as always well to the fore. She promptly dropped a $50 dollar bill into one of the tambourines, saying, 'I know what a perfectly ghastly season it has been for you Spanish dancers.'

Told by Glenda Jackson on BBC Radio *Quote... Unquote* (1983). Also recounted in Dorothy Herrmann, *With Malice Towards All* (1980).

—— 8 ——

Bankhead said, 'I tell you cocaine isn't habit-forming and I know because I've been taking it for years.'

Written by Bankhead herself in *Tallulah* (1952). Also quoted in Lillian Hellman, *Pentimento* (1974).

—— 9 ——

Bankhead went to see Maurice Maeterlinck's play *Aglavaine and Selysette* on 3 January 1922 in the company of Alexander Woollcott. She told him: 'There's less in this than meets the eye.'

Quoted in Alexander Woollcott, *Shouts and Murmurs* (1922). But it is an old formula. In his journal for 1 May 1783, James Boswell attributed a version to Richard Burke, the son of Edmund: 'I suppose *here* less is meant than meets the ear.'

Isobel BARNETT

(1918–80) (Lady Barnett) Scottish-born broadcaster, best known for her appearances as a panellist on BBC TV's *What's My Line?* in the 1950s. She was also popular as a public speaker. After being found guilty on a shoplifting charge, she took her own life.

—— 10 ——

In about 1953, Lady Barnett paid a visit to the United States and came across a most ladylike advertising slogan for a deodorant spray called Stopette. It was: 'Makes your armpit your charm pit!'

Related in her book *My Life Line* (1956). See also VAUGHAN-THOMAS 187:1.

Sir James BARRIE

(1860–1937) Scottish playwright, paralysingly shy
except with children.

—— 1 ——

William Nicholson once noticed that Barrie always ordered Brussels sprouts but invariably left them on the side of his plate. He asked him why. 'I cannot resist ordering them,' Barrie replied, 'The words are so lovely to say.'

Reported in *The Sunday Referee* (5 December 1927).

—— 2 ——

Barrie put H. G. Wells on the spot. 'It is all very well to be able to write books,' he said to him once, 'but can you waggle your ears?'

Quoted in J. A. Hammerton, *Barrie: The Story of a Genius* (1929). Wells couldn't, apparently.

—— 3 ——

Barrie was producing one of his own plays and was approached by a young actor who was having difficulty with interpreting his part. Barrie told him, 'Try and look as if you had a younger brother in Shropshire.'

Quoted in Lady Cynthia Asquith, *Diaries 1915–18*, entry for 6 January 1918. The story also occurs in John Aye, *Humour in the Theatre* (1932) where the advice is, 'I should like you to convey that the man you portray has a brother in Shropshire who drinks port.'
From about the same period there is said to have been a stage direction (from another dramatist): 'Sir Henry turns his back to the audience and conveys that he has a son' (quoted in Michael Holroyd, *Bernard Shaw, Vol. 3: 1918–1950*, 1991).

—— 4 ——

There is a story told about Barrie's advice to a young writer who did not know what title to give his work. 'Are there any trumpets in it?' Barrie asked, and got the answer 'No'. 'Are there any drums in it?' he asked. 'No.' 'Then why not call it *Without Drums or Trumpets*?'

Untraced, but when I heard Ludovic Kennedy tell the story about Barrie in 1991, the title suggested was, rather, *No Horses, No Trumpets*. A similar story is told about the French playwright, Tristan Bernard (1866–1947) in Cornelia Otis Skinner's *Elegant Wits and Grand Horizontals* (1962). Somebody did take the advice: the English translation of Alec Le Vernoy's Second World War memoir was entitled *No Drums, No Trumpets* (1983).

Ethel BARRYMORE

(1879–1959) American actress. Sister of John and
Lionel.

—— 5 ——

Barrymore was told that another actress had begun a new marriage by making a full confession of her past to the new husband. 'What honesty! What courage!' somebody said. Commented Ethel, 'What a memory!'

Told by Ronald Fletcher (1979).

John BARRYMORE

(1882–1942) American actor on stage and screen.

—— 6 ——

In a visitors' book at a theatrical digs, he wrote: 'Quoth the raven . . .'

So attributed on BBC Radio *Quote...Unquote* (1977), but often ascribed to other performers. See also CAMPBELL 48:3.

—— 7 ——

Katharine Hepburn, sighing with relief after she had completed filming *A Bill of Divorcement* with Barrymore in 1932, said, 'Thank goodness I don't have to act with you any more.' Barrymore replied: 'I didn't know you ever had, darling.'

So ascribed on BBC Radio *Quote...Unquote* (1979).

—— 8 ——

Driven to fury by the coughing of members of a theatre audience, Barrymore picked up a large sea bass and threw it in their direction, saying: 'Busy yourselves with that, you damned walruses, while the rest of us proceed with the play.'

Quoted in Bennett Cerf, *Try and Stop Me* (1944). Cerf has it that the incident occurred when Barrymore was playing Fedor in *The Living Corpse*, a version of Tolstoy's *Redemption*, in 1918.

6th Marquess of BATH

(1905–92) English aristocrat, owner of Longleat House, Wiltshire, and a pioneer of the stately homes business. He opened the first British wildlife park including the 'lions of Longleat' in the 1960s.

—— 1 ——

The Marquess and his second wife, Virginia, were desperate to have a child and were reminded that nearby was the Cerne Abbas giant, an ancient fertility symbol carved in the chalk on the Wiltshire Downs. According to which story you believe, they either made love on the tip of the giant's substantial member, or merely sat on it. Either way, it worked. The result was Lady Silvy Thynne – whose second name is Cerne.

Sources for this story include: *Harpers & Queen* **(June 1992).**

Lilian BAYLIS

(1874–1937) English theatre manager, founder of the Old Vic (1912) and Sadler's Wells (1931).

—— 2 ——

Her professional life was a perpetual struggle over money. Once Baylis was overheard pleading with the Good Lord to come to her aid, praying: 'O God, send me some good actors – cheap!'

Related by Russell and Sybil Thorndike in *Lilian Baylis* **(1938).**

—— 3 ——

She complained about dramatic critics: 'They form too quick an impression of work it has taken my dear producer and his boys and girls a whole week to prepare.'

Quoted in a show about her work, at the Old Vic (March 1976).

—— 4 ——

Of some poor unfortunate ingénue, she remarked witheringly: 'Quite a sweet little Goneril, don't you think?'

Quoted in the same show.

—— 5 ——

The actress Mary Kerridge went for an audition at the Old Vic. Baylis was told, 'There's a Miss Kerridge in the stalls.' She replied, 'Well, why doesn't someone clear it up?'

Told by Hilary Pritchard on BBC Radio *Quote... Unquote* **(1977). Hotly denied by Miss Kerridge herself.**

—— 6 ——

One day she fell over in the street. 'That's Lilian Baylis of the Old Vic,' said a bystander. '. . . and Sadler's Wells,' added the prostrate form, insistently.

Source not known.

'BEACHCOMBER'

(J. B. Morton) (1893–1979) British humorous writer.

—— 7 ——

One day Morton was walking down a crowded Fleet Street with Rupert Hart-Davis, the publisher. He suddenly went up to a pillarbox and shouted into the slot: 'YOU CAN COME OUT NOW!'

Recounted in *The Lyttelton Hart-Davis Letters* **(for 5 February 1956) where it was said to have happened '20 years ago'. (This is the vocal equivalent of the graffito 'HELP!' written on the slot as though from the inside of the pillarbox.)**

—— 8 ——

Morton sometimes complained that the readers of *The Daily Express* (in which his column appeared) were unable to distinguish between his comic musings and the real news. Once he filled up space with: '*Stop Press*. At 3.55 p.m. yesterday there was a heavy fall of green Chartreuse over South Croydon.' Next morning he received six letters from people saying they had been in South Croydon that very afternoon and not a drop of green Chartreuse had fallen.

Recounted by the same source.

Sir Thomas BEECHAM

(1879–1961) English orchestral conductor, about
whom anecdotes are legion.

—— 1 ——

Beecham was travelling in the no-smoking carriage of a train when a woman passenger lit a
cigarette with the words, 'You won't object if I smoke?'
To which Beecham replied, 'Certainly not – and you
won't object if I'm sick.' It was in the days when the
railways were still privately owned. 'I don't think
you know who I am,' the woman angrily pointed
out. 'I am one of the directors' wives.' To which
Beecham riposted: 'Madam, if you were the director's *only* wife, I should still be sick.'

**Pass the Port (1976) ascribes these two barbs to
Beecham, but a story about the Marquess of
Hartington ('Harty-Tarty')(1833–1908), who became
the 8th Duke of Devonshire, is told in Anita Leslie,
Edwardians in Love (1972): 'When a man entering
his railway carriage put the question, "Do you
mind if I smoke a cigar?" Hartington serenely
answered: "No, my dear sir, provided you don't
mind me being sick".'**

—— 2 ——

Said Beecham: 'I have always laid it down as a
golden rule that there are only two things requisite so far as the public is concerned for a good
performance. That is, for the orchestra to begin
together and end together. In between it doesn't
matter much.'

**These are his actual words as recorded on an LP: *Sir
Thomas Beecham in Rehearsal* (WRC SH 147).**

—— 3 ——

To a lady cellist Beecham said: 'Madam, you have
between your legs an instrument capable of
giving pleasure to thousands – and all you can do is
scratch it.'

**Quoted by Fred Metcalf in *The Penguin Dictionary
of Modern Humorous Quotations* (1986), without
source.**

—— 4 ——

Beecham's sister had a friend called Utica
Wells. Out walking together one day, Beecham
informed Utica, 'I don't like your Christian name. I'd
like to change it.' Replied she, 'You can't do that, but
you can change my surname.' And so they were
married.

**Recounted in Daphne Fielding, *Emerald and Nancy*
(1976).**

—— 5 ——

Returning to his hotel in Manchester one night,
Beecham encountered a familiar-looking woman
in the foyer. He thought he must know her but could
not think of her name. Recalling that the woman had
a brother, he inquired politely how this brother was
and whether he was still doing the same job. 'Oh
yes,' the woman replied, 'He is very well – and still
the King.'

**Recounted in Atkins & Newman, *Beecham Stories*
(1978), but without source.**

—— 6 ——

In the 1930s, conducting for the Camargo Society,
Beecham took the Dance of the Cygnets from *Swan
Lake* at about four times the normal speed. Said he,
'That made the buggers hop!'

**Recounted by Sarah Woodcock in *Images of Show
Business* (ed. James Fowler, 1982). The version in
Atkins & Newman has the work in question as the
Polovtsian Dances from *Prince Igor* during a
Diaghilev ballet season.**

—— 7 ——

Beecham was conducting a rehearsal when he
suddenly stopped and said, 'Figure eight . . . the
Second Oboe was late!' And the First Oboe said, 'Sir
Thomas, the Second Oboe hasn't arrived yet.' 'Oh, I
see,' replied he, 'Well, when he arrives, will you tell
him that he's late . . .'

**Told by Sir Peter Ustinov on BBC Radio *Quote...
Unquote* (1991).**

Sir Max BEERBOHM

(1872–1956) English writer and caricaturist.

—— 8 ——

Going backstage after a particularly disastrous
opening night, Beerbohm is supposed to have
reassured the leading lady with the compliment:
'My dear, good is not the word.'

**Ascribed to Beerbohm on BBC Radio *Quote...
Unquote* (1979), but later also to Bernard Shaw.**

—— 9 ——

Answering serious abuse of an essay that had
appeared in Volume 1 of *The Yellow Book* (1894),
Beerbohm turned his attention to the critics themselves in Volume 2. 'It is a pity,' he wrote, 'that critics

should show so little sympathy with writers, and curious when we consider that most of them tried to be writers themselves, once.'

The final comma has been described as one of the most effective in all literature.

Hilaire BELLOC

(1870–1953) French-born British poet and writer.

—— 1 ——

During the 1930s, Belloc was travelling by train when he encountered a man reading a copy of his *History of England*, a book he considered to be less than good, and one of many pot-boilers he produced in his later life. Asking the man how much he had paid for it, and fishing the money out of his pocket, Belloc then proceeded to fling the book out of the carriage window.

A. N. Wilson in *Hilaire Belloc* (1984) notes that he had heard this story 'from many sources, but never seen it substantiated'.

Robert BENCHLEY

(1889–1945) American humorist and drama critic for *Life* and *The New Yorker*.

—— 2 ——

When the play *Abie's Irish Rose* ran for so long on Broadway (1922–7), Benchley found that he was incapable of saying anything new about it in the capsule criticisms that he had to supply each week. So he put 'See Hebrews 13:8.' The text he alluded to reads: 'Jesus Christ the same yesterday, and today, and for ever.'

Recounted in Diana Rigg, *No Turn Unstoned* (1982). When *A Chorus Line* ran for an even longer time on Broadway (1975–90), the space for it in *The New Yorker*'s listings was given over to reprints of paragraphs from *War and Peace*. Or so I think.

Tony BENN

(1925–) English Labour politician of left-wing tendency. A minister in the Labour governments of the 1960s and 70s, he became popularly known as 'Loony Benn' for the vigour with which he embraced technology and for the mildly eccentric way in which he presented himself. Known originally as Anthony Wedgwood Benn, he managed to disclaim the Stansgate viscountcy when it descended upon him. Gradually he shortened his name (and his *Who's Who* entry) until it was of a more voter-friendly size.

—— 3 ——

Benn became the modern equivalent of a music-hall joke on account of his supposedly 'loony' policies. His brother David, a BBC producer, was made well aware of this when he had to pay a visit to someone in a mental hospital. As he was going on to stay with friends, David had a small weekend case with him and arranged in advance for a minicab to collect him from the hospital and take him to the railway station.

After the visit, David emerged, clutching his case, and instructed the driver to take him to the station. To make conversation he said, 'I've just been visiting a friend of mine, you know.'

The driver merely nodded and said, 'Aye' as if to humour him. They drove on a bit further. David then added: 'I work for the BBC, you know.' The driver again nodded at this far-fetched claim and said, 'Oh aye.'

The climax came when David announced after a further pause, 'My brother is the Minister of Technology. You may have heard of him. He's Tony Benn . . .'

I believe David Wedgwood Benn told this story against himself. I must have heard it in the early 1970s.

A. C. BENSON

(1862–1925) English schoolmaster and poet ('Land of Hope and Glory'). Eventually Master of Magdalene College, Cambridge.

—— 4 ——

When he was a housemaster at Eton, on being told that, rather unfortunately, a murder had been committed in the College and one of the boys killed, Benson posed the inevitable question in a somewhat strange way. He inquired: 'What dangerous clown has done this?'

> This version was told by Humphrey Lyttelton (an Old Etonian) on BBC Radio *Quote...Unquote* (1988). Earlier it had been told on the programme in 1986 by Steve Race who happened to have the headmaster of Eton sitting next to him (who did not dispute the tale). However, Kenneth Tynan in a 1948 review in *A View of the English Stage* gives it as an 'Alexander Woollcott story' of merely 'a schoolmaster' who, coming upon a mutilated torso in the Lower Third dormitory, remarked: 'Some dangerous clown has been here.'
>
> Humphrey Lyttelton's father, George, apparently resolves the matter in *The Lyttelton Hart-Davis Letters* (for 23 February 1956): 'Woollcott records in one of his books his high appreciation when my colleague [at Eton] Booker was summoned one Sunday afternoon to his kitchen where his cook had been murdered, and on seeing the body, asked "What dangerous clown has done this?"'

BEREAVED PEOPLE

―――― 1 ――――

I once knew of some people called Sands. They lived overlooking the seaside and Mr Sands decreed in his will that when he died he was to be cremated and his ashes scattered over the, er, *sands*. And so it turned out, though not quite in the way he expected.

Shortly after the cremation, a small group of his relatives was seen trooping down to the shore carrying the casket containing his ashes. After they had stood in silent prayer for a minute or so, the lid was removed from the casket. At that very moment, a gust of wind whipped the ashes out of the casket and blew them all over the family.

But Mr Sands had had his wish – even if his ashes were scattered over the Sands rather than over the, er, sands.

> I heard this story in the early 1970s. I have changed the name of the family.

―――― 2 ――――

The bereaved widow allowed one of her late husband's friends to say 'a few words' after the cremation service was over. He started by saying that the last time he had been at that crematorium there had been some swallows flying about. He then went on to say how he had gone on a bird-watching expedition with the deceased, and so on. He ended – the cremation took place in early January – by saying: 'Now Mr G—, and the swallows, have departed to a warmer climate.'

> Told to me by the Reverend P. G., Oxford (1982).

―――― 3 ――――

There was an Englishman whose wife died while they were on a visit to France. Wanting a black coat to attend her funeral, the husband went into a shop and asked for a *capote noire*, explaining that his wife had died unexpectedly. Commented the shopkeeper: '*Oh, Monsieur! Quelle attention délicate!*'

> Source untraced, but before 1986. (If it helps, perhaps I should explain that whereas *capote* means 'greatcoat', *capote anglaise* is French slang for a condom.)

Lord Charles BERESFORD

> (1846–1919) Naval officer who rose to the rank of Admiral. An intimate of Edward VII when Prince of Wales.

―――― 4 ――――

In the days of lust in stately homes, Lord Charles went prowling down the corridors one night, tiptoed into one particular bedroom, and jumped into the vast bed, crowing 'Cock-a-doodle-doo!' as he did so. When the lamp was lit, after a good deal of confusion, he found himself between the Bishop of Chester and his wife.

> Recounted in Anita Leslie, *Edwardians in Love* (1972). She adds: 'The situation seemed very difficult to explain and he left the house before breakfast next morning.'

See also BERNERS 29:4.

Irving BERLIN

(1888–1989) Russian-born American composer
and lyricist.

—— 1 ——

During the Second World War, Winston Churchill was mightily impressed by the quality of press summaries he was receiving from the British Embassy in Washington DC and inquired who had written them. He was told simply 'I. Berlin'. This referred to Isaiah Berlin who was then a well-known Fellow of All Souls and of New College, Oxford, and on his way to becoming a philosopher of great distinction.

Some weeks later, in February 1944, the Prime Minister gave a small lunch party and duly invited Berlin along, having heard that he was in London. All went well until Churchill turned to Berlin and asked him for his views on when the war would end and on the re-election prospects of President Roosevelt. Berlin began a rather rambling account of his oddly ill-informed views on these topics, which were rather at odds with the sharp tone of the brilliant reports Churchill had been receiving from Washington.

Only gradually did it dawn on those present, that the 'Mr I. Berlin' they were listening to was Mr *Irving* Berlin who had lately arrived in Britain to entertain American troops.

> This delightful mistake is recounted at greater length in 'A Tale of Two Berlins' in John Colville's *Footprints in Time* (1976) – based in turn on Colville's diary entry for 9 February 1944 which is included in Vol. 2 of his *The Fringes of Power: Downing Street Diaries* (1987). The fact that the mistake occurred had earlier been made known by Ian Mackay in *The News Chronicle* (3 January 1946): 'We are told that [Irving Berlin] kept his end up magnificently, even if it involved a bit of swift syncopation now and then.'

Lord (Gerald) BERNERS

(1883–1950) English composer, writer, painter and eccentric. In John Betjeman's article on Berners in *The Dictionary of National Biography*, it states: 'He never made a public speech in his life, except for the three short sentences with which he opened the Faringdon cinema.'

—— 2 ——

Berners's paternal grandmother, Lady Bourchier, was very fond of birds and encouraged robins, tits, nuthatches and sparrows to come to her windows and be fed. She claimed to have tamed a pair of bluetits to come and eat out of her hands though nobody had ever seen them do this. However, one day, the boy Berners did catch a glimpse of them and he remembered causing a mild sensation by rushing into the drawing-room where several members of the family were sitting, and crying out excitedly, 'I say! I've just seen Grandmother's tits!'

> An early citing of this *double entendre* – it must have been about 1890 – and recorded by Berners in *First Childhood* (1934).
> Compare also what I recall Lady Hayter, wife of the Warden of New College, Oxford, saying to a group of irreverent freshmen in February 1964. In the Warden's Lodgings is a valuable Quatrain Chest. Carved on the top is a depiction of the only battle the Belgians have ever won, or some such feature. Iris Hayter, who was very keen that all of us freshmen should view such college treasures, piped up: 'Now then, has everybody seen my chest?'

—— 3 ——

One of Berners's acquaintances had the impertinent habit of saying to him, 'I've been sticking up for you.' He repeated this once too often and Berners replied, 'Yes, and I have been sticking up for you. Someone said you aren't fit to live with pigs and I said you were.'

> This version appears in Edith Sitwell, *Taken Care Of* (1965). Compare the caption to a cartoon by A. Wallis Mills in *Punch* (28 June 1905): '*Lady A.* "HERE COMES THAT DREADFUL MAN WHO SAT NEXT TO ME AT DINNER. HE HASN'T THE MANNERS OF A PIG!" *Mrs B.* "HOW FUNNY! I THOUGHT HE *HAD!*"'

—— 4 ——

A pompous woman, complaining to Berners that the head waiter of a restaurant had not shown her and her husband immediately to a table, said, 'We had to tell him who we were.' Berners, interested, inquired, 'And who were you?'

> Version from Edith Sitwell, *Taken Care Of* (1965). Also told about John Betjeman. However, Patrick Balfour in *Society Racket* (1933) noted: 'I discovered the other day that [this] remark, attributed to a modern wit (and a true wit), Lord Berners, was in fact made by Lord Charles Beresford.'

—— 1 ——

After somewhat improbable rumours had been circulating that he was to marry Violet Trefusis, the 'friend' of Virginia Woolf and Vita Sackville-West, Berners put a notice of his travels in the newspapers, as was then the custom. It read, 'Lord Berners has left Lesbos for the Isle of Man.'

Told in *The Sunday Telegraph* (11 September 1983).

—— 2 ——

When people took to referring to the Prince of Wales rather knowingly as 'the P. of W.', Berners took great delight in doing the same. It was only after people wondered how on earth *his* 'P. of W.' could have been doing things most untypical of *their* 'P. of W.', that Berners explained, in all innocence, that he had, of course, been referring to the Provost of Worcester.

Source unknown.

—— 3 ——

Berners wrote a delightful parody of W. B. Yeats's 'The Lake Isle of Innisfree' which goes:

I will arise and go now, and go to Innisfree,
And tell them, at the little Inn,
That there'll be twenty-four for tea.
Twenty-four ladies of the Band of Hope,
United in their hatred of the Pope,
Each one declaring loudly she would rather
Serve the Devil than the Holy Father.
The bee-loud glade may hum with sounds, I fear,
Other than the murmur of the bee.
I do not fancy they'll be very welcome there –
At Innisfree.

This was sent to me by Philip Lane of Cheltenham in 1984. I know no more of its provenance.

—— 4 ——

Berners put this sign up at his home, Faringdon House, in Oxfordshire: 'ANYONE THROWING STONES AT THIS NOTICE WILL BE PROSECUTED'.

Quoted in *The Independent on Sunday* (25 July 1993). Compare David Frost's narration from BBC TV's *The Frost Report* (c. 1966): 'For many of us, authority is summed up by the sign that one of the team found on the Yorkshire Moors which said simply, "It is forbidden to throw stones at this notice."'

Sarah BERNHARDT

(1844–1923) French actress, regarded as one of the greatest of all time.

—— 5 ——

To be carpingly accurate, she never played Hamlet strutting about on her wooden leg. After she had her amputation, she performed sitting down. Nevertheless, that should not be allowed to spoil the story of the comment passed between two members of the audience at one of her later appearances. When there were three heavy thumps on the stage – the traditional starting signal for French tragedy – one said, 'Ah, here comes the Divine Sarah now . . .'

Told by Roy Hudd on BBC Radio *Quote...Unquote* (1978). Ned Sherrin, *Theatrical Anecdotes* (1991), has it as Jean Cocteau greeting the three knocks on the stage with, '*C'est elle!* [Here she is!]'

—— 6 ——

One night Bernhardt essayed the role of Cleopatra in Shakespeare's *Antony and Cleopatra* during a London season in the reign of Queen Victoria. In the scene where Cleopatra receives the news of Mark Antony's defeat at the battle of Actium, she stabbed the messenger who brought her the news, 'stormed, raved, frothed at the mouth, wrecked some of the scenery in her frenzy and finally, as the curtain fell, dropped in a shuddering convulsive heap.'

As the applause died down, an American visitor overhead a middle-aged British matron saying to her friend in the next seat, 'How different – how very different from the home life of our own dear Queen!'

So attributed by Irvin S. Cobb in *A Laugh a Day Keeps the Doctor Away...* (1921).

—— 7 ——

When asked by a reporter what she thought of the Ten Commandments, Bernhardt replied: 'Zey are too many.'

Recalled in *The Lyttelton Hart-Davis Letters* (for 9 November 1957).

—— 8 ——

In the early years of the century, Bernhardt was playing in Manchester and was being taken for a drive in the countryside by a friend when they came across a noisy and vigorous football match. Being a wet day, all the players were covered in mud. Bernhardt, swathed from head to foot in white furs, stood on her seat and watched the contest with eager interest. When it was over she sat down and sank back into her cushions, exclaiming, 'I adore this cricket; it's so utterly *English*!'

Recounted in *The Manchester Guardian* (13 July 1937) about an incident that occurred 'some thirty years ago'.

Sydney BERNSTEIN

(1899–1993) English businessman and media tycoon. Founder of Granada Television. Made a Life Peer in 1969.

—— 1 ——

After many years as a film producer and cinema owner, Bernstein applied for one of the first commercial television franchises in Britain. He was successful in winning the Northern region (which at first included Lancashire and Yorkshire). Some time later he explained to the Manchester Publicity Association why he had chosen the North rather than London or the Midlands: 'It was brought about by two maps: a population map of Great Britain and a rainfall map. Any sensible person, after studying these two maps for a few minutes, would realise that if commercial TV is going to be a success anywhere in the world, it would be in the industrial North of England.'

Recalled in Caroline Moorhead, *Sydney Bernstein* (1984).

—— 2 ——

At 7.30 p.m. on 3 May 1956, Granada Television went on the air from Manchester with the words, 'From the North, this is Granada – on Channel 9.' The evening ended with a typical Bernstein gesture – a programme saluting the rival BBC, its stars and founders.

Recalled in ibid.

—— 3 ——

P. T. Barnum, the American showman and circus proprietor, was Bernstein's idol from an early age. So much so that *in every office* of the various branches of the Granada empire there was placed a signed portrait of Barnum. This was to remind everyone – especially some of the more refined producers in the TV company – that showmanship was or should be at the heart of the operation. In other words, whatever sort of programme you did,

it was all show business. If anyone chose to remove the portrait from the wall, it would mysteriously be replaced overnight. The unstated suggestion was that if you removed it, it would be replaced, and your desk and job would be thrown out instead.

Personal recollection of my time working for Granada TV in Manchester and London, 1966–7.

Bernardo BERTOLUCCI

(1940–) Italian film director.

—— 4 ——

Bertolucci appeared in person at the Academy Awards ceremony in 1988 and received an Oscar for his film, *The Last Emperor*. His use of the English language was less than award-winning, however. He said: 'If New York is the Big Apple, tonight Hollywood is the Big Nipple.' In an attempt at clarification, he added: 'It is a big suck for me.'

Report in *The Guardian*, April 1988.

Sir John BETJEMAN

(1906–84) English poet, enthusiast for Victorian architecture, and national teddy-bear.

—— 5 ——

Betjeman married Penelope, the daughter of Field Marshal Lord Chetwynd, in 1933. Being only 27 himself, he was a little doubtful as to how he should address his future father-in-law. Chetwynd soon put him at his ease. 'Well, Betjeman,' he said, 'if you're going to marry my daughter you needn't go on calling me "sir". Call me "Field Marshal".'

Recounted in *The Observer* (8 February 1959).

Aneurin BEVAN

(1897–1960) Welsh Labour politician to whom the epithet 'fiery' is usually applied.

—— 1 ——

During the Second World War, Churchill had to announce to the House of Commons that the British had, rather illicitly, taken bases in the Azores. He apparently thought he could gloss it over with a splendid speech, so he rose and said, 'I must ask the House now to come with me back over four hundred years of our eventful history…' Nye Bevan interrupted: 'Good God, he's looked into his in-tray at last!'

Told by Wynford Vaughan-Thomas on BBC Radio *Quote…Unquote* (1980).

—— 2 ——

Bevan was one of the – if not the – first to formulate a specific criticism of middle-of-the-roaders: 'We know what happens to people who stay in the middle of the road. They get run over.'

Quoted in the *Observer* (9 December 1953). According to Kenneth Harris, *Thatcher* (1988), Margaret Thatcher later said to James Prior: 'Standing in the middle of the road is very dangerous, you get knocked down by traffic from both sides.' And a TV play called *A Very British Coup* (1988) had a fictional Prime Minister saying, 'I once tried the middle of the road … But I was knocked down by traffic in both directions.'

Ernest BEVIN

(1881–1951) British Labour politician, much admired but dropped his aitches.

—— 3 ——

On being told that another Labourite was 'his own worst enemy', Bevin replied: 'Not while I'm alive, he ain't.'

Reputedly levelled at Aneurin Bevan, Herbert Morrison, Emanuel Shinwell and others, and quoted by Michael Foot in *Aneurin Bevan* (Vol. 2, 1973). Foot footnoted: 'Perhaps once [Bevin] had made it he recited it about all of them. Impossible to determine who was the original victim.' Douglas Jay in *Change and Fortune* (1980) adds that it was, 'Made, I have little doubt, though there is no conclusive proof, about Bevan [being the victim] … I could never discover direct evidence for this oft-told story.'

—— 4 ——

Bevin was Foreign Secretary in the British Labour Government of 1945–51 – a considerable achievement for a man, born in poverty, who had been orphaned at the age of seven. He only began to take an interest in foreign affairs when serving in Churchill's war cabinet during the Second World War. Previously, Bevin had been a robust, down-to-earth trade unionist but he now hoped that his conciliatory approach could be applied to world peace. When asked about his foreign policy, he announced: 'My policy is to be able to take a ticket at Victoria Station and go anywhere I damn well please.'

Quoted in the *Spectator* (20 April 1951). Francis Williams in his biography of Bevin (1952) has a slightly different version – said to a diplomat about the most important objective of his foreign policy: 'Just to be able to go down to Victoria station and take a ticket to where the hell I like without a passport.'

BIBLIOPHILES

—— 5 ——

The late John Sparrow was fond of quoting 'the book collector's caveat', which goes: 'Never lend a book; never give a book away; never read a book.'

Quoted in his obituary in *The Independent* (4 February 1992).

BISHOPS

—— 6 ——

An Anglican bishop contemplating a gathering of clergymen remarked, 'The see gives up its dead.'

Alluding to Revelations 20:13, 'The sea shall give up its dead.' Ascribed on BBC Radio *Quote…Unquote* (1984) by the Reverend Roger Royle to Henry Montgomery-Campbell, Bishop of London (1956–61). In a letter broadcast on *Quote…Unquote* (1985), Prof. Maurice Hugh-Jones ascribed the remark to 'a Bishop of Lichfield'.

—— 7 ——

It is said that in 1944, the priest of a Roman Catholic church in Putney wanted to call a statue of the Virgin Mary 'Our Lady of Putney', but his bishop demurred, saying, 'If the Germans land, they will go into the church and look at the statue and be able to tell where they are.' Accordingly, the pedestal of the statue bears the inscription: 'Our Lady of Hereabouts'.

Source unknown. Included in my *Say No More!* (1987).

—— 1 ——

An archetypal joke, based on a double pun, is the one about being 'in bed with my favourite Trollope'. An early sighting occurs in Chips Channon's diary (4 April 1943) where we read: 'At Wells we went over the Cathedral, and then to the Palace where we lunched with the Bishop . . . Much talk of Barchester, "there is nothing I like better than to lie on my bed for an hour with my favourite Trollope", the Bishop said, to everybody's consternation.'

'Trollop' has meant a 'slut, morally loose woman' since the 17th century. Compare BLYTON 34:4.

—— 2 ——

Two men who had been rivals since their schooldays eventually ended up as a bishop and an admiral. At the height of this eminence, they met at Paddington station. The bishop, not recognizing his old schoolmate but perceiving from his uniform that he was an official of some sort, addressed him with the words: 'Tell me, my man, which platform is it for Reading?' The admiral, perceiving not only who the bishop was but that he was kitted out in all his finery, replied: 'I don't know, *madam* – and should you be travelling in your condition?'

Told in *Pass the Port* (1976) and by Kingsley Amis on BBC Radio *Quote...Unquote* (1979).

—— 3 ——

Henry Montgomery-Campbell, when Bishop of Guildford (1949–56), was presiding over a retreat house called Farnham Castle. One of the clergymen became bored with the retreating and nipped out to do some shopping in Farnham town. As he departed he bumped into the bishop and felt he owed him some explanation. 'My Lord,' said he, 'the Holy Spirit has moved me to go down to the town and do some shopping . . .' Replied the bishop: 'Then I feel bound to tell you that at least one of you is wrong . . . it's early closing.'

This appeared in *Pass the Port Again* (1980), though without the bishop's name. Told by the Reverend Roger Royle (1984).

See also CLERGY.

Cilla BLACK

(1943–) English pop singer and Liverpudlian personality.

—— 4 ——

Her name is really Priscilla *White*, but a newspaper report in the early 1960s printed it wrong, and that's how it has stayed.

As explained to Roy Plomley on BBC Radio *Desert Island Discs* (24 August 1964).

Eubie BLAKE

(1883–1983) American ragtime composer, lyricist ('Charleston Rag', 'I'm Just Wild About Harry') and boogie-woogie pianist.

—— 5 ——

On reaching his 100th birthday, having smoked since he was six and always refusing to drink water, Blake said, 'If I'd known I was gonna live this long, I'd have taken better care of myself.' He died five days later.

Quoted in *The Observer* (13 February 1983). Earlier, in 1973, Adolph Zukor, the founder of Paramount Pictures, had said on reaching his centennial: 'If I'd known how old I was going to be I'd have taken better care of myself.' He survived even longer – until 1976.

Jasmine BLIGH

(1913–91) British television's first female announcer when the BBC opened its regular service from Alexandra Palace in 1936.

—— 6 ——

In the early days of television, the floor managers became fed up with having to give hand signals to performers such as Bligh. This was because they thought the signals were coarse and rather tiresome (in radio, such cues had always been given by the flashing of a green light). So, at the BBC's studios at Alexandra Palace, they rigged up a little engine which they tried out, slipping it round Jasmine Bligh's ankle, out of shot. The idea was that when they pressed a button in the control gallery, it would provid a little pulse that would cue the performer. The first time they used it, Ian Atkins was directing. 'Cue, Jasmine!' he said. They pressed the little button, and she said, 'AAARGH! Good evening.'

Recounted by Sir Huw Wheldon on BBC Radio *Quote...Unquote* **(1985).**

BLURB WRITERS

Most authors write their own blurbs – or at least approve what is written about them on the covers of their books. So presumably these two knew what they were doing . . .

—— 1 ——

'William Kotzwinkle is a former department store Santa Claus who has taken leave of his senses to write a remarkable series of short stories.'

To *Elephant Bangs Train* **(1971).**

—— 2 ——

'Mr Smith, who is half Pueblo Indian, lives in New York City . . .'

To Martin Cruz Smith, *Gorky Park* **(1981).**

Enid BLYTON

(1897–1968) English children's author, prolific and popular, though latterly condemned by the politically correct police.

—— 3 ——

Every letter written to *Blue Peter*, BBC Television's long-running children's show, receives an *individual* reply. The reason for this, according to Biddy Baxter, the programme's editor from 1962 to 1988, was because of Enid Blyton. As a six-year-old, Baxter had written two fan letters to the children's author. The first letter, a hymn of praise, received a wonderful reply from Blyton – 'very chatty and with her own address on the top – I felt she was writing to me. But, being a typical child, I wrote again three days later. I got back exactly the same letter. I remembered for ever how awful I felt that day.'

Recounted in *Kingsgate*, **Durham University's alumni magazine (September 1992).**

—— 4 ——

Kenneth Horne got into trouble on *Beyond Our Ken* (BBC radio, early 1960s) when he said that there was nothing he liked more of a cold winter's evening than to curl up on the hearthrug with Enid Blyton. The writer's husband evidently created a great fuss, threatened to sue, and the line was excised from the repeat broadcasts.

Told to me in 1963 by Eric Merriman who had written the offending joke. Compare BISHOPS **33:1.**

Sir Dirk BOGARDE

(1921–) English film actor and novelist. Bit of a worrier.

—— 5 ——

At Bogarde's Rank Organisation audition, Earl St John said to him: 'Nice of you to come, but your head's too small for the camera, you are too thin, and . . . I don't know what it is exactly about the neck . . . but it's not right.'

Recounted by Bogarde in *Snakes and Ladders* **(1978), the second volume of his autobiography.**

—— 6 ——

In 1960, Bogarde played the title role in the Hollywood biopic *Liszt*. As he tells it, one of the lines in the script was: 'Hiya, Chopin, this is my friend George Sand. She's a great friend of Beethoven's.'

From ibid. However, Bogarde seems to have been successful in mocking the line, as it does not appear in the film.

Steve BONARJEE

(1912–) English broadcasting executive. An Anglo-Indian of prematurely ancient appearance, Bonarjee is credited with launching the BBC radio *Ten O'Clock* programme, the forerunner of ITN's *News at Ten*. He also launched many names – giving Robin Day, for example, his first broadcasting job.

—— 1 ——

A distinguished opera singer came in to Bonarjee's department to be interviewed for the *Today* programme. Unaided by an agent, she personally read through her contract, noting the various rates of payment for repeat broadcasts in S. E. Asia, Australasia, and so on. Then coming to 'S. W. Bonarjee' at the bottom of the contract, she demanded, 'And where precisely *is* South-West Bonarjee?'

Heard when I was working for him in the late 1960s.

—— 2 ——

Although *Ten O'Clock* (which later became *The World Tonight*) was an influential programme and a great training ground, it was itself a rather staid institution. It always consisted of four interviews – usually with pundits rather than the newsmakers themselves. This contrasted with the styles of other regular current-affairs programmes on the air at that time. Accordingly, I devised a little joke to characterize them. I asked, how would Radio 4 respond to the unlikely prospect of the Duke of Edinburgh losing his trousers in public?

Ten O'Clock, I said, would interview the editor of the Court Circular in *The Times*. The *Today* programme would send Monty Modlyn to interview a braces manufacturer in the East End of London. *Radio Newsreel* would have a report from a radio car parked outside the place where the incident had occurred. And *The World at One*? Ah – this was rather a sharp touch – *The World at One* would interview the Duke of Edinburgh . . .

From my diary (16 April 1969). This story was sold to *The Guardian*'s 'Miscellany' column (for three guineas) by someone called Tim Pitt. When the joke appeared on 23 April, Jack de Manio repeated it on the *Today* programme. People seemed oddly reluctant to see the criticism in it. Humphrey Carpenter, then working for the then functioning BBC Radio Durham, added the following: 'How would Radio Durham cover the story? They'd try and find someone in Durham who had ever been to London, and interview them.'

BORES

—— 3 ——

There is a celebrated anecdote of an actor who bored his listener to tears with a relentless monologue about his latest performance in a play. Then, contritely, he suddenly broke off. 'But I'm talking all about myself,' he apologized winningly. 'Let's talk about *you*. How did *you* like me in the part?'

As told by Godfrey Smith in *The Sunday Times* (31 July 1983).

Reginald BOSANQUET

(1932–84) English TV newscaster. Oxford-educated, he was with ITN from its start in 1955, eventually becoming a reasonably much-loved national figure presenting *News at Ten*. His slurred delivery was attributed to a form of facial paralysis he had once suffered but few believed this was the only reason. The onset of colour television focused attention on his toupee. The nation sat on the edge of its seat while wondering where Reggie would put the emphasis on the words in his script.

—— 4 ——

Once, when filming in Africa, Reggie had to stoop to enter a mud hut. The cameraman who was following – possibly Cyril Page – suddenly became aware of a fearsome hairy beast on the floor and stamped heavily upon it. Reggie complained vociferously that his hairpiece was ruined and he wouldn't be able to wear it in vision.

Heard at ITN in *c.* 1967. And, no, I'm not going to repeat the story about the nude photographs taken of Reggie when he was swimming in Loch Ness while making a report on the monster.

—— 5 ——

During a national fire brigade strike in 1977, Reggie had to read a news item which told of an emergency call made to the Army. It was from an old lady whose cat was stuck up a tree. The Army fire engine duly arrived – it was a Green Goddess – a soldier shinned up the tree and rescued the moggie. Reggie went on to report that, unfortunately, as they were backing out of the garden, they accidentally ran over the cat they had just rescued, and so killed it. Alas, he allowed the whisper of a grin to pass over his face and the switchboard was flooded with protest calls. His excuse was that he had had a lopsided grin on his face since birth.

> In his autobiography *Let's Get Through Wednesday* (1980), Bosanquet denied that he had so much as moved a muscle after reading the story and added: 'It is interesting that someone in the newsroom should have found this nugget of a tailpiece in what can normally be expected to be thoroughly humourless – a Ministry handout. And I should mention that what is said to have happened afterwards is definitely not true. The firemen did *not* push the cat into the dear lady's letter-box with a note of apology.' Also recounted in *TV Times* (21 September 1985).

—— 1 ——

On the occasion of his noisy resignation from ITN in November 1979, Reggie wrote a goodbye poem to his on-screen newscasting partner, Anna Ford:

If I suffer from eccentricity
Do I have *egg*centricity
On my face?

I may not be here tomorrow.
Can I borrow
All of your best wishes?

> Quoted on BBC Radio *Quote...Unquote* (1979), source unknown. Reggie embraced the bottle fulltime after this resignation and had a few embarrassing years as a professional personality before eventually dying of cancer.

Sir Adrian BOULT

(1889–1983) English orchestral conductor. A man born to conduct Elgar, indeed looking quite like him.

—— 2 ——

As conductor of the BBC Symphony Orchestra, Boult frequently ran up against official parsimony. On one occasion, when planning to conduct a piece requiring two piccolo players, he was told that only one could be afforded. He complained to his boss, Charles Carpendale, who reflected for a moment and then suggested a compromise: 'How about using one piccolo,' he urged, 'and placing it closer to the microphone?'

> Told in Andrew Boyle, *Only the Wind Will Listen: Reith of the BBC* (1972).

—— 3 ——

Sir Adrian was rehearsing an amateur orchestra before an evening concert which he had agreed to conduct. When he asked for one of the set pieces and began to conduct it, some of the members, perhaps overawed by his presence, began to play a different one. After stopping them, he said quietly, 'I think we have time to rehearse both pieces separately.'

> Told to me by Joan Hewitt of Winscombe, Avon (1992) whose mother was in the orchestra.

Clara BOW

(1905–65) American film actress, known as the 'It Girl' – to describe her vivacious sex appeal – after appearing in the film *It* (1928).

—— 4 ——

Bow wrote these words on a photograph that she gave to her fiancé, Harry Richman: 'To my gorgeous lover, Harry. I'll trade all my It for your that.'

> Quoted in Bob Chieger, *Was It Good for You, Too?* (1983).

Sir Maurice BOWRA

(1898–1971) English academic with a booming voice. Warden of Wadham College, Oxford.

—— 5 ——

At the funeral of Humphrey Sumner, the Oxford historian and Warden of All Souls, in 1951, Bowra intoned: 'Sumner is a-going out/Loud sing boo-hoo.'

> Quoted by Alan Bennett on BBC Radio *Quote...Unquote* (1982). This alluded to the 13th-century rhyme, 'Sumer is icumen in,/Lhude sing cuccu!'

—— 6 ——

About his affection for a rather plain young lady, Bowra said: 'Buggers can't be choosers.'

> Quoted in Jan Morris, *The Oxford Book of Oxford* (1978).

—— 1 ——

There was until quite recently a small spot reserved by the River Cherwell in Oxford for dons to swim in the nude. Some young wags decided to go up the river in a punt in order to be able to see their tutors so disporting themselves. They braved the rapids and came into the quiet patch of the river where these rather corpulent dons were sitting naked on the sward. As the old gentlemen saw their pupils going past, they all – except Bowra – covered their loins with their hands. Bowra put his hands over his *eyes* – and explained to his colleagues, 'In Oxford I'm known by my face . . .'

Told by A. N. Wilson on BBC Radio *Quote... Unquote* (1990).

—— 2 ——

When told of the forthcoming wedding of John Bayley and Iris Murdoch in 1956, Bowra opined: 'Splendid couple – I should know – slept with both of them.'

This story was certainly around in 1963 when John Bayley became my tutor at New College (and my moral tutor, too . . .).

BOX-OFFICE PERSONNEL

—— 3 ——

Traditionally, one is not supposed to have very much sympathy with people who run theatre box offices. They can be off-hand in person, quite apart from being unget-at-able over the telephone. Nevertheless, I did feel a smidgin of sympathy when I had to ring up the Royal Court Theatre to book tickets for Alan Bennett's play called – and that's the problem – *Kafka's Dick*.

'Have you got two tickets for the 24th?' is what I actually said, rather than, 'Have you anything for Kafka's Dick?'

I am told that when the National Theatre announced Girardoux's *The Trojan War Will Not Take Place*, box-office staff were often asked what they were going to put on instead.

Similarly, when the NT announced *Rosencrantz and Guildenstern are dead*, they received many kind words of sympathy.

From my column in *Sunday Today* (29 September 1986).

Brendan BRACKEN

(1st Viscount Bracken) (1901–58) Irish journalist and Conservative politician. British Minister of Information during the Second World War. A close associate of Winston Churchill who, on this account, some held must have been his father.

—— 4 ——

When Bracken became Minister of Information, a journalist told him, 'I don't believe a word you say, Brendan. Everything about you is phoney. Even your hair, which looks like a wig, isn't.'

Version from Charles Edward Lysaght, *Brendan Bracken* (1979).

Marlon BRANDO

(1924–) American actor who reportedly played the title role in *The Godfather* with his mouth full of orange peel or cotton wool, to give the requisite bloated effect. The rest of his body, by this time, needed no such aids.

—— 5 ——

When I was dining at Le Grand Véfour restaurant in London, there was such a deathly hush that I was able to listen to a conversation between two fairly mature colonial types, both well travelled, seated near by. He apparently lived in Guernsey; she had a hard voice like that of Lady Barnett. He admitted he had been to see the film *Last Tango in Paris* (then just released) and she pressed him to explain what Brando got up to in the famous 'butter' sequence. I wondered whether he was going to explain it to the whole restaurant. 'Well, they got very excited about the butter,' he suggested diplomatically. 'But why?' she pressed on. 'Did he *throw* it at her?'

From my diary (26 April 1973).

Alfred BRENDEL

(1931–) Austrian pianist, London-based. Wears sticking plaster over his finger-tips so that they do not slide off the keys.

—— 1 ——

It is said that Brendel once stunned an expectorating concert audience at a pianissimo point by announcing, 'I can hear you, but you can't hear me,' – thus ensuring absolute silence for the remainder.

As told in *The Observer* (20 May 1991).

Bernard BRESSLAW

(1933–93) English comedy actor, a benign giant.

—— 2 ——

Bresslaw's thicko remark 'I only arsked' was quite the most popular British TV catchphrase of the late 1950s. It came from Granada's *The Army Game*. A story is told of the day when the team first appreciated that they had a catchphrase on their hands. It is said that Milo Lewis, the director, was rehearsing a scene in which the lads from Hut 29 realized that though they had been moved to a new camp, they still hadn't escaped the clutches of the sergeant-major (played by William Hartnell). 'Quite a reunion!' the sergeant-major commented. Private 'Popeye' Popplewell (the Bresslaw character) inquired, 'Can we bring girls?' 'No, you can't,' replied the sergeant-major. 'I only arsked!' said Popplewell.

At this point, Milo Lewis is said to have exclaimed enthusiastically, 'We've got a catchphrase!' The others chorused, 'You mean . . .?' 'Yes,' replied Lewis, '"Can we bring girls?"'

Told to me by Barry Cryer in *c.* 1979.

Alan BRIEN

(1925–) British journalist and author.

—— 3 ——

Who said 'Violence is the repartee of the illiterate'? When I put this question to Brien on *Quote...Unquote*, he said: 'I don't think I've heard it before . . . modernish? . . . it can't be very old. Bernard Shaw would be too good for it. Perhaps it's Chesterton, is it?'

In fact, he had written it himself in an article for *Punch* in February 1973.

The incident occurred on BBC Radio *Quote... Unquote* in 1985.

Benjamin BRITTEN

(1913–76) English composer. Made a Life Peer in 1976.

—— 4 ——

Britten was famously close to Peter Pears, the tenor. One day they were walking along the windswept beach at Aldeburgh, where they lived, and Britten turned to his friend and said, 'Peter, I don't know how to tell you this . . .'

Pears turned sensitively to Britten and replied, 'What is it, Ben? What have you got to tell me?'

But still the words wouldn't come. They walked a little further down the beach until finally Britten found the words to announce: 'Peter, I think we're going to have . . . another opera.'

A story retold in *The Daily Mail* around the time of Britten's death in 1976.

BROADCASTERS

—— 5 ——

More than one BBC announcer has fallen down on the job when saying the words 'British Broadcasting Corporation'. One actually went the whole hog and heard himself talking about the

'British Broadcorping Castration'.

> Told by Ronald Fletcher on BBC Radio *Quote... Unquote* (1976).

—— 1 ——

A disc jockey on Irish radio was having difficulty in reading a request postcard sent in by a listener. He said, 'I've got a request here from Sean O'Flaherty of County Sligo who was 111 recently . . . isn't that amazing? Must be the oldest man in the whole of Irel . . . Oh no . . . who was "ill" recently.'

> Well, that's the way I tell it, and I did hear something like it once when I was driving around Ireland listening to RTE, but as my diary for 18 June 1973 reminds me, what the disc jockey actually said first was '11 recently'. I have been telling my version since 1984 at least (when I told it on BBC TV's *Wogan*). Barely a week goes by now without my hearing it told by someone else. But it is not just another Irish joke.
> Earlier, by a strange chance, Jack de Manio in *To Auntie With Love* (1967) had warned of death-traps for announcers when reading cricket scores and given this example: 'Finally, to end the news, here are the cricket scores – Edrich 22, Hutton 47, Compton ill. I beg your pardon I'll read that again. Edrich 22, Hutton 47, Compton 111.'

—— 2 ——

One of my most treasured moments from the wireless comes from about 1980 and was when a foreign correspondent was referring to the Kurdish autonomy movement in Iran and Iraq. He said, 'There is the danger of civil war if the Kurds don't get their way.'

> This only goes to confirm one theory about the roots of humour, that people don't make up jokes, the jokes are there in the English language waiting to be let out. Ronald Pearsall in his survey of Victorian humour, *Collapse of Stout Party* (1975) relates that this joke was alive and well 'a hundred years ago'. 'In New College common room, Walter Thursby, don and explorer, related how he had scaled Mount Ararat. The snow was not so bad as expected, he explained, but because of marauding tribes a guard of Kurdish soldiers had been provided. Later Arthur Riding went up to him and commented: "I understand you took some Curds with you to show the whey."' In addition, *Punch* had the punning headline 'Kurds and their ways' on 12 February 1881 (Vol. LXXX).

—— 3 ——

Long ago, when he was on BBC Radio 1, the disc jockey Johnnie Walker read out a request postcard from a listener who, he said, lived in:

> Bury Street,
> Edmunds,
> Suffolk.

> Heard by myself, *c.* 1971.

—— 4 ——

A BBC announcer in London was introducing a light music group called The Chameleons and throughout the programme pronounced the 'ch' as in 'charm'. At the end, the leader of the group walked up to him and merely said, 'Chunt!'

> Told to me by Bernard Keeffe (1990).

—— 5 ——

Sympathize with the natural history broadcaster who told listeners that, 'In winter bullfinches are best fed on bacon rinds and great tits like coconuts.'

> Told by Ronald Fletcher on BBC Radio *Quote... Unquote* (1979).

—— 6 ——

On a radio tour of a farm in Kent where a new system of mechanical milking was being tried, the commentator noticed that there was one cow still being milked by hand. So he asked the farmer why it, too, was not attached to the machine. Came the reply: 'You couldn't do that. This be old Daisy. Her be a wrinkly-titted old sod!'

> Probably 1930s. As related by Wynford Vaughan-Thomas in *Trust to Talk* (1980).

—— 7 ——

David Bellan, a BBC Radio 2 announcer: 'And now a record dedication for Mrs Ethel Smith who is 100 years old today – but I'm told she's dead with-it.'

> From a listener's letter, quoted by 1982.

—— 8 ——

An American radio announcer once gave the message: 'This portion of *Woman on the Run* is brought to you by Phillips' Milk of Magnesia . . .'

> Quoted in *Time* Magazine (30 March 1981). One of the 'bloopers' collected and anthologized by Kermit Schafer.

—— 1 ——

I was once being interviewed on television about graffiti, a subject on which I used to be able to speak for many hours without notes. Suddenly, Jenni Murray, the charming interviewer, asked me in her best Robin Day manner: 'And tell me, have *you* ever done it in a lavatory?'

> Recounted in my *The Gift of the Gab* (1985). The incident occurred at BBC Southampton on 30 September 1980. Unfortunately, Jenni realized what she had said, dissolved into a fit of giggles, and we had to start the interview again.

—— 2 ——

Another time, I was touring Australia, giving interviews on the same topic, and was beginning to wonder whether I would ever get asked an *original* question about graffiti. Then, one morning in an Adelaide radio station, I was. The interviewer asked me: 'And, Nigel, is there a *season* for graffiti?'

> What did this mean? Did he suppose there was a sort of rutting season for graffiti-writers, that when the sap rose they reached for their spray-cans? I cannot, off-hand, recall my answer. This was in November 1981. Recounted in my *Gift of the Gab* (1985).

—— 3 ——

LBC, Britain's first commercial radio station to go on the air (in 1973), had a curious design fault: none of the studio doors had a window. Thus it was not possible for anyone to look through the doors and see if it was all right to enter the studios. As always happens, the worst thing possible occurred in the midst of a very serious news bulletin. A newsreader was reporting a bomb blast at Green Park Underground station in London, when the studio door could be heard opening to reveal the sound of a studio cleaner gaily entering with vacuum cleaner at full throttle.

> From a recording of the incident, *c.* 1974.

—— 4 ——

Ed Stewart was introducing a BBC Radio 2 show and had been asked to play a romantic record for an old lady celebrating her 89th birthday. He said, 'Here's one entitled, "Until It's Time for You to Go".'

> Included in my *Foot in Mouth* (1982).

—— 5 ——

A Cambridge don of an older generation had been in the habit of speaking scornfully of some of his younger colleagues whom he feared were prostitut-ing their vocation by giving talks on the radio. One day he was astonished to be invited to broadcast himself, the invitation ending with the words, 'Fee 20 guineas'. The don sent off a telegram of acceptance, adding: 'Should I send the 20 guineas in advance?'

> Included in this form in *Pass the Port* (1976).

—— 6 ——

In a BBC *Music and Movement* programme for children (which, happily for posterity, was recorded), a woman presenter said: 'We are going to play a hiding and finding game. Imagine we've got some balls. They might be hidden. You don't know where I'm going to hide your balls. Now, are your balls high up or low down? Close your eyes a minute and dance around, and look for them. Are they high up? Or are they low down? If you have found your balls, toss them over your shoulder and play with them . . .'

> From a recording of the incident. Jack de Manio in *Life Begins Too Early* (1970) seems to indicate that this immortal broadcast took place *c.* 1950.

—— 7 ——

Harry Kershaw (1918–92), British television writer and producer, was principally connected with Granada TV's *Coronation Street*, with which he was associated for 28 years. Granada also used to produce a programme called *All Our Yesterdays* which reran old newsreel clips from 25 years previously. When asked how long he thought *Coronation Street* could last, he would reply, 'As long as life itself . . . and then another 25 years on *All Our Yesterdays*.'

> From Barry Hill's obituary of Kershaw in *The Independent* (4 May 1992).

—— 8 ——

Rabbi Goldberg, the Chief Rabbi of Manchester, came in to Granada TV for an interview and I looked after him. Mike Ryan, the producer, came bowling up and asked him what his Christian name was. The Rabbi replied, without batting an eyelid, 'My Christian name is Selwyn.'

> From my diary for 1967.

—— 9 ——

In the late 1970s, Alan Towers was working for BBC TV's *Nationwide* programme as a reporter, from his base at Pebble Mill in Birmingham. One assignment took him to Croydon where lived Herbie, a duck who had been taught to run alongside a skateboard and leap on – travelling 5m (15ft) or more without assistance. Towers was the reporter on the consequent film which won an award from the Royal Television Society and became part of television folklore.

> In July 1993, Towers had to write to defend his place in television history when *The Independent on Sunday* wrongly ascribed the skate-boarding duck story to *News at Ten*. He was correct in thinking that this had become an archetypal example of TV news trivia. However, there are many other examples. In 1967, when I occupied the adjacent desk to Alan in the newsroom at Granada TV in Manchester, I believe the archetypal story of this type was – apart from parrots that played the piano – what I have always referred to as 'the beer-drinking cow'.

See also COMMENTATORS, NEWSREADERS.

Eleanor BRON

(1940–) English actress, initially in revue-type material on TV.

—— 1 ——

alking with a friend in Soho one day, Bron retrieved from her handbag a postcard from another mutual friend who had gone to Guyana. As she handed it to him, the present friend said, 'You have beautiful wrists, you know.'

'Don't be ridiculous,' she said. 'They're huge.'

'Yes,' he agreed, 'but your hands are so enormous that it doesn't matter . . .'

> Related by her in *The Pillow Book of Eleanor Bron* (1985).

Rupert BROOKE

(1887–1915) Glamorous English poet who died of blood poisoning during the First World War.

—— 2 ——

According to Arthur Marshall, Brooke had pre-hensile toes and could pick up a tennis ball with his foot. How useful this must have been, mused Arthur, when the need arose to fish them out of Grantchester mere. He could also seize a matchbox with one foot and strike a match upon it with the other.

> This interesting information was given as a Useful Fact for setting conversational balls rolling, in an article 'Master Beeton' included in *Sunny Side Up* (1987). Also mentioned by Marshall on BBC Radio *Quote...Unquote* (1987), so it must be true.

Anita BROOKNER

(1928–) English novelist and art historian. Often to be seen travelling by bus.

—— 3 ——

Brookner was, it could be said, a 'woman of a certain age' when she achieved public recognition by winning the Booker Prize for Fiction with her novel *Hotel du Lac* in 1984. Irritated by speculation over her precise years and, in particular, by the 'increasing churlishness' of *The Times* in alluding to her age and that of Erica Jong – an age which she withheld from publications like *Who's Who* – she eventually penned a letter to *The Times* (in 1985) saying, 'I am 46, and have been for some years past.'

> Compare No. 99 in the original *Joe Miller's Jests* (1739): 'A Lady's Age happening to be questioned, she affirmed, she was but *Forty*, and call'd upon a Gentleman that was in Company for his Opinion; Cousin, said she, do you believe I am in the Right, when I say I am but *Forty*? I ought not to dispute it, Madam, reply'd he, for I have heard you say so *these ten Years*.'

George BROWN

(later Lord George-Brown) (1914–85) English
Labour politician for whom the euphemism 'tired
and emotional' might well have been invented,
and probably was. For a while, though, he was the
life and soul of the Party.

—— 1 ——

During his time as Foreign Secretary (1966–8),
Brown rather bibulously teetered across the room
to one of the guests at a reception, sank on his knees
and cried out, 'Lovely creature in scarlet, dance with
me! You *lovely* creature in scarlet . . .' And the guest
turned and said, 'I'm the Apostolic Delegate and I
don't think you're in any condition to dance with
me.'

This is the version told by Kenneth Williams on
BBC Radio *Quote...Unquote* (1979), though without naming Brown. He added, 'It must be true
because I read it in *The Sunday Times*. I checked
with Alan Brien about it.' Earlier it had appeared in
Pass the Port (1976), safely consigned to 'a South
American country', the politician unnamed, and
the put-down: 'First, you are drunk, secondly the
music is the National Anthem, and finally, I am the
Cardinal Archbishop.'

In Peter Paterson's biography, *Tired and Emotional: The Life of Lord George-Brown* (1993), the
story is set in Brazil, Brown is named, the creature
is in crimson, and the put-down is administered by
the Cardinal Archbishop of Lima (who was on a
visit from Peru). Paterson, although hearing from
a 'distinguished former member of the Foreign
Office' who claimed to have been present at the
reception was, unfortunately, unable to prove the
veracity of this story. In fact, Brown never seems to
have visited Brazil. Another version of the tale has
it occurring at a state function in Vienna and the
put-down administered by the Cardinal Archbishop thereof.

In *The Kenneth Williams Diaries* (1993), it was
further revealed that Williams had acquired the
story from a friend, the actor Gordon Jackson, in
December 1970 in the form of a newspaper cutting
detailing some of Brown's eccentricities and taken
from *The Sunday Times*.

—— 2 ——

After an incident in which he was photographed
falling in the gutter outside the Houses of Parliament and had announced he was quitting the Labour Party, *The Times* commented in a leading article,
'Lord George-Brown drunk is a better man than the
Prime Minister [Harold Wilson] sober.'

Source: *The Times*, 4 March 1976. *The Times* Magazine (23 May 1993), while mentioning that

Woodrow Wyatt claimed to have made the remark
in 1963, also revealed that William Rees-Mogg had
actually come up with the sentence, as editor, in
1976: 'I wrote it. I remember it well. Bernard Levin
was sitting in my outer office. I showed it to Bernard
and said: "I don't really think I can print that, do
you?" Bernard replied: "If you *don't* print it, I shall
never speak to you again." Perhaps Woodrow's
memory is playing him up . . .'

Compare what Andrew Bonar Law is reported to
have said: 'Asquith, when drunk, can make a better speech than any of us when sober' (Longman,
Guide to Political Quotations; 1985). Also the
story told by John Beevers in *The Sunday Referee*
(19 February 1939): 'About ten years ago there was
a famous scene in the House. Mr Jack Jones was
speaking. Lady Astor entered and sat down opposite him. He stopped speaking, turned to her and
said: "I am not drunk. I have had so many insults
from this lady I resent it. She does not talk to me
straight. She talks under her breath." The Deputy
Speaker then said how glad he would be if the
honourable lady would keep quiet. Mr Jones continued: "It is a common thing for the honourable
lady to talk under her breath about drunkenness
when I am speaking. I will tell her straight in her
teeth that I am a better man when I am drunk than
she is when I am sober." And the House laughed
its head off.'

Coral BROWNE

(1913–91) Australian-born actress, chiefly on the
stage in the UK and US. In 1974, she married the
actor Vincent Price. They made a wonderful
couple.

—— 3 ——

Browne went to see the National Theatre production of Seneca's *Oedipus* in 1968. At one point the
stage disclosed a huge golden phallus around which
the company danced. (Irene Worth even had to
embrace it and stroke it.) Browne turned to her
companion, Charles Gray, and commented reassur-
ingly: 'Nobody we know, dear.'

The anecdote was confirmed by Coral Browne
herself in a Channel 4 documentary in December
1990. Told on BBC Radio *Quote...Unquote* (1981).

—— 4 ——

Browne was with a gay actor she didn't think
much of who was looking for a part for himself
in Shakespeare's *King Lear*. Taking the text from him
and flipping through the pages she eventually
pointed to a stage direction in Act V and said: 'Here
you are, dear, how about "A Camp, near Dover"?'

Told to me by Roger Hammond in 1983. Sometimes the actor in question is said to have been her first husband, Philip Pearman (d. 1964), and that she said it to him when they were lying in bed and she was learning her lines as Regan.

—— 1 ——

Appearing at Stratford, Ontario, Browne was having trouble with a wig and when Tyrone Guthrie asked what the matter was, she told him: 'It's like looking through a yak's arse!'

From her obituary in *The Independent* (31 May 1991).

—— 2 ——

Browne appeared as herself in Alan Bennett's TV play *An Englishman Abroad*, based on her encounter in Moscow with the exiled spy Guy Burgess. A Hollywood writer told her that although he had enjoyed the play, he didn't think the writing was up to scratch. Aghast at this slight, Browne put the American in his place on the question of writing: 'Listen, dear, you couldn't write "f***" on a dusty venetian blind.'

Quoted by Alan Bennett in *The Sunday Times Magazine* (18 November 1984), and the story confirmed by Browne in a Channel 4 documentary, December 1990.

—— 3 ——

To a friend who spotted her emerging from Brompton Oratory, Browne implored: 'Don't talk to me, dear, I'm in a state of f****** grace.'

Told to me by an anonymous correspondent (*c.* 1987).

—— 4 ——

When a man attempted to get into a taxi that Browne had already hailed and boarded, the driver said to him, 'Sorry, mate, this lady's already hired me.' The man asked, 'Which lady?' So Browne rolled down the window and said, 'This f****** lady, mate!'

Told to me by Roger Hammond in 1983. Confirmed by a Channel 4 documentary, December 1990.

—— 5 ——

An actor with whom she was rehearsing caught Browne's fancy. Informed by a colleague that she was *most* unlikely to get anywhere with that particular man, she bet the colleague a pound that she would. Next morning, the colleague who had

accepted the bet asked her, loudly and meaningfully, in the presence of the other actor, 'Well, dear, do you owe me anything?' Browne replied, disappointedly: 'Seven and six.'

Told to me by Roger Hammond in 1983.

—— 6 ——

Taking part as Volumnia in a production of *Coriolanus*, Browne waspishly suggested that what the rabble might be shouting at one point was: 'Three o'clock, Duke of York's theatre, they're burning Dulcie Gray!'

Told to me by Martin Jarvis in 1991.

—— 7 ——

Of the ageing actor Sir Godfrey Tearle's romance with the then young actress Jill Bennett, Browne commented: 'I could never understand what he saw in her, until I saw her eating corn on the cob at the Caprice.'

In Ned Sherrin, *Cutting Edge* (1984), anonymously, and in Ned Sherrin, *Theatrical Anecdotes* (1991), with the participants named.

Lenny BRUCE

(1925–66) American satirical comedian.

—— 8 ——

Bruce once leapt out of a second-storey window crying, 'I'm Superjew!' If it was a suicide bid, it was unsuccessful. He merely sustained a broken leg.

Quoted in *The Observer* (21 August 1966).

BUILDERS

—— 9 ——

A friend of mine told me of a builder who was carrying out very extensive work for him and said, 'You know that estimate we talked about, Mr White?' (Note the careful use of 'talked about' rather than 'agreed'.)

'Yes, yes,' said my friend.

'Well, "24", I think we was talking about?'

'Yes, yes,' said my friend. '"24".'

'Well, I thought I'd better warn you, what with one thing and another, that it now looks as though it will be nearer to "32" . . .'

'Ah, "32", eh?' said my friend. 'I wonder if you could be a bit more specific? How much nearer will it be to "32"?'

'Er, well,' replied the operative, 'Not to put too fine a point on it, and what with one thing and another, "46" . . .'

Told to me by Jonathan White, c. 1983.

George BURNS

(1898–) American comedian who starred with his wife Gracie Allen in delightful TV shows. After her death, he specialized in jokes about his extreme longevity.

—— 1 ——

'Acting is about honesty,' said Burns. 'If you can fake that, you've got it made' – so says Fred Metcalf in *The Penguin Dictionary of Modern Quotations* (1986). Michael York has the more familiar version in *Travelling Player* (1991): 'The secret of acting is sincerity – and if you can fake that, you've got it made.'

> However, Kingsley Amis in a devastating piece about Leo Rosten in *Memoirs* (1991) has the humorist relating 'at some stage in the 1970s' how he had given a Commencement address including the line, 'Sincerity. If you can *fake that* . . . you'll have the world at your feet.' So perhaps the saying was awash before Burns received the credit. Or perhaps Rosten took it from him? An advertisement in *Rolling Stone, c.* 1982, offered a T-shirt with the anonymous slogan: 'The secret of success is sincerity. Once you can fake that you've got it made.'

—— 2 ——

Asked by William Safire of *The New York Times* about the origin of the saying, 'When the man shows up at the door to return the pictures, you've got to go', Burns explained: 'You see, I'm an old vaudeville actor – I'm going back 65 or 70 years – and in those days, your contract had a cancellation clause in it. If the manager didn't like your act, he was able to cancel you after your first show. All the actors carried their own pictures, so after the first show, if the manager knocked on your door and gave you

back your pictures, you started packing.'

Burns (then in his 90s) added: 'When the Guy knocks on my door with the pictures, I'm not going to answer.'

Related to me by Charles G. Francis (1992).

George BUSH

(1924–) American Republican President, chiefly notable for his language-mangling 'Bushisms' – sayings which seemed to hint at meaning but seldom delivered it.

—— 3 ——

During his 1984 vice-presidential campaign, Bush let slip several male-chauvinist remarks. In a TV debate with the Democratic contender, Geraldine Ferraro, he said, patronizingly, 'Let me help you with the difference, Mrs Ferraro, between Iran and the embassy in Lebanon'. He then compounded this offence by referring to the debate in an aside to a docker: 'We tried to kick a little ass last night.'

> **Sources: *The Times* (19 October 1984) and *Time* (22 October 1984). Barbara Bush joined in, too. Of Mrs Ferraro, Mrs Bush said, '[She is] a four million dollar *****. I can't say it, but it rhymes with "rich".'**

—— 4 ——

During the 1988 presidential election campaign, Bush had occasion to point out his half-Mexican grandchildren. Unfortunately he referred to them as 'the little brown ones'.

Reported in *The Independent* (17 August 1988).

—— 5 ——

After touring the Auschwitz death camp, Bush said, 'Boy, they were big on crematoriums, weren't they?'

Reported in *The Independent* (19 August 1988).

—— 6 ——

Bush was a junk-food junky. It was said that he crunched chocolate bars on his breakfast and was addicted to pork scratchings. One of the few policies he stood firm on concerned broccoli. 'It tastes like a medicine,' he declared and banned it from his official plane, Air Force One. When this caused ructions among broccoli growers (who unloaded a 10-ton juggernaut on the White House steps), he warned, 'Wait till the country hears how I feel about cauliflower.'

He followed this up by declaring his distaste for carrots also. He denounced them as 'orange broccoli'.

Reported in *The Independent on Sunday* (25 March 1990).

—— 1 ——

When he was President, Bush paid a visit to an old people's home. After chatting to patients for a little while, he asked one of them, 'And do you know who I am?' 'No,' came the reply from one old biddie, 'but if you ask in reception I'm sure they will be able to tell you.'

Told by Derek Parker in *The Author* (Summer 1993).

BUS PASSENGERS

—— 2 ——

'On the bus the other day a woman with a baby sat opposite, the baby bawled, and the woman at once began to unlace herself, exposing a large red udder, which she swung into the baby's face. The infant, however, continued to cry and the woman said, "Come on, there's a good boy – if you don't, I shall give it to the gentleman opposite."'

This passage comes from *The Journal of a Disappointed Man* by 'W. N. P. Barbellion', first published in 1919. I included it in my *Eavesdroppings* (1981) but subsequently discovered that – like so much else – this much-quoted remark probably began life as a *Punch* cartoon caption. In the edition of 11 May 1904 (Vol. 126), 'THE UNPROTECTED MALE' shows a man in an omnibus being addressed thus: 'Mother (after vainly offering a bottle to refractory infant) "'ERE, TIKE IT, WILL YER! IF YER DON'T 'URRY UP, I'LL GIVE IT TO THE GENTLEMAN OPPOSITE!"'

—— 3 ——

I was sitting on top of a No. 29 bus which had stopped outside the old Wood Green Town Hall on its way to Palmers Green in 1938–9. A cockney factory girl said to her friend: 'So I sez to 'im "Oh", and 'e sez "Oh, it's 'Oh', is it?" and I sez, "Yes, it is 'Oh'."'

'This was a story often repeated over the years with varying intonations by my friend Dorothy

Reynolds, the actress' – stated Mrs G. H. Alston, Lewes in a letter to me in January 1980. Peter Jones had quoted it on *Quote...Unquote* in the summer of 1979, mentioning where it had come from. I included it in my *Eavesdroppings* (1981).

—— 4 ——

The following letter was received by the General Manager of a Motor Omnibus Service 'north of the Trent'. It was written from 'The Royal Infirmary': 'Dear Sir, I was prevailed upon by my husband, last Saturday, to make a journey in one of your motor omnibuses, and I am very pleased indeed that I did so, for during the journey down, a floating kidney, which has for many months resisted the best medical skill of this city, settled into its normal position and I have been free from pain ever since.

'Should you desire to communicate with me, please do so at the above address, where I am being treated for a lacerated throat due to swallowing my false teeth upon the return journey. Yours truly, A VERY GRATEFUL PASSENGER.'

Told in the *Journal of the Municipal Tramways Association* in 1924. Sent to me by Rosemary Thacker, Librarian of the National Tramways Museum, in 1991.

R. A. BUTLER

(Lord Butler of Saffron Walden) (1902–82) English Conservative politician who, in time, came to be referred to as 'the Best Prime Minister We Never Had'.

—— 5 ——

After attacks on the government of Sir Anthony Eden in the closing days of 1955, Butler was about to board an aircraft when he was asked 'by a Press Association man', 'Mr Butler, would you say that this is the best Prime Minister we have?' As Butler put it in his autobiography *The Art of the Possible* (1973), 'My hurried assent to this well-meant but meaningless proposition was flashed around the world, indeed it was fathered upon me. I do not think it did Anthony any good. It did not do me any good either.'

Samuel BUTLER

(1835–1902) Author of *Erewhon* and *The Way of All Flesh*.

—— 1 ——

Butler, though dying, was engaged in the purchase of the freehold of a house in Hampstead. To Alfred Emery Cathie, his clerk, 'servant and friend', he said, 'Have you brought the cheque book, Alfred?' Butler took off his spectacles and put them down on the table. 'I don't want them any more,' he said, his head fell back, and he died. 'Have you brought the cheque book, Alfred?' has subsequently become a family catchphrase in certain households.

As for example that of the actress Sian Phillips (as recounted by her on BBC Radio *Quote...Unquote*, 1993). Biographical details from Philip Henderson, *Samuel Butler: the Incarnate Bachelor* (1953).

Ernie BYFIELD Jr

(*fl.* 1950) American businessman.

—— 2 ——

The son of the American hotel owner (1889–1950) was asked why he – such a young man – was running three big hotels. He replied, 'Well, I happened to run into my father in the lobby and he took a liking to me.'

Source unknown. The father is credited in *Who's Who in American History* with popularizing tomato juice as a beverage.

Max BYGRAVES

(1922–) English entertainer.

—— 3 ——

At one time Bygraves was on every impressionist's list. His drying-the-hands gesture, his cockney drawl, his assumed conceit were a gift to impressionists. And one impressionist, Mike Yarwood, made a gift to Bygraves – his catchphrase, 'I wanna tell you a story', which Yarwood created. Anyway, as Bygraves used to say in his act, 'I was down at a seaside resort the other day and they were having a Max Bygraves impersonation contest, so I decided to give it a go. I came fifth.'

Told to me by Bygraves in a radio interview (1980). Compare the story told about Charlie Chaplin entering a look-alike competition in Monte Carlo – he came third (L. Lucaire, *Celebrity Trivia*, date unknown).

—— 4 ——

Bygraves was in Jersey, going to appear in his show: 'When I put my glasses on and put a hat on, I can get along the street quite well without being recognized. I don't mind being stopped and asked for an autograph – I quite enjoy it – but sometimes when you want to get on, you want to get round a store . . . I can really disguise myself and nobody knows who I am. Anyway, I was in this store, buying some cigars, and the girl who was serving me didn't recognize me, and a lady sidles up to me and she says, "I recognize yer! . . . 'I wanna tell you a story' . . . We know who you are, *Frankie!*"'

From the same radio interview (1980).

C

Michael CAINE

(1933–) English actor, mostly in films. If he had failed at this, he would have made a wonderful London cab-driver.

—— 1 ——

Caine was born in 1933 with the name Maurice Micklewhite. He was influenced in his choice of stage name by a film he'd seen called *The Caine Mutiny*.

Simon CALLOW

(1949–) English actor and director.

—— 2 ——

With his booming voice and actorish persona, Callow doesn't have to climb very far to go over the top. At least, however, he is self-aware. 'There was the time,' he recalls, 'when I went out in my fedora and a rather big coat to hail a taxi. The taxi-driver said to me, "Where to?" and I said, "The National Theatre". He gave me a look and he said, "Where else?" And I *suppose* I understood what he meant . . .'

From an interview in *The Independent on Sunday*, 23 February 1992.

Commander A(rchibald) B(ruce) CAMPBELL

(1881–196?) British broadcaster who was a regular participant in the radio *Brains Trust* of the 1940s. He was a retired naval officer turned anecdotalist.

—— 3 ——

Campbell was taking part in an earlier version of the programme when it was still called *Any Questions* (in 1941). Donald McCullough, the chairman, said to the panel: 'Mr Edwards of Balham wants to know if the members of the Brains Trust agree with the practice of sending missionaries to foreign lands.' Professors Joad and Huxley gave their answers and then Campbell began, 'When I was in Patagonia . . .'

In a book which used the phrase as its title, Campbell recalled: 'I got no further, for Joad burst into a roar of laughter and the other members of the session joined in. For some time the feature was held up while the hilarity spent itself. For the life of me I could not see the joke . . . Even today (1951), years after, I can raise a laugh if I am on a public platform and make an allusion to it.'

Quoted in *The Bloomsbury Dictionary of Popular Phrases* (1990).

Mrs Patrick CAMPBELL

(1865–1940) English actress of formidable reputation.

—— 4 ——

Mrs Pat was sitting in the stalls with the director of a new play watching a new young actress rehearsing. The actress broke off and said, 'I wonder if it would be a good idea here, Mrs Campbell, if while they were talking I was arranging some flowers?' 'That's quite a good idea, my dear, do that,' came the reply, to everyone's surprise. Then later, the actress suggested, 'I was wondering if, before I said my line, I could have a coat which I took off?' 'Yes, do that, my dear.' The director turned to Mrs Pat and said, 'Clever girl, isn't she?' And Mrs Campbell said, 'Yes, *very*. What a pity she won't be with us after lunch . . .'

Told by Antony Jay on BBC Radio *Quote...Unquote* (1990).

—— 1 ——

An elderly scientist was droning on to Mrs Pat about ants – 'They are wonderful little creatures. They have their own police force and their own army.' Mrs Pat could bear it no longer. She leaned forward and said, with an expression said to be 'of the utmost interest and in a voice like damson-coloured velvet': 'No navy, I suppose?'

Recounted in Margot Peters, *Mrs Pat* (1984). James Agate in *Ego 7* (for 11 February 1944) has it from someone called Bobby Andrews.

—— 2 ——

A taxi driver once attempted *not* to carry Mrs Pat and a disagreeable pooch called 'Moonbeam' in his vehicle. But she climbed in nevertheless and commanded, 'The Empire Theatre, my man, and no nonsense!' The dog decided to misbehave *en route* and the taxi driver chose to point out the large damp patch on the floor of his cab. Mrs Pat was having none of it. 'Moonbeam didn't pee,' she said loudly. '*I* did!'

Bennett Cerf, *Shake Well Before Using* (1948), has an early version of this story.

—— 3 ——

After a dull weekend, Mrs Pat took pen in hand and wrote in the hostess's elaborate visitor's book, 'Quoth the raven'.

This version is from Bennett Cerf, *Shake Well Before Using* (1948). See also BARRYMORE 24:6.

Alfredo CAMPOLI

(1906–91) Italian violinist, chiefly in Britain.

—— 4 ——

He was known professionally as 'Campoli'. The reason for this, as he used to say himself, was that if announced along the lines of, 'Alfredo Campoli is now going to play . . .', he thought people tended to hear, 'I'm afraid old Campoli is now going to play . . .'

An addition from Monica Parkhurst to *The Independent*'s obituary (30 March 1991).

Eddie CANTOR

(1892–1964) American comedian, in vaudeville and films.

—— 5 ——

When Cantor heard that Norma Shearer, the actress wife of Irving Thalberg, had produced a son, he sent a telegram of the utmost point to the noted Jewish film producer: 'Congratulations on your latest production. Sure it will look better after it has been cut.'

Told by Larry Adler on BBC Radio *Quote...Unquote* (1977).

Don CARNEY

(1897–1954) American broadcaster.

—— 6 ——

From 1928 to 1949, 'Uncle Don' was the host of a popular children's show on radio station WOR, broadcasting over a large part of the United States. He spent his life trying to deny that he had ever let slip one of the most famous clangers of all when, thinking he was off the air, he had said, 'I guess that'll hold the little bastards . . .'

I have also seen this attributed, without any justification, to Derek McCulloch, 'Uncle Mac' of BBC *Children's Hour* (as by the *Daily Star* 24 April 1985).

Jimmy CARTER

(1924–) American Democratic President. A peanut farmer from Plains, Georgia, Carter had a fearsome wife (Rosalynn, 'The Steel Magnolia') with whom he held hands publicly, a folksy mother (Miz Lillian), a drunken brother (Billy) and a faintly embarrassing daughter (Amy – whose views on world affairs he was wont to quote publicly). His stature increased after he was voted out of office after one term.

—— 7 ——

During his campaign for the presidency, Carter gave an interview to *Playboy* in which he said: 'I've looked on a lot of women with lust. I've committed adultery in my heart many times. God recognizes I will do this and forgives me.'

The American electorate, perceiving a useful working relationship with the Almighty, voted Carter in to the White House.

From his interview with *Playboy* (November 1976).

—— 1 ——

In 1978, Carter was due to visit West Germany and wanted to come up with a slogan as memorable as John F. Kennedy's 1963 *'Ich bin ein Berliner'*. Unfortunately, he resisted an impish suggestion allegedly made by Gerald Rafshoon, his communications adviser, that he should go instead to Frankfurt and declare, *'Ich bin ein Frankfurter'*.

Told in *Time* Magazine (24 July 1978).

—— 2 ——

On his first visit to a Russian bloc country – Poland – Carter wanted to make a good impression. In his prepared remarks, he told the Poles, 'I have come to learn your opinions and understand your desires for the future.' The American interpreter translated these phrases, somewhat surprisingly, as, 'I desire the Poles carnally.'

Report-ed in *The Evening Standard* (30 December 1978).

—— 3 ——

Seeking re-election, Carter addressed the Democratic Convention and was booed twice – an unprecedented reaction on such an occasion. He made fluffs and errors, which augured badly for his future. Wishing to evoke one of the great Democratic politicians who never made it to the White House, he wanted to mention the name of Hubert Horatio Humphrey. Instead, what he said was, 'Hubert Horatio Hornblower'.

Reported in *The Daily Mail* (16 August 1980).

—— 4 ——

Some years after Carter's star had faded, Queen Elizabeth the Queen Mother was reported to have complained drolly about his behaviour: 'He is the only man, since my dear husband died, to have the effrontery to kiss me on the lips.'

Quoted in *The Observer* (13 February 1983).

Lord CASTLEROSSE

(1891–1943) Irish peer, later the 6th Earl of Kenmare. The court jester of Lord Beaverbrook's court. When asked on the golf-course what his handicap was, he replied, 'Drink and debauchery'.

—— 5 ——

The massive Castlerosse was being upbraided by Lady Astor about the size of his stomach. 'What would you say if that was on a woman?' she asked. 'Madam,' he replied politely, 'half an hour ago it was.'

Recounted by Godfrey Smith in his *Sunday Times* column during 1980.

Nurse Edith CAVELL

(1865–1915) English nurse who was shot by the Germans for helping Allied prisoners escape during the First World War.

—— 6 ——

James Pryde, the artist (1866–1941), was watching the unveiling of the statue of Cavell outside the National Portrait Gallery in London and evidently thought it a poor likeness. As the drapes fell away, he remarked, 'My God, they've shot the wrong person!'

Letter from Derek Hudson of Hindhead (1977). The statue was unveiled in 1920.

Jonathan CECIL

(1939–) English actor, son of the writer and academic Lord David Cecil.

—— 7 ——

When asked what he wanted to be when he grew up, Cecil replied: 'I'm going to be neurotic like my daddy.'

I recall being told this at New College, Oxford, in about 1963. Both father and son had strong connections with the college. Kingsley Amis in his *Memoirs* (1991) wonders whether it wasn't rather Hugh Cecil, the younger son, who said it. Accord-

ing to Ned Sherrin, *Theatrical Anecdotes* (1991), Jonathan appeared as a fairy in a New College production of *A Midsummer Night's Dream* and was interviewed by a reporter from *The Oxford Mail* who also asked what he wanted to be when he grew up. The reply: 'An aesthete, like Daddy.' So which of these is the original or correct version, I know not. Perhaps he said both.

Charles CHAPLIN

(later Sir Charles) (1889–1977) British-born film comedian of universal fame. Wrote an appallingly conceited autobiography.

—— 1 ——

At the end of the First World War, General Nivelle, hero of Verdun, made a tour of the United States. When he reached Los Angeles, a big public reception was held so that he could meet members of the movie colony. Among those invited were Charles Chaplin and Will Rogers. Chaplin was oddly nervous about meeting this great war hero and confided in Rogers that he had absolutely no idea how he would start up a conversation. Advised Rogers, 'Well, you might ask him if he was in the war, and which side he was on . . .'

Told in Irvin S. Cobb, *A Laugh a Day Keeps the Doctor Away* (1921).

Prince CHARLES

(1948–) Heir to the British throne. A more sensitive plant than some in his family, but he unwisely admitted on one occasion that talking to plants was a good thing (for the plants, that is).

—— 2 ——

At their wedding in July 1981, Charles's bride, Lady Diana Spencer, vowed: 'I, Diana Frances, take thee Philip Charles Arthur George to be my wedded husband' – accidentally transposing the first two of his Royal collection of names. Not to be outdone, Prince Charles, instead of saying 'and all my worldly goods with thee I share' vowed 'all *thy* goods with thee I share . . .'

From a recording of the ceremony.

—— 3 ——

The Prince was making a speech in the open air to an audience of 13,500 schoolchildren in Western Australia. His theme was good manners and he quoted a homily dating from 1897: 'Swearing is contemptible and foolish . . . Ill temper can disorder the mind . . .'

A few seconds into his prepared speech, the blustery wind whipped the top sheet of paper away. 'Oh God, my bloody bit of paper,' he exclaimed.

Reported in *The Times* (9 April 1983).

—— 4 ——

After the birth of his second son, Prince Harry, in September 1984, Prince Charles said, 'We have nearly got a full polo team now.'

—— 5 ——

Presenting the Thomas Cranmer Schools Prize, organized by the Prayer Book Society, in 1989, Prince Charles delivered an attack on the 'dismal wasteland of banality, cliché and casual obscenity' of everyday language. 'Is it entirely an accident,' he wondered, 'that the defacing of Cranmer's Prayer Book has coincided with a calamitous decline in literacy and the quality of English?' He went on to deliver a rendering of Hamlet's 'To be or not to be' speech in modern English:

Well, frankly, the problem as I see it
At this moment in time is whether I
Should just lie down under all this hassle
And let them walk all over me.
Or, whether I should just say: 'OK,
I get the message', and do myself in.
I mean, let's face it, I'm in a no-win situation,
And quite honestly, I'm so stuffed up to here with the
Whole stupid mess that, I can tell you, I've just
Got a good mind to take the quick way out.
That's the bottom line. The only problem is:
What happens if I find that when I've bumped
Myself off, there's some kind of a, you know,
All that mystical stuff about when you die,
You might find you're still – know what I mean?

Full marks to the Prince's speechwriter. Text from *The Independent* (20 December 1989). Compare CLERGY 57:1.

G. K. CHESTERTON

(1874–1936) English novelist, poet and critic.

—— 1 ——

Chesterton was noted for being disorganized and absent-minded. On one occasion, heading off by train to make a speech, he had to get out and send his wife a telegram saying, 'Am in Market Harborough. Where ought I to be?'

> Often misquoted as 'Am in Wolverhampton'. According to one biographer, Maisie Ward, in *Return to Chesterton* (1944), a hundred different places have been substituted for 'Market Harborough'. Chesterton's wife, Frances, on this occasion cabled the answer: 'Home' – because, as she exclaimed, it was easier to get him home and start him off again. Yes, Market Harborough was the original, and is confirmed by Chesterton himself in his *Autobiography* (1936).

—— 2 ——

During the First World War, a patriotic hostess pointedly asked Chesterton, 'Why are you not out at the Front?' He replied to her, gently: 'Madam, if you go round to the side, you will find that I am.'

> An old story, recounted for example by A. N. Wilson in *Hilaire Belloc* (1984).

CHILDREN

—— 3 ——

A child in class, when asked to draw a picture of the Holy Family, produced a picture in which Mary and the baby sat on a recognizably donkeyish steed, led by Joseph. On the ground nearby lay a black blob. 'What is that?' asked the teacher. 'The flea,' answered the artist. 'What flea, dear?' asked the puzzled teacher. 'The one the Angel told Joseph to take.' Eventually, puzzled but not liking to challenge an imaginative child, the teacher checked out her Bible. And there it was: Matthew 2:13 '. . . the angel of the Lord saying, Arise, and take the young child and his mother, and flee into Egypt . . .'

> Letter from Robina S. Dexter of Liverpool, April 1992. She had had it from her mother, a kindergarten teacher. A well-known story.

—— 4 ——

The little girl made a classic comment to the little boy when he dropped his trousers for her to have a look – 'My,' she said, 'that's a handy little gadget.'

> In my book *Babes and Sucklings* (1983), I said this remark had reached me from several sources – 'One says it involved "the daughter of a friend", another says "it was told me by a friend who was a teacher about the local primary school at which he taught", and a third specifically says it concerned "our 2-year-old son".' In 1992, Miss Pera J. Bain of Brighton, having heard me allude to 'handy little gadgets' on the radio, wrote to say she had first heard it in 1941 when she was in charge of Inspection at a very small factory in Woking, staffed entirely by women. 'The Tool-Setter came from Scotland . . . Relatives of hers lived in a croft on one of the outer islands. They had one small daughter, Alison, who rarely saw another child. But they had a visit from relatives who had one small boy. Shortly after arrival this child said he needed the lavatory, so Alison was told to show him the bathroom. Which she did and presently she was heard to say, "*That's* a handy little gadget ye have there."' Indeed, I think some of the other versions I have heard were spoken with a Scots accent – even to the point of re-phrasing it, 'a handy *wee* gadget'.

—— 5 ——

Overheard outside the junior section of a public library. Two little girls were talking and one remarked, 'Yes, we've moved into a house now, so me and my brother have got a bedroom each.' Then she added, thoughtfully: 'But Mummy and Daddy still have to share.'

> I quoted this from a *Quote...Unquote* listener in *Eavesdroppings* (1983), but I fear it had whiskers on it even then. With the tag, 'Mum still has to sleep with dad', it had appeared in *Pass the Port Again* (1980).

—— 6 ——

A schoolteacher in New Zealand had given her class of ten-year-olds a list of words which were to be used, one at a time, in a short passage to demonstrate their exact meaning. One word was 'Frugal' which a clever boy clearly knew had something to do with saving. He wrote: 'A beautiful princess was at the top of a tall tower. She saw a handsome prince riding by. "Frugal me, frugal me," cried the beautiful princess. So the handsome prince climbed the tall tower and he frugalled her and they lived happily ever after.'

> This story from a correspondent in Truro appeared in my *Foot in Mouth* (1982). She said the schoolteacher in question was her niece. However, the story had already appeared in *Pass the Port* (1976).

—— 1 ——

A seven-year-old girl was watching her mother put on some face cream and asked, 'Mummy, is that the cream they show on the television that makes you beautiful?' When Mummy told her it was, she commented, after a thoughtful pause, 'It doesn't work very well, does it?'

Told in my *Babes and Sucklings* (1983) but I see that a version had earlier appeared in *Pass the Port* (1976). A *Punch* joke, originally, in all probability.

—— 2 ——

A little girl was splashing a little boy in the swimming pool. 'I'm going to duck you,' said she. Replied he, 'No chance. You can't even say it proper.'

Told by Lord Oaksey on BBC Radio *Quote... Unquote* (1986).

—— 3 ——

S amuel Butler recorded this in his notebook: 'The little Strangs say the "good words", as they call them, before going to bed, aloud and at their father's knee, or rather in the pit of his stomach. One of them was lately heard to say "Forgive us our Christmasses, as we forgive them that Christmas against us."'

Samuel Butler's *Notebooks* were compiled between 1874 and 1902 and have been published.

—— 4 ——

T here can be few who have not heard of the little boy who called his teddy bear 'Gladly' because of the line in the hymn which goes (for childish ears, at least): 'Gladly, my cross-eyed bear . . .'

Known by the 1960s, certainly. John Hopkins used the phrase as the title of one part of his TV drama *Talking to a Stranger* in 1966. Other childish mishearings on religious themes include 'Blessed art thou, a monk swimming', 'Harold be Thy name', 'Suffered under bunch of spiders', 'Hail, Mary, blessed art thou swimming' and my own 'Holy Golfball'.

Agatha CHRISTIE

(later Dame Agatha) (1890–1976) English detective novelist and playwright.

—— 5 ——

C hristie's play *The Mousetrap* has famously become the longest continuously-running stage play in the world. When it was first tried out in 1952 in Nottingham before coming to the West End, the part of Detective Sergeant Trotter was played by Richard Attenborough. He recalls that the cast was worried that the second act wouldn't work and a good deal of agonizing over it went on. Christie, taking her leave on one occasion, remarked, 'I should stop worrying and get off to bed. I think we might get quite a nice little run out of it . . .'

Quoted in *The Times* (22 November 1982) – but Attenborough had been telling the story long before, as on a BBC Radio *Home This Afternoon* broadcast (1966). In that, he has her say, 'Darlings, I think we might get quite a little run', though one wonders if the 'darlings' wasn't himself coming through.

Sir John CHRISTIE, Bt.

(1882–1962) English arts administrator, founder of the Glyndebourne Opera.

—— 6 ——

W hen his wife was rushed to hospital with acute appendicitis on their honeymoon, she woke up the morning after the operation to find him in bed with her. 'I got bored,' he explained, 'so I thought I'd have my appendix out too and keep you company.'

Recalled by his son, Sir George Christie, in *The Observer* (3 May 1992).

Randolph CHURCHILL

(1911–68) English journalist and politician who had the difficult task of attempting to follow in his father Winston's impressive footsteps. Noël Coward remarked of him: 'Dear Randolph, utterly unspoiled by failure.'

—— 7 ——

W hile reading the Bible from cover to cover in response to Evelyn Waugh's bet of £10 that he could not do so, Churchill was heard exclaiming periodically, 'Isn't God a shit!'

From *The Diaries of Evelyn Waugh* (1976), entry for 11 November 1944.

—— 1 ——

Churchill wrote apologetically to a hostess whose dinner party he had ruined with one of his displays of drunken rudeness: 'I should never be allowed out in private.'

Recounted in Brian Roberts, *Randolph* (1984). Writing a letter to his father (16 October 1952), Churchill called this a 'mot' he had coined about himself.

—— 2 ——

He was not only a drunk and a bully, he was a bounder. On one occasion, in bed with someone else's wife, Churchill rang up the woman's husband. 'Guess who I'm in bed with!' he barked at the man. '. . . Doris!'

(Or some such name.) Told to me by Sir Osbert Lancaster when recording an obituary of Churchill for the BBC in 1968. On re-reading my diary entry for 6 June 1968 I see that what Lancaster actually told me was that he himself had once gone into a room and found Randolph in bed with a blonde. 'He reached for the telephone and rang up Lord Castlerosse and said, "Guess where I am! In bed with Doris!" Doris being, I gather, Lady Castlerosse . . .'

I need hardly say this was not part of the obituary. Malcolm Muggeridge (so it is said) did, however, push forward the boundaries of obituaries in *The Times* when he wrote of Randolph (7 June 1968): 'At social gatherings he was liable to engage in heated and noisy arguments which could ruin a dinner party, and made him the dread of hostesses on both sides of the Atlantic. The tendency was exacerbated by an always generous, and occasionally excessive alcoholic intake.'

Sir Winston
CHURCHILL

(1874–1965) English Conservative prime minister, about whom there are more stories, probably – and certainly more quoted remarks – than any other public figure this century. A few of the marginally less familiar:

—— 3 ——

David Lloyd George is reputed to have said of Churchill: 'He would make a drum out of the skin of his mother the louder to sing his own praises.'

Told by Peter Kellner (1987).

—— 4 ——

George Bernard Shaw sent Churchill two tickets for the first night of *St Joan* (which was in 1924), with a note explaining, 'One for yourself, the other for a friend – if you have one.' Churchill sent them back, regretting he would be unable to attend the first night, but saying he would like some tickets for the second night – 'If there is one'.

I first received this anecdote in a letter from Nancy and Tony Morse of Blackley, Manchester in 1978 and I have no idea where they found it, though it is in *Pass the Port* (1976). Peter Hay in *Theatrical Anecdotes* (1987) says that it was told by his grandfather when Hay was growing up in London (1950s). I have also seen a version involving Noël Coward and Churchill. According to Michael Holroyd, *Bernard Shaw, Vol. 3* (1991), Shaw's secretary, Blanche Patch, dismissed this story as a journalistic invention.

—— 5 ——

At Christmas 1944, Churchill paid a visit to Athens. This resulted in the appointment of Archbishop Damaskinos as Regent of Greece and General Plastiras as Prime Minister. Of the latter, Churchill commented: 'Well, I hope he doesn't have feet of clay, too.'

Quoted in Leon Harris, *The Fine Art of Political Wit* (1966). In *Geoffrey Madan's Notebooks* (1981 – but Madan died in 1947), Churchill's remark is quoted as: 'A bewhiskered ecclesiastic, and a certain General Plastiras. I hope his feet are not of clay.'

—— 6 ——

A bishop told Churchill that his palace had no less than forty bedrooms in it. Churchill commented: 'Oh dear – and only Thirty-Nine Articles to put in them.'

Letter from Martin Hawkins of London SW2 (1979).

—— 7 ——

During a debate in the House of Commons a Labour MP called Paling interrupted Churchill during a speech and called him a 'dirty dog'. Churchill looked over his glasses at him and said, 'And you know what dirty dogs do to palings . . .'

Told by Jimmy Reid on *Quote...Unquote* (1982). If this is true, then it must have involved the Rt Hon. Wilfred Paling (1883–1971), a former colliery checkweighman who became a Labour MP and Postmaster-General (1947–50).

——— 1 ———

Churchill had some words of advice for those in public life who attracted the attention of the press. 'Never be photographed with a glass in your hand,' he said and added, after a pause, 'especially if it's an empty glass.'

> This was said to Sir David Hunt, his Private Secretary during Churchill's second prime-ministership, who told me in 1993. Evidently, Churchill went on to refer to an election at Dundee when he was defeated by a teetotaller.

——— 2 ———

Sir Stafford Cripps flourished under Churchill's leadership during the Second World War but afterwards rejoined the Labour Party and became Chancellor of the Exchequer. As well as presiding over austere policies, he was a long, thin streak of austerity to look at, too. Having had enough of his views at a dinner party, Churchill cried: 'Who will relieve me of this Wuthering Height?'

> In Willans & Roetter, *The Wit of Sir Winston* (1965).

——— 3 ———

When Sir Alfred Munnings was President of the Royal Academy in 1949, one of the guests at the annual dinner was Winston Churchill, who had just been admitted to the Academy. Munnings supposedly ruffled the politician's feathers by saying in his speech: 'Seated on my left is the greatest Englishman of all time. I said to him just now: "What would you do if you saw Picasso walking ahead of you down Piccadilly?" – and he replied: "I would kick him up the arse, Alfred."'

> Thus a report in *The Times* Diary (29 March 1983). Alas, the BBC recording of the event fails to confirm that Munnings ever said this. Not a born speaker, to put it mildly, what Munnings said was: 'Once he said to me, "Alfred, if you met Picasso coming down the street, would you join with me in kicking his something-something?" I said, "Yes, sir, I would!"'
> *The Times* report also suggested that, 'as the laughter died, Munnings yelled at the top of his voice: "Blunt, Blunt [i.e. Sir Anthony Blunt, the art connoisseur later unmasked as a traitor] – you're the one who says he prefers Picasso to Sir Joshua Reynolds!"' If Munnings did yell this, he was very quiet about it because the barb is not audible on the recording.

——— 4 ———

In a speech at Cardiff in 1950, Churchill chose to parody official jargon which had become all the rage under the then Labour government and which had redesignated 'homes' as 'accommodation units'. He referred to 'Accommodation Unit Sweet Accommodation Unit'.

> Recorded in Leslie Frewin, *Immortal Jester* (1973).

——— 5 ———

On his 80th birthday (30 November 1954), both Houses of Parliament presented Churchill with a portrait painted by Graham Sutherland. He did not like it but accepted the portrait with a gracefully double-edged compliment: 'The portrait is a remarkable example of modern art. It certainly combines force and candour. These are qualities which no active member of either House can do without or should fear to meet.'

Lady Churchill's dislike of the portrait took a more practical form: she had it destroyed.

> Another of Churchill's remarks on the same portrait was, 'I look as if I was having a difficult stool' – quoted in Ted Morgan, *Somerset Maugham* (1980) but earlier in *The Lyttelton Hart-Davis Letters* (for 20 November 1955). Other versions of this criticism are: 'How do they paint one today? Sitting on a lavatory!' (said to Charles Doughty, secretary of the committee which organized the tribute), and 'Here sits an old man on his stool, pressing and pressing.'

——— 6 ———

When Churchill was a very old man, he paid one of his infrequent visits to the House of Commons. An MP, observing him, remarked, 'After all, they say he's potty.' Muttered Churchill, 'They say he can't hear either.'

> Quoted in William Manchester, *The Last Lion* (1983).

——— 7 ———

Towards the end of his life, Churchill was sitting in the House of Commons smoking room with his fly-buttons undone. When this was pointed out to him, he said: 'Dead birds don't fall out of nests.'

> Also told in *The Lyttelton Hart-Davis Letters*, Vol. 2 (1979) (from a letter dated 5 January 1957, where the reply is: 'No matter. The dead bird does not leave the nest.')

CINEMA-GOERS

—— 1 ——

In the days of silent films, two elderly women were in an Edinburgh picture house watching a thriller. As the explanatory titles came up on the screen, one of the women was reading them aloud to her companion. When the situation reached its climax, came the subtitle, and then the voice: 'The thick plottens,' it said.

> Told to me by Mrs Dora Thomas of Edinburgh, in 1979.

—— 2 ——

The biographer, Robert Lacey, was in a Bristol cinema with his wife Sandi, watching the Ken Russell film of D. H. Lawrence's *Women in Love*. At the conclusion of the memorable scene in which Alan Bates and Oliver Reed wrestle with each other totally naked and then lie exhausted on the carpet, a woman in the audience was heard to comment: 'Nice carpet!'

> Told by Robert Lacey on BBC Radio *Quote... Unquote* (1978).

—— 3 ——

Overheard during a showing of the film *The Sound of Music*: one old lady saying to another, 'Isn't this the bit we like?'

> Quoted in my *Say No More!* (1987).

—— 4 ——

Overheard after a New York screening of the original four-hour version of the film *Heaven's Gate* in 1980: 'If we'd gone on Concorde we'd be in Paris now.'

> Recounted by Dick Vosburgh on BBC Radio *Quote...Unquote* (1980).

—— 5 ——

A Jewish woman told her friend: 'I've just been to Dr Zhivago and, do you know, it cost me £5.50!' Replied the other: '£5.50! That's outrageous. What is he, some sort of specialist?'

> Told by Kenneth Williams on TV-am *Good Morning Britain* (19 January 1985). In *The Diaries of Kenneth Williams* (1993) – the entry for 31 July 1978 – he has another version in which Golda Meir, the Prime Minister of Israel, went to a cinema box office and was told it would cost '1.50 to see *Dr Zhivago*' and she expostulates, 'What is he? Some sort of specialist?'

CIVIL SERVANTS

—— 6 ——

A minister making a speech in the House of Lords inadvertently read out an annotation which a civil servant had scrawled on his brief: 'This is a rotten argument but it should be enough for their Lordships on a hot summer afternoon.'

> From Lord Home's memoirs, *The Way the Wind Blows* (1976).

—— 7 ——

A civil servant in the Department of the Environment scribbled in the margin of a document written by a senior, 'P.O.F.' This was short for 'Pompous Old Fool'. However, when the senior noticed the initials and asked what they meant, the junior, with great presence of mind, quickly replied, 'Put On File'.

> Told to me by the civil servant in question, 1980s.

General Mark CLARK

(1896–1984) American soldier.

—— 8 ——

During the Second World War, prior to the Allied landings in North Africa, Clark was landed secretly on the coast of Algeria to make contact with friendly French officials and pro-Allied conspirators. He narrowly escaped being captured by the Vichy French police. Unfortunately, there was a mix-up as to which beach Clark should land on, with the result that the reception committee consisted of a man who inquired whether the General would like to meet his pretty sister. The interpreter gave such a strong negative that the man got the wrong idea and said, hastily, 'My brother then?' At which point the General (who had not been following the conversation) said, 'Ask him if he can get us the harbour-master.' The man replied, 'My brother will come cheaper.'

> Told to me by T. A. Dyer of London SW12 (1992) who points out that a similar sequence of misunderstandings occurs between Heracles and Dionysus at the beginning of Aristophanes' *The Frogs*.

John CLEESE

(1939–) English comic actor and writer of stature
(well, he has long legs).

—— 1 ——

The Cleese family name was originally *Cheese* until his father, presumably tired of ridicule, changed it. But the new name proved difficult to convey to people over the telephone. In the 1980s Cleese claimed that when booking tables at restaurants he would adapt the name to suit the nationality of the restaurant. Hence if he was booking a table in an Italian restaurant he would say he was 'Signor Formaggio' – which is the Italian for . . . Mr Cheese.

Cleese himself told me the first bit in 1973.

CLERGY

—— 2 ——

In the early days of British radio, a leading churchman was conducting a live religious service, conscious that he had to modulate his voice to make it more acceptable for a studio than for a church. After he had concluded the broadcast with the Grace, he commented to the producer, 'I don't think that was too loud, do you?' Unfortunately, part of this came over the air as, '. . . the fellowship of the Holy Ghost, be with us all evermore . . . I don't think!'

Told to me by the Reverend Vernon Sproxton, *c*. 1955.

—— 3 ——

An old Nonconformist minister chose as his text Psalm 42 v.1: 'As the hart panteth after the waterbrooks, so panteth my soul after Thee, O God.' His discourse, the minister said, would be divided into three parts – 'the pants of the hart, the pants of the Psalmist, and, finally, pants in general.'

Source unknown.

—— 4 ——

When an order of service was printed at one particular church it revealed this interesting sequence of musical items:

Solo: 'Death where is thy sting?'
Hymn: 'Search me, O God.'

Source unknown.

—— 5 ——

At a village kirk in the Scottish Highlands, the minister was much given to interminable impromptu prayer but occasionally lost his train of thought. 'Oh Lord,' he entreated, 'Thou that paintest the crocus purple . . .' Here, his inspiration failing him, he rapidly concluded: '. . . paint us purple, too.'

Told to me by J. M. Dick-Cunyngham (1984).

—— 6 ——

How appropriate it was that for a marriage service the minister had chosen from the Methodist Hymnal the one beginning 'Here I Raise My Ebenezer'.

Told to me by David Ashton, Pontefract, West Yorkshire (1979).

—— 7 ——

At the wedding of an elderly woman who had buried her first two husbands and was now marrying for the third time, a hymn was sung which contained these first two lines:

I know not what awaits me;
God kindly veils my eyes.

Told to me by Edna Cluley, Camberley, Surrey (1992).

—— 8 ——

I do not know who wrote this 'Home Counties version' of the Lord's Prayer, but it sums up the delightful confusion occasioned by certain lines in the prayer and directs one's religious thoughts in wholly new directions . . .

Our Farnham which art in Hendon, Harrow be thy Name. Thy Kingston come. Thy Wimbledon, in Erith as it is in Heston.
    Give us this day our Leatherhead. And forgive us our Westminsters. As we forgive them that Westminster against us. And lead us not into Thames Ditton; But deliver us from Ealing: For

thine is the Kingston, the Purley, and the Crawley,
For Iver and Iver. Crouch End.

This version was printed in my *Say No More!*
(1987). Correspondence in the magazine *Oxford
Today* (Hilary/Trinity terms 1990) produced a
number of variations and a date of composition
somewhere in the 1930s, but no author. Peter Hay
in *Business Anecdotes* (1988) includes a faintly
similar parody written in 1930s America by a Ford
Motors worker before unionization. It begins:

Our Father, who art in Dearborn, Henry be thy
    name.
Let payday come. Thy will be done in Fordson
    as it is in Highland Park . . .

—— 1 ——

Ivor Brown wrote an officialese version of the
Lord's Prayer, which included: 'We should be
obliged for your attention in providing for our own
nutritional needs, and for so organizing distribution
that our daily intake of cereal filler be not in short
supply . . .'

Quoted in *The Lyttelton Hart-Davis Letters* (Vol.
6, 1984) for 30 November 1961.

—— 2 ——

Was there ever really an Anglican priest who
prayed: 'Dear God, as you will undoubtedly
have read in the leader column of *The Times* this
morning . . .'?

Recalled by Anna Ford (a clergyman's daughter)
on BBC Radio *Quote...Unquote* (1977).

—— 3 ——

At the wedding of two young people, instead of
saying, 'Lawfully joined together', the priest
said, 'Joyfully loined together'.

Told me by Barbara Reeve of Chelmsford (1982).

—— 4 ——

The following are actual texts from the Author-
ized Version of the Bible (except where stated).
How many clergymen have attempted to preach
sermons based on them, it is hard to say. Certainly
some have been preached, if only for a dare:

And he said unto her, Give me, I pray thee, a little
water to drink; for I am thirsty. And she opened a
bottle of milk. – Judges 4:19.

So we boiled my son, and did eat him. – 2 Kings
6:29.

Go not empty unto thy mother in law. – Ruth 3:17.

For only Og king of Bashan remained of the rem-
nant of giants; behold, his bedstead was a bedstead
of iron. – Deuteronomy 3:11.

He got in underneath the Elephant and thrust at it
from below and killed it. It fell to the ground on top
of him, and there he died. – 1 Maccabees 6:46
(Apocrypha).

And all the people sat in the street trembling
because of this matter, and for the great rain. – Ezra
10:9.

My God, my soul is vexed within me . . . one deep
calleth another, because of the noise of the water-
pipes. – Psalm 42:7/9 (Book of Common Prayer
version).

And the lot fell upon Matthias. – Acts 1:26.

And he spake to his sons, saying, Saddle me the
ass. And they saddled him. – 1 Kings 13:27.

Even a child is known by his doings. – Proverbs
20:11.

He delighteth not in the strength of the horse: he
taketh not pleasure in the legs of a man. – Psalms
146:10.

And Isaiah said, Take a lump of figs. And they laid
it on the boil, and he recovered. – 2 Kings 20:7.

And Adonibezak said, Three-score and ten kings,
having their thumbs and their great toes cut off,
gathered their meat under my table. – Judges 1:7.

He saith among the trumpets, Ha, Ha. – Job 39:25.

And I will take away my hand, and thou shalt see
my back parts. – Exodus 33:23.

As she sat on the ass, she broke wind, and Caleb
said, 'What did you mean by that?' She replied, 'I
want to ask a favour of you.' – Judges 1:14 (New
English Bible).

See also BISHOPS 32:6 and MONTGOMERY 137:3.

Bill CLINTON

(1946–) American saxophone-playing Democratic President. Deferential to his wife, Hillary.

—— 1 ——

Clinton was a Rhodes Scholar at Oxford towards the end of the Swinging Sixties. In 1992, while seeking the Democratic nomination, he appeared on TV with a rival candidate, Jerry Brown. The two men were asked if they had ever violated state, federal or international laws. Clinton admitted that while at Oxford between 1968 and 1970 he had used marijuana 'a time or two – and I didn't like it'. He also added, '*I didn't inhale* – and I didn't try it again.'

Report in *The Times* (30 March 1992).

Brian CLOUGH

(1935–) Loquacious English football manager and former footballer.

—— 2 ——

After watching his Nottingham Forest team defeat Queen's Park Rangers 5–2 in the Littlewoods Cup, Mr Clough rushed on to the pitch to eject spectators from it. In full view of television cameras, he proceeded to clout offenders and clip them round the ear. An anonymous wit described this procedure as a case of 'the shit hitting the fan'.

Untraced. The incident occurred in January 1989. Clough was banned for the rest of the season from watching his team from the touchlines.

Irvin S. COBB

(1876–1944) American humorist and writer.

—— 3 ——

When Cobb was a reporter on the New York *World*, he had to work under Charles E. Chapin, whom he found to be a difficult boss. Arriving at the office one day, Cobb was told that Chapin was off sick. Inquired he: 'Nothing trivial, I trust.'

Recounted in Ralph L. Marquard, *Jokes and Anec-

dotes (1977). Possibly the origin of this oft-told tale. Compare, from *Ego 3* by James Agate (entry for 20 November 1936): 'The week's good thing. A journalist saying that his editor was ill, Lionel Hale murmured, "Nothing trivial, I hope!"'

James Burke appearing on BBC Radio *Quote...Unquote* (1979) had this to say: 'A long time ago I was making a film in a hospital and two medics went by. One said, "I can't remember exactly what he died of – but I do recall it wasn't anything serious."' I suppose it is possible that the medic did actually repeat the old line. It is, after all, quite a reasonable thing to say, seen in a certain light.

Richard COBB

(1917–) English academic with great interest in matters French. One-time Professor of Modern History at Oxford.

—— 4 ——

In 1984, Cobb was chairman of the judges for the Booker Prize for Fiction. At the awards presentation in October, he told the distinguished literary audience about the qualities of the winning novel: 'In an operation of this kind, one would not go for a Proust or Joyce – not that I would know about that, never having read either.'

Sir Jack COHEN

(1898–1979) English supermarket retailer.

—— 5 ——

The belief, firmly held by some, that the name of Cohen's 'Tesco' supermarkets is an acronym standing for 'The Express Supermarket Company' is incorrect. In the early days, the tea for the stores was provided by a Mr T. E. Stockwell. 'Tesco' derives from this man's initials coupled with the 'co' of 'Cohen'.

Source: Adrian Room, *Dictionary of Trade Name Origins* (1982).

—— 6 ——

Cleverer wordplay on the name 'Cohen' occurs in the armorial bearings of Tesco Stores (Holdings) Ltd – a coat of arms granted in 1979. The English translation of the motto is 'May the traders be convivial together.' The Latin is: *'Mercatores Coenascent'*.

Source unknown.

Harry COHN

(1891–1958) American film producer.

—— 1 ——

John, as head of Columbia studios, was greatly disliked in Hollywood but there was a large turnout at his funeral. An observer remarked, 'It only proves what they always say – give the public something they want to see, and they'll turn up to see it.'

> This version is from Oscar Levant, *The Unimportance of Being Oscar* (1968). Lillian Hellman in *Scoundrel Time* (1976) has it said by the comedian George Jessel as 'Same old story: you give 'em what they want and they'll fill the theatre.' Also attributed to the comedian Red Skelton.

Horace de Vere COLE

(*fl.* 1910) English hoaxer of the Edwardian era. He arranged a ceremonial visit to Cambridge by 'the Sultan of Zanzibar' (impersonated by himself) and was received with great ceremony by the Mayor and councillors. In 1910, he topped this with a visit to HMS *Dreadnought*, the flagship of the Home Fleet, by 'the Emperor of Abyssinia'.

—— 2 ——

Cole is believed to have been the original person to have accosted a man in the street and asked him if he would kindly hold the end of a tape measure. He then went round the corner and found another volunteer to hold the other end. Cole then left them to get on with it.

Oral tradition.

—— 3 ——

On another occasion, Cole spotted a group of workmen digging up the road in Oxford. Accordingly, he went along to the police station and told the sergeant that a group of wicked under-graduates – dressed as workmen – were digging up the High Street. He then rattled down to the High Street, told the workmen that a group of wicked undergraduates dressed as policemen would shortly be arriving, and withdrew a short distance to observe the conflagration that inevitably ensued.

> Oral tradition. This may be a confusion with some other hoaxer, as Cole was not an Oxford man. The confusion may have arisen since another Cole story is that he once arrived in Piccadilly Circus in London with some friends and pretended to dig up the road. They then watched as London ground to a halt around them. (This version was mentioned in *The Independent* Magazine (2 September 1989.) Compare also the story related by Dacre Balsdon in *Oxford Life* (1957) about the time when Oxford police imported plain-clothes men to deal with undergraduate brawls. One laid hands on an undergraduate and said, 'I am a plain-clothes policeman.' The undergraduate replied: 'And so, my dear sir, am I.' Then the trouble started.

Sybil COLEFAX

(1874–1950) English society hostess. Co-founder of the interior decorating business, Colefax and Fowler.

—— 4 ——

She had very bad handwriting. It was said that the only hope of deciphering her invitations was to pin them up on the wall and run past them.

> Reported in *The Lyttelton Hart-Davis Letters* (Vol. 1, 1978). Letter of 13 November 1955.

Norman COLLINS

(1907–82) English broadcasting executive (with the BBC and then a founder of ITV) and novelist – *London Belongs To Me* (1945). Invented the pejorative phrase 'steam radio'.

—— 5 ——

In the 1959 General Election, Collins was drafted in to produce the party political broadcasts by the incumbent Prime Minister, Harold Macmillan – not the most natural of performers. The first thing Collins noted was Macmillan's guardsman-like bearing and suggested that he should give his final broadcast *standing up.* 'Oh, I see,' said the Prime Minister, 'but am I allowed to?'

The next thing that concerned Collins was that Macmillan was looking stiff and inhibited. So he told him that his voice was sounding hoarse and a drop of port was the best medicine. Macmillan acquiesced and drank a glass. Then Collins demanded one more rehearsal to get the timing exactly right. At the end of it, Macmillan said, 'I hope I shall do it better when I do it live tonight.' Replied Collins, 'Prime Minister, you have already done it and you have been recorded.' 'You are a remarkable fellow,' said Macmillan. 'This is like going to the dentist to have a tooth drawn and being told it is already drawn.'

Recounted in Michael Cockerell, *Live from Number 10* (1988) and Alastair Horne, *Macmillan 1957–1986* (1989).

COMEDIANS

—— 1 ——

One of the great show-business stories is about the two pros – and I assume they were comedians – who met one another. One asked the other how he was doing. 'Marvellous!' he replied. 'I've just finished a sensational series on TV – top of the ratings every week!'

'Ah, yes,' replied the other pro, 'I'm afraid I didn't hear about that.'

'And on top of that, I made a record which went straight to the top of the charts.'

'I didn't hear about that either, I'm afraid,' said the other pro.

'Yes, and I also wrote my autobiography which is top of the bestsellers' list.'

'I didn't hear about that,' was the reply.

'Oh yes, and I just did two weeks at the Palladium – sold out every night.'

'Didn't hear about that.'

'The only disappointment was, I did a charity concert at Chingford and died a death . . .'

'Ah, yes,' said the other pro, brightening, 'I heard about *that*!'

This version was told by Bill Cotton when head of Light Entertainment group, BBC Television, at a BBC Lunchtime Lecture on 11 January 1977. The moral he drew from it was that, 'in terms of failure, news spreads fast and people have long memories.'

—— 2 ——

A man was walking along the road with a lemon held close to his right ear. When challenged to explain this strange behaviour, he did so. 'You've heard of a hearing aid?' he asked. 'Yes,' replied the challenger. 'Well,' said the man, 'This is a lemonade.'

I would say I first heard this joke in the 1950s. John Osborne, recalling variety comedians of that era in *Almost a Gentleman* (1991), puts it in the mouth of the cockney comic, Scott Sanders, who was 'loud, brisk, seldom funny and looked as if he knew it'. He was one of the comedians Osborne drew to the attention of the company of his play *The Entertainer* (1957). These actors included Sir Laurence Olivier who was to play the failed comedian Archie Rice with great success on stage and screen.

—— 3 ——

'Apart from that, Mrs Lincoln, how did you enjoy the play?' was probably the world's first sick joke – or perhaps 'sickish' would be more precise. I wonder when it first arose? Oddly enough, *The Oxford English Dictionary* (2nd edition) mentions it twice with 1959 datings. Under the word 'cruellie' (a cruel joke) it quotes from *The News Chronicle* (6 July 1959): 'The famous American "cruellie" joke – example: "But what did you think of the play, Mrs Lincoln?" – is on the way out.' And defining 'sick humour, joke etc.', it quotes from *Punch* (2 September 1959): 'The prototype of sick jokes is one that goes "But apart from that, Mrs Lincoln, how did you enjoy the play?"'

'Sick humour' – with this name – appears to have been first identified in the 1950s. I have a hunch that the joke does not date from any earlier decade.

As for variations on the same: somewhere or other I have heard that on the evening in 1963 when news of President Kennedy's assassination reached London, the British Academy of Film and Television Arts was holding a dinner or awards ceremony of some kind. At this gathering, Bernard Braden, the Canadian-born broadcaster, is said to have wondered (publicly or privately, I don't know) how long it would be before people started joking, 'Apart from that, Mrs Kennedy, did you manage to do much shopping?'

Oral tradition and my uncertain recollection.

—— 4 ——

In *Punch* for 8 May 1901 under the possibly ironic headline 'THE VERY LATEST' appears this joke: 'When did the lobster blush? When he saw the salad dressing.'

Daring, eh?

COMMENTATORS

—— 1 ——

Did you hear the story about the man who put an advertisement in the paper, having lost his dog? The dog apparently had every disadvantage a beast could possibly have. It had an ear and possibly a leg missing. It was blind. It had lost its sense of smell. Probably hard pad came into it. And the dog had, of course, been doctored. According to the advertisement, it answered to the name of 'Lucky'.

You may encounter this joke in all kinds of places. In 1984, I noticed it was in the script of Frederic Raphael's TV series *Oxbridge Blues*. I myself had earlier twice told the story on TV – on Channel 4 a few minutes into 1 January 1984 and, before that, on ITV on 30 November 1983. I had taken it from a cutting sent to me from the Lost and Found Column of the *Westmorland Gazette* dated 19 August 1983, which stated:

LOST – CARTMEL AREA
BALD ONE-EYED GINGER TOM
Crippled in both back legs,
recently castrated, answers to name
of "Lucky".

Replies to
BOB BATEY
PIG & WHISTLE
CARTMEL

Was this apparently genuine ad how it had all started? I managed to track down Mr Batey in March 1987 to ask if his advertisment had really appeared and, if so, had he had any luck in recovering his poor Lucky (a cat, not a dog, you notice). Well, no. Mr Batey, you see, was a bit of an entertainer – comedy magic was his speciality – and he'd put the ad in the paper to, well, liven things up a bit in the Cartmel area. And no, no, the joke wasn't original even in 1983 and I have no idea where *he* got it from.

Except that in the special edition of *Punch* published to mark the magazine's 150th anniversary (in 1991), a section was devoted to the newspaper clippings sent in by readers to the 'Country Life' column. Among the examples cited (but without date of publication given) was one from 'P. Butler' who had found this in the 'Trinidad Guardian': 'LOST – Bull Terrier, has three legs, blind in left eye, missing right ear, broken tail, recently castrated. Answers to the name of Lucky.' Back to dogs, you see. Will we ever know if this was an original advertisement?

—— 2 ——

A BBC radio commentator in the early 1930s was describing the disembarking of the then Duke and Duchess of York from a destroyer. They were taking a long time about it, chatting to the captain on the bridge, and so on, and he had to throw in every fact he could think of to keep going. Then he intimated that the couple would be coming ashore shortly as the Duchess had just left the bridge. Yet still nothing happened and the commentator unfortunately went on, 'Well, I think something really *is* about to happen now, as an immense amount of water is pouring from the ship's side . . . and here is the Duchess returning to the bridge . . .'

Related by Jack de Manio in *To Auntie With Love* (1967).

—— 3 ——

A commentator at the funeral of King George VI in 1952 heard himself say with horror: 'And now here comes the main body of the procession.'

Told by Antony Jay on BBC Radio *Quote...Unquote* (1990).

—— 4 ——

Introducing Harry Carpenter on some sports programme in 1973, Frank Bough is reputed to have said: 'Harry commentator is your carpenter.'

Quoted by Clive James in *The Observer* (13 May 1973).

—— 5 ——

During the 1978 World Cup, after several mentions of the hole in footballer Asa Hartford's heart, commentator David Coleman described him as: 'A whole-hearted player'.

Quoted by Clive James in *The Observer* (11 June 1978).

Shirley CONRAN

(1932–) English journalist, writer (*Superwoman*) and novelist.

—— 1 ——

The bit that most people remember from her novels is the scene in *Lace* (published 1982) in which a goldfish features in the sexual activities of an Arab prince and one of the book's heroines. According to Conran's ex-husband – now Sir Terence Conran, the designer – she was told the idea by him. 'I'd been to this extraordinary wild, midsummer party in Finland,' he told *The Independent*. 'A group of young men went into the lake and came out with nets filled with sticklebacks. They then introduced these little fish into the, er, private parts of some vodka-soaked ladies . . .'

From an interview by Hunter Davies in *The Independent* (16 March 1993).

Peter COOK

(1937–) English humorist. The inspirer of a generation of comic writers and performers.

—— 2 ——

Attempting to start up a dinner-party conversation, Cook asked the person seated next to him, 'What are you doing at the moment?' The person replied, 'Writing a book.' To which Cook rejoined, '. . . Neither am I.'

This story was told by Richard Ingrams on BBC Radio *Quote...Unquote* (1984), though I gather that Cook later said he did not claim it to be original.

Alastair COOKE

(1908–) English-born American broadcaster and journalist. Known in Britain for his radio *Letter from America*, which has run, seemingly, since time began. In the US, Cooke is known principally as the host of TV's *Masterpiece Theater* in which he introduces (and explains) classic, quality (mostly British) TV productions.

—— 3 ——

A reader wrote to *The New York Times* saying she had grown up admiring Cooke's calm erudition but had had trouble as a small child sitting with her parents and watching *Masterpiece Theater* when the announcer said the show would be introduced by 'Alice the cook'.

A story relayed to me by Stephan Chodorov (1993).

Calvin COOLIDGE

(1872–1933) American Republican President. Numerous tales attest to his reticence – hence the nickname 'Silent Cal'.

—— 4 ——

A story about Coolidge's taciturnity was told by his wife. A woman sat down next to him at a dinner party and said, 'You must talk to me, Mr Coolidge. I made a bet with someone that I could get more than two words out of you.' Coolidge replied: 'You lose.'

This made an early appearance in Gamaliel Bradford, *The Quick and the Dead* (1931).

—— 5 ——

Said someone: 'He opened his mouth and a moth flew out.'

Mentioned on BBC Radio *Quote...Unquote* (1985). This would appear to be a variant on the remark often directed at mean people – that they opened their wallets and a moth flew out.

—— 6 ——

Coolidge went to church alone one Sunday because his wife was unable to go with him. She asked him on his return what the sermon was about. 'Sin,' he replied. 'But what did he say about it?' Coolidge said, 'He was against it.'

This made an early appearance in John Hiram McKee, *Coolidge Wit and Wisdom* (1933). Mrs Coolidge said this was just the sort of thing he would have said. Coolidge himself said it would be funnier if it were true.

Lady Diana COOPER

(1892–1986) English beauty. Born Lady Diana
Manners. It seems to be generally assumed that
she was the result of a liaison between Violet,
Duchess of Rutland (wife of the 8th Duke) and
Harry Cust.

—— 1 ——

In her old age and before obtaining a Disabled
Driver's disc, Lady Diana used to park on double
yellow lines and leave (usually successful) notes to
parking wardens, like these: 'Dear Warden – Taken
sad child to cinema – please forgive'; 'Dear Warden
– Only a minute. Horribly old (80) and frightfully
lame. Beware of the DOG [in reality a chihuahua]';
'Disabled as you see – lunching on guard – Diana
Cooper, Sir Martin Charteris's AUNT!' [this was
outside St James's Palace]; 'Dearest Warden – Front
tooth broken off: look like an 81-year-old Pirate, so at
dentist 19a. Very old, very lame – no metres [meters].
Have mercy!'

**Her son, John Julius Norwich, collected some of
these notes and published them as part of the 1979
selection in *Christmas Crackers* (1980). Another
version of the first of the above: in *The Lyttelton
Hart-Davis Letters* (Vol. 6), Rupert Hart-Davis in a
letter dated 11 November 1961 says he borrowed
Lady Diana's Mini and found a piece of paper
under the windscreen-wiper stating, 'HAVE
MERCY. AM TAKING SAD CHILD TO
CINEMA.'**

—— 2 ——

During the interval of a Covent Garden gala to
mark the 100th birthday of Sir Robert Mayer, the
musical benefactor, Lady Diana (then aged 86) recalled being approached by 'an extremely pleasant
lady' who seemed vaguely familiar. Trying to put a
name to the face, she struggled womanfully on, until
the dreadful truth dawned: it was the Queen. 'I sank
into a curtsey and said, "I'm terribly sorry, Ma'am,
but I didn't recognize you without your crown on".'

**This version from *The Daily Telegraph*, 21 June
1986. Andrew Barrow in *International Gossip* (1983)
dates the incident precisely to 5 June 1979 and
gives the Queen's response as: 'It's Sir Robert's
evening. I left it at home.' There is nothing new
about this sort of error. The old, short-sighted Lord
Portarlington is supposed to have told Queen Victoria, 'I know your face quite well, but dammit I
cannot put a name to it!' (recalled in Robert Rhodes
James, *Rosebery*, 1963).**

Sir Noël COWARD

(1899–1973) English entertainer and writer,
nicknamed 'The Master'.

—— 3 ——

In the revival of his play *Hay Fever*, which Coward
directed at the National Theatre in 1964, Edith
Evans always said one line wrong. 'On a clear day
you can see Marlow' was invariably changed by her
to: 'On a *very* clear day . . .' Coward would not let her
get away with it. Said he: 'Edith, dear, the line is "On
a clear day you can see Marlow." On a *very* clear day
you can see Marlowe and Beaumont *and* Fletcher as
well . . .'

**The earliest showing of this story would appear to
be in Dick Richards, *The Wit of Noël Coward*
(1968).**

—— 4 ——

A typical story about Coward goes like this (as
told to me by an actress in 1979): 'Diana Wynyard
said to Coward, "I saw your *Private Lives* the other
night. Not very funny." He replied: "I saw your Lady
Macbeth the other night – very funny!"'

**In fact this dates back to a 1920s dinner party when
Lady Diana Cooper told Coward that she had not
laughed once at his early comedy *The Young Idea*
(London, 1922). 'How strange,' Coward replied.
'When I saw you acting in *The Glorious Adventure*
[a film about the Great Fire of London], I laughed
all the time!' This exchange is quoted in *The Noël
Coward Diaries* (note to 13 March 1946). Compare
the story recounted in *Sheridaniana, or Anecdotes
of the Life of Richard Brinsley Sheridan* (1826): the
playwright Richard Cumberland took his children
to see Sheridan's *The School for Scandal* and kept
reprimanding them when they laughed at it – 'You
should not laugh, my angels; there is nothing to
laugh at.' When Sheridan was informed of this
long afterwards, he commented: 'It was very un-
grateful in Cumberland to have been displeased
with his poor children for laughing at my comedy;
for I went the other night to see his tragedy, and
laughed at it from beginning to end.'**

—— 5 ——

As an 18-year-old, just out of RADA, Richard
Attenborough went to audition for the part of
the young stoker in Coward's film *In Which We Serve*.
Extremely nervous, he was instantly gratified when
the Master arrived with his entourage and announced, 'You won't know me, but I'm Noël Coward.
You, of course, are Richard Attenborough.'

Attenborough later commented, 'I felt ten feet tall and immensely grateful.'

Recounted by Attenborough in *The Sunday Telegraph* (22 August 1965).

—— 1 ——

When told that some producer whom he did not admire had blown his brains out, Coward commented, 'He must have been an incredibly good shot.'

Told in Dick Richards, *The Wit of Noël Coward* (1968).

—— 2 ——

At the pre-London opening of *Quadrille* (1952) in Brighton, Coward asked local inhabitant, TV personality Gilbert Harding, 'What did you think of my show?' Harding confessed, 'I'm afraid I slept through it.' Noël Coward: 'Don't worry about that, dear fellow, I've slept through *so* many of yours.'

In Wallace Reyburn, *Gilbert Harding* (1978).

—— 3 ——

When Coward was making the film *Bunny Lake Is Missing* in 1965 he encountered the American actor Keir Dullea, who said, 'Oh, Mr Coward, I am so proud to have you in my film. I am Keir Dullea.' And Coward said, 'Keir Dullea, gone tomorrow.'

Told by Sheridan Morley on BBC Radio *Quote...Unquote* (1989).

—— 4 ——

Watching the 1953 Coronation on TV in London, Coward was asked who the little man was riding in a carriage with the portly Queen of Tonga. In fact, it was the Sultan of Kelantan, but Coward answered: 'Her lunch.'

This famous story made an early appearance in Dick Richards, *The Wit of Noël Coward* (1968). It is often told differently and may well be apocryphal. About the only thing to be said for certain is that Coward did spend most of Coronation Day watching TV – he says so in his diaries. According to Ned Sherrin, *Theatrical Anecdotes* (1991), Coward always denied the story, 'not least because she [Queen Salote] was a personal friend and would have been very upset'. Sherrin suggests that Emlyn Williams was the perpetrator and, curiously, casts Emperor Haile Selassie in the role of 'the lunch' (he did not even attend the Coronation).

—— 5 ——

Meeting the American playwright Edna Ferber in the Algonquin Hotel, New York, Coward remarked on her trouser suit. 'You look almost like a man,' he unwisely commented. 'So do you,' she replied.

Told by Martin Jarvis on BBC Radio *Quote...Unquote* (1980).

—— 6 ——

Of the musical *Camelot* on Broadway, in December 1960, Coward said: 'It's like *Parsifal* without the jokes.'

Or 'It's about as long as *Parsifal*, and not as funny', in Dick Richards, *The Wit of Noël Coward* (1968). In *The Noël Coward Diaries* (entry for 16 December 1960) he merely relates how he took Marlene Dietrich to the first night and found the show 'disappointing ... music and lyrics uninspired and story uninteresting'.

—— 7 ——

Coward was once asked why he had champagne for breakfast. His reply was, 'Doesn't everyone?'

Told to me by J. Petty of Bradford (1977).

—— 8 ——

Opening a Red Cross bazaar in Oxford, Coward began, 'Desperately accustomed as I am to public speaking . . .'

Quoted in Dick Richards, *The Wit of Noël Coward* (1968).

—— 9 ——

Laurence Olivier's then five-year-old daughter Tamsin asked Coward what two dogs were doing together. Coward produced a masterpiece of creative explanation: 'The doggie in front has suddenly gone blind, and the other one has very kindly offered to push her all the way to St Dunstan's.'

Quoted by Kenneth Tynan in *The Observer* (1 April 1973), but with 'push *him* all the way to St Dunstan's', interestingly.

—— 10 ——

An anxious actor rushed up to Coward after a dress rehearsal and demanded, 'Could you see my wig-join?' Replied Coward, 'Perfectly, dear boy, perfectly.'

Source untraced.

—— 1 ——

When the American actor Chuck Connors introduced himself to Coward by saying, 'I am Chuck Connors', Coward replied, 'Of course you are, dear boy, of course you are.'

Told by Spike Milligan on BBC Radio *Quote...Unquote* (1979) though using the name 'John Wayne'. Connors is the more likely original, however.

—— 2 ——

Coward was known as 'The Master' throughout the theatrical profession and beyond, from the 1940s onwards, though not to his close friends. He professed not to like his nickname (perhaps because it had already been associated with Somerset Maugham) and – when asked to explain it – would reply, 'Oh, you know, jack of all trades, master of none.'

John Mills in his autobiography *Up in the Clouds, Gentlemen, Please* (1980), put in a bid to have first given Coward the name when they were both involved in a production of *Journey's End*.

—— 3 ——

Taking part in a TV interview with Patrick Garland on his 70th birthday, Coward admitted to a lack of formal education. He said, 'I learnt all I know at Twickenham Public Lavatory . . . er . . . Library.'

From my diary for 7 December 1969. In *The Diaries of Kenneth Williams* (1993), he also recounts the tale and has the lavatories in question as 'Battersea'. He suggests that Coward added, 'Oh dear! Quite a Freudian slip there, I'm afraid . . .'

—— 4 ——

The screenwriter William Fairchild gave Daniel Massey a questionable line to speak when the actor was playing Coward in the film *Star*. When an unknown woman greets Coward with the words, 'I know you, Mr Coward, but I'm sure you don't know me', he replies: 'It's an incredible, but increasingly common phenomenon, I fear.' In real life, Coward could be more teasing. When American matrons accosted him with, 'Oh, Mr Coward, you don't know me . . .', he was inclined to answer, 'But, of course, I do. And how is Mabel?'

The 'Mabel' bit was told to me by Kenneth Williams in 1964. With 'Muriel', that line is in Dick Richards, *The Wit of Noël Coward* (1968). In Wallace Reyburn, *Gilbert Harding* (1978), it is back to 'Mabel'.

—— 5 ——

Coward is one of various authors credited with the nickname for which Edward Woodward is famous in the acting profession and about which he is understandably modest. It is 'Fart in the Bath' – which is supposed to describe the sound made when 'Edward Woodward' is pronounced.

Conceded to me – with great reluctance – by Edward Woodward himself, in 1985.

—— 6 ——

In 1962, after Coward had been to see Lionel Bart's musical *Blitz!* – which was all about London in the Second World War and chiefly notable for the elaborate moving scenery by Sean Kenny – he commented: 'Just as long as the real thing and twice as noisy'.

Quoted in Sheridan Morley, *Spread a Little Happiness* (1987).

—— 7 ——

Beryl Reid met Coward at a party when he was very old and she said to him, 'Oh, Noël, isn't it awful, we'll all be dead soon.' And Coward said, 'Oh, my darling, you mustn't worry. After we die, you must remember, little bits of you go on growing, you know. Your nails go on growing, and the hair on your chest goes on growing . . .'

Beryl Reid protested, 'Not the hair on *my* chest, please!'

And Coward said, 'Oh, Beryl, you give up hope *so* easily . . .'

Told by Francis Matthews on BBC Radio *Quote...Unquote* (1993).

CRITICS

—— 8 ——

A very brilliant character actress had turned in an outstanding performance in one of those slippered and dressing-gowned roles. A very eminent critic said afterwards that he was going to give her an absolutely wonderful notice. But when the newspaper appeared, the actress was terribly upset to read, 'The brilliant Miss ****** was magnificently lousy in the role of ******.'

The director of the play took up the cudgels on the actress's behalf and spoke to the critic. 'Oh, I'm terribly sorry,' said he. 'I phoned the notice in, and they left the "b" off!'

Told by Peter Wood on BBC Radio *Quote...Unquote* (1993).

—— 1 ——

When Charlton Heston directed and took one of the title roles in a film of Shakespeare's *Antony and Cleopatra*, it was a flop. One of the tabloids headlined its thumbs-down review: 'The Biggest Asp Disaster in the World'.

Recounted in Ned Sherrin, *Theatrical Anecdotes* (1991).

—— 2 ——

A film critic is said to have reviewed *Ben-Hur* (1959) with the words, 'Loved Ben, hated Hur.'

Source untraced.

—— 3 ——

A critic in *The New Statesman* once commented that watching Bette Davis in the film *Another Man's Poison* (1951) was 'like reading Ethel M. Dell by flashes of lightning'.

Source untraced. The line is credited to Frank Hauser in *Halliwell's Film Guide*.

—— 4 ——

In 1969, when the film of *The Battle of Britain* was completed, a special showing was arranged in an Air Force mess overseas at which some of those present had participated in the real event. As they headed for the bar at the end of the film, one of these pilots was heard to mutter: 'Not as good as the play'.

Told to me by T. R. H. Lyons of Buckfastleigh, Devon (1980).

—— 5 ——

Michael Billington, the theatre critic of *The Guardian* for many years, went to review a revival of the musical *Godspell* at the Young Vic in 1981. He wrote: 'Heralded by a sprinkling of glitter-dust and much laying on of microphones, *Godspell* is back in London at the Young Vic. For those who missed it the first time, this is your golden opportunity: you can miss it again.'

Recounted in Diana Rigg, *No Turn Unstoned* (1982).

Michael CURTIZ

(1888–1962) Hungarian-born American film director.

—— 6 ——

During the filming of *The Charge of the Light Brigade*, Curtiz ordered the release of a hundred riderless steeds by shouting: 'Bring on the empty horses!' David Niven and Errol Flynn fell about with laughter at this. Curtiz rounded on them and said, 'You and your stinking language! You think I know f*** nothing. Well, let me tell you, I know f*** all!'

Recounted in the second volume of David Niven's autobiography to which he gave the title *Bring On the Empty Horses* (1975).

1st Marquis CURZON

(1859–1925) English viceroy and politician.

—— 7 ——

Curzon is said to have commented on his first trip by bus: 'This omnibus business is not what it is reported to be. I hailed one at the bottom of Whitehall and told the man to take me to Carlton House Terrace. But the fellow flatly refused.'

This is among the 'Curzonia' included in *The Oxford Book of Political Anecdotes* (1986), though it is not quite clear what the original source was. Compare the story told about Sir Herbert Beerbohm Tree, the actor, which must have occurred at the same sort of period. Antony Jay tells me that his father (who was an actor) used to say that Tree hailed a *taxicab* and told the driver to take him home. 'Where's that?' the driver asked, understandably. To which Tree replied: 'Why should I tell you where my beautiful house is?'

As always, the origin of the tale could lie in *Punch*. On 10 April 1901, there was a cartoon by Everard Hopkins with this caption:

A GIRLISH IGNORANCE
Lady Hildegarde, who is studying the habits of the democracy, determines to travel by Omnibus.
***Lady Hildegarde:* "CONDUCTOR, TELL THE DRIVER TO GO TO NO. 104, BERKELEY SQUARE, AND THEN HOME!"**

—— 1 ——

A correspondent suggested, *en passant*, that it was Curzon who originated the saying 'She should lie back and enjoy it'. I puzzled over this for a number of years, unsure in what circumstances he might have said it and how it could ever be verified. Then I came across what he may *really* have said (and perhaps my correspondent may be forgiven for his confusion). According to *The Oxford Book of Political Anecdotes* (1986), when instructing his second wife on the subject of love-making, Curzon said, 'Ladies never move.'

No precise source is given, however. The book of *New Statesmen* competition winners called *Salome Dear, Not With a Porcupine* (1982 – edited by Arthur Marshall) prefers, 'A lady does not move' (and proceeds to provide the circumstances in which it *might* first have been said). Note, however, that a completely different source for the story is given by Rupert Hart-Davis in *The Lyttelton Hart-Davis Letters* (for 19 August 1956) while researching Cora, Lady Strafford, a thrice-married American: 'Before one of her marriages (perhaps the second – to Lord Strafford) she thought it would be a good thing to get a little sex-instruction, so she went over to Paris and took a few lessons from a leading cocotte. On her wedding night she was beginning to turn precept into practice when her bridegroom sternly quelled her by saying: "Cora, *ladies don't move!*"' Alas, he does not give a source for this version either.

René CUTFORTH

(1909–84) English broadcasting reporter and journalist who ended up doing TV adverts for butter (or was it margarine?) in Australia.

—— 2 ——

When Cutforth was a BBC radio reporter, it is said that he emerged from Broadcasting House and found a crowd gathered round a man who had been knocked down by a motor car. But how was he going to find out who the man was and if there was any story? He went up to the police officer who was holding back the crowd and said, 'Let me through, officer, it is my duty as an ordained minister of the church.' He then knelt, with hands clasped, by the body of the injured man, discovered that he was a diplomat from one of the embassies near by, and earned a few guineas selling the information to the news agencies.

Quoted in Gerald Priestland, *Something Understood* (1986).

—— 3 ——

Cutforth was something of a master at claiming expenses. On many occasions he claimed for expensive lunches with a certain general from the Polish Embassy in London. A diligent BBC accountant was suspicious about this and looked up the general in the Diplomatic List. There was no such person at the Polish Embassy. Accordingly, Cutforth was challenged over the veracity of his expenses claim. He was unfazed. 'I am very shocked,' he said. 'The man is clearly an impostor and I shall have nothing more to do with him.'

Told by Martyn Lewis at a lunch in Cardiff (1991).

Bette DAVIS

(1908–89) American actress.

—— 1 ——

Of a certain starlet who put herself about a bit, Davis said: 'I see – she's the original good time that was had by all.'

Quoted in *Halliwell's Filmgoer's Book of Quotes* **(1973/8).**

Frances DAY

(1908–?) American-born singer and actress in British musicals. By the 1950s she was being described as a 'veteran sex symbol . . . breast-waving and leggy'. Could also put on a squeaky voice.

—— 2 ——

It was generally agreed that Day's off-stage activities were as energetic as her public performances. When she arrived late for rehearsal looking somewhat the worse for wear, Bud Flanagan was moved to remark: 'Little Day, you've had a busy man'.

Quoted in Wallace Reyburn, *Gilbert Harding* (1978).

DEAD PEOPLE

—— 3 ——

One old woman is reported to have said to another, 'Yes, I had him cremated and his ashes made into an eggtimer.'
The other asked, 'Why an eggtimer?'
And the first replied: 'Well, he never did any work while he was alive, so he might as well do some now he's dead.'

A traditional exchange. In J. B. Priestley's *English Journey* (1934), he recounts attending a lunch club in Manchester where commercial travellers told stories. He repeats one: 'A weaver up Blackburn way had just lost her husband. "Where yer going to bury 'im?" a neighbour asked her. "Ah'm not going to bury 'im," she replied. "Ah'm going to 'ave 'im cremated," she replied. The neighbour was impressed. "But whatever will yer do wi' th'ashes?" she inquired. "Ah'll tell yer what Ah'm going to do wi' th'ashes," said the widow. "Ah'm going to 'ave 'em put into an eggtimer. Th'owd devil wouldn't ever work when 'e wer alive, so 'e can start doing a bit now 'e's dead."'
Priestley comments: 'That still seems to me a very good story, even though I am no longer under the influence of beer and Bury Black Puddings. It is a fair sample of Lancashire's grimly ironic humour.'

—— 4 ——

A young newspaper reporter in the North of England found himself ushered into a front parlour and shown the body of a recently-deceased man. Unable to think of anything suitable to say to the bereaved wife, he remarked, 'Looks well, doesn't he?' Replied she, 'He ought to be. He only came back from Blackpool on Monday.'

Sometimes told by – or about – the broadcaster Robert Robinson. In Chapter 12 of Robinson's detective novel *Landscape With Dead Dons* (1956), he himself puts this experience in the mouth of a character called Bum: 'Corpses always turned me up – even when I was doing Bereaved Households on the old Maida Vale *Intelligencer* . . . I remember once I was drinking tea in one of these front rooms with a middle-aged lady who'd just lost her husband, and she asked me if I'd like to have a look at him . . . Over we went to the coffin . . . Well, you don't really know what to say, do you, so I said, "He looks well, doesn't he?" and she said, "He ought to. We only came back from Brighton last week."'
However, there is an even older version. In Irvin S. Cobb's *A Laugh a Day Keeps the Doctor Away* (1921), story number 254 tells of 'two sympathic friends' calling at a house of mourning in the Bronx. The bereft husband of the late Mrs Levinsky sat alongside the casket. 'Doesn't she look wonderful?' said one of them. The widower replied, 'Why shouldn't she look wonderful? Didn't she spend the whole winter in Palm Beach?'

—— 1 ——

An English couple were on holiday in Spain with the wife's grandmother. Shortly before they were due to drive back across France, the grandmother died. Knowing there would be a lot of red tape and fuss at border control points – and realizing that they could be back home in England after fifteen hours of steady driving – the couple decided to hide the old lady's body in a carpet, fix it on the roof rack of their car, and take a chance.

But first they agreed to stop for lunch before crossing the border into France. When they finished their meal and walked out of the restaurant, they discovered that their car had been stolen.

This is one of the most famous examples of 'urban myths'. Paul Smith in *The Book of Nasty Legends* (1983) records that it has been popular throughout Europe and North America since the Second World War. Alfred Hitchcock used the theme in 'The Diplomatic Corpse' (part of the TV *Alfred Hitchcock Presents* series, 1955–61) and it is related over dinner in Roger Peyrefitte's novel *La Fin des Ambassades* (1953).

Tom Burnam in *More Misinformation* (1980) calls it 'The Dead Grandma in the Station Wagon' story and notes that Robert H. Woodward, writing in the American *Northwest Folklore* (Summer 1965), points to a possible origin in *The Grapes of Wrath* (1939), John Steinbeck's novel in which the Joads do carry the body of Grandma Joad about with them after she dies.

A very early record of the tale occurs in James Lees-Milne's diary entry for 15 December 1942 (published in his *Ancestral Voices*, 1975): 'I dined at the Ritz with . . . Morogh Bernard [who] told a true story about a Belgian friend of his who, with a rich aunt, escaped in a closed car when the Germans invaded Belgium. The aunt, who was very delicate, died in the car. The niece could not stop to bury her for obvious reasons . . . so the niece put her aunt on the roof of the car wrapped in some valuable rugs. At last she was able to stop at a café, and get out for a meal . . .' You can guess the rest.

See also BEREAVED PEOPLE 68:3–69:1.

DEBATERS

—— 2 ——

A motion for debate that is an old stand-by of school debating societies – at least, so I recall from the 1950s – is the one proposing that instead of the Pilgrim Fathers landing on the Plymouth Rock, the Plymouth Rock should have landed on the Pilgrim Fathers.

H. L. Mencken in his *Dictionary of Quotations* (1942) has this in the form, 'How much better it would have been if the Plymouth Rock had landed on the Pilgrim Fathers' – and ascribed to an 'Author unidentified'.

Charles DE GAULLE

(1890–1970) French soldier and president. Tall and Concorde-nosed. My uncle, who received a medal from him, was convinced he wore corsets.

—— 3 ——

On 18 June 1940, de Gaulle made his first broadcast over the BBC from London. This is credited with launching the French wartime Resistance. It began, in French, 'I, General de Gaulle, now in London, call on all French officers and men who are at present on British soil, or may be in future, with or without arms . . . to get in touch with me . . .' Unfortunately, no one appears actually to have heard the broadcast – although many soon heard *about* it.

De Gaulle was extremely annoyed to find that the BBC hadn't even bothered to make a record of it, though he was persuaded to repeat his rallying cry a week later in a second broadcast which *was* recorded.

Sources: Leonard Miall, talk 'In at the Start' (No. 1), broadcast on BBC Radio (1982); *The Independent*, 17 June 1990.

—— 4 ——

On either the first or the second occasion he arrived at the BBC for a broadcast, de Gaulle so impressed a French-speaking announcer who was already in the studio that the announcer leapt up to shake the great man's hand and struck his head on the overhead microphone. It is said that de Gaulle began his broadcast, in consequence, with the microphone still swinging to and fro in front of him.

Correspondence in *The Independent* Magazine, 23 June/7 July 1990.

—— 5 ——

A prophetic remark was attributed to de Gaulle after attending President Kennedy's funeral in 1963. Of Jackie Kennedy he was supposed to have said: 'I can see her in about ten years from now on the yacht of a Greek petrol millionaire.' In 1968, she married Aristotle Onassis.

> In *Fallen Oaks* (1972), André Malraux recalls de Gaulle as having said, rather, 'She is a star, and will end up on the yacht of some oil baron.' When later reminded that he had said this, de Gaulle told Malraux: 'Did I say that? Well, well ... Fundamentally I would rather have believed that she would marry Sartre. Or you!'
> Compare this story from *Pass the Port* (1976): Chairman Mao Zedong, the Chinese leader, was asked whether the world would have been any different if Nikita Khrushchev had been assassinated in 1963 instead of President Kennedy. Mao thought for a moment and then replied, 'I think there would have been one difference. I very much doubt whether Mr Aristotle Onassis would have married Mrs Khrushchev.'

Yvonne DE GAULLE

(d. 1979) French wife of the above.

—— 1 ——

The nickname of '*Tante Yvonne*' [Aunt Yvonne] came from her homely nature. On the day of one of the assassination attempts against her husband, she had bought two chickens in aspic. She took them with her when she accompanied the President in his car. Her first question after finding out that her husband was all right was to ask if anything had happened to the chickens in aspic.

> Source untraced.

—— 2 ——

Lunching with friends at the time of her husband's retirement, Madame de Gaulle was asked what she was looking forward to in the years ahead. 'A penis', she replied without hesitation. The embarrassed silence that followed was broken by the former president. 'My dear, I don't think the English pronounce the word like that. It is 'appiness.'

> Exactly as told in Robert Morley, *Book of Bricks* (1978), but probably applied to 'Tante Yvonne' simply because she was a famous Frenchwoman. The same pronunciation is delivered as a joke in the film version of Terence Frisby's *There's A Girl in My Soup* (1970) – by a French hotel manager welcoming a honeymoon couple. In *The Diaries of Kenneth Williams* (1993), the entry for 10 April 1966 has it as told by Michael Codron and involving

Lady Dorothy Macmillan. She asks Mme de Gaulle if there is any desire she has for the future and the reply is, 'Yes – a penis.'

Jack DE MANIO

(1914–88) English radio announcer and then presenter, whose speciality was getting the time-checks wrong when presenting the breakfast-time *Today* programme on the BBC Home Service/ Radio 4, from 1958 to 1971.

—— 3 ——

Trailing a forthcoming programme on the BBC Home Service, de Manio unfortunately mispronounced the name 'Niger' and told a rather shocked Britain (not to mention parts of Africa which happened to be tuned in) that, 'After the news at nine o'clock, you may like to know that there will be a talk by Sir John MacPherson on "The Land of the Nigger" ...'

> In *To Auntie With Love* (1967), de Manio devotes considerable space to describing all the ramifications, personal and international, of this wonderful boob. It occurred on 29 January 1956.

—— 4 ——

One morning, having been given a list of items to announce for *Music in Miniature*, a programme which included Prokofiev's 'Prelude in C', de Manio carefully wrote the piece down as 'Prelude "In Sea"'. The producer hadn't the heart to stop him delivering it with the appropriate relish.

> Told to me by that producer, Bernard Keeffe, in 1990.

—— 5 ——

When the troubles in Northern Ireland first blew up in the late 1960s, they were described initially as part of a 'civil rights' dispute. One morning just before the *Today* programme went on the air, de Manio was recording an interview 'down the line' with a pundit in Belfast. As was then the practice, his questions had been written out beforehand by his producer. He faithfully read them out, but then spotting the phrase 'civil rights', he obviously wondered, 'What's this, what's this?' and actually asked, 'Is there a large coloured population in Northern Ireland?' Fortunately, it was just before the programme started so the producer was able to lop the question off.

Told to me by the producer involved, and recorded in my diary, 21 January 1969.

—— 1 ——

A *frisson* passed across the nation's breakfast tables when de Manio was doing the concluding back-reference to an interview with a clergyman who had condemned wife-swapping in a parish magazine which just happened to have the title *Cockcrow*. What de Manio said was: 'The Reverend ****** on what Mr Fletcher MP calls our "sex-ridden society". And I can't wait to get my cock ... er ... my copy of *Cockcrow*!'

Recorded in my diary 21 July 1969. I believe Mrs Mary Whitehouse duly complained, not so much about de Manio's slip as about the item being done at all.

—— 2 ——

O ne morning when the *Today* programme was due to start its first edition at 7.15, the announcer handed over to de Manio, but instead what listeners heard was the voice of Tim Matthews, a regular contributor to the programme. Matthews explained that de Manio wasn't there. He (Matthews) had just been walking past when the producer had handed the script to him and told him to introduce the programme. Half-way through the opening announcement, de Manio was then heard entering the studio and explaining, rather desperately, 'I got stuck in the loo.' Then in slightly more measured tones, he explained, 'I had a slight bit of ... trouble.'

From a recording of the incident, *c.* 1969.

—— 3 ——

I nterviewing a newly-appointed woman assistant governor at a man's prison, de Manio asked: 'Do you think the prisoners will regard you as a good screw?'

Told to me by a correspondent, *c.* 1980.

—— 4 ——

A t the height of his fame, de Manio was modelled, holding a microphone, for display in Madame Tussaud's waxworks in London. By the early 1980s, however, he had not quite suffered the usual Tussaud indignity of being melted down and turned into someone else. Rather he stood in the reception hall, *sans* microphone, unidentified and, by most people, unrecognized.

My own observation, *c.* 1983.

Judi DENCH

(1934–) English actress, mostly in classical roles on the stage. Awarded the DBE in 1988.

—— 5 ——

D ench's daughter Finty looked like following in her mother's footsteps one Christmas when she landed the part of the innkeeper's wife in a school nativity play. For weeks, her parents heard nothing but the lines of the innkeeper's wife repeated day in, day out. A visitor to the house asked what sort of play she was in. 'A nativity play,' explained Finty. What was it about? Finty replied: 'Well, you see, it's about this innkeeper's wife...'

Told by Dench on BBC Radio *Quote...Unquote* (1982). Compare, however, the story about the long-out-of-work actor who was given the part of the doctor in *A Streetcar Named Desire* by Tennessee Williams when it was revived by a theatre company in Chicago. The character only comes on at the end and has very few lines. Nevertheless, when a relative asked the actor what the play was about, he replied: 'It's about a doctor who comes to New Orleans because he's received a telephone call from a young lady whose sister is having a nervous breakdown.' As told in William Redfield, *Letters from an Actor* (1967).

—— 6 ——

P laying Juliet at the Old Vic, in a production directed by Franco Zeffirelli, Dench was crouching in a heap and crying at the death of Tybalt. When she came to the line, 'Where are my father and my mother, nurse?', her actual father, a doctor, stood up and said, 'Here we are, darling, in Row H!'

Told by Judi Dench (1982).

Michael DENISON

(1915–) Debonair English actor.

—— 7 ——

A performance of Denison's was once favoured with a review in the *Tailor and Cutter* pointing out that he had an 'inadequate central vent'.

Told by Frank Keating on BBC Radio *Quote...Unquote* (1986).

Peter DEWS

(1929–) English theatre and TV drama director. Revered by many for his BBC TV series *An Age of Kings* (1960), which brilliantly presented Shakespeare's English history plays tailored for the small screen.

—— 1 ——

In a long and successful career as a theatre director, Dews has had ample opportunities to collect overheard reactions to his own productions. After *Vivat! Vivat Regina!*, which he directed at Chichester and which ends with the execution of Mary Queen of Scots, he overheard a female member of the audience say: 'Do you know, it's extraordinary -- exactly the same thing happened to Monica.'

In a letter to me dated 10 January 1980, Dews called this anecdote 'absolutely true. I heard it with my own ears.' Ned Sherrin, *Theatrical Anecdotes* (1991) mistakenly puts it after Dews's 1969 production of *Antony and Cleopatra* at Chichester.

Anne DIAMOND

(1954–) Pert English TV presenter, notably with TV-am, the breakfast-television station.

—— 2 ——

The potential hazards of having to sight-read from a teleprompting device were brought home to Diamond in 1985. Following a disastrous fire which killed many people in a football ground stand at Bradford, an appeal for funds was launched. Among the fund-raising activities was a re-recording of the Gerry and the Pacemakers hit 'You'll Never Walk Alone'. One morning, Diamond managed to stop herself in time from reading what it said on the Autocue: 'You'll Never Walk Again . . .'

Told to me by Anne Diamond (May 1985).

DIANA, Princess of Wales

(1961–) English wife of Prince Charles. Formerly Lady Diana Spencer.

—— 3 ——

Lady Diana was not noted for her scholastic achievements when she attended Riddlesworth Hall school in Norfolk. But she did hold the record for not going to the loo. She went three days without doing so. This probably stood her in good stead when carrying out arduous Royal duties later in life.

Told to me by someone who was in a position to know (1984).

—— 4 ——

The Countess Spencer is said to have said of her step-daughter, 'If you mention Afghanistan to her, she'll think it a type of cheese.'

Source untraced, but reported by 1987.

—— 5 ——

Making small talk to a priest she met during a visit to Italy in 1985, she asked him, 'Do you a pray a lot?'

Source untraced.

Richard DIMBLEBY

(1913–65) English broadcaster, notable for fronting current affairs programmes and for his commentaries on great state occasions.

—— 6 ——

On 1 April 1957, Dimbleby introduced a TV film report on *Panorama* about that year's exceptionally heavy spaghetti harvest on the borders of Switzerland and Italy. The crop was shown hanging vertically from laurel bushes (having been affixed there first with Sellotape). Not everyone noticed the calendar on Dimbleby's desk as he closed the programme.

The hoax is fully recounted in *Richard Dimbleby, Broadcaster* (1966).

—— 7 ——

On the evening of 27 May 1965, Dimbleby was taking part in a live broadcast from Berlin of highlights from a Royal visit there. Several times there had been technical breakdowns between Berlin and West Germany. His producer told him, 'Hold everything. We're not on the air. London isn't getting us.' Thus thinking that his words were not being broadcast, Dimbleby let slip the oath, 'Jesus wept!' This would have passed unnoticed if London had not been receiving him loud and clear.

Related by the producer, Richard Francis, in *Richard Dimbleby, Broadcaster* **(1966).**

—— 1 ——

During a *Panorama* programme, Dimbleby said 'RSPCA' when he meant 'NSPCC'. Many viewers phoned in to point out his error. At the end of the programme he said: 'The more intelligent among you will have realized what I meant. Goodnight.'

Source untraced.

DIPLOMATS

—— 2 ——

A former British ambassador to France was asked by *Paris Match* what he would like for Christmas if he could have absolutely anything he wanted. The ambassador at first demurred and said no, no, he couldn't possibly, but eventually made his choice. The next issue of *Paris Match* duly carried its feature 'What the world would like for Christmas' in which Mikhail Gorbachev said he wanted an end to the arms race, Ronald Reagan opted for peace on earth, and so on. Finally there was the British ambassador: 'A small box of crystallized fruits, please.'

This joke made an appearance late in its life in Lynn Barber's column in *The Independent on Sunday* **on 29 December 1991. I was well familiar with it, as Jonathan James-Moore, later to become the BBC's Head of Light Entertainment (Radio), used it invariably as his warm-up joke in the early 1980s. The earliest version of it I have found occurs in** *Pass the Port* **(1976), but it also appears in Geoffrey Moorhouse,** *The Diplomats* **(1977) where it is told as the result of a Washington radio station telephoning various ambassadors in December 1948. In this version, the British ambassador, Sir Oliver Franks, was the one who said, 'I'd quite like a box of crystallized fruits.'**

—— 3 ——

The Master of an Oxford college was once asked to provide a brief reference for an undergraduate who was intending to join the diplomatic service. He simply wrote, 'X is not a homosexual. In every other respect he is ideally suited to a career in the Foreign Office . . .'

Told by R. G. in a letter (1993).

Frances DOBLE

(1902–69) English actress.

—— 4 ——

At the first night of Noël Coward's play *Sirocco* in 1927, the leading lady – Doble – was so thrown by the booing audience at the close that she launched into the only speech she had memorized. It began: 'Ladies and gentlemen, this is the happiest moment of my life . . .'

Quoted by Cole Lesley in *The Life of Noël Coward* **(1976).**

Robert DONAT

(1905–58) English actor, born in Manchester of Polish descent.

—— 5 ——

In the 1930s, a critic described Donat as a 'half-Greek god who had winged his way from Olympus'. His response was to sigh, 'Actually, I'm a half-Pole who's winged his way from Withington, Manchester.'

Quoted by Emlyn Williams in *George* **(1973).**

Diana DORS

(1931–84) Blonde, curvy, English film actress.

—— 6 ——

She was born – and this will come as a mighty revelation to all those who don't know it – Diana Fluck. Her father was the railway station master, or some such, in a tiny Somerset village. Anyway, when fame and fortune descended upon her in the 1950s, the well-known star was invited back to open the village fête.

The vicar – who had to introduce her – was very conscious of the fact that he would have to mention the name by which she was still known to all in the village and how serious it would be if by any chance he mispronounced 'Fluck'.

He worried about it, right up to the moment when he had to speak. He concluded his introduction with the words: 'And now here she is, the woman the whole world knows as "Diana Dors" but whom we will always remember as our own Diana Clunt . . .'

A tale first heard by me in the late 1960s, I should think.

Robert DOUGALL

(1913–) English broadcaster, notable as a gentlemanly television newsreader for the BBC.

------ 1 ------

People were queuing in a large department store at Wolverhampton when Dougall was signing copies of the autobiography he wrote when he retired from the BBC. One woman, obviously very excited at seeing Dougall in the flesh, was heard to say to her friend, 'It's *just* like him, isn't it?'

Told to me by Margaret Bell of Cannock (1981).

Kirk DOUGLAS

(1916–) American film actor with a remarkable dimple.

------ 2 ------

I once had to interview Douglas at very short notice, so I had not had a chance to read through the cuttings and background material before it was time for me to be shown up to his room at the Dorchester Hotel in London. I asked him questions off the top of my head and he answered them thoughtfully and with many vivid touches.

At the end, Douglas showed me to the door and bade me farewell. As I padded off down the corridor, I couldn't help hearing him say to his publicity person, 'That was a really good interview, wasn't it? Such a good interviewer.'

Was it possible that he had not closed the door before making the remark so that I was bound to hear it? Just another sign of his great professionalism, rather. When I eventually did get to go through the

cuttings of his previous interviews, I discovered that every single one of his observations and stories had been conveyed to other interviewers before me – in some cases many years previously.

The interview took place on 17 July 1975.

Mike DOUGLAS

(1925–) American TV chat-show host, not the actor son of Kirk.

------ 3 ------

'Idiot boards' are large pieces of card held up just out of camera range to help TV performers remember their words. Douglas, host of a very successful daytime talk show on American television, was once recording an interview with Kirk Douglas (no relation). The first question on the idiot board was about Kirk's latest picture – 'IS IT AN EPIC MOVIE?' it said. When they started recording, Mike peered at the idiot board and asked Kirk, in all seriousness, 'Tell me, Kirk, is it an *Eric* movie?' (Kirk, to give him his due, replied that, well, yes, it was an Eric movie . . . if that's how Mike wanted it . . .)

Told to me by David Frost, c. 1984.

Sir Alec DOUGLAS-HOME

(1903–) British politician. He renounced his peerage as the Earl of Home in order to become Conservative Prime Minister (1963–4), under this name. He became Lord Home of the Hirsel in 1974.

------ 4 ------

His looks more or less guaranteed that the otherwise amiable Douglas-Home would be a disaster on television. He recalled the following exchange with a make-up woman as she plied her trade prior to a prime ministerial broadcast: 'Can't you make me look better than I do on television? I look rather scraggy, like a ghost.'

'No.'

'Why not?'

'Because you have a head like a skull.'

'Doesn't everyone have a head like a skull.'
'No.'

Quoted in Michael Cockerell, *Live from Number 10* (1988).

—— 1 ——

I was once round at the Homes' London flat – a curious blend of baronial and G-plan – recording an interview with Sir Alec. Lady Home made herself scarce while we recorded the interview but reappeared at the end, clutching her foot. 'I dropped the kitchen table on it,' she explained, 'but I didn't like to cry out in case it spoiled the recording . . .'

From my diary for 24 July 1969. Such selflessness echoes what happened to an earlier Conservative Prime Minister's wife. 'One evening [Mrs Disraeli] drove to Westminster with him. She knew that, that night, he had a very important speech to make. When Disraeli was leaving, her fingers got trapped in the carriage door. She suffered excruciating pain but never uttered a word because she did not want to upset him and thereby spoil his speech' – D. H. Elletson, *Maryannery: Mary Ann Lincoln and Mary Anne Disraeli* (1959).

—— 2 ——

Sir Alec once received a telegram saying, 'TO HELL WITH YOU. OFFENSIVE LETTER FOLLOWS.'

Quoted in William Safire, *Safire's Political Dictionary* (1978).

Charlie DRAKE

(1925–) Diminutive English comedian.

—— 3 ——

After Drake had been given his first seven-minute slot in a BBC radio show in 1946, he wrote himself 800 fan letters. He took the tube from the Elephant and Castle, getting off at each stop to post several letters to the BBC. He thought that the BBC would be so overwhelmed that they would offer him his own show. A few days later, his mum handed him a fat parcel. It contained all the letters, unopened. It was a rule of the BBC that they never opened personal correspondence.

Reported by Russell Twisk in *Radio Times* (7 December 1967).

Marchioness of DUFFERIN AND AVA

(1907–) English aristocrat (née Maureen Guinness), married to the 4th Marquess from 1930 to 1945 and then to two other gentlemen, lastly Judge John Maude QC. Curiously, she continued to call herself by the style of her grandest husband, not the most recent. Said to be the original of 'Maudie Littlehampton' in Osbert Lancaster's cartoons.

—— 4 ——

Under the name of 'Maureen Dufferin and Ava', she ordered a taxi to pick her up from her home (round the back of Harrods, I believe) and take her to an important event. When the taxi arrived, the driver duly asked for 'Maureen Dufferin and Ava'. She came down and got in, but the driver – despite much urging from the Marchioness – declined to set off. Explained he: 'I'm waiting for Ava . . .'

Source untraced.

Jimmy DURANTE

(1893–1980) American comedian noted for his big nose, hence his nicknames 'Schnozzle' or 'Schnozzola'.

—— 5 ——

In 1935, Rodgers and Hart, Hecht and MacArthur wrote one of their less successful shows, *Jumbo*, which involved the use on stage of practically an entire circus. At one point, a sheriff is repossessing the circus and Jimmy Durante comes on with a full-grown real-life elephant; the sheriff asks him, 'Hey, where are you going with that elephant?' and Durante replies with sublime serenity, 'What elephant?'

Told to me by Pete Atkin (1979). The line was revived in the film *Jumbo*, 1962, with the joke specifically credited to Charles Lederer.

T. W. EARP

(1892–1958) English art critic.

—— 1 ——

Earp matriculated at Exeter College, Oxford, in 1911. *The Oxford English Dictionary* (Second Edition) produces a couple of citations (one, be it noted, from J. R. R. Tolkien) to demonstrate that this man gave rise to the use of the word 'twerp' to mean a 'foolish fellow'. It is not totally clear what Mr Earp did to make his unfortunate gift to nomenclature. If it was his gift – it is not proven.

Earp became President of the Oxford Union after the First World War and was, so it seems, the very opposite of a rugby-playing 'hearty'. Roy Campbell (in *Portugal*, 1957) spoke of Earp kindling 'Goering-like wrath . . . in the hearts of the rugger-playing stalwarts of Oxford . . . by being the last, most charming, and wittiest of the "decadents".'

Romilly John in *The Seventh Child* (1932) provides a description of Earp as a soft-spoken, gently humorous man, his hair close-cropped, his head shaped like a vegetable, 'who had taken his lack of ambition to the extreme of becoming an art critic' – or, at least, this is how the information appears in Vol. 2 of *Augustus John* (1975) by Michael Holroyd.

Anthony Powell in *Messengers of Day* (1978) adds that Earp had a 'thin, trembling voice'. As he had been ineligible for military service in the First World War, he had remained at Oxford and become Secretary and almost sole member of every conceivable Oxford club. Earp is buried at Selborne, Hampshire.

The Speaker of the House of Commons added the word 'twerp' to the list of unparliamentary expressions in May 1987.

James Chuter EDE

(later Lord Chuter-Ede) (1882–1965) English Labour politician. He was Home Secretary from 1945 to 1951 – in the days when Home Secretaries had names like Chuter Ede.

—— 2 ——

On a visit to one of His Majesty's prisons, which being under his care, Chuter Ede was encouraged to make a short speech to a group of inmates. The prisoners must have been deeply reassured when he began his remarks by saying: 'I'm so glad to see you all here . . .'

Told by Lord Elwyn-Jones on BBC Radio *Quote...Unquote* **(1987).**

Sir Anthony EDEN

(later 1st Earl of Avon) (1897–1977) British Conservative prime minister, reputedly of great sex appeal but also prone to carpet-chewing.

—— 3 ——

When Eden was Prime Minister and Harold Macmillan the Chancellor of the Exchequer, both men had to come to terms with appearing on television as a tool of the politician's trade. To help him with his first ministerial broadcast, the urbane Prime Minister rather curiously sought the aid of a BBC studio manager called Johnny Day who had a rich cockney accent and gloried in the use of rhyming slang. The reason was, a few weeks before, Day had instructed Macmillan in a Budget broadcast. 'Right, cock, over 'ere,' he had said. 'Boys, give me a piece of Duke of York.' He put a chalk mark on the blue carpet. 'Right, that's where you put your daisy roots. Now you look at the camera and go "blah, blah, bah". Then they've got a caption, you look at it and go "blah, blah, blah" again. Right?'

Macmillan acquiesced. Thus Eden sent in a request, 'Can John Day be present when I do my broadcast?'

Recounted in Michael Cockerell, *Live from Number 10* **(1988), based on a reminiscence by James Cellan-Jones.**

Thomas Alva EDISON

(1847–1931) American inventor. Among his thousand or so inventions were the gramophone and the incandescent light bulb.

—— 1 ——

However good Edison may have been as an inventor, he did not always have a good instinct for the prospects of other people's inventions. In 1926, he said, 'I have determined that there is no market for talking pictures.'

Quoted in Stuart Berg Flexner, *Listening to America* (1982).

—— 2 ——

In addition, Edison seems not to have been too confident of his own inventions. He said on one occasion: 'The phonograph is not of any commercial value.'

Quoted in *Time* Magazine (13 August 1984).

EDUCATIONISTS

—— 3 ——

A bravura toast, given at the centenary of a college, was: 'Here's to pure scholarship. May it never be of any use to anyone!'

Told by Oonagh Lahr (1993). John Julius Norwich commented that his father, Duff Cooper, used to quote this as being a toast to Higher Mathematics.

King EDWARD VII

(1841–1910) British sovereign who liked his pleasures.

—— 4 ——

When the future King said to his lover, the actress Lillie Langtry, 'I've spent enough on you to buy a battleship', she replied, 'And you've spent enough in me to float one.'

Source untraced.

—— 5 ——

The King had an obsessive interest in correct attire. On one occasion when a courtier unwisely appeared in a loud check suit, the King said: 'Goin' rattin', Harris?'

Told by Miles Kington on BBC Radio *Quote...Unquote* (1986). Compare SALISBURY 164:4.

—— 6 ——

When the King died, Lord Kinnoull's little daughter, who had witnessed the funeral procession, refused to say her prayers that night. 'It won't be of any use,' she explained, 'God will be too busy unpacking King Edward.'

Recounted in Lord Riddell, *More Pages from My Diary 1908–14* (1934).

King EDWARD VIII

(later the Duke of Windsor) (1894–1972) The British sovereign who abdicated to marry the woman he loved.

—— 7 ——

Within days of the Abdication – in December 1936 – schoolchildren were singing:

Hark, the herald angels sing
Mrs Simpson's pinched our king.

A letter from Clement Attlee on 26 December 1938 included the information that his daughter Felicity had produced this 'ribald verse which was new to me' – quoted in Kenneth Harris, *Attlee* (1982). Iona and Peter Opie in *The Lore and Language of Schoolchildren* (1959) comment on the rapidity with which this rhyme spread across the country. The constitutional crisis did not become public until 25 November, the King abdicated on 10 December, 'yet at a school party in Swansea given before the end of term ... when the tune played happened to be "Hark, the Herald Angels Sing", a mistress found herself having to restrain her small children from singing this lyric, known to all of them, which cannot have been composed more than three weeks previously.'

—— 8 ——

It was not very difficult to understand what the King saw in Mrs Simpson. However, a lesser-known aspect of her charms is indicated by the view that, 'She could make a matchstick seem like a

Havana cigar' – which was, perhaps, important to the man in question.

Told to me by a Royal biographer in 1981. Also, in 1975, a journalist related how one of the rumours concerning the Duke of Windsor was that he used to enjoy watching society ladies having it off with footmen because 'his own parts were so small'.

Diana EDWARDS-JONES

(*fl.* 1968) English hard-swearing TV director, chiefly at ITN.

—— 1 ——

In a studio discussion at ITN which was being directed by Edwards-Jones, both interviewer and interviewee had earpieces (perhaps they were being joined by a third party from another location). Something was wrong, however, and this meant that Edwards-Jones's instructions to the interviewer were also heard by the interviewee. She said to the interviewer, 'Ask the old fart to give us some [voice] level'. And the Archbishop of Canterbury said, 'I think she means me.'

Told by Martyn Lewis in a speech at Cardiff (1991).

Albert EINSTEIN

(1879–1955) German-Swiss-American mathematical physicist.

—— 2 ——

Einstein was a keen amateur violinist. One day he was practising sonatas at home with the pianist Arthur Rubinstein. Someone overheard Rubinstein pointing out a late entry on Einstein's part. 'Albert,' he was saying, 'can't you count?'

The earliest version of this story I have encountered is in Oscar Levant, *The Unimportance of Being Oscar* (1968). He places it in Princeton, New Jersey, when Einstein was lecturing there and playing his violin in string quartets.

ELDERLY PEOPLE

—— 3 ——

One elderly person was overheard saying to another: 'If anything should happen to either of us, you may take it that I'm definitely going to live in Bournemouth.'

This version of an old story appeared in *Pass the Port Again* (1980). In my *Eavesdroppings* (1981), I called it 'traditional' and gave it as said on a park bench: 'When one of us passes on, I shall move south to live with my daughter.' There is nothing new, etc.: in *Samuel Butler's Notebooks* (which covered the years 1874–1902) there appeared the entry: 'Warburg's old friend . . . said to Warburg one day, talking about his wife, who was ill, "If God were to take one or other of us, I should go and live in Paris."'

—— 4 ——

A 100-year-old woman was asked whether she still had any worries. 'No, I haven't,' she replied. 'Not since my son went into an old folks' home.'

Source forgotten.

—— 5 ——

The family patriarch was on the way out. As he lay on his deathbed, the family gathered round. Sleepily, the old man opened his eyes and asked, 'Is Johnny here?' The eldest son quietly asserted that, yes, he was there. 'And is my good boy, Tommy, also here?' The good boy, with a lump in his throat, made it clear to his father that he, too, was there. 'And what about Henry? Is he here?' Yes, the said Henry piped up – he was there. And so on, down through the family, the roll call continued, until all the children, male and female, had been accounted for.

The patriarch still didn't look very pleased. 'If you're all here,' he finally said, very tetchily, 'Then who's minding the store?'

This punchline is found in many joke books as far back as Irvin S. Cobb, *Many Laughs for Many Days* (1925). It was used as the title of a Jerry Lewis film in 1963.

—— 6 ——

There are three rules of life for men over sixty-five: 'Never pass up a chance to pee, never trust a fart, and never waste an erection even if you're on your own.'

Told by a well-known radio disc-jockey, who should know (1993).

—— 1 ——

More useful advice – from an over eighty-five. The Reverend H. J. Bidder, aged 86, sat silently, with a crumpled face, all through dinner and then promulgated the following: '(1) Never drink claret in an east wind. (2) Take your pleasures singly, one by one. (3) Never sit on a hard chair after drinking port.'

Recalled in *Geoffrey Madan's Notebooks* (ed. Gere & Sparrow, 1981). Madan died in 1947.

Queen ELIZABETH II

(1926–) British sovereign who acceded to the throne in 1952. Will be remembered for her entertaining Christmas broadcasts, her handbags and corgis.

—— 2 ——

In a magazine article in 1958, Lord Altrincham said the Queen's style of speaking (*not* her voice) was 'frankly a pain in the neck' and what she was given to say suggested a 'priggish schoolgirl, captain of the hockey team, a prefect and a recent candidate for confirmation'. For his pains, Altrincham was slapped in the face by a member of the League of Empire Loyalists.

Altrincham's remarks appeared in *The National and English Review* (August 1958). He later disclaimed his peerage and became known as John Grigg.

—— 3 ——

Not so long after Princess Margaret's wedding to Anthony Armstrong-Jones in 1960, the photographer, the Queen was speaking to a guest at one of her garden parties. 'What is your profession?' she asked, interested as ever in the world around her. 'I'm a photographer, ma'am,' the man replied. 'Oh, how interesting,' said Her Majesty, 'I have a brother-in-law who is a photographer . . .' 'Even more of a coincidence,' said the man, 'I have a brother-in-law who's a queen!'

This story comes round quite often. In *The Kenneth Williams Diaries* (1993) it is recorded on 1 May 1963 and said to be 'current at the moment'.

—— 4 ——

When asked to attend a performance of Mozart's *The Marriage of Figaro*, the Queen replied, 'Is that the one about the pin?'

Indeed, it is, though it is a little odd that she should have remembered this small moment. Source untraced.

—— 5 ——

Reading a speech in Australia during 1977, the Queen said, 'In the 25th reign of my year . . .' Shortly afterwards she started wearing spectacles.

Reported in BBC Radio *Quote...Unquote* (24 December 1977).

—— 6 ——

When an intruder called Michael Fagan made his way into the Queen's bedroom at Buckingham Palace in 1982, Her Majesty, by all accounts, behaved with exemplary coolness. On the other hand, when Elizabeth Andrews also turned up, the royal chambermaid exclaimed – with a beguiling blend of shock and courtesy: 'Bloody hell, *Ma'am*, what's he doing here?'

Quoted in *The Daily Mail* (July 1982).

—— 7 ——

The Queen demonstrated formidable tact when asked by a small Commonwealth person during a Christmas broadcast whether she believed in Father Christmas. She was ready for it, and replied simply: 'I like to believe in Father Christmas.'

Soundtrack of the broadcast (25 December 1989).

Queen ELIZABETH the Queen Mother

(1900–) Wife of King George VI and mother of Queen Elizabeth II. The 'Queen Mum' is universally loved, though not, it is said, by all of her servants.

—— 8 ——

A tale of two department stores. When visiting a children's hospital, the Queen Mother asked a little boy where he lived. 'Behind 'Arrods,' came the answer. 'And where do you live?' the boy asked her in turn. She replied, 'Behind Gorringes'.

Recounted by Ruth Zollschan in a letter to *The Guardian* (15 December 1986).

Duke ELLINGTON

(1899–1974) American bandleader, pianist and composer.

—— 1 ——

It wasn't all music-making for Ellington. He had other interests – or, rather, he had one. A musical about his life ran into difficulties because originally it had spoken introductions trying to point up the contrast between the 'public' and the 'private' Ellington. Mercer Ellington, his son, quietly pointed out that there was only one aspect to both: 'He spent his whole life chasing pussy.'

Told to me by a New York lawyer in 1981. The musical that *didn't* result from this observation was *Sophisticated Ladies*.

Lord ELWYN-JONES

(1909–89) Likeable Welsh jurist and Labour politician. His wife, Polly Binder, died – touchingly – a matter of weeks after him.

—— 2 ——

In the days of King Idris, Elwyn-Jones went out to Tripoli in Libya to defend a man. As soon as he arrived, the trial was postponed for a week. Elwyn-Jones was worried about this because he was due to defend in a murder trial at Cardiff Assizes the following week and he wasn't sure of the date. So he cabled his clerk, 'Please send me date of Cardiff murder trial.' The next morning, the British Ambassador in Tripoli rang up Elwyn-Jones and said, 'What on earth is going on? A cable addressed to you has been opened by Security, reading: "Cable received. Murder fixed for Wednesday".'

Told by him on BBC Radio *Quote...Unquote* (1987).

EMBARRASSED PEOPLE

—— 3 ——

A woman was overheard at Eton saying: '. . . And as he'd had a long run down, he asked for the bathroom. When he was shown into it, he suddenly looked and there was his hostess in the bath. He couldn't think what was the correct thing to say, so he said, "You *are* looking well."'

C. D'O. Gowan of Ulverston related this snippet of conversation to me in 1980. It was picked up when he was a housemaster at Eton and he and his wife were walking round Agar's Plough on 4 June. But what should the man have said? That same year, I decided to consult Douglas Sutherland, author of the *English Gentleman* series of books. He advised: 'I beg your pardon, *sir!*'

This sounded much better, and I subsequently found confirmation that it was the correct response when reading a 1932 novel, *Charming Manners* by 'John Michaelhouse' (a pen name of the Reverend Joseph McCulloch). In the story, a group of Oxford undergraduates happen upon half-a-dozen naked nymphs dancing in the sunlight on the banks of the River Cherwell. 'We all collapsed in the punt at once, there being no chance of saying, "Sorry, gentlemen" in the approved style.'

In François Truffaut's film *Baisers Volés* (1968), the character played by Delphine Seyrig says that she was taught the difference between tact and politeness – if a man surprises a naked lady in the bathroom, politeness is to say 'Sorry', tact is to say, 'Sorry, sir.'

The boot is on the other foot, so to speak, in a glancing comment in E. M. Forster's *A Room with a View* (1908): 'Mr Beebe [the clergyman] was not able to tell the ladies of his adventure at Modena, where the chambermaid burst in upon him in his bath, exclaiming cheerfully, "Fa niente, sono vecchia" [It doesn't matter, I'm an old woman].'

—— 4 ——

A woman answered a box number in a newspaper offering a bed-sitter that sounded better than the one she had. Two days later, her landlady came in with the letter in her hand. She said, 'I see you are thinking of moving . . .'

Told to me by the woman involved, *c.* 1982.

—— 5 ——

The Oxford Library Club – 'for Retired Professional People and Others Interested' – was all agog to hear its guest speaker, Dr P. R****t, on the subject of 'Old Age, Absent-Mindedness and Keeping Fit'. Alas, he forgot to turn up.

Told to me by a member of the club, *c*. 1984.

—— 1 ——

Alan Melville told a story involving his Aunt Kate: 'She had a visit one tea-time from an old friend she hadn't seen for a very long time. It turned out that the old friend had "got religion" and when she came she announced to Aunt Kate that she had found Christ. Aunt Kate said the right things – that she was delighted to hear it, you know – and the old friend went on and on and on about it. Eventually, to Aunt Kate's great embarrassment this lady said, "Shall we go down on our knees and say a prayer together?" And Aunt Kate said in a panic – and she didn't mean it to be a "funny" – "Oh, I don't think so, dear, we've just Hoovered the carpet!"'

As told by him on BBC Radio *Quote...Unquote* (1983).

—— 2 ——

He (who has tried to catch his companion's name, and wishes to find it out indirectly): 'BY THE WAY, HOW DO YOU *SPELL* YOUR NAME?' She: 'J-O-N-E-S'.

This is the caption to a cartoon in *Punch* (Vol. 122, 8 January 1902) and is presumably the forerunner of embarrassment jokes concerning name forgetting and non-recognition, such as BEECHAM 26:5 and COOPER 63:2.

—— 3 ——

A number of years ago, to say the least, an audience of tittering sixth-formers (including myself) believed it had stumbled upon a prime example of the Freudian slip. We were attending what was known as a Film Appreciation Lecture in the Philharmonic Hall, Liverpool. The speaker was a distinguished film director whose name fortunately I have forgotten, and he was introducing one of his distinguished films. In a throwaway line, he informed us he had just been with Dirk Bogarde in the South of France or somewhere, 'And we've been disgusting together ... er ... discussing ... oh God!'

I fear the name of the film director may be coming back to me. I think it was Roy (Ward) Baker introducing a showing of his film *Morning Departure* (1950). He subsequently directed Bogarde in *The Singer Not the Song* (1960), which would fit the time scale.

ENGLISH PERSONS

—— 4 ——

'If an Englishman gets run down by a truck, he apologizes to the truck.'

A terribly true joke told by the American comedian Jackie Mason in 1992.

—— 5 ——

An Englishman sat unmoved all through Pavlova's dying-swan dance until, near the end, a feather detached itself from her costume and fell to the ground. He said but one word: 'Moulting'.

Reported by Arnold Bennett and recounted in *The Lyttelton Hart-Davis Letters* (for 28 March 1957).

—— 6 ——

Mrs Edmund Warre was the wife of the Headmaster of Eton at the time of the sinking of the *Titanic* in 1912. She broke the news to him with remarkable understatement: 'I am sorry to hear there has been a bad boating accident.'

Recounted by George Lyttelton in *The Lyttelton Hart-Davis Letters* (for 7 December 1955). He adds, 'She came in, quivering slightly with age and dottiness. . . An odd but very characteristic way of describing the sinking of the largest ship in the world and the death of 1400 people.'

Peg ENTWISTLE

(1908–32) American actress.

—— 7 ——

Disappointed by lack of success at the studios, this actress climbed to the top of the 15-m (50-ft) letter H in the HOLLYWOOD sign overlooking Los Angeles, threw herself off it and died.

Source: article in *The Independent* Magazine (4 May 1991).

ENVIRONMENTALISTS

—— 1 ——

I once heard about a very environmentally-minded couple who did all the right energy-saving things, grew their own vegetables and recycled everything in sight. So successful were they that they had sufficient cash in hand to enable them to run a second car.

—— 2 ——

A slogan that might have done with a little more thought in its creation was: 'Every penny you spend will help the World Wildlife Fund's Tropical Rain Forest Campaign.'

Current in *c*. 1982.

—— 3 ——

A man was desperately searching for something beneath the light of a lamppost. A neighbour came out to help him and asked what he was looking for. 'A $50 bill that dropped out of my pocket,' said the man. 'Do you know where you dropped it?' inquired the neighbour. 'Yes,' said the man, 'it was about ten yards up the street.' 'Then why are you looking for it here under the street lamp?' asked the neighbour. 'Because the light here is much better,' said the man.

Told by Charles G. Francis (1991). This is really a story about research or discovery, but it is included under 'Environmentalists' because it was originally invoked by a large US oil company under pressure from state governments to reformulate its gasoline to help combat air pollution. The company felt that the answer to the problem lay elsewhere – with automobile manufacturers, not least – and so thought that, like the man in the story, the governments were looking for the right answer in the wrong place.

Dame Edith EVANS

(1888–1976) English actress of distinctive voice and great personality, even if she will always be first remembered for her enunciation of the word 'handbag' as Lady Bracknell in Wilde's *The Importance of Being Earnest*.

—— 4 ——

In April 1951, Evans opened in N. C. Hunter's play *Waters of the Moon*, with Sybil Thorndike. After the play had been running for 12 months, the H. M. Tennent management announced to Evans that she would be getting a whole new wardrobe from Pierre Balmain. Said she of Thorndike, her supposed rival: 'If I'm to have a new frock, I insist that Sybil has a new cardigan.'

Related by Sheridan Morley in *Sybil Thorndike: A Life in the Theatre* (1977). Kenneth Tynan told it slightly differently in *Woman's Journal* (1956). In his version, 'Binkie' Beaumont offered to fly Evans to Paris for a completely new wardrobe by Pierre Balmain, and Evans said, 'If I go to Paris, Sybil must have a new cardigan.'

On the subject of her relations with Thorndike, Evans is also supposed to have said: 'I don't know whether I like her [Sybil] or not, but I've named my new bicycle after her' (told by Denise Coffey on BBC Radio *Quote...Unquote*, 1979).

—— 5 ——

The pot calling the kettle black etc.: when it was suggested to Evans that Kenneth Williams should be in the cast of a play with her, she told the impresario that she viewed this with great apprehension. 'Why him?' she asked. 'Well, he's right for the role.' 'But he's got such a peculiar voooooiiiiicccce!'

Told to me by Kenneth Williams on 29 October 1964, when I was interviewing him for an Oxford publication. In *The Kenneth Williams Diaries* (1993), he reports it a year earlier on 24 October 1963 as 'a story going round'. In that version the impresario is named as Binkie Beaumont. Williams adds: 'It's only funny when the impersonation of her is good.'

—— 6 ——

When urging a young actress to get on with her scene, Evans announced, rather disarmingly: 'I'm a very old lady. I may die during one of your pauses.'

Told by Denise Coffey (1979).

—— 7 ——

When asked by a young actress how to set about speaking her lines, Evans advised: 'Say everything as if it is improper.'

Told by Rula Lenska on BBC Radio *Quote...Unquote* (1980). In Donald Sinden's *A Touch of the Memoirs* (1982), he has it thus: 'If she could not think what to do with a line, she spoke it as if it was obscene. One has only to think of her delivery of "A handbag!" in *The Importance of Being Earnest* to know what she meant.'

—— 1 ——

When a young actor wished her luck before a radio broadcast, Evans reproved him, saying: 'With some of us it isn't luck.'

Related by Bryan Forbes in *Ned's Girl* (1977).

—— 2 ——

When a Fortnum and Mason salesgirl insisted on fetching her threepence change, Evans said: 'Keep the change, my dear, I trod on a grape as I came in.'

Related in ibid.

—— 3 ——

Told that Nancy Mitford was staying at a friend's house in order to finish a book, Evans remarked, 'Oh, really? What exactly is she reading?'

I put this in my book *Quote...Unquote* (1978), source forgotten. Alexander Walker, in a letter to me (dated 23 September 1985), claimed to have overheard Evans saying this to Katharine Hepburn during the filming of *The Madwoman of Chaillot* (*c.* 1968).

—— 4 ——

Rehearsing in Hammersmith one day, Evans heard talk of some people 'who were living in Barnes'. She inquired, 'Couldn't they afford a house?'

Told by Patricia Hodge (1986).

—— 5 ——

Shortly after being awarded the DBE, she was addressed by a call-boy with the words, 'Ten minutes, Miss Evans'. She exclaimed: '*Miss* Evans! It'll be Edie next!'

Told by Terry Wogan on BBC Radio *Quote ...Unquote* (1980). Ned Sherrin in *Theatrical Anecdotes* (1991) locates this specifically at Riverside Studios when a stagehand said helpfully, 'This way, dear.' Evans said: 'Dear? They'll be calling me "Edie" next.'

—— 6 ——

Sir Peter Ustinov recalls rehearsing with Dame Edith. He says, 'She had a very special way of suggesting that there were certain unauthorized presences in the theatre, people who shouldn't have been there. And she said to the auditorium – while wearing that jockey hat she affected – "Are we all of the family?"'

Told by him on BBC Radio *Quote...Unquote* (1992).

—— 7 ——

Evans had been excluded from some improvisational exercises during a rehearsal at the Old Vic because it was thought she might not approve. In time, however, a peculiar noise emerged from where she was sitting in the auditorium. A voice inquired anxiously, 'Dame Edith, what's the matter?' She replied, 'I'm being a handbag.'

Told to me by a correspondent in 1981.

—— 8 ——

When asked to add Lady Macbeth to her repertoire, Evans declined, saying it was out of the question. 'I could never impersonate a woman with such peculiar notions of hospitality!'

Related in Richard Huggett, *The Curse of Macbeth* (1981).

EXCUSE-MAKERS

—— 9 ——

The buffet car steward on an InterCity express announced: 'For the benefit [*sic*] of the passengers, only cold meat and salad will be on the menu for dinner tonight. This is due to the buffet car being the wrong way round . . .'

Told to me by David L. Coggins of Blackburn, Lancashire (1986).

Marianne FAITHFULL

(1947–) English pop singer and actress.

—— 1 ——

From 1967 to 1970, Faithfull was the girlfriend of Rolling Stone Mick Jagger. When he and Keith Richard appeared in court on drugs charges in June 1967, it was revealed that during the police raid a 'young lady' (Faithfull) dressed only in a fur rug had been observed. A rumour swept the country that the police had interrupted an orgy in which Jagger had been licking a Mars bar inserted in a special part of her anatomy.

> As Philip Norman noted in *The Stones* (1984), 'The Mars bar was a detail of such sheer madness as to make the story believed, then and for ever after.'

—— 2 ——

When Faithfull made an unexpectedly convincing stage debut at the Royal Court Theatre, London, in Chekhov's *The Three Sisters*, a disappointed member of the audience was overheard saying: 'If she's not awful soon, I'm leaving.'

> Told on BBC Radio *Quote...Unquote* (1979). On the other hand, this may be a borrowing from a story which concerns Elizabeth Taylor's appearance at a fund-raising poetry reading in New York. Here, Bea Lillie, sitting in front of Emlyn Williams, whispered to her companion, 'If she doesn't get bad pretty soon, people are going to start leaving' – quoted in Melvyn Bragg, *Rich: The Life of Richard Burton* (1988).

W. C. FIELDS

(1880–1946) American vaudeville and film comedian.

—— 3 ——

In the days before he became a comedian, Fields was for a time a newspaper vendor in Philadel-

phia. As you might anticipate, he had a somewhat eccentric way of promoting his wares. 'Bronislaw Gimp,' he might say, 'Bronislaw Gimp acquires licence for two-year-old sheepdog. Details on page 26.' It is said that many citizens of Philadelphia bought copies out of simple curiosity.

> **Source untraced (but known by 1986).**

—— 4 ——

Fields once inserted a small paragraph in *Variety* stating: 'W. C. Fields wishes a Happy Christmas to all his friends but one.'

The consternation that ensued boggled all imagination.

> In a letter from C. R. W. (1993). Compare the dedication that appeared in Jan Morris's book *The Oxford Book of Oxford* (1978): 'DEDICATED GRATEFULLY TO THE WARDEN AND FELLOWS OF ST ANTONY'S COLLEGE OXFORD. EXCEPT ONE.'

—— 5 ——

Although he once joked that he would like as an epitaph, 'On the whole I'd rather be in Philadelphia', the nearest to a memorable deathbed utterance Fields produced before his demise on Christmas Day 1946 was when the actor Thomas Mitchell, to his amazement, found the comedian thumbing through a Bible. When Mitchell asked him what he was doing, Fields answered, 'Looking for loopholes'.

> Fields's actual last words were: 'Goddamn the whole friggin' world and everyone in it but you, Carlotta' (a reference to his mistress) – Robert Lewis Taylor, *W. C. Fields: His Follies and Fortunes* (1950).

FILM PEOPLE

—— 6 ——

The film 'Oscar' or 'Academy Award' is said to take its name from a comment made by

Margaret Herrick when she was a secretary at the American Academy of Motion Picture Arts and Sciences. On seeing the statuette (awarded since 1928), she declared: 'Why, it looks just like my Uncle Oscar' – i.e. one Oscar Pierce, a wheat-and-fruit grower.

Source: my *Why Do We Say...?* (1987) and *The Oxford English Dictionary* (2nd edition).

—— 1 ——

In the epic *Quo Vadis*, Leo Genn as Petronius is relaxing at his villa outside Rome. The character is then given this line to say: 'Why don't you come down to Sicily for the weekend, Marcus? And bring the children.'

Unverified.

—— 2 ——

Spike Milligan claims that when *Quo Vadis* was released in 1951, the producers felt that it was absolutely vital to have a love theme which could sell lots of records as well as promoting the picture. Hence, they commissioned a song with the title 'Quo Vadis I Love You'.

In fact, no such song exists, although there is a 'Love Theme from *Quo Vadis*' to which someone might have attached these words.

Ian FLEMING

(1908–64) English novelist and newspaperman.
The creator of 'James Bond', with whom he shared
several traits.

—— 3 ——

During the Second World War, Fleming worked in 'black propaganda' with the journalist Sefton Delmer. One of their schemes – which, alas, was never put into action – was to broadcast an instruction to the German people. They would be told that, in order to allow German scientists to ensure that the war was having no deleterious effect on their digestive tracts, a mass examination of faeces was being arranged. In short, the German people was being asked to save its shit. This would then be collected at various designated points. It would be suggested that the best thing for them to do was to deposit the shit in letter boxes.

Told to me by Sefton Delmer in March 1972.

Ronald FLETCHER

(1910–) English BBC radio newsreader and
announcer. He was also featured in 1950s radio
shows with Bernard Braden. From 1976 he read
the quotations on BBC Radio's *Quote...Unquote*.

—— 4 ——

As Fletcher himself admitted, on reaching the end of a news bulletin he once declared: 'That is the end of the forecast. Now a look at the weather.'

Told on BBC Radio *Quote...Unquote* (1979).

—— 5 ——

Fletcher's end-pieces from the Braden shows were treasured by many who heard the original broadcasts. They were written for him by such luminaries as Frank Muir and Denis Norden. For example, he would say things like: 'Isn't it wonderful that a cat has two holes in its fur just where its eyes are?' Possibly his most famous utterance was: 'It is an offence to have a wireless on too loud these still summer evenings. It can annoy your neighbour. An even better way is to throw a dead cat on the lawn . . .'

Recalled in Bernard Braden, *The Kindness of Strangers* (1990). In fact, the first of these owes a good deal to Georg Christoph Lichtenburg (1742–99) who wrote: 'The thing that astonished him was that cats should have two holes cut in their coat, exactly at the place where their eyes are.' I also wish I had the text of another of Fletcher's homilies on the effects of loud radios – 'in which he advised us to test the offensiveness of our radios by leaning out of the window ... "a little more; a little bit more; just a bit more . . . oh, I beg your pardon"' – (letter from Charles Lewsen, 1979.)

—— 6 ——

Fletcher never threw off the urge to gamble. In his early days he had lost all the money his grandfather had left him, in an unsuccessful business venture, and that is when he turned to the BBC. At one stage he was in debt to a bookmaker for several thousand pounds and the bookmaker offered to write off the debt if Ronnie promised never to back another horse. That night he went to the dog track. On another occasion he offered a bank manager his BBC salary as collateral for a loan. When Ronnie told the manager what the salary was, he replied, 'Would a pound be all right?'

Based on the reminiscences of Eric Nicol, as related in Bernard Braden, *The Kindness of Strangers* (1990).

—— 1 ——

Radio newsreaders have two keys which they can operate while on the air. The cough key cuts out the microphone so that the throat can be cleared. The other key enables contact to be made with the control cubicle through the otherwise soundproof glass.

At the height of the Soviet invasion of Czechoslovakia in August 1968, I recall watching Fletcher read the ten o'clock news on Radio 4. At the conclusion of a lengthy report containing any number of impossible Czech names, all pronounced with dazzling confidence and nary a stumble, Fletcher pressed down both keys and remarked to those in the control cubicle, 'How about that then?'

My memory of the occasion.

—— 2 ——

During the first series of *Quote...Unquote*, Fletcher was, unusually for him, making very heavy weather of the script and fluffing heavily. At one point, he made a complete balls-up. What was astonishing was his explanation. 'You must excuse me,' he said, 'My wife has got the flu.'

This was during the recording on 10 February 1976.

Anna FORD

(1943–) English TV newscaster with ITN and BBC.

—— 3 ——

In 1983, Ford was one of the unhappy quintet of presenters with whom TV-am, the breakfast television station, went on the air. Within weeks, the station was in trouble and Peter Jay, who had headed the company's bid for the franchise, was ousted by its financial backers. Ford broke ranks and talked to the press, declaring that, 'There's been a great deal of treachery . . . History will expose those who have been most treacherous.'

Quoted in Michael Leapman, *Treachery? The Power Struggle at TV-am* (1984).

—— 4 ——

After Ford herself had been ousted – ostensibly for breach of contract in talking to the press – she expressed her indignation at Jonathan Aitken MP, who had assumed Peter Jay's post, by throwing a glass of white wine over him at a party. She explained (though not to him), 'He had just ruined my life. He broke my contract and I lost my job.'

In ibid.

Gerald R. FORD

(1913–) American Republican president from 1974 to 1977, and noted for his physical and verbal slips. It was said famously of him (by Lyndon Johnson), 'He can't fart and chew gum at the same time.' Also, 'He couldn't find the seat of his pants with both hands.'

—— 5 ——

Ford said, 'Whenever I can, I always watch the Detroit Tigers on radio.'

Quoted in *Time* Magazine (30 March 1981).

—— 6 ——

The clanger that finally scuppered his chances of a further term occurred in the 1976 TV debates with his challenger, Jimmy Carter. Said Ford, 'There is no Soviet domination of Eastern Europe and there never will be under a Ford administration.'

Pressed to elaborate on this surprising view he said, 'I don't believe that the Poles consider themselves dominated by the Soviet Union . . . It has its own territorial integrity.' After a couple of clarifying statements, Ford finally admitted, 'I was perhaps not as precise as I should have been.' Quoted in my *Sayings of the Century* (1984).

Wallace FORD

(1897–1966) English actor who went to Hollywood in the early 1930s and ended up playing character parts.

—— 7 ——

After a number of 'semi-leads', Ford was condemned to a succession of supporting roles in Hollywood films and decided that his gravestone epitaph should read, 'At last – I get top billing.' This inscription was duly put on his grave. Then along came a graffiti artist who chalked above it, 'Clark Gable and Myrna Loy supported by . . .'

Told by Terence Frisby on BBC Radio *Quote...Unquote* (1979).

John FOTHERGILL

(1876–1957) English publican who was quite well known in the 1920s and 30s, particularly as landlord of the Spread Eagle at Thame, and wrote a couple of books about his experiences, including *An Innkeeper's Diary*.

—— 1 ——

On one occasion, Fothergill was trying to off-load some pudding on a customer, and said: 'Would you like to try some of our excellent chapel harlot?'

The customer, unperturbed, is said to have asked whether this was any relation to 'Thame Tart'.

Sir Norman FOWLER

(1938–) English Conservative politician, formerly journalist. For many years Social Services Secretary under Margaret Thatcher, Fowler then resigned 'to spend more time with his family' and subsequently became Conservative Party Chairman. A noted user of after-shave.

—— 2 ——

Fowler ran an anti-AIDS campaign as Social Services Secretary and it was rumoured in Whitehall that, in some discussion, he had asked, 'What *is* oral sex?'

Referred to in *The Independent on Sunday* (26 May 1991). Quoted in *Sunday Today* (11 January 1987).

Clare FRANCIS

(1946–) Petite English yachtswoman and then born-again novelist.

—— 3 ——

When I was at Oxford, I appeared in an undergraduate revue with Clare who at that stage had been to the Royal Ballet School, was currently at St Clare's, a sort of Oxford finishing school, and displayed few signs of being a future intrepid lone woman yachtsperson. I took her to a ball in the spring of 1964. I think it was on that occasion I asked her what her father did – which was still the sort of question one asked girls in the early 1960s – and I

think she told me he was an electrician. It was only many years later, by which time Clare had been transformed into an intrepid, lone etc., that I discovered her father had actually been Chairman of the London Electricity Board.

My memories of the incident.

Sir Richard FRANCIS

(1934–92) English broadcasting producer and executive, including Managing Director of BBC Radio (1982–6). Subsequently, Director-General of the British Council.

—— 4 ——

Dick Francis loved gadgets. Having organized much of the 1960s British TV coverage of US space missions, he took to wearing several wristwatches up his left arm, giving the local time in several countries. He also indulged in NASA-speak, saying 'Affirmative' instead of 'Yes', and so on. When he was organizing the BBC's coverage of the 1970 British General Election, a film editor offered him some exclusive footage of one of the polling stations. 'Negative', replied Francis, and the programme budget was charged with 400 feet of negative colour film stock.

From Leonard Miall's obituary in *The Independent* (29 June 1992), though Miall concedes that the story may be apocryphal. Still, I can recall my first meeting with Dick Francis in about 1977. He had a prominent wire coming out of one ear and it was explained to me that this dated from his time as BBC Controller in Northern Ireland when he was permanently tuned into a transistor so that he would know where the latest bomb had gone off.

Bill FRASER

(1907–87) English actor who played 'Snudge' in the ITV series *Bootsie and Snudge*, as well as working in the legitimate theatre.

—— 5 ——

When Fraser was waiting to be demobbed at the end of the War, he formed a touring company to keep the troops entertained. By the time he got back to camp, he found he'd been demobbed two weeks previously. 'Well, Fraser,' his CO said, 'What are you going to do in civvy street?' 'The theatre,' Fraser replied. 'Oh dear, dear. They've blown up all the piers, haven't they?'

Fraser's own version appeared in *Radio Times* (24 January 1974).

Brenda FRICKER

(1944–) Irish character actress who won an Academy Award for 'Best Supporting Actress' for her role in *My Left Foot* (1989).

—— 1 ——

Fricker sagely commented on an apparent dual nationality that afflicts some Irish people in the world's eyes: 'When you're lying drunk at the airport, you're Irish. When you win an Oscar, you're British.'

Quoted in *The Observer* (8 April 1990).

Sir David FROST

(1939–) English TV interviewer and entertainer, originally host of the satirical show *That Was The Week That Was.*

—— 2 ——

Following his debut as a satirist and at the time he was about to launch himself as a more serious TV chat-show host, Frost demonstrated the drawing power of TV when, on 7 January 1966, he invited to breakfast at the Connaught Hotel in Mayfair not only the Prime Minister, Harold Wilson, but also the Bishop of Woolwich, Lord Soper, Len Deighton the novelist, and newspapermen Cecil King, David Astor and Charles Wintour. Paul McCartney had also been invited but had a previous engagement.

—— 3 ——

Willie Rushton, who had appeared with Frost from the beginning of *That Was The Week That Was* in 1962, discovered that one of the secrets of

being a globe-trotting, wisecracking TV superstar lay in a folder to be found in Frost's luggage. It was labelled 'Airport ad-libs'.

Source untraced.

—— 4 ——

During the taping of his world-exclusive interviews with ex-President Nixon in 1977, even Frost was disconcerted to be on the receiving end of some Nixonian small talk. After a week-end break, Nixon welcomed him back on a Monday morning with, 'Well, did you do any fornicating this week-end?'

Quoted in David Frost, *They Gave Me A Sword* (1978).

—— 5 ——

When the Nixon interviews were being launched, I myself interviewed Frost for the BBC Radio *Today* programme. He was in Los Angeles and suffering from jet-lag, the time difference, and possibly from the end product of the local Californian vines. Anyway, at some point he said to me: 'The art of the quill has been practised since Caxton – *and probably before . . .*'

The interview was broadcast on 5 May 1977. A number of listeners drew my attention to this interesting historical assessment but, curiously enough, I had already noticed it.

—— 6 ——

In the stormy opening weeks of the TV-am breakfast station of which he was a founder/presenter, Frost slipped away to marry his second wife, Lady Carina Fitzalan-Howard, the daughter of the Duke of Norfolk. On his return, he quipped – possibly ad-lib – to waiting reporters, 'We have been on a working honeymoon.'

From an untraced newspaper report, March 1983.

—— 7 ——

Lady Carina broke it to her favourite nun, Mother Wilson, that she had met the man she wanted to marry. The nun asked if he was religious. 'Oh, yes,' replied the wife-to-be, 'he thinks he's God Almighty.'

Quoted in *The Sunday Times* (28 July 1985).

Clark GABLE

(1901–60) American actor.

—— 1 ——

When Gable was filming in Britain, he preferred to stay with the Yeatman family – it will be remembered that Julian Yeatman was co-author of the humorous classic *1066 and All That* – instead of at a hotel. Yeatman's son recalls Gable looking into a mirror, taking his false teeth out, and saying sadly, 'America's sweetheart!'

Related by Frank Muir in *The Oxford Book of Humorous Prose* (1990).

—— 2 ——

The verdict on Gable's first screen test was: 'Ears too big' and comments on the size thereof did not cease when he did manage to break into films. Howard Hughes said, 'His ears made him look like a taxicab with both doors open' and Milton Berle called him 'The best ears of our lives'.

Sources include: Charles Higham and Joel Greenberg, *Celluloid Muse* (1969) and Leslie Halliwell, *The Filmgoer's Book of Quotes* (1973).

Greta GARBO

(1905–90) Swedish-born American film actress, reclusive for most of her life.

—— 3 ——

After such films as *The Torrent* and *Flesh and the Devil*, Garbo decided to exploit her box-office power and asked Louis B. Mayer for a rise – from $350 to $5,000 dollars a week. Mayer offered her $2,500. 'I tink I go home,' said Garbo. She went back to her hotel and stayed there for a full seven months until Mayer finally gave way.

At one time, the phrase 'I tink I go home', spoken in a would-be Swedish accent, was as much part of the impressionist's view of Garbo as 'I want to be alone'. One version of how the line came to be spoken is told by Norman Zierold in *Moguls* (1969), as above.

Alexander Walker in *Garbo* (1980) recalls, rather, what Sven-Hugo Borg, the actress's interpreter, said of the time in 1926 when Mauritz Stiller, who had come with her from Sweden, was fired from directing *The Temptress*: 'She was tired, terrified and lost . . . as she returned to my side after a trying scene, she sank down beside me and said so low it was almost a whisper, "Borg, I think I shall go home now. It isn't worth it, is it?"'

Walker comments: 'That catch-phrase, shortened into "I think I go home", soon passed into the repertoire of a legion of Garbo-imitators and helped publicize her strong-willed temperament.'

A caricatured Garbo was shown hugging Mickey Mouse in a cartoon film in the 1930s. 'Ah tahnk ah kees you now' and 'Ah tink ah go home', she said. This cartoon was, incidentally, the last item to be shown on British television before the transmitters were closed down on the brink of war (1 September 1939).

—— 4 ——

Howard Dietz plucked up courage and invited Garbo out for a dinner date 'on Monday night'. Garbo declined, saying, 'How do I know I'll be hungry on Monday night?'

Told by Benny Green on BBC Radio *Quote...Unquote* (1989).

Andrew GARDNER

(1932–) Tall British broadcaster, for many years an ITN newscaster and then with Thames TV.

—— 5 ——

Like many news broadcasters, Gardner practised hard to pronounce correctly the name of the Nigerian premier, Sir Abubakar Tafawah Balewa. 'Sir Abubakar Tafawah Balewa', he would say, over and over again, trying to get it right. Then, just as the pronunciation was perfect, they shot 'Sir Abubakar Tafawah Balewa' in a coup.

Related by Gardner on ITV's *It's Alright on the Night*, 1980s. Balewa died in 1966.

John Nance GARNER

(1868–1967) American Democratic vice-president.

—— 1 ——

Garner was vice-president from 1933 to 1941 during F. D. Roosevelt's first two terms and famously said of his job that it wasn't 'worth a pitcher of warm piss' – though this was quickly bowdlerized to 'warm spit'. On another occasion, Garner was walking down the halls of the Capitol at a time when the circus was in Washington. A fellow came up to him and introduced himself. 'I am the head clown in the circus,' he said. Very solemnly, Garner replied, 'And I am the vice-president of the United States. You'd better stick around here a while. You might pick up some new ideas.'

Theo Lippman Jr in *The San Francisco Chronicle* (25 December 1992) provided this story.

GENTLEMEN

—— 2 ——

Some young soldiers were being given a homily by their platoon sergeant on the subject of 'public duties' – that is, how they should behave when they were out of the barracks and moving about among civilians. Said he: 'A gentleman always gives up his seat to a lady in a public convenience.'

A correspondent in 1976 observed to me that this 'old music-hall joke' appears in Gerald Kersh's book *They Die With Their Boots Clean* (1941), a record of his experiences in the Guards.

—— 3 ——

Definition of an English gentleman: 'Useful at a hunt ball. Invaluable in a shipwreck.'

Source not known.

King GEORGE V

(1865–1936) British sovereign who acceded to the throne in 1911.

—— 4 ——

After a long life spent doing public duties, the King summed up his experience thus: 'Never miss an opportunity to relieve yourself; never miss a chance to sit down and rest your feet.'

His son, the Duke of Windsor, was later to ascribe this remark to 'an old courtier' but it seems likely that it was said by George V himself. A correspondent who wished to remain anonymous told me in 1981 that a naval officer of her acquaintance who was about to accompany Prince George, Duke of Kent, on a cruise, was asked by George V to make sure that the Prince was properly dressed before going ashore. He also advised: 'Always take an opportunity to relieve yourselves.' Another correspondent suggests that it was an equerry's first advice to the new King George V; yet another that Edward VII was the first to say this when he was Prince of Wales. On the other hand, more than a century earlier, the Duke of Wellington had said: 'Always make water when you can.'

Compare also the remark of Samuel Freeman, who served in the US Supreme Court from 1862 to 1890. He advised: 'Never walk when you can ride, never sit when you can lie down.' Winston Churchill is reported to have said: 'Never stand when you can sit and never sit when you can lie down.'

—— 5 ——

When Harold Nicolson was writing the official life of George V (it was published in 1952), he had access to papers written in the King's own hand which were in the possession of the Royal Archives. From these, Nicolson was surprised to discover that the monarch had been unable to spell the word 'prerogative' correctly. Considering that the 'royal prerogative' of British sovereigns – their rights which are not subject to restriction – has been much discussed since the 17th century, this was a curious lapse in the King's English.

I forget how I heard this (in the early 1970s), though I do recall that Sir Harold Nicolson was rather embarrassed at having stumbled upon such a morsel.

—— 6 ——

In his published diary, Harold Nicolson described a problem he was having when writing the life of the King. He was all right as a 'gay young midshipman'; he might be all right as a 'wise old king'; but the period in between when he was Duke of York and lived at Sandringham was difficult to deal with. 'For 17 years,' concluded Nicolson, 'he did nothing at all but kill animals and stick in stamps.'

Extracted from Harold Nicolson, *Diaries and Letters 1945–1962* (entry for 17 August 1949).

—— 1 ——

George V went to the opera every year and the only opera he ever saw was *La Bohème*. Sir Thomas Beecham once bravely asked why this one was his particular favourite. 'Because it's much the shortest,' replied the King.

Recounted in *The Lyttelton Hart-Davis Letters* (for 4 November 1956).

—— 2 ——

A rare example of a royal joke comes from the period before George V's death. In December 1935, it was revealed that Sir Samuel Hoare, the Foreign Secretary, had come to an arrangement with M. Laval, his French counterpart, whereby Abyssinia was virtually to be consigned to the Italians behind the League of Nations' back. The Hoare–Laval Pact had been concluded in Paris when Sir Samuel was passing through on his way to a holiday in Switzerland. In the furore that followed he had to resign. The King joked: 'No more coals to Newcastle, no more Hoares to Paris.'

He may just have been repeating a remark that was current anyway and is unlikely to have said it to Hoare himself, despite Lord Avon's recollection of what the King told him in *Facing the Dictators* (1962).

—— 3 ——

When they came to ask his permission to call the new Cunard liner *Queen Victoria*, they prefaced their request with an indication of their intention to honour the very greatest of British queens. 'Oh, well, May will be very pleased,' he replied. And so they had to call it *Queen Mary* instead.

Quoted in William Manchester, *The Last Lion* (1983).

King GEORGE VI

(1895–1952) British sovereign who acceded to the throne in 1936 on the abdication of his brother, Edward VIII.

—— 4 ——

A Labour minister dining with the King at Buckingham Palace in the late 1940s, was asked if he would like a cigar. 'Oh no, thank you,' he said, 'I only smoke on special occasions.'

I was told this story in about 1975. In Theo Aronson, *Royal Ambassadors* (1976), he tells a similar story about the King's tour of Canada before the War. He remarked that a local mayor was not wearing a mayoral chain. 'Oh,' explained the mayor, 'but I only wear it on special occasions.'

Sir John GIELGUD

(1904–) English actor, principally of classical roles on the stage, but also in many films. Knighted in 1953. The great and good actor is known throughout and beyond the theatrical profession for his dropped bricks. People find him all the more endearing because of this little peccadillo. Indeed, one gets the impression that half the actors in England are hovering by Sir John, waiting for him to let one drop. A tiny sample, one of which at least is absolutely genuine:

—— 5 ——

James Agate writing in his diary for 25 September 1935 (published in *Ego*) tells of lunching at the Ivy with Curt Dehn, his lawyer, who asked the name of the man lunching opposite. 'I said, "John Gielgud." Dehn said, "It's a rum sort of head. The profile's Roman Emperor, but the rest is still at Eton."'

Thus the process of describing Gielgud began. My favourite attempt, much later, was by Anthony Shaffer, the playwright. 'Of course,' he said, 'he's a *camel*.'

The Shaffer comment is from my diary (19 November 1974).

—— 6 ——

Writing to James Agate from Liverpool on 17 April 1942, Gielgud, who was touring in *Macbeth*, noted: 'There was a very nice misprint in the *Liverpool Echo* on Wednesday, paying tribute to our broad comedian George Woodbridge, who plays the Porter, as "an engaging Portia". I could not forbear to murmur that the quality of Mersey is not strained.'

An early appearance of the 'Mersey' joke, in *Ego 5* (1942).

—— 1 ——

Shortly after receiving his knighthood, Gielgud had an unfortunate run-in with the police. *The Times* in reporting this information either innocently or guardedly printed it thus: 'John Gielgud, aged 49, described on the charge sheet as a clerk, of Cowley Street, Westminster, was fined £10 at West London yesterday . . . He had been self-employed for a number of years and earned approx. £1,000 a year.'

Report in *The Times* (22 October 1953).

—— 2 ——

Gielgud once described Edith Evans and Peggy Ashcroft as, 'Two leading ladies, the like of whom I shall never meet again.'

Quoted in Bryan Forbes, *Ned's Girl* (1977) and apparently confirmed by Gielgud. This was in a speech, delivered when he was flustered, after he had directed the 1932 Oxford University Dramatic Society production of *Romeo and Juliet*, with Ashcroft as Juliet and Evans as the Nurse.

—— 3 ——

Herbert Marshall was a British actor who made a name for himself in Hollywood during the 1930s despite losing a leg in the First World War. He was between marriages when – or so the story has it – Gielgud encountered him with the words: 'Ah, Herbert, foot-loose in Hollywood, I see . . .'

Recounted by John Mortimer on BBC Radio *Quote...Unquote* (1979).

—— 4 ——

Gielgud was being interviewed late at night on a local television show in St Louis, Missouri. Peter Ustinov, who just happened to be there watching it go out, recalls how Sir John was asked who had been the greatest influence on his early career. He replied: 'Claude Rains. But I don't know what happened to him afterwards. I think he failed and went to America.'

Recounted in Peter Ustinov, *Dear Me* (1977).

—— 5 ——

Gielgud was giving last-minute instructions to the cast of a production which required the men to wear tights. Having presumably noticed some pretty odd sights in tights over the years, he insisted that all the males in the cast should wear jockstraps (athletic supports). A little voice popped up and inquired, 'Sir John, does that include people like me with only small parts?'

Told to me by Charles Richardson and recorded in my diary on 18 July 1966.

—— 6 ——

A man came to congratulate Gielgud in his dressing room after a performance. 'I am very pleased to meet you,' said Sir John recognizing the man's face, 'I used to know your son. We were at school together.' The man responded coldly, 'I don't have a son. It was *I* who was at school with you.'

Recounted in Robert Morley, *Book of Bricks* (1978).

—— 7 ——

Sir John told the theatre director Patrick Garland that he was going down to Chichester to do a play with Robin Phillips whom he did not know. 'I hear he's very young,' commented Sir John. '*I* know him very well,' replied Garland. 'He's about my age.' To which the Gielgudism was: 'Oh, he's not so young then.'

Recounted by Patrick Garland in 1979.

—— 8 ——

During rehearsals for Peter Brook's production of Seneca's *Oedipus* at the National Theatre in 1968, the cast was required to go through many days of primal screaming and other aids to great drama. The actors were then required to prepare an improvisation based on the most terrifying thing they could imagine. Gielgud did not comply, so he said, because there was nothing he could think of. But then he spoke up: 'Actually, there is something that is absolutely terrifying . . . we open in ten days.'

Told by Myfanwy Talog (1983). In a Channel 4 programme screened in January 1993, Sir John appeared to ascribe the threat 'We open next week' in this sort of context to Dame Edith Evans.

—— 9 ——

Gielgud ventured into opera direction at the Coliseum but was finding rehearsals a touch exasperating. When the orchestra struck up the overture to Mozart's *Don Giovanni*, he rushed down the centre aisle shouting, 'Oh, do stop that awful music!'

Recounted thus by Alan Bennett on BBC Radio *Quote...Unquote* (1983). According to Ned Sherrin, *Theatrical Anecdotes* (1991), Gielgud acknowledges this story but places it during his production of Berlioz, *The Trojans*.

—— 1 ——

Lunching with the actress Athene Seyler, Gielgud fell to bemoaning his lot. 'These days I seem to spend all my time in the company of these old bags of stage and screen – Monday, Fay Compton, Tuesday, Sybil Thorndike, Wednesday, Athene Seyler . . .' Then realizing what she might be thinking, he added quickly: 'Of course, I don't mean *you*, Athene!'

Told by Kingsley Amis on BBC Radio *Quote...Unquote* (1979). Compare the version from John Mortimer, *In Character* (1983): 'Gielgud once had lunch with a writer called Edward Knoblock. "Do you see that man coming in?" Gielgud said. "He's the biggest bore in London – second only to Edward Knoblock." And then, in a terrible attempt to put matters right, he added hopelessly, "Not you, of course. I mean the *other* Edward Knoblock."'

—— 2 ——

Gielgud went to see the first performance of Richard Burton's Hamlet. According to the story, the performance was not of the best but nevertheless Gielgud felt obliged to go backstage and congratulate Burton whilst concealing his true feelings about what he had seen. On entering Burton's dressing room, he discovered that the actor was in a state of undress. Gielgud meant to say, 'I'll come back when you're dressed.' What he is reported to have said, was: 'I'll come back when you're better . . .'

Burton played Hamlet at the Old Vic in the 1953–4 season, directed by Michael Benthall. If, however, this was the production that Gielgud himself directed (New York, 1964) then John Mortimer's version (*In Character*, 1983) makes more sense: '"We'll go to dinner when you're ready," was what Gielgud honestly meant to say to Burton in the dressing room: but that loquacious subconscious rushed into the open with, "We'll go to dinner when you're better".' This is the version that also appears in Melvyn Bragg, *Rich: The Life of Richard Burton* (1988).

—— 3 ——

Walking home from the theatre one night during the Blitz, Gielgud happened to glance up at the moonlit barrage balloons. 'Oh dear,' he murmured to his companion, 'our poor boys must be terribly lonely up there.'

Version from John Mortimer, *In Character* (1983).

—— 4 ——

Another actor was discussing with Gielgud a colleague who was described as being 'a frightful curmudgeon, really impossible . . . let's face it, he's got a chip on his shoulder because he's a failure.' Gielgud's reaction to this was, 'Yes, but you're a failure, and you haven't got a chip on your shoulder . . .'

Told by P. J. Kavanagh (1984).

—— 5 ——

On the disastrous first night of Gielgud's Othello at Stratford – in which the scenery fell down and an actor cut his hand – the play had taken 4½ hours with some scenes still to go. Ian Bannen, who was playing Iago, attempted to reduce the running time of the tragedy by announcing, 'Rodrigo's dead, my lord' when Rodrigo still had two scenes to go. Gielgud replied, '*Dead*, says thou?' Bannen as Iago replied, 'Well, not dead. Just not very well, my lord.'

Told in Melvyn Bragg, *Rich: The Life of Richard Burton* (1988). The production was in 1961.

Frank GILES

(1919–) English newspaperman. Foreign Editor of *The Sunday Times* for many years and later Editor.

—— 6 ——

Giles's wife was Lady Katharine Sackville who, being the daughter of an Earl, retained her title though married to a plain 'Mr'. On a visit to Rome they received an invitation from the British ambassador which was incorrectly made out to 'Mr and Mrs Frank Giles'. Giles thought he ought to point out the error, rang the British Embassy and said, 'She's not exactly *Mrs* Giles, you see.' 'Oh, never mind,' said an embassy official, 'bring her along anyway. We're not at all stuffy here.'

A version of this appeared in *The Los Angeles Times* (15 December 1981).

Eric GILL

(1882–1940) English sculptor and letterer.
Somewhat goat-like in his private life.

—— 1 ——

When the BBC moved to the splendid new Broadcasting House in Portland Place, London, in 1932, it had commissioned Eric Gill to sculpt a statue of Prospero and Ariel to stand in a niche above the main entrance. The relevance of these two figures was not entirely clear and Gill wondered whether Ariel was supposed to be a pun on 'aerial'.

Leslie French, the actor, who was currently playing the Shakespeare character of Ariel at the Old Vic was Gill's main model for Ariel, right down to the penis. Gill worked on the figures *in situ* and finally the Governors of the BBC trooped along and examined them behind a tarpaulin. They requested that Ariel's genitals should be diminished.

> Sources include: Fiona MacCarthy, *Eric Gill* (1989). Louis Marder in *His Exits and His Entrances* (1963) tells a slightly different story: that Sir John Reith, the BBC Director-General, had complained of the size of Ariel's genitals and the matter was sent to arbitration. Sir Israel Gollancz and Israel Zangwill, Shakespeare scholars, were deputed to investigate. They decided that Ariel would have been 13 years old. A medical doctor was then drawn in who decreed that the genitals as Gill had originally sculpted them were too generous. They were diminished.

Hermione GINGOLD

(1897–1987) British actress mostly in faintly grotesque character parts.

—— 2 ——

It is said that a small boy once pointed at Miss Gingold and asked, 'Mummy, what's that lady *for*?'

> I first heard of this remark being applied to Gingold in 1980, but she is only one of several people to whom it has been aimed: 'It was an anonymous little girl who, on first catching sight of Charles James Fox, is supposed to have asked her mother: "What is that gentleman for?" One asks the same question of Mr [Douglas] Hurd' – Alan Watkins, *The Observer* (29 May 1988).
>
> '"What," a little girl is supposed to have asked her mother, pointing at Sir John Simon, a pre-war

chancellor, "is that man for?" What, she might now ask, pointing at the Labour faithful assembling in Brighton today, is that party for?' – editorial, *The Independent on Sunday* (29 September 1991).

In fact, the remark, out of the mouth of a not-quite babe or suckling, is a convenient stick with which to beat anyone the speaker wishes to reduce in importance. It is particularly useful when taunting politicians. The Watkins extract above goes on: 'Why is [Hurd] where he is in this particular government? He has never been wholly in sympathy either with Mrs Thatcher or with her version of Conservatism.'

But is it possible to say where the taunt originated? The remark about Charles James Fox might possibly have evolved from what the young Viscount Eversley (born 1794) is reported to have said on hearing Fox speak in Parliament: 'What is that fat gentleman in such a passion about?' This was recorded by G. W. E. Russell in *Collections and Recollections* (1898). If that is the origin, the remark has undergone a considerable shift in meaning.

Derek Parker, editor of *The Author*, recalled: 'Quentin Bell told me (in a radio programme I did) that he had originated the phrase "What is that lady *for*?" at the age of four or five on seeing Lady Ottoline Morrell arrive, more than usually eccentrically dressed, on top of a cart, at Garsington'. If so, this would have been about 1914.

Yes, but Michael Grosvenor Myer of Cambridge produced what I believe is the true original. It is the caption to a *Punch* cartoon from the edition of 14 November 1906. Drawn by F. H. Townsend, who was art editor of the magazine at the time, it shows the question 'MUMMY, WHAT'S THAT MAN FOR?' being posed by a small boy about a bemonocled man carrying a bag of golf clubs.

Grace Wyndham GOLDIE

(1900–86) English TV executive.

—— 3 ——

A formidable presence behind many BBC TV current affairs productions in the 1950s/60s – especially *Tonight* and *That Was the Week That Was* – Goldie was once described as being a 'woman with a whim of iron'.

> Whoever coined this about Goldie was not being entirely original. Oliver Herford wrote in *Excuse it Please* (1929): '"Perhaps it is only a whim," said the Queen. The King laughed mirthlessly. "King Barumph has a whim of iron!"'

Sam GOLDWYN

(1882–1974) American film producer. Most Goldwynisms – idiotic sayings from a Polish-born man who never quite got to grips with the English language – are apocryphal. His son, Samuel Goldwyn Jr, has a list of 28 sayings which may be genuine – and most of these are too well known to be repeated again here . . .

—— 1 ——

How he got the name Goldwyn: when a Pole arrived in the United States bearing an unpronounceable monicker – Schmuel Gelbfisz – an immigration official renamed him 'Goldfish'. Eventually he realized the trick that had been played on him and took the name 'Goldwyn'. How did he choose that? Goldfish had formed a partnership with Selwyn. When Goldfish changed his name, he took the first syllable of his 'Goldfish' and the second syllable of 'Selwyn' to make Goldwyn. Had he taken the first syllable of 'Selwyn' and the second syllable of 'Goldfish', he would have had 'Selfish'.

The last sentence derives from Howard Dietz, *Dancing in the Dark* (1974).

—— 2 ——

Goldwyn was having a disagreement with Jack L. Warner over a labour dispute involving Busby Berkeley. The choreographer had been discovered moonlighting for Warner Brothers. Goldwyn said to Warner, 'How can we sit together and deal with this industry if you're going to do things like that to me? If this is the way you do it, gentlemen, include me out!'

Context from an interview with Sam Goldwyn Jr, *TV Times*, 13 November 1982. As if to confirm this one, Goldwyn Sr, speaking at Balliol College, Oxford, on 1 March 1945, said, 'For years I have been known for saying "Include me out" but today I am giving it up for ever.'

—— 3 ——

Some friends had gone down to the harbour to see Goldwyn off on a transatlantic trip. He waved down to his friends on the quayside and shouted, 'Bon voyage!'

Quoted by Lillian Hellman in *Pentimento*, 1974.

—— 4 ——

When Goldwyn was told by the head of his script department that they could not film Lillian Hellman's play *The Children's Hour* because it dealt with lesbians, Goldwyn said, 'OK, we make them Albanians.'

Re-told by Philip French, *The Observer*, 10 May 1992. Sounds pretty unlikely. This made an early appearance in Edmund Fuller, *2500 Anecdotes for All Occasions* (1943) with the contentious script Radclyffe Hall's *The Well of Loneliness* and the reply: 'All right – where they got lesbians, we'll use Austrians.'

—— 5 ——

At a postwar banquet for Field Marshal Montgomery, Goldwyn rose and proposed a toast to 'Marshall Field Montgomery'. After a stunned silence, Jack L. Warner corrected him, 'Montgomery Ward, you mean.'

Quoted in Lillian Hellman, *Pentimento* (1974). (Marshall Field is a Chicago department store; Marshall Field III (d. 1956) was the founder of the *Chicago Sun* newspaper. Montgomery Ward is a leading US mail-order chain.)

Yakubu GOWON

(1934–) Nigerian soldier and president, until he was deposed in 1975.

—— 6 ——

In the early 1970s, Gowon, at that time president of Nigeria, came to London on a state visit. Welcomed by the Queen at Victoria Station, he had barely sat down in a carriage for the short drive to Buckingham Palace, when one of the Royal horses gave vent to an ear-splitting, tail-lifting fart. The Queen was very put out by this, as well she might be, and turned to President Gowon, saying, 'Oh, I do apologize . . . not a very good start to your visit!' 'Oh, please don't apologize' said Gowon. 'Besides, I thought it was one of the horses . . .'

I believe I first read this in *Private Eye* in the 1970s. In *Of Kings and Cabbages* (1984), Peter Coats has this exchange between King Edward VII and his nephew, the Kaiser.

2nd Earl of GOWRIE

(1939–) English Conservative politician, art dealer, Chairman of the Arts Council, and things like that.

—— 1 ——

At the Conservative Party Conference in 1981, a then upwardly-rising politician called Edwina Currie was taking part in a debate on law and order. To illustrate some point or other she held aloft a pair of handcuffs. Subsequently, Gowrie admitted to having felt 'a bat's squeak of desire' for Mrs Currie at this moment.

Up to this point, the most notable use of the expression had been in Evelyn Waugh's novel *Brideshead Revisited* (1945): 'I caught a thin bat's squeak of sexuality, inaudible to any but me.'

Lew GRADE

(1906–) Russian-born British theatrical agent who became a prominent TV and film impresario. Rarely to be seen without a large cigar, his chief gift to the world was *The Muppets* TV show. He also ventured into prestige productions. Created Lord Grade in 1976.

—— 2 ——

A small child asked Grade, 'What does two and two make?' Grade replied: 'Are you buying or selling?'

Apocryphal, according to Grade, but an essential piece of Gradiana. Quoted in *The Observer* during 1962.

—— 3 ——

In his early days in 'the business', Grade went backstage at the Finsbury Park Empire to congratulate one of the acts he had admired. 'Fantastic, great, terrific!' he enthused. 'How much are you getting? What! Only £25 a week? You're mad. I can get you £40 a week. Who's your agent?' Came the reply: 'You are, Mr Grade.'

A story Grade admits to. Quoted in Hunter Davies, *The Grades* (1981).

—— 4 ——

ATV, the TV company over which Grade presided for many years, was about to present a *Golden Hour of Entertainment* as a great new artistic spectacular. Crowed Grade: 'I tell you we've got every big name taking part you've ever heard of – Callas, Picasso, Barenboim, Stradivarius . . .'

Apocryphal. Quoted in Hunter Davies, *The Grades* (1981).

—— 5 ——

To Franco Zeffirelli, who had explained that the high cost of the film *Jesus of Nazareth* was partly because there had to be twelve apostles, Grade said: 'Twelve! So who needs *twelve*? Couldn't we make do with *six*?'

Quoted in *Radio Times*, October 1983. Compare the story of the crass John B. Stetson (1836–96), producer at the Globe Theatre in Boston, Mass., long ago. Watching the rehearsal of a Passion play he said, 'Apostles are they? What's the good of twelve on a stage this size? Let's have fifty' – John Aye, *Humour in the Theatre* (1932).

—— 6 ——

When it was revealed that the actor playing Christ in the same film was living with a woman to whom, at that time, he was not married, Grade exclaimed: 'What about it? Do you want me to crucify the boy?'

Oral tradition.

—— 7 ——

In 1980, Grade produced a famously expensive and unsuccessful film called *Raise the Titanic*. He is supposed to have commented ruefully, 'It would have been cheaper to lower the Atlantic.'

Alas, on TV-am's *Frost on Sunday* (23 November 1987), Grade denied having said it. What he had actually said was, 'I didn't raise the Titanic high enough.'

Cary GRANT

(1904–86) British-born American film actor.

—— 1 ——

A magazine writer preparing a profile of Grant sent a cable to his agent inquiring, 'HOW OLD CARY GRANT?' Grant sent the reply himself: 'CARY GRANT FINE. HOW YOU?'

Oral tradition. Told by Barry Cryer, BBC Radio *Quote...Unquote* (1979).

Harley GRANVILLE-BARKER

(1877–1946) English playwright, actor and producer.

—— 2 ——

Coaching an actor he gave the instruction: 'Try and look as if you had read Shelley in your youth.'

Quoted in Lady Cynthia Asquith, *Diaries 1915–18* (entry for 6 January 1918).

Graham GREENE

(1904–91) English novelist, playwright, critic.

—— 3 ——

A magazine ran a competition for the best parody of Greene's style. A week after the prize-winning entry had been published, Greene wrote to say that he was delighted with the winning entry, but felt that two other competitors had deserved prizes. He had sent in all three himself. What was more, they were not parodies, but passages from some of his early novels that he had excised as not being good enough.

This is as reported in *Book-of-the-Month Club News*, October 1949. According, however, to Frank Muir in *The Oxford Book of Humorous Prose* (1990), Greene appears to have played the same trick more than once. In 1965, under the name 'Malcolm Collins', he entered a *New Statesman* competition for the best parody of a Graham Greene biography of his brother Hugh, then Director-General of the BBC. (Graham's parody won him honourable mention; the winner, however, was Hugh himself, writing as 'Sebastian Eleigh'.) E. O. Parrott, in *Imitations of Immortality* (1986), also finds a 'verse autobiography' written by Graham Greene under the pseudonym 'H. A. Baxter'. This appeared in *The New Statesman* on 7 April 1961.

Wallace 'Bill' GREENSLADE

(d. 1961, aged 48) Portly English BBC radio newsreader and announcer. Noted for unbending sufficiently to introduce many editions of *The Goon Show*.

—— 4 ——

One night Greenslade appeared somewhat tiddly when reading the nine o'clock news on the BBC Home Service. There were the expected complaints. After a dignified pause, a 'BBC spokesman' commented wisely, 'All of us have our off-days, and this was one of Mr Greenslade's.'

From my own memory of newspaper reports at the time – mid-1950s. In Jack de Manio's *To Auntie With Love* (1967), a 'BBC spokesman' is quoted as having said, on a similar occasion about another, 'Newsreaders never get drunk, but they are sometimes very upset.'

D. W. GRIFFITH

(1875–1948) American film director of such epics as *Intolerance* and *The Birth of a Nation*.

—— 5 ——

During the making of one epic film, Griffiths is supposed to have ordered: 'Move those ten thousand horses a trifle to the right. And that mob out there, three feet forward.'

Quoted in Josef von Sternberg, *Fun In a Chinese Laundry* (1966).

Sir Alec GUINNESS

(1914–) English actor, notable in many leading character roles and for his ability to disguise his appearance – without ever being able to conceal a rich parsonical voice.

—— 1 ——

His cadaverous appearance as 'Professor Marcus' in *The Lady Killers* was based on that of the critic, Kenneth Tynan, who had appeared (with singular lack of success) in a Guinness production of *Hamlet* a few years previously.

> **Source: Philip Kemp, *Lethal Innocence: The Cinema of Alexander Mackendrick* (1991). See also** TYNAN **185:4.**

—— 2 ——

Guinness once offered this important advice to all actors: 'Always remember before going on stage, wipe your nose and check your flies.'

> *Time* **(11 May 1987) preferred the version: 'Blow your nose and check your fly'. Michael Freedland in *Kenneth Williams* (1990) has it as comment to KW after Guinness had apparently tried to jostle KW out of public view and behind a potted palm during *Hotel Paradiso* (KW's flies being undone). As this incident is not recorded in *The Kenneth Williams Diaries* (1993), I am inclined to doubt it.**

Sacha GUITRY

(1885–1957) French actor.

—— 3 ——

Waspishly, he is supposed to have provided an epitaph for another French film star: 'Here lies Yvonne Printemps, silent at last.' To which she is supposed to have responded with: 'Here lies Sacha Guitry, stiff at last.'

> **Source unknown.**

Edmund GWENN

(1875–1959) Welsh-born character actor, especially in Hollywood.

—— 4 ——

When someone said to Gwenn, on his deathbed, 'It must be hard, very hard, Ed?', he replied: 'It is. But not as hard as farce.'

> **Quoted in *Time* Magazine (30 January 1984). One version has it that the visitor was Jack Lemmon. Compare the remark attributed to David Garrick: 'Any fool can play tragedy but comedy, sir, is a damned serious business.'**

King HAAKON VII

(1872–1957) King of Norway from 1905 onwards, following his country's secession from Sweden. During the Nazi occupation in the Second World War, Haakon lead the Norwegian resistance in London.

—— 1 ——

The exiled king used the BBC's facilities in London to broadcast to his people back home. He would arrive unaccompanied at the studios and try to cause no fuss – hence the archetypal BBC commissionaire story he gave rise to. 'I am King Haakon of Norway' he told one such commissionaire on arrival. 'Ah, yes' replied the commissionaire and started hunting for the visitor's name among various lists in front of him. Obviously he was having no success in finding the distinguished visitor's name, so he probably said, 'Half a mo', guv,' and dialled a number, no doubt to consult with a higher authority. 'Oh, yes,' he said, 'got a visitor here. Can't find any record of who's expectin' 'im. 'E's the king of . . .' Then putting one hand over the mouthpiece, he asked, "Scuse me, guv, which country did you say you was king of?'

This traditional story was told by Martin Jarvis on BBC Radio, *Quote...Unquote* (1979), in consequence of which I received a letter from a Mr I. Thompson of London, dated 15 April 1980. Mr Thompson said he had been on duty at Bush House on that very evening: 'The Norwegian King had an appointment at B[roadcasting] H[ouse] for recording for transmission purposes – no doubt some very senior official was waiting to welcome him there. The King was driven in error to Bush House (Norwegian broadcasts normally went out from there). There were two reception desks at Bush, one for tenants other than BBC . . . and the other for BBC. King Haakon approached the former first. Someone got a little confused and the BBC Duty Editor learned that the King of *Sweden* was at reception. This piece of news caused some alarm. However, everything was sorted out and King Haakon duly made his recording. So it seems that your version has been somewhat corrupted down the years.'
In Jack de Manio's *To Auntie With Love* (1967), the story is related as having involved a female receptionist who mistakenly rang up the *Dutch* section and said, 'Well I've got your King here. He says he wants to broadcast.'

John HABGOOD

(1927–) English Anglican Archbishop of York.

—— 2 ——

John Peart-Binns, the archbishop's biographer, unearthed a letter written by Habgood when he was eight years old. 'Dear God,' it began, 'If you feel lonely up in the sky would you like to come down and stay with us? You could sleep in the spare room, and you could bathe with us, and I think you would enjoy yourself. Love, John'.
Addressed to 'Our Father Which Art in Heaven' it was opened by the Post Office and marked 'Return to sender', which, as Peart-Binns commented, has fewer theological implications than 'Gone away' or 'Unknown at this address'.

Reported in *The Sunday Telegraph* (31 May 1987).

Lord HAILSHAM

(1907–) English lawyer and Conservative politician. He renounced his viscountcy to become plain Quintin Hogg and to make himself available for the prime ministership, which he did not get, in 1963. He was created Lord Hailsham in 1970.

—— 3 ——

Any Lord Chancellor in procession is an impressive figure. Bewigged and gowned, he is preceded by a mace bearer, a purse bearer (who carries the magnificently embroidered bag which used to hold the Great Seal of England), and is followed by a train bearer. There is a story that once, processing through the corridors of Westminster, Lord Hailsham spotted a friend and called out his

Christian name, 'Neil!', whereupon a number of American tourists fell to their knees in reverence.

As told by John Mortimer in *Character Parts* (1986). Earlier in *Pass the Port Again* (1980).

Lord HALIFAX

(1st Earl of Halifax of 2nd creation) (1881–1959) English Conservative politician.

—— 1 ——

A civil servant made a marginal comment on an official document that was circulating in the Foreign Office but instead of putting what he thought – i.e. 'Balls!' – he chose the more diplomatic words, 'Round objects!' When the document passed before the eyes of the then Foreign Secretary – Lord Halifax – he inquired who this Mr Round was and what precisely were the grounds for his objection?

Told by Kingsley Amis on BBC Radio *Quote...Unquote* (1978). A version involving Winston Churchill and Pug Ismay is told in *Pass the Port Again* (1980).

Marvin HAMLISCH

(1944–) American composer and pianist.

—— 2 ——

W ill Rogers, the folksy American comedian, was famous for saying, 'When I die, my epitaph is going to read, "I never met a man I didn't like."' This only partly goes to explain why in New York in 1987, a car sticker was observed proclaiming, 'Will Rogers never met Marvin Hamlisch.'

Reported in *The Independent*, 15 May 1987.

Susan HAMPSHIRE

(1938–) English actress, always remembered for having played 'Fleur' in the BBC TV *Forsyte Saga* in the 1960s.

—— 3 ——

W hen the word 'dyslexic' became popular for people with reading difficulties or 'word blindness', Hampshire, suffering from it herself, became one of those most often quoted in public on the topic. Others who had worked with her and had never noticed her having any trouble were unkindly wont to remark: 'I knew Susan Hampshire before she was dyslexic.'

Source conveniently forgotten, *c.* 1982.

Sheila HANCOCK

(1933–) Perky British actress, least famous for being married to John Thaw, a younger actor who nevertheless looks older. Latterly, a director.

—— 4 ——

I t is a tradition of the theatre that the last line of a play is not spoken during rehearsals – in fact, not until the first public performance. Otherwise, bad luck will result. Consequently, there is scope for forgetting the line or for the end of the play never really being rehearsed. When Hancock was playing in rep at the Bromley New Theatre, she was not only the female lead but also the assistant stage manager. Hence, it was not until the first performance that anybody faced the problem of how she was to release herself from a clinch with her lover on-stage left and exit off-stage right to lower the curtain. Resourceful as ever, she unclinched herself and said, 'Excuse me, I must go and clean my teeth.'

As told by Hancock in *Ramblings of an Actress* (1987).

—— 5 ——

T aking part in Shakespeare's *The Winter's Tale* for the Royal Shakespeare Company, Hancock sometimes found it rather difficult to concentrate when she returned after a long wait off-stage in the second part. One night, in the scene in which she, as Paulina, restored Hermione to the reformed Leontes, she came to the lines:

I, an old turtle,
Will wing me to some withered bough.

Unfortunately, she had a complete black-out and after a long, groping pause, substituted the word 'twig' for 'bough'.

> As told by Hancock in *Ramblings of an Actress* (1987). 'The whole company dissolved in giggles,' she adds, 'shamefully ruining the end of the play for the bewildered audience.'

William HARDCASTLE

(1918–75) English newspaper editor then radio current-affairs presenter, especially of *The World at One* on BBC Radio.

—— 1 ——

Hardcastle never really left behind the written word or, to put it another way, he was never entirely at ease as a performer. Nevertheless, his breathless delivery was redolent of the news-gathering process at its most hectic. If only one could recapture in print the full force of the occasion when he found himself completely incapable of uttering the name of the African politician 'Hebert Chitepo'. Or of the time when Hardcastle bounced on to the air and announced himself, 'This is William *Whitelaw* with *The World at One*'.

> From recordings of these incidents.

Gilbert HARDING

(1907–60) English radio quizmaster and panellist. The first major TV personality of the 1950s. Always described as 'irascible' and noted for his impatience with the less intelligent, Harding was clearly embarrassed by being cast as a 'professional personality' when he felt capable of doing better things.

—— 2 ——

Just after the Second World War, Harding was journeying from Toronto, Canada (where he was briefly the BBC's representative) to New York to attend a reunion of war correspondents at CBS News. On crossing the border at Buffalo, he was extremely irritated at having to answer an interminable immigration questionnaire. So much so that when he came to the question, 'Is it your intention to subvert the government of the United States?', he scrawled, 'Sole purpose of visit!'

> This story was largely told by Wynford Vaughan-Thomas (as in *Trust to Talk*, 1980). In some accounts, Wynford was accompanying Harding to the reunion. Wallace Reyburn had it in *Gilbert Harding: A Candid Portrayal* (1978) and sets the story in the American consulate in Toronto.

—— 3 ——

Again just after the War when the BBC was still trying to find the right outlet for his talents, Harding was given an interview to do with Mae West for *In Town Tonight*. It was to take place in the BBC wartime studio created from the underground Monseigneur Cinema at Marble Arch, London. After the rehearsal, Mae West's PR man gave Harding an unwelcome slap on the back and boldy suggested that he ought to try and sound a bit more 'sexy'.

Harding's reply went as follows: 'If, sir, I possessed the power of conveying unlimited sexual attraction through the potency of my voice, I would not be reduced to accepting a miserable pittance from the BBC for interviewing a faded female in a damp basement.'

> Quoted by Wynford Vaughan-Thomas in *Gilbert Harding By His Friends* (1961). Circumstantial details from V-T's *Trust to Talk* (1980).

—— 4 ——

Harding was invited to the official opening of the BBC Television Centre in 1960 and observed the Director-General, Hugh Greene, talking in a group with two of his predecessors, Sir William Haley and Sir Ian Jacob. 'Ah,' said Harding, 'either the Holy Trinity or Pip, Squeak and Wilfred.' Then he added: 'The latter, I fear.'

> Quoted in Paul Ferris, *Sir Huge* (1990).

—— 5 ——

Within three years of his death, the model of Harding displayed in the Brighton waxworks had been melted down and turned into Christine Keeler.

> This is the concluding fact in Wallace Reyburn's *Gilbert Harding: A Candid Portrayal* (1978).

Augustus HARE

(1834–1903) English man of letters.

—— 1 ——

Somerset Maugham once asked Hare, whose practice was to read aloud to his household from the *Book of Common Prayer*, why he omitted all passages glorifying God. 'God is a gentleman,' Hare replied, 'and no gentleman cares to be praised to his face.'

Quoted in *The Observer* (10 November 1991).

Sir Rex HARRISON

(1908–90) English actor and frequent husband
('Sexy Rexy').

—— 2 ——

Two members of the audience of Harrison's greatest success, *My Fair Lady*, were coming out of Drury Lane after the show. One remarked, 'Of course, Rex Harrison isn't his real name, you know.' The other person replied: 'Rex Harrison isn't whose real name?'

Told by Benny Green on BBC Radio *Quote...Unquote* (1989). In fact, Rex Harrison *was* his real name. I have also heard the story told involving Laurence Olivier – but that was his own name, too.

—— 3 ——

Famously prone to farting, even before he was an old man, Harrison, in his later years, became equally famous for ill-advised attempts to disguise what he had done. Evidently, when he broke wind on stage, there was no mistaking the fact. It was about as inaudible as a stage whisper. Fellow cast members would instantly begin to titter and eventually ended up crying with uncontrollable laughter as Harrison indulged in increasingly hammy stage coughing – which only served further to identify himself as the culprit. The ultimate indignity, caused by this unwise course of action, was that a substantial portion of Harrison's obituary in *The Independent* was devoted to this unfortunate failing.

Told in *The Independent* (3 June 1990).

Sir Norman HARTNELL

(1901–78) English couturier and dressmaker to the
Queen.

—— 4 ——

Hartnell was staying with some very horsey people. When he admired an ornament on the mantelpiece, the daughter of the house informed him, 'Mummy won that with one of her jumpers.' Hartnell replied, 'If I sent her the wool, would she make me one?'

Told to me by T. A. Dyer (1993). I am not sure what connection, if any, this has with that most well-known of graffiti – 'My mother made me a homosexual', under which was written in another hand, 'If I got her the wool, would she make me one?' (which was in circulation by 1979).

Russell HARTY

(1934–88) English broadcasting producer (of arts programmes) and TV personality who had his own chat shows on ITV and BBC. Originally a schoolmaster, he had a cosy, North-country style, often indistinguishable from camp.

—— 5 ——

An example of his interviewing style: Harty asked a bemused Hermione Gingold whether her elderly dog could still masticate properly. Replied she: 'He does whatever nature intended, Mr Harty.'

Recounted by Compton Miller, *Who's Really Who* (1983).

—— 6 ——

At the height of his fame, Harty went into a branch of Marks and Spencer in London and bought six pairs of underpants (or, as he characteristically put it, 'those things you wear underneath what you wear over them'). When he got to the check-out desk, he overheard a woman who had been following him 'like a kind of pilot fish' through the store, saying to her friend: 'Fancy him buying underpants . . .'

Told by Harty on BBC Radio *Quote...Unquote* (1983).

—— 1 ——

Invited to open a garden fete, Harty took along as his companion the actress Madge Hindle who was appearing at the time in the TV soap *Coronation Street*. Harty became aware of people backing away from them after the vicar who was introducing Harty happened to say, 'We're very pleased to see that he's brought along with him the famous Myra Hindley . . .'

Told by Russell Harty in the 1980s. (Myra Hindley was one of the Moors Murderers.)

—— 2 ——

After Harty had played host to Johnny Weiss-muller, the former Olympic athlete and film Tarzan, on his London Weekend Television chat show, the two were coming out of the studios when they were confronted by a posse of small boys waving autograph books. Seeing Harty and the actor – who was 6ft 11in (or something) and broad of shoulder – one little kid asked, 'Hey, which one of you two guys is Tarzan?'

Told by Harty in the book *Russell Harty Plus* (1974).

—— 3 ——

Harty received what he took to be a fan letter from a woman TV viewer who wrote: 'My parrot Joey gets a small erection every time you appear and I think you are getting better.'

Told by Harty in *Russell Harty Plus* (1974).

Ralph Macdonald HASTINGS

English playwright and critic.

—— 4 ——

In the 1930s and 40s, the Questors Theatre in the London suburb of Ealing established a reputation for outstanding (what would now be called) fringe theatre. Hastings was one critic who rather resented being dragged away from the traditional beat of Shaftesbury Avenue and the West End. In a memo to the editor of the *Daily Express*, he wrote: 'Sir, I respectfully submit that I am your dramatic critic for London, not Asia Minor.'

Recounted by Adam Benedick in *The Independent* (4 March 1991). Compare the story told about A. B. Walkley of *The Times*: according to *The Lyttelton Hart-Davis Letters* (for 19 February 1956), he was sent tickets for a play at Richmond, and returned them to the editor with a note saying, 'I was engaged as *The Times* dramatic critic for central London, not for Asia Minor.' And James Agate's version (from *Ego 4*, for 25 July 1938): 'Richmond Theatre. This is what Basil [*sic*] Macdonald Hastings called being the dramatic critic for Asia Minor.' Basil (1881–1928) was presumably the father of Ralph and also combined precariously the two professions of playwright and critic.

Sir Edward HEATH

(1916–) British Conservative prime minister, bachelor musician, yachtsman and curmudgeonly elder statesman.

—— 5 ——

Once upon a time, Heath's trademark was the heaving shoulders with which he mirthlessly greeted a joke. For a while this tended to make up for the countless tales of his abruptness. At the Conservative Party Conference in 1966, I remember him coming into a makeshift ITN studio for an interview and – noticing it was rather hot and stuffy – his saying immediately, 'Haven't you people heard of air-conditioning?'

Invited to dinner by the dons of Exeter College, Oxford, Heath retired with them to the Senior Common Room for post-prandial drinks and then, looking at his watch, declared, 'There's an organ recital at Balliol I want to hear . . . come on.'

When Heath was still Leader of the Opposition, a BBC Radio producer went to interview him in his hotel room during a Conservative Party Conference. When it was over, Heath asked (to the producer's surprise), 'Would you like some tea?' (probably expecting the answer 'No'). The producer, a man of independent mind, said, 'Yes'. So Heath rang for room service and requested, 'Tea for one. And a half-bottle of champagne for me.'

Told to me by the people involved, *c*. 1972.

Ted HEATH

(1900–69) British band leader who founded (in 1944) the first British swing band capable of comparison with America's best.

—— 1 ——

One of Heath's trumpet-players decided to move on after 12 years with the band and told the boss: 'Ted, I really would like to move on.' 'You're leaving?' said Heath, obviously annoyed. 'After only 12 years? Listen, if I'd known you were going to be a fly-by-night, I'd never have booked you in the first place.'

Told by Tony Brandon on BBC Radio *Where Were You in '62?* (1982).

Sir Robert HELPMANN

(1909–86) Australian dancer, choreographer and actor.

—— 2 ——

Helpmann was once asked whether the 1960s fashion for stage nudity would ever extend to dance. 'No,' he replied. 'You see, there are portions of the human anatomy which would keep swinging after the music had finished.'

Quoted in Elizabeth Salter, *Helpmann* (1978). Earlier, in *The Frank Muir Book* (1976), Helpmann had been quoted after the New York opening of the nude revue *Oh! Calcutta!* as having said, 'The trouble with nude dancing is that not everything stops when the music stops.'

—— 3 ——

Being an Australian, Helpmann was devoted to taking his ballet company on tour to some of the least accessible corners of that rugged continent. Once he had to dress and get made up for a performance in the changing room of a football club somewhere in the outback. Helpmann was discovered standing on a chair, holding a hand-mirror, and applying his make-up by the light of the one naked bulb that dangled from the ceiling. Said he: 'Really, I just don't know how the footballers manage with *their* make-up.'

Told by Sally Miles on BBC Radio *Quote...Unquote* (1984). In *The Diaries of Kenneth Williams* (1993), he has a version in which Helpmann is changing in the 'umpires' room of a huge sports stadium' and is dressed as Oberon.

—— 4 ——

Helpmann went to see a performance of *Hamlet* by a touring company and at a matinée noticed that the lady playing Queen Gertrude 'should have played it a few years earlier'. He was heard to say, 'I hope they cut that line about "Go not to thy uncle's bed" because, frankly, she'd never make it.'

Told by Robin Bailey (1985).

—— 5 ——

On a tour of Australia with Katharine Hepburn, Helpmann began to tire of Hepburn's incessant chatter, not to mention her characteristic accent. Seeking to get away from her, Helpmann went off to the beach and was really enjoying himself when suddenly he heard her calling him, 'Barb! Barb!' He told himself he mustn't look. 'Barb! Barb!' came the cry again. Helpmann thought this was just too much. He opened his eyes and saw – 'Barb! Barb!' – that it was a kookaburra.

Told by Victor Spinetti on BBC Radio *Quote...Unquote* (1990).

Katharine HEPBURN

(1909–) American film actress.

—— 6 ——

The great actress was once observed shovelling snow outside her New York residence. 'Hey, aren't you Joan Crawford?' someone called out. 'Not any more,' replied Hepburn.

Source untraced. Compare THESIGER 180:1. In addition, almost any famous person worth his or her salt has at some time, apparently, been asked the question, 'Hey, didn't you used to be —— ——?'

Sir Alan ('A. P.') HERBERT

(1890–1971) English independent politician and humorous writer.

—— 1 ——

When Herbert made his maiden speech in the House of Commons in 1935, he was congratulated on it by Winston Churchill. 'Call that a maiden speech? I call it a brazen hussy of a speech.'

I heard Herbert himself do his Churchill impression when recounting this remark during a speech at my school (30 October 1962).

—— 2 ——

Herbert had a daughter called Crystal. She was called this because she was either conceived or born on the night that the Crystal Palace burned down (on 30 November 1936).

Told by Malcolm Muggeridge on BBC Radio *Quote...Unquote* (1977) but, understandably, I have had difficulty in confirming this story.

Gordon HEWART

(Baron Hewart) (1870–1943) English lawyer, politician and Lord Chief Justice of England (1922–40). He famously enunciated the principle that justice should not only be done but be *seen* to be done.

—— 3 ——

When he was in the House of Commons, Hewart was answering questions on behalf of David Lloyd George. For some time, one afternoon, he had given answers in the customary brief parliamentary manner – 'The answer is in the affirmative' or 'the answer is in the negative'. After one such noncommittal reply, several members arose to bait Hewart with a series of rapid supplementary questions. He waited until they had all finished and then replied: 'The answer is in the plural!'

Recounted in Robert Jackson, *The Chief* (1959). Compare the response given by Sir Edwin Lutyens, the architect, to a Royal Commission: 'The answer is in the plural and they bounce.'

—— 4 ——

Referring to the 19th hole at golf, Hewart asked, 'Is that the hole they call the "alco-hole"?'

Quoted in Robert Jackson, *The Chief* (1959).

—— 5 ——

Hewart's most famous and shortest after-dinner speech was given in reply to a toast to 'His Majesty's Judges' at an important dinner in London. Unfortunately, there were several long-winded and unfunny speakers before him and by the time Hewart rose to speak, he was exasperated. So this is what he said: 'When I accepted the invitation to respond to this toast I was not certain at what stage of the evening I should be required to speak. So I prepared two speeches – a short one and a longer one.' With this, he looked at the clock. 'As the night is young, I propose to deliver them both. I will give you first the shorter speech – "Thank you." Now I will deliver the longer speech – "Thank you very much."' And he sat down.

Recounted in Robert Jackson, *The Chief* (1959).

—— 6 ——

F. E. Smith, 1st Earl of Birkenhead, once taunted Hewart about the size of his stomach. 'What's it to be – a boy or a girl?' Replied Hewart: 'If it's a boy, I'll call him John. If it's a girl, I'll call her Mary. But if, as I suspect, it's only wind, I'll call it F. E. Smith.'

I printed that anecdote in my book *Quote...Unquote* (1978). The story had come to me the previous year from a *Quote...Unquote* listener who said (with wonderful precision) that it had been told to her brother 'by a stranger in a bus queue in Harrogate in 1923'. (Smith died in 1930.)

According to Humphrey McQueen in *Social Sketches of Australia* (1978), the antipodean version has Sir George Houstoun Reid (1845–1918) replying, in answer to the question, apropos of his stomach, 'What are you going to call it, George?': 'If it's a boy, I'll call it after myself. If it's a girl, I'll call it Victoria after our Queen. But if, as I strongly suspect, it's nothing but piss and wind, I'll call it after you.'

In *Pass the Port Again* (1981 ed.) the exchange occurred between Lord Haldane and Winston Churchill, as also according to John Parker, *Father of the House* (1982), where the exchange is specifically located at the Oxford Union in 1926. *The Faber Book of Anecdotes* (1985) has the US version: President Taft (d. 1930) making the retort to Senator Chauncey Depew (d. 1929).

Thor HEYERDAHL

(1914–) Norwegian explorer and author – *The Kon-Tiki Expedition* (1950) and so on.

—— 1 ——

Few authors have been as assiduous in promoting their books as Heyerdahl. On a visit to London in the 1970s, he had a packed day of interviews with newspapers and magazines, radio and television. Towards the end of it he was due to leave the studios of Thames Television in the Euston Road and go on to do a live radio interview at the BBC's Broadcasting House. A taxi was laid on to take 'Thor Heyerdahl' the short journey and as soon as the TV programme was over he went straight out to the taxi waiting outside.

'Sorry, guv, don't think it's for you, this one,' said the driver.

Heyerdahl, puzzled, went back to the reception where they assured him that it must be the one. So he went back to the cab and asked the driver, 'They say you're the one to take me to the BBC.'

'Don't think so, guv. I'm waiting for four airedales.'

Story current in the late 1970s.

Stuart HIBBERD

(1893–1983) English radio newsreader and announcer from the earliest days of the BBC.

—— 2 ——

Reading the news once, concerning some volcanic eruption, Hibberd is supposed to have spoken of 'floods of molten lager flowing down the mountainside'.

Told in Jack de Manio, *To Auntie With Love* (1967).

Sir Seymour HICKS

(1871–1949) English actor-manager.

—— 3 ——

It was said that whereas Irving and Garrick had been *tours de force*, Hicks had been forced to tour.

Told by Sheridan Morley on BBC Radio *Quote...Unquote* (1989). Peter Hay, *Theatrical Anecdotes* (1987) also finds both 'Olivier is a *tour de force* but Wolfit is forced to tour' *and* Mrs Patrick Campbell saying to Lillian Braithwaite, 'You are a perfect *tour de force* and here I am forced to tour.' Ned Sherrin in *Theatrical Anecdotes* (1991) has the Campbell version (reported by Emlyn Williams) said when Braithwaite was playing a role based on Campbell in Ivor Novello's *Party* (1932) (when Braithwaite was in the West End but the real Campbell off to the provinces). And Sherrin has the Olivier version as a recycling by Hermione Gingold's writers for a revue in the 1940s.

Benny HILL

(1924–92) English television comedian with a worldwide following.

—— 4 ——

Hill never married, though much of his humour was saucy and he was often pictured in the company of pretty girls. He was asked by an interviewer how many of the Hill's Angels dancing troupe he had been to bed with. 'Off the record,' he confided, 'I haven't made love to one of those girls. I think her name was Sandra.'

Recalled in David Lister's obituary of Hill in *The Independent* (22 April 1992).

Charles HILL

(Lord Hill of Luton) (1904–89) English doctor, politician and broadcaster. As the anonymous BBC 'Radio Doctor' of the 1940s, he often seemed to growl in his distinctive deep, fruity voice, about the condition of the nation's bowels. He later became successively chairman of both the ITA and the BBC.

—— 5 ——

Hill called on the principal medical officer of the Board of Education who suggested to him that the prune was a black-coated worker and that the phrase might be useful to him in his broadcasts. It was, and became one of his stock phrases.

Related by Hill in *Both Sides of the Hill* (1964).

—— 1 ——

The switching of Hill from the chairmanship of the Independent Television Authority (as commercial TV's regulatory body was then called) to that of the BBC in 1967 was a politically-motivated act by the then Prime Minister, Harold Wilson, who wanted Hill to set the BBC's house in order. The news was sprung upon the BBC's Acting Chairman, Robert Lusty, by the Postmaster-General, Edward Short. He was told that the new BBC Chairman was to be Charles *Smith*. Short's private secretary quickly corrected the name to Charles Hill.

Recounted by Leonard Miall in *The Independent* **(24 July 1991).**

—— 2 ——

When Hill complained to David Attenborough about his cool reception at the BBC, when he came over from 'the other side' as Chairman, Attenborough explained that for the BBC it was rather like inviting Rommel to take over the Eighth Army before the battle of El Alamein. When Hill asked whether he was suggesting Rommel wasn't a good general, Attenborough replied, 'No, but we'd like to know he's fighting for the same things as us.'

A version is quoted in Lord Hill, *Behind the Screen* **(1974). Sir Robert Lusty in his autobiography (***Bound To Be Read***, 1975) claimed to have made a similar analogy, though not directly to Hill himself. Leonard Miall discussed the rival claims in** *The Independent* **(31 July 1991).**

Sir Edmund HILLARY

(1919–) New Zealand mountaineer.

—— 3 ——

The first two climbers to reach the summit of Mount Everest, the world's highest mountain, in the Himalayas, were Hillary and his Sherpa guide, Tenzing Norgay. They were members of the British-led expedition of 1953. In his autobiography *Nothing Venture, Nothing Win* (1975), Hillary described what happened when they came down from the summit: 'George [Lowe] met us with a mug of soup just above camp, and seeing his stalwart frame and cheerful face reminded me how fond I was of him. My comment was not specially prepared for public consumption but for George . . . "Well, we knocked

the bastard off!" I told him and he nodded with pleasure . . . "Thought you must have!"'

Macdonald HOBLEY

(1917–87) Suave English TV announcer of the 1940s and 50s – the days when BBC ones appeared in vision, he invariably in a dinner jacket.

—— 4 ——

Introducing a live Party Political Broadcast (indeed, one of the first of its kind anywhere in the world) in 1949, he sat in Studio A at Alexandra Palace with one of the leading politicians of the day by his side. He said: 'Here to speak on behalf of the Labour Party is Sir Stifford Crapps . . .'

Recounted by him on innumerable occasions, including BBC Radio *Where Were You in '62?* **(1983).**

David HOCKNEY

(1937–) Bespectacled English artist of great international popularity.

—— 5 ——

The title of Hockney's 1961 painting 'We Two Boys Together Clinging' is from a poem by Walt Whitman. The picture shows two figures clinging together indeed surrounded by various inscriptions including the numerals '4.2'. This is code for 'Doll Boy' – i.e. Cliff Richard. Hockney had been amused to come across a newspaper headline which stated: 'TWO BOYS CLING TO CLIFF ALL NIGHT LONG'. Although the article concerned a climbing accident and not a sexual fantasy, the reference gives an added resonance to the picture.

Described by Marco Livingstone in *David Hockney* **(1981).**

—— 6 ——

Hockney once told on TV of how and why he decided to bleach his hair and become the blond bombshell he is today. It was in response to a television advertisement he saw late one evening in New York City. 'Blondes have more fun,' it said. 'You've only one life. Live it as a Blonde!' He immediately jumped up, left the apartment, found an all-night hairdresser there and then and followed the advice of the advertiser, Lady Clairol.

As recounted by a reviewer in *The Listener* (1983).

Dustin HOFFMAN

(1937–) American stage and screen actor of diminutive stature. First came to general notice by his performance in the film *Midnight Cowboy* (1969).

—— 1 ——

Reviewing Hoffman's performance as Willy Loman in Arthur Miller's *Death of a Salesman*, Frank Rich of the *New York Times* wrote: 'I was overwhelmed by the tragic smallness of Dustin Hoffman's Willy.'

Quoted in *The Observer* (28 May 1989).

See also OLIVIER 146:3.

Gerard HOFFNUNG

(1925–59) German-born British cartoonist, musician and eccentric. Although he looked and sounded like an old man, he was a mere 34 years old when he died. His famous speech at the Oxford Union on 4 December 1958 was on the motion 'Life begins at 38'.

—— 2 ——

One of the most-remembered lines from his Oxford Union speech concerns letters supposedly received from Tyrolean landladies about the desirability of their properties: 'There is a French widow in every bedroom (affording delightful prospects) . . .'

How nice to hear an old joke revisited! In the Reverend Francis Kilvert's diary (entry for 7 October 1871) he says: 'The *Hereford Times* has misprinted our report of the Clyro Harvest Festival as follows, "The *widows* were decorated with Latin and St Andrew's crosses and other beautiful devices in moss with dazzling flowers." This was irresistible and the schoolmaster roared with delight.'

Stanley HOLLOWAY

(1890–1982) English actor, chiefly remembered for his performance as Alfred Doolittle in the stage and screen versions of the musical *My Fair Lady*.

—— 3 ——

Asked on his deathbed by his son whether, looking back on a long and crowded life, he had any lasting regrets, Holloway replied: 'Yes – the fact that I never got the Kipling Cake commercials.'

Related by Sheridan Morley in a *Theatreprint* quiz, some time before 1986.

HONEYMOONERS

—— 4 ——

When I was introducing the BBC Radio 4 *Today* programme, there was an item on it about a man who raised buff Orpingtons, a breed of poultry. He had devoted much of his life to this hobby, but in his middle years he had found time to take unto himself a wife. For the honeymoon, they went – and this, as far as I can tell at this distance, was the point of the story – to Orpington.

After their return, the blushing bride and groom were interviewed against a background of clucking buff Orpingtons. All proceeded merrily until the interviewer ventured to ask the bride: 'And when you were on your honeymoon, did he show you his buff Orpingtons?'

I very much hope I declined – as presenter – to add anything after this interview.

Remembered from about 1977.

Herbert HOOVER

(1874–1964) American Republican president (1929–33).

—— 5 ——

Sir Isaiah Berlin is fond of doing a one-word imitation of Herbert Hoover, which goes: 'Eighteenthly . . .'

According to John Julius Norwich (1992).

Anthony HOPE

(Sir Anthony Hope Hawkins) (1863–1933) English novelist (chiefly known for *The Prisoner of Zenda*).

—— 1 ——

The opening night of J. M. Barrie's play *Peter Pan* in 1904 was received with tremendous enthusiasm, but there was one dissenter. The scene of the 20 'Beautiful Mothers' who have come in answer to an advertisement for adopting the 'Lost Boys' (which was cut from the play after the first season) caused Anthony Hope, who was in the audience, to exclaim: 'Oh, for an hour of Herod!'

Told in Andrew Birkin, *J. M. Barrie and the Lost Boys* (1979). An earlier outing for this remark occurred one hundred years previously when 'Master Betty', the child acting prodigy, was all the rage in London theatre. Dorothea Jordan, the actress mistress of the Duke of Clarence, surveying the throng of juvenile would-be imitators of 'Master Betty', exclaimed, 'Oh, for the days of King Herod!' – Anne Matthews, *Anecdotes of Actors* (1844).

Kenneth HORNE

(1907–69) Bald, urbane, avuncular English entertainer, chiefly known for his BBC radio comedy shows *Much Binding in the Marsh, Beyond Our Ken* and *Round the Horne*.

—— 2 ——

There was another Kenneth Horne (1900–75), a playwright (*Love in a Mist*, and so on), and the two were and still are frequently thought to have been the same person. During the Second World War, even more confusingly, they were both in the RAF and both wing commanders (can you believe this?). This led to a major, life-changing development for one of them, at least. Marjorie Thomas had met Horne (the playwright) at some social function and attempted to contact him by telephone at the Air Ministry. She was put through to Horne (the entertainer).

'Wing Commander Horne,' replied he.

'Oh, hallo, is that Kenneth Horne?' asked she.

'It *is*.'

'I hope you will remember me. We met at a party two weeks ago. Now I'm giving a little party and would love you to come.'

Horne (the entertainer), unable to resist, duly turned up and was immediately *not* recognized by Marjorie Thomas as the man she had met previously (i.e. Horne the playwright). He took her out to dinner and she eventually became his third wife.

Told to me (1984) by Judy Farrar, daughter of Horne (the playwright). Also described by Norman Hackforth in *Solo for Horne* (1976).

HOSTS AND HOSTESSES

—— 3 ——

Dr Vaughan, one-time headmaster of Harrow school, evolved a useful phrase designed to get rid of boys he had entertained at breakfast, when he had had enough of them. From G. W. E. Russell in his *Collections and Recollections* (1898): 'When the muffins and sausages had been devoured . . . and all possible school-topics discussed, there used to ensue a horrid silence . . . Then the Doctor would approach with cat-like softness, and, extending his hand to the shyest and most loutish boy, would say, "Must you go? Can't you stay?" and the party broke up with magical celerity.'

It was later twisted to, 'Must you stay? Can't you go?' For example, as the caption to a *Punch* cartoon in the edition dated 18 January 1905. The Governor of Madagascar is saying it, referring to the prolonged stay of the Russian Admiral Rodjestvensky at Madagascar when on his way to meet the Japanese Fleet.

—— 4 ——

A hostess dealt with a maddeningly garrulous guest by sharply saying to him: 'While you've got your mouth open, would you ask the maid to serve dinner?'

Told to me by Miss V. Ruth Bennett of Swindon (1980).

—— 5 ——

At a certain dinner party, when a young, nervous girl lit up a cigarette after the soup, without asking permission to do so, the hostess said icily, 'We seem to have finished', and led the party from the room. That was the end of the dinner.

I first came across this cautionary tale in Katharine Whitehorn's *Observer* column (27 July 1980), though I have subsequently found it told about a *duke* in

Francis Meynell's *The Week-end Book* (1955). From the way Meynell tells it, it was an old tale even then. I have also heard it adorned with the additional detail of the cook throwing a tantrum over the ruination of her meal, and with the moral drawn that it is an excellent illustration of the way in which manners that are intended to put people at their ease can be used rather to humiliate an innocent or uninitiated person. The girl who lit up is said to have run off in tears and had to leave the house next day.

―― 1 ――

What should one call the lavatory in polite society? A young girl had been to a luncheon party and half-way through the luncheon she had turned to the hostess and said 'Could you tell me where the bathroom is?' And the hostess had said, 'Out of the door, second on the right'. So she'd gone along and when she got there she found that that was exactly what it was, a bathroom with a bath and a wash-hand basin. So she decided to lock herself in and use the wash-hand basin for a purpose other than for which it was intended.

Consequently, her weight pulled the basin off the wall. She crashed to the ground, being knocked out and concussed with the basin on top of her, and had to be rescued fifteen minutes later by the host who had to break down the door to get in.

Was the hostess deliberately being a bitch by sending the girl to the one place she'd asked for, but which is considered in some circles to be an acceptable term to describe the loo? Told to me by Una-Mary Parker in 1991 for the BBC Radio series *Best Behaviour*. She assured me that it was a true story which she had been told when she was teaching etiquette at a girls' school. The story resurfaced in *The Guardian* as one of its 'Urban Myths' series on 13 March 1993.

Harry HOUDINI

(1874–1926) Hungarian-born American escapologist.

―― 2 ――

Orson Welles, as a small boy, was introduced to Houdini, who taught him to do a simple trick with a red handkerchief and then counselled him, 'Never perform any trick until you have practised it a thousand times.' Welles went away and duly practised the handkerchief trick the requisite thousand times. When Welles next met Houdini, a manufacturer of magic called Carl Bremer was showing him a new vanishing lamp trick. Welles was utterly shocked when he heard Houdini say, 'Fine, Carl, I'll put it in the act tonight.'

Told by Frank Brady in *Citizen Welles* (1989).

―― 3 ――

While appearing in Montreal, Houdini was visited in his dressing room by three students from McGill University. Although over fifty years old, Houdini was still very proud of his physique and invited one of the young men to punch him in the stomach. Alas, the blow came before he had had time to brace himself. His appendix was ruptured and he died within a fortnight.

Recounted in Roy Busby, *British Music Hall: A Who's Who 1840–1923* (1976).

Sir Geoffrey HOWE

(later Lord Howe) (1926–) Welsh Conservative politician.

―― 4 ――

In November 1982, when Howe was Chancellor of the Exchequer, he was travelling by rail on an overnight sleeper and had his trousers stolen. He merely commented, 'I have more than one pair of trousers', and it was left to an anonymous colleague – probably a fellow member of the Cabinet to say, 'I am thrilled about the loss of your trousers... because it revealed your human face.'

This would seem to be quite a reliable quote, as it was repeated by Lady Howe in a magazine interview two years later.

Howard HUGHES

(1905–76) American film producer, industrialist and, latterly, weirdo recluse.

―― 5 ――

When he was in Hollywood, Hughes was producing a historical epic when a young assistant boldly pointed out some inaccuracy in t he text or the costume or the scenery. 'It makes a complete nonsense,' said the assistant. 'I'll go to the library and check it for you, if you like.' 'No,' pronounced Hughes, wisely, 'never check an interesting fact!'

Source untraced.

Hubert HUMPHREY

(1911–78) American Democratic politician. Lyndon Johnson's vice-president.

—— 1 ——

Commenting on a failed assassination attempt against President Gerald Ford, Humphrey might have phrased his remarks a little differently. He said: 'There are too many guns in the hands of people who don't know how to use them.'

Quoted in 1981.

HYGIENISTS

—— 2 ——

It was said that Queen Elizabeth I was remarkably advanced for her time in matters of hygiene. Indeed, she was in the habit of taking a bath once a month – 'whether she need it or no.'

David Cottis wrote to me (1992): 'This sounds to me like a case of an old line becoming attached to a famous person. Certainly, the story has been told of people other than the Virgin Queen. Indeed, it is quoted as an anti-Semitic joke by no less an authority than Sigmund Freud in *Jokes and their Relation to the Unconscious* (1905)':

Two Jews were conversing about bathing. 'I take a bath once a year,' said one, 'whether I need one or not.'

David Cottis adds (amusingly) that Freud explains (helpfully), 'It is clear that this boastful assurance of his cleanliness only betrays his sense of uncleanliness . . .'

HYMNOLOGISTS

—— 3 ——

In the late 19th century religious words were sometimes put to popular tunes of the day – with unusual results. Particularly was this the case where the hymns had repetitive choruses in which the congregation joined and especially so when the last line was broken up and repeated as a refrain. In one they sang:

O catch the flee,
O catch the flee,
O catch the fleeing sinner, Lord.

In another the sopranos sang,

I want a man
I want a man
I want a mansion in the skies.

To which the tenors responded,

Come down Sal
Come down Sal
Come down Salvation from the skies.

And, finally, there was:

O take thy mourning pil,
O take thy mourning pil,
O take thy mourning pilgrims home.

Original letter from Peter C. Peck of Polegate (1991). Others from the Reverend Christine J. Hey of Mansfield, Notts. and Florence Wilkinson of Menston, West Yorkshire (1992).

I

INDEXERS

—— 1 ——

Book indexers lead lives of quiet dedication, if not desperation, as they ply their trade for little reward. They do, however, have opportunities to insert subtle jokes which one day, possibly, a reader may happen to stumble across.

In the Index (Vol. XI, 1983) of the Latham and Matthews edition of *The Diary of Samuel Pepys*, there is delightfully quiet, possibly unconscious, humour to be found in the entry for one of Pepys's mistresses. Here it is, slightly abbreviated:

BAGWELL, Mrs, wife of William: her good looks, 4/222; P plans to seduce, 4/222, 266; visits, 4/233–4; finds her virtuous, 4/234; and modest, 5/163; asks P for place for husband, 5/65–6, 163; P kisses, 5/287; she grows affectionate, 5/301–2; he caresses, 5/313; she visits him, 5/316, 339; her resistance collapses in alehouse, 5/322; amorous encounters with: at her house, 5/350–1; 6/40, 162, 189, 201, 253, 294; 7/166 . . . asks for promotion for husband, 6/39–40; P strains a finger, 6/40; has sore face, 7/191; servant dies of plague, 7/166.

All human life is there . . .

—— 2 ——

In the diary, also, Pepys several times mentions an eating house in Old Palace Yard, London, called 'Heaven' (there was also one called Hell). This enables him to write (possibly without realizing it): 'And so I returned and went to Heaven' (28 January 1660). In the Latham and Matthews edition (Vol. 1, 1970), the editors explain this reference on its first appearance and then, in a subsequent footnote, put: 'For heaven, see above.'

IRISH PEOPLE

—— 3 ——

An Englishman had spent all evening telling Irish jokes in the pub. Suddenly, a man at the next table leaned over indignantly and said, 'Oi! You telling Irish jokes! I think you should know that I'm Irish.' To which the Englishman answered apologetically, 'Oh, I'm terribly sorry, pal! If I'd known, I'd have told them more slowly . . .'

Told to me by Joan Smith of Manchester in 1981, saying that a friend of hers called Ken was the Englishman in question.

—— 4 ——

Sir Huw Wheldon once recalled how he had asked an Irishman's advice at which of two restaurants to dine. He said the Irishman thought hard for a moment and then answered: 'If you go to the one, you would wish you had gone to the other.'

Told in 1985.

—— 5 ——

Oh, what the hell, surely I need to put a few choice Irish jokes in here? 'The Irish don't know what they want and won't be happy till they get it.' 'What's an Irish contraceptive like?' – 'Hand me that ball of wool and I'll knit you one.' 'Did you hear about the Irishman who was laying turf on an Englishman's lawn? The Englishman had to keep reminding him, "Green side *up*, Paddy, green side *up*!"' 'What did the Irishman call his pet zebra?' – 'Spot.' 'Did you hear about the Irishman who won the Nobel Prize for Agriculture? He was out standing in his field.' 'How do you tell which is the bride at a Kerry wedding?' – 'She's the one wearing the white gumboots.' 'Did you hear about the first Irish space shot? They attempted to put the first man on the sun.'

That's quite enough.

J

Glenda JACKSON

(1936–) English stage and screen actress, who won Oscars for her performances in *Women in Love* and *A Touch of Class*. At one time she was noted for being unable to keep her clothes on in films. Entered Parliament as Labour MP for Hampstead in 1992.

––––– 1 –––––

Playing the character Nina in Eugene O'Neill's *Strange Interlude*, Jackson was rather baffled by one of the playwright's legendarily lengthy stage directions. It went: 'She walks into the room. She stops. All the blood rushes from her face. A faint flush begins at the base of her neck, rises upward. Her eyes dilate. Their extraordinary turquoise blue become black, then pale green.'

Recounted by her on BBC Radio *Quote...Unquote* (1990).

David JACOBS

(1926–) English broadcaster who seemed fatherly even when presenting TV's *Juke Box Jury* in the 1960s.

––––– 2 –––––

After being told by a BBC executive that he was being dropped from chairing the *Any Questions* radio programme after many years on the job (1968–84), Jacobs was taken out to lunch. Said Jacobs, 'You've put the knife between my shoulder blades, but you might have spared me the fork.'

Having suffered similarly, Jack de Manio once said: 'When the BBC wants to sack you, they take you out to lunch.'

Martin JARVIS

(1941–) English actor. A dashing juvenile lead until he was into his fifties but, at the same time, outstanding in character parts. The foremost radio 'reader' and an ubiquitous voice-over artist.

––––– 3 –––––

Taking part in Somerset Maugham's *The Circle* at the Haymarket Theatre in London, Jarvis played the part of a husband who had summoned his wife's lover for a confrontation. As the lover entered and closed the door, Jarvis saw that the ornate door handle came off in his hand. The actor playing the lover was laughing and, of course, they could not look each other in the eye. As it happens, Jarvis's next line was: 'Has it struck you that you are destroying my home?'

Told by Jarvis on BBC Radio *Quote...Unquote* (1979).

David JASON

(1940–) English (mostly) comedy actor who finally achieved the status of a TV star as Del Boy in *Only Fools and Horses* and Pa Larkin in *The Darling Buds of May*.

––––– 4 –––––

For many years in the early 1970s, Jason appeared regularly in BBC Radio's faintly satirical series *Week Ending*. A proper actor, who likes thorough rehearsal and direction, he was less at home in a world where he had to read scripts straight off the page. On one occasion, in some sketch about storms around the coast of Britain, he had to utter the line, 'Alert Aberdeen!' What came out of his mouth, however, was '*Albert* Aberdeen!' and this became his nickname on the programme.

From my memories of being told about the incident when I joined the programme in 1971.

—— 1 ——

Self-effacing off-screen, Jason tends to avoid show business croneyism and lives in the country. He has been known to take his three-legged dog for a walk round the village while himself wearing dark glasses. His neighbours think this is a less than successful attempt at disguise when you have a three-legged dog.

Told in *The Independent* (19 December 1992).

JEWISH PEOPLE

—— 2 ——

A Jewish joke: How do we know that Jesus was a Jew? 1. He lived at home until he was 30. 2. He went into his father's business. 3. His mother thought he was the Messiah. 4. He thought his mother was a virgin.

Told to me by Rabbi Cliff Cohen (1985). This particular rabbi had recently been sacked by his synagogue because of his over-fondness for telling jokes.

—— 3 ——

During the Six Day War of 1967, an Israeli soldier stood up and called across to an Arab on the other side: 'Stand still, won't you – these bullets cost money!'

Told to me by Michael Almaz (1969).

—— 4 ——

A Jewish mother bought her beloved son two shirts as a present. He went straight upstairs and put one of them on, then reappeared before his mother. 'Oh,' she said, disappointedly, 'you don't like the other one? . . .'

Told to me by Michael Almaz (1969), since when I have regarded it as the perfect Jewish joke.

Augustus JOHN

(1878–1961) Welsh-born artist who reinvented the Bohemian life. It is said that he automatically patted children on the head just in case they turned out to be his.

—— 5 ——

Out swimming one day, as a young man, John dived into shallow water and cut his head on a rock. As Virginia Shankland subsequently wrote: 'He hit his head whilst diving and emerged from the water a genius!'

As noted by Michael Holroyd in Volume 1 of his biography of John (1974), Shankland's comment appeared on the back of a Brooke Bond Tea Card as one of a series of 'Fifty Famous People' (no date available). Compare the George Melly version from BBC Radio *Quote...Unquote* (1977): 'I understand he was a sober and pleasant young man until he fell on his head in Wales, whereupon he became the slap-dash goat of his later years.'

Lyndon B. JOHNSON

(1908–73) American Democratic president who brought an earthy Texan manner to the White House.

—— 6 ——

On a visit to the LBJ ranch, the then West German Chancellor, Ludwig Erhard, said, 'I understand that you were born in a log cabin, Mr President.' 'No, Mr Chancellor,' replied Johnson, 'I was born in a manger.'

Quoted in Alfred Steinberg, *Sam Johnson's Boy* (1968).

—— 7 ——

Before he became President, Johnson was Senate Majority Leader and evidently took great delight in teasing fellow Senator, Everett Dirksen, about LBJ's latest toy, a car telephone. When Johnson left for home, he would see the conscientious Dirksen still at work, so he would ring up from the car, always beginning with the query, 'Guess where I'm calling you from, Ev?' The answer was always the same: 'From my car telephone'.

Dirksen became so annoyed by this that one day he got himself a car phone and when he saw Johnson leaving, he ran down to his own car and called up the LBJ car. 'Guess where I'm calling you from, Lyndon?' he asked. Johnson paused and then said, 'Hold on a minute, Ev. My other phone's ringing . . .'

Original source untraced. This story has probably been told about other pairs engaged in one-upmanship.

—— 1 ——

LBJ once said of the media that, if one morning he walked on top of the water across the Potomac River, the headline that afternoon would read, PRESIDENT CAN'T SWIM.

Quoted in *Time* (28 December 1987). This is a joke that politicians just love. Neil Kinnock, when leader of the British Labour Party, said: 'Worried about my media coverage, I consulted a fortune-teller. She told me to perform miracles, so I walked across the Thames. Next day the *Sun* headline ran: Neil Kinnock fails to swim river.' (Quoted in *Sunday Today*, 17 May 1987). The Right Reverend Desmond Tutu, Archbishop of Cape Town tells a joke about himself: 'Tutu and State President P. W. Botha are in a boat in Table Bay when a storm blows up. Tutu says: "It's all right, I'll get help" and walks across the water. The next day in the Afrikaans paper, the headline is: "*Tutu Kan Nie Swem Nie*" – Tutu can't swim.' (Quoted in *The Observer* Magazine, 20 March 1988).

—— 2 ——

After reviewing some Vietnam-bound Marines, LBJ moved towards a helicopter for his return journey to the White House. An officer helpfully pointed out another chopper, saying, 'That's your helicopter over there.' 'Son,' replied LBJ, 'they are all my helicopters.'

Quoted in Hugh Sidey, *A Very Personal Presidency* (1968).

Paul JOHNSON

(1928–) English writer and journalist who took the traditional path from Left (editor of *The New Statesman*) to Right ('Why, oh, why?' editorialist).

—— 3 ——

In about 1977, when Johnson was still 'on the turn', so to speak, a waiter at a London club remarked of him, 'He eats more oysters than the dukes.'

Reported in the William Hickey column of *The Daily Express*.

—— 4 ——

Jonathan Miller said of the red-haired Johnson, that he looked like 'an explosion in a pubic hair factory'.

Quoted in Alan Watkins, *Brief Lives* (1982).

Brian JOHNSTON

(1912–93) Ebullient English cricket commentator, chiefly on radio.

—— 5 ——

Johnston's most famous broadcasting moment was when he said, 'There's Neil Harvey at leg slip with his legs wide apart, waiting for a tickle.'

Recounted by Johnston on innumerable occasions.

—— 6 ——

Commentating on the Oval Test against the West Indies in 1976 with Michael Holding bowling to Peter Willey: 'The bowler's Holding, the batsman's Willey.'

Recounted by Johnston on BBC Radio *Quote...Unquote* (1980). On another occasion in the commentary box, Trevor Bailey had been singing the praises of Peter Willey when he suddenly produced the remarkable admission: 'I am, of course, a great Willey supporter.'

Peter JONES

(1920–) Brilliant English character actor in TV shows like *The Rag Trade*. Equally superb when he adopts a slightly crusty, bemusedly aged persona as 'himself' on panel games.

—— 7 ——

In the early 1950s, Jones partnered Peter Ustinov in what came to be regarded as one of the classic radio comedies, *In All Directions*. Unfortunately, for ever after, all that interviewers seemed to want to talk to Jones about was that partnership with Ustinov. Jones countered with this story: 'I dreamt that I had died and, just before ascending into heaven, I floated down to Piccadilly Circus where there was a news vendor with a placard with, I was surprised to see, a mention of my demise. It said, "FRIEND OF PETER USTINOV DEAD".'

Told to me by Jones before 1979, I think. In *Laughter in the Air* (1976), Barry Took presents the story in a lengthier version, supposedly concocted by Jones for a speech he made at a Press Association dinner. Here the placard states, 'PETER USTINOV BEREAVED'.

I wouldn't like to have to break it to Peter Jones but in the biography circulated in 1991 by (now) *Sir*

Peter Ustinov's press agent, it stated that *In All Directions* was 'his own show' in which Ustinov 'produced and co-starred with Peter *James.*'

—— 1 ——

Jones had just started to appear in the TV series *Mr Big* when he was accosted by a lady in the street: 'Oh, Mr Jones, I do so enjoy your programme. It's so *mediocre* – something in it for the whole family.'

Recounted by him on BBC Radio *Quote...Unquote* (1979).

JOURNALISTS

—— 2 ——

Also including editors, sub-editors, correspondents and hacks.

There is a definition of a journalist: 'Someone who stays sober right up to lunch-time.'

Quoted by Godfrey Smith on BBC Radio *Quote...Unquote* (1985).

—— 3 ——

An absurd aspect of the war correspondent's job in broadcasting – having to find people who have experienced the horror of war but who are also capable of putting that horror into words – is encapsulated in a question heard during the war in the Congo (*c.* 1960). Thousands of frightened Belgian civilians were waiting for a plane to take them to safety from the newly independent ex-Belgian colony when a BBC television reporter walked among them with his camera team and asked, 'Has anyone here been raped and speaks English?' The incident was reported by Edward Behr who commented: 'The callous cry summed up for me the tragic, yet wildly surrealist nature of the country itself.'

Recounted by Behr in his book with the title *Anyone Here Been Raped and Speaks English?* (1978).

—— 4 ——

When Rupert Murdoch took over the American *San Antonio News* in the 1970s, one headline became the paradigm of his new style. Reputedly a bee with a fatal sting had been sighted in South and Central America. Hence the famous headline, 'KILLER BEES HEAD NORTH'.

Quoted in Michael Leapman, *Barefaced Cheek* (1983).

—— 5 ——

Typographical errors – 'typos' – come thick and fast when newspapers are produced quickly and cheaply. The New York *American* once printed the term 'battle-scared hero' and, for some reason, 'corrected' this in later editions to 'bottle-scarred hero'.

Quoted in Nat J. Ferber, *I Found Out* (1939).

—— 6 ——

A woman accused of being a common prostitute said in court, 'Prostitute I am, common I am not.' *The Daily Telgraph* headlined this, 'TART REPLY'.

Quoted in *The Sunday Telegraph* (25 November 1984).

—— 7 ——

The story is told of a Belfast businessman who was playing an innocent round of golf when a donkey came up and attacked his wife. He gallantly came to the rescue and the incident was thought newsworthy by the editor of the local newspaper. An account appeared under the headline, 'BELFAST GOLFER BEATS ASS OFF WIFE WITH NIBLICK.'

Source unknown.

—— 8 ——

'Things that might have been expressed differently' was the title of a *Punch* series at the turn of century. Well, the editor of *The Leicester Mercury* told me of an occasion when a young man had obviously found life in Leicester too exciting and had decided to take his own life. He had not succeeded, however, and was left clinging by his fingernails from the window ledge of a tallish building in the city centre. The *Mercury*, on that occasion, unfortunately rushed into print and advised its readers that the young man – hanging by his fingernails – 'had declined all offers of food and drink'.

Told to me by Neville Stack in May 1983.

—— 9 ——

Dr (later Sir) Vivian Fuchs was leader of the Commonwealth Antarctic Expedition (1956–8). For a while his surname gave a certain amount of pleasure to impish headline writers in the press. Actual examples include: 'DR FUCHS OFF TO SOUTH ICE', 'FUCHS OFF AGAIN' and 'DR FUCHS FIFTY TO-DAY'.

The first two of these are reproduced in Fritz Spiegl, *The Black on White Misprint Show* (1967).

—— 1 ——

A possibly apocryphal headline referring to a mental patient who raped two laundry-workers and escaped was: 'NUT SCREWS WASHERS AND BOLTS'.

Current by 1978.

—— 2 ——

Another possibly apocryphal headline, said to have appeared in a British newspaper – presumably during the Second World War – was 'EIGHTH ARMY PUSH BOTTLES UP GERMANS'.

Recounted on BBC Radio *Quote...Unquote* (1979).

—— 3 ——

'EQUITY BLACKS OTHELLO' did actually appear in *The Daily Telegraph* when British Actors' Equity prevented the American actor James Earl Jones from playing the role in the West End.

In about 1979.

—— 4 ——

'CHIP SHOP OWNER BATTERED MAN' was a headline that did actually manage to appear in *The Gateshead Post*.

In about 1979.

—— 5 ——

'NUDIST WELFARE MAN'S MODEL WIFE FELL FOR THE CHINESE HYPNOTIST FROM THE CO-OP BACON FACTORY' definitely appeared in *The News of the World*.

From 1970.

—— 6 ——

'COLETTE: GRAND OLD LADY OF FRENCH LETTERS' is said to have appeared in *The Scotsman*.

Prior to 1979.

—— 7 ——

'STEPS TO HELP HILL FARMERS URGED'. I saw this myself in *The Dundee Courier & Advertiser*.

In about 1979.

—— 8 ——

'ANTARCTICA: CHILE NAVY RESCUES CRUISE PASSENGERS AFTER LINER GOES AGROUND.' Quite understandable, really.

This appeared in *The Times* (12 February 1972).

—— 9 ——

'SEX CHANGE MONK ONCE A ROYAL FOOTMAN' definitely once appeared in *The Yorkshire Evening Post*.

Prior to 1979. Compare the apocryphal 'TEENAGE DOG-LOVING DOCTOR-PRIEST IN SEX-CHANGE MERCY DASH TO PALACE' mentioned in *The Lyttelton Hart-Davis Letters* (Vol. 4, 1959).

—— 10 ——

A famous litany describing British newspapers according to their readers goes like this: *The Times* is read by the people who run the country. *The Guardian* is read by the people who would like to run the country. *The Financial Times* is read by the people who own the country. *The Daily Telegraph* is read by the people who remember the country as it used to be. *The Daily Express* is read by the people who think the country is still like that. *The Daily Mail* is read by the wives of the men who run the country. *The Daily Mirror* (which itself once tried to run the country) is read by the people who think they run the country. *The Morning Star* is read by the people who would like another country to run the country. *The Sun* – well, Murdoch has found a gap in the market, the oldest gap in the world.

In this form the list was ascribed to 'An Advertising Copywriter' and quoted on the cover of Fred Hirsch and David Gordon, *Newspaper Money: Fleet Street and the Search for the Affluent Reader* (1975). For once, however, it is possible to be quite precise about the origin of a piece of folklore. As Miles Kington described in *The Times* (20 January 1984), the piece was written by Kevin Grant and based on an idea by the broadcaster and former newspaper editor, Brian Redhead. All one can say as to dating is that it was obviously compiled before the Hirsch/Gordon book in 1975 and, equally, before the launching of *The Daily Star* in 1978. The line about *The Sun* sometimes takes a different form – 'The Sun is read by people who don't care who runs the country, as long as they can keep on looking at naked titties.' Or something similar.

James JOYCE

(1882–1941) Irish novelist.

—— 1 ——

Joyce dictated parts of his novel *Finnegan's Wake* to an amanuensis – Samuel Beckett. During one such session there came a knock on the door. 'Come in,' Joyce called out. Beckett wrote the words down. Later, when the work was read back to him, he asked Beckett, 'What's that "Come in"?' 'That's what you said,' said Beckett. 'Well then, let it stand,' said Joyce.

Recounted in Richard Ellman, *James Joyce* (1959).

JUDGES

—— 2 ——

At the height of Beatlemania, when the papers were full of pieces about the Fab Four every day, a High Court judge lifted the flap of his wig quizzically and inquired of counsel, 'Who *are* the Beatles?'

This is the archetypal judge's remark – often, of course, a question posed when the judge knows the answer, in order to further his reputation for fustiness and aloofness from the concerns of ordinary citizens. But did any judge actually ever ask it? I believe not. What I think happened was that an assumption was made that, when the The Beatles came along, judges would ask the question – just as they had always done and still do.
   In 1990, the year of the football World Cup, Mr Justice Harman actually asked, 'Who is Gazza? Isn't there an operetta called *La Gazza Ladra*?' Indeed, there is – but that has nothing to do with the footballer Paul 'Gazza' Gascoigne. A century before, in 1889, Mr Justice Stephen had asked, 'What is the Grand National?' (but he was eventually committed to a lunatic asylum). In *Geoffrey Madan's Notebooks* (ed. Gere & Sparrow, 1981 – but Madan died in 1947), Lord Hewart is credited with: 'Precedent compels me to ask: what is jazz?' In fiction, A. P. Herbert's Mr Justice Snubb asked: 'What is a crossword?' I am encouraged to believe in the apocryphal nature of the Beatles remark by a report in *The Guardian* on 10 December 1963 (when Beatlemania was rampant). A QC representing the Performing Right Society at a tribunal in London in a case concerning copyright fees at pop concerts objected to a suggestion that tribunal members should attend a pop concert to see and hear what it was like. Instead, they listened to a recording of a Beatles' concert. Another QC remarked to the court: 'You will only have to suffer two or three minutes.' The *Guardian* headline over its report of all this was: '*What is a Beatle?*' which, as I say, appears to be a case of the old question being applied to a new phenomenon. But it is not an actual quotation.

—— 3 ——

Marty Feldman, the comedian, was called as a witness in the *Oz* magazine obscenity trial in the summer of 1971. He managed the rare feat of turning the tables on a difficult judge – Judge Michael Argyle – by asking: 'Am I speaking loud enough for you, judge? Sorry, am I waking you up?'

Quoted in Tony Palmer, *The Trials of Oz* (1971).

—— 4 ——

Possibly in order to lighten the atmosphere at the *Gay News* blasphemy trial in July 1977, Judge Alan King-Hamilton advised the jury, 'You might like to know that I've just been informed that Australia are four for one.'

Quoted in BBC Radio *Quote...Unquote* (1978).

—— 5 ——

There was a judge who had the job of sentencing two gentlemen who were discovered in an attitude of unusual friendliness under Waterloo Bridge. Instead of just sentencing them, he said: 'You two men have done a most disgusting and immoral and depraved and terrible act. And what makes it so much worse is that you chose to do it under one of the most *beautiful* bridges in London.'

Told innumerable times by John Mortimer but, in particular, on BBC Radio *Quote...Unquote* (1979).

—— 6 ——

When a jury at the Old Bailey acquitted four of the defendants on conspiracy and arms charges, Judge Alan King-Hamilton told them that their verdict was, 'Remarkably merciful in the light of the evidence'.

The trial was in December 1979.

—— 7 ——

When Thurgood Marshall was retiring as a justice of the US Supreme Court, he was asked the clichéd question, 'How do you feel?' He replied: 'With my hands'.

Quoted in *Texas Lawyer* (6 January 1992).

Otto KAHN

(1867–1934) American banker.

—— 1 ——

Kahn was a convert to Christianity. One day he was walking up Fifth Avenue in New York with a banker who had a hunchback. Kahn pointed to the Temple Emmanuel Synagogue and remarked, 'I used to be a Jew.' 'Yeah,' said the other, 'and I used to be a hunchback.'

Told by Larry Adler on BBC Radio *Quote...Unquote* (1977).

George S. KAUFMAN

(1889–1961) American playwright and screenwriter.

—— 2 ——

Of an actor with the interesting name Guido Nadzo, Kaufman came up with the devastatingly final comment: 'Guido Nadzo is nadzo guido.'

Quoted in Scott Meredith, *George S. Kaufman and the Algonquin Round Table* (1977).

John F. KENNEDY

(1917–63) American Democratic president.

—— 3 ——

Harold Macmillan liked to suggest that when he was prime minister and Kennedy was president there was something of a father-son relationship between them. If so, the mind can merely boggle at the remark Kennedy made at their third or fourth meeting. He said to the world-weary (and, indeed, famously cuckolded older man), 'I wonder how it is with you, Harold? If I don't have a woman for three days, I get a terrible headache.'

Quoted in Alastair Horne, *Macmillan 1957–1986* (1989). In a letter from Venice (3 July 1961), Nancy Mitford told her sister the Duchess of Devonshire (and related by marriage to the President): 'They say on the beach that if [Kennedy] doesn't ** every day he has a headache.'**

—— 4 ——

On 26 June 1963, Kennedy proclaimed a stirring slogan outside the City Hall in the then newly-divided city of West Berlin. 'All free men, wherever they may live, are citizens of Berlin, and, therefore, as a free man, I take pride in the words *Ich bin ein Berliner*.' Ben Bradlee noted in *Conversations with Kennedy* (1975) that Kennedy had to spend 'the better part of an hour' with Frederick Vreeland and his wife before he could manage to pronounce this and the other German phrases he used. In fact, *Ich bin Berliner* would have been sufficient to convey his meaning. By saying *Ich bin* ein *Berliner*, Kennedy unwittingly drew attention to the fact that in Berlin, *ein Berliner* is the name given to a type of sponge cake. So it was rather as if the proud boast of free men everywhere was 'I am a doughnut.'

I first drew attention to this matter on Channel 4 TV *Countdown* in November 1984. I can't recall who put me up to it. Compare CARTER 49:1.

Oleg KERENSKY

(1930–93) English ballet and theatre critic. Grandson of Alexander Kerensky, the Russian prime minister at the time of the October Revolution.

—— 5 ——

Oleg was turned down for military service in Britain on account of his eyesight, but he loved to tell of the interview he had with a bright-eyed, moustachioed RAF officer during the selection procedure. '"Kerensky", eh? Not an English name?' he asked, perceptively. 'No', replied, Oleg, 'in fact it is Russian.' 'You were born in Russia?' asked the RAF man. 'No,' replied Oleg, 'but my father and grandfather were. They had to leave Russia, you see.' 'Ah,' wondered the RAF man, 'that wouldn't have been for any *political* reasons, by any chance?' 'Yes, in fact it was,' replied Oleg. 'You see, my grandfather was the prime minister.' 'Prime minister, eh!' exclaimed the RAF man, still bright-eyed and beaming. Then after a moment's pause, he added: '. . . . Jolly good!'

Recounted by Dick Taverne at Oleg's memorial service, London (14 October 1993).

Nikita KHRUSHCHEV

(1894–1971) Soviet politician.

—— 1 ——

In 1956, Khrushchev paid an eventful visit to Britain in the company of Marshal Bulganin ('B and K'). At Oxford, Khrushchev visited New College chapel and – famously disliking modern art – viewed the Jacob Epstein statue of the risen Lazarus with marked distaste. Next morning, back in London, at Claridge's, he declared that he had not slept well. 'I had nightmares from that terrible statue at Oxford,' he said.

Reported in Sir William Hayter, *A Double Life* (1974). Hayter, as British ambassador to Moscow, accompanied Khrushchev on his visit to New College (of which Hayter himself became Warden in 1958). Khrushchev's initial derogatory remarks about the statue were overheard by a journalist and printed. Epstein fired off a telegram: 'Tell your guest to keep off art criticism, which he does not understand, and stick to his own business, which is murder.'

Rudyard KIPLING

(1865–1936) English writer and poet, who took his unusual first name from the fact that his parents spent their honeymoon near Rudyard Lake in Derbyshire.

—— 2 ——

There is a joke which goes, 'Do you like Kipling?' To which the response is, 'I don't know, you naughty boy, I've never kippled.' Insofar as one can ever point to the origin of a joke, this did appear as the caption on a comic postcard drawn by Donald McGill, probably dating from the 1930s.

Henry KISSINGER

(1923–) German-born American secretary of state.

—— 3 ——

For one not endowed with obvious good looks, Kissinger developed a curious reputation as a 'swinger' in the early 1970s when he was a national security adviser. He attributed this to the fact that 'power is the ultimate aphrodisiac'. Some of the women who appeared on his bachelor arm were more equivocal. Barbara Howar said, 'Henry's idea of sex is to slow the car down to 30 miles an hour when he drops you off at the door.'

The 'aphrodisiac' remark was reported in *The New York Times* (19 January 1971) and Howar's in Barbara Rowes, *The Book of Quotes* (1979).

Ronald KNOX

(1888–1957) English theologian, priest and writer.

—— 4 ——

Sometimes told as though *about* Father Knox, though in fact only a story told *by* him, is the one about the English priest who had never got beyond fourth-form French and who was asked if he would like to take confession at Notre Dame in Paris on Easter Sunday. A little old lady from the streets of Paris came into the confessional and started babbling out all the sins she had committed. The priest, who did not understand a word of it, was overheard mumbling, 'Ah, *vouz avez, avez-vous?'*

A version told by Leslie Thomas on BBC Radio *Quote...Unquote* (1982) – from which several inaccuracies have been removed.

—— 1 ——

Knox once related how it had been alleged by a friend of the family that when Knox was a mere four years old and suffering from insomnia, he was asked how he managed to occupy his time at night. He answered, apparently, 'I lie awake and think about the past.'

Quoted in Ronald Knox, *Literary Distractions* (1941).

—— 2 ——

When he was headmaster of Shrewsbury, Knox is said to have divided the school reports he had to sign into two piles. On those in one pile he wrote, 'Trying', on the those in the other, '*Very trying'.*

Told by Dr Eric Anderson, headmaster of Eton, on BBC Radio *Quote...Unquote* (1986).

Fritz KREISLER

(1875–1962) Austrian-born American violinist.

—— 3 ——

A society hostess had jibbed at Kreisler's fee of $5000 for a recital and added, as though in mitigation, that he would not after all be required to mingle with the guests. 'In that case, madam,' Kreisler answered brightly, 'the fee would only be $2000.'

Told in Bennett A. Cerf, *Try and Stop Me* (1944). Also ascribed to other famous musicians and singers.

Harry KURNITZ

(1907–68) American screenwriter in Hollywood. He wrote *Witness for the Prosecution* and much else.

—— 4 ——

Kurnitz had a thing about large cars. One day his own splendid limousine broke down as he was on his way to Paris and he was forced to take a lift in a Volkswagen. When he was asked what he thought about it, he replied: 'I've been in bigger women'.

Quoted in Ned Sherrin, *Theatrical Anecdotes* (1991). One senses that this must have influenced Woody Allen in his remark (quoted 1993): 'Hey, the last time I was inside a woman was when I went up the Statue of Liberty'.

L

Elsa LANCHESTER

(1902–86) English film actress.

—— 1 ——

Of Maureen O'Hara, Lanchester reputedly said, 'She looked as though butter wouldn't melt in her mouth. Or anywhere else.'

Told by Kenneth Williams on BBC Radio *Quote...Unquote* **(1978).**

Theatrical LANDLADIES

—— 2 ——

Comedians Morecambe and Wise were often faced with the difficult task of what to write in the visitors' books that theatrical landladies traditionally asked their guests to sign. If they did not like the digs, Morecambe and Wise would settle for the wonderfully equivocal: 'We shall certainly tell our friends.'

Source untraced.

—— 3 ——

Arthur Rigby Jr was a character actor, best remembered as the desk-sergeant for many years in TV's *Dixon of Dock Green*. As a young man, Rigby was once staying in theatrical digs and found that the landlady's daughter not only made eyes at him but also ended up in his bed from Monday night to Sunday morning. The landlady made absolutely no mention of a situation of which she must have been aware – except that when Rigby got his bill on Sunday morning it included, 'Ten shillings for extra vegetables', a charge he otherwise had not incurred.

Told by Rigby's nephew, the actor William Franklyn, on BBC Radio *Quote...Unquote* **(1983).**

See also BARRYMORE 24:6.

LAPLANDERS

—— 4 ——

In Joe Orton's radio play *The Ruffian on the Stair*, the hero is describing what is obviously a homosexual experience and an outraged Irishman says, 'There is no word in the Irish language for what you've been doing.' And the retort is: 'In Lapland they have no word for snow.'

Recalled by John Lahr on BBC Radio *Quote...Unquote* **(1980). The play was first broadcast in 1964. (Someone wrote to point out that, on the contrary, the Lapps have scores of words to describe snow . . .)**

D. H. LAWRENCE

(1885–1930) English novelist, poet and writer.

—— 5 ——

Many years after it was originally clandestinely published, Lawrence's infamous novel *Lady Chatterley's Lover* was reissued in the United States by Grove Press (I think it may have been in the 1940s). Rather oddly, this edition was reviewed in the pages of *Field and Stream*, a journal aimed at followers of outdoor pursuits. In part, the review stated: 'This fictional account of the day-by-day life of an English gamekeeper is still of interest to outdoor-minded readers, as it contains many passages on pheasant-raising, the apprehending of poachers, ways to control vermin, and other chores and duties of professional gamekeepers. Unfortunately, one is obliged to wade through many pages of extraneous material in order to discover and savour these sidelights on the management of a Midland estate, and in this reviewer's opinion, the book cannot take the place of J. R. Miller's *Practical Gamekeeper*.'

Quoted in the seventh volume of Rupert Furneaux's *Famous Criminal Cases* **(1962) in its account of the Penguin Books/***Lady Chatterley*** trial.**

T. E. LAWRENCE

(1888–1935) 'Lawrence of Arabia' – Anglo-Irish
soldier and Arabist.

—— 1 ——

In Cairo, a woman exclaimed, 'Ninety-two this morning, Colonel Lawrence! Ninety-two. What do you say to that?' Lawrence replied: 'Many happy returns of the day.'

I have never heard of Lawrence making any other attempt at humour. This comes from *Geoffrey Madan's Notebooks* (ed. Gere & Sparrow, 1981).

LAWYERS

—— 2 ——

A Yorkshire miner put in a very late claim for compensation. The judge told his counsel: 'Your client is no doubt aware of *vigilantibus, et non dormientibus, jura subveniunt?*' The counsel replied: 'In Barnsley, m'lud, they speak of little else.'

This much-told legal joke takes any number of forms. In *Pass the Port Again* (1980), there is a version told involving Serjeant Sullivan – 'the last serjeant of the Irish Bar to practise in the English courts'. This I take to be Alexander Martin Sullivan (1871–1959). Here, the legal tag is *'Assignatus utitur jure auctoris'* and the place where they speak of little else is Ballynattery.

—— 3 ——

Did you hear about the overworked law student who confused arson with incest and ended up setting fire to his sister?

Related in *The Lyttelton Hart-Davis Letters* (for 13 November 1955).

John LE MESURIER

(1912–83) English character actor whose mournful features appeared in numerous film comedies and also in TV's *Dad's Army*.

—— 4 ——

It seems that Le Mesurier may have been as much of a ditherer in real life as he often was on the screen. He once received news that a friend of his was in difficulties and was threatening suicide in some distant place. When asked by a fellow actor what he was doing about it, Le Mesurier replied that he was going to ring up the potential suicide – 'I'll do it after six o'clock.' 'But why wait till then?' the other actor demanded. 'He might have done it by now . . .' 'Yes,' replied Le Mesurier, 'but calls are cheaper after six o'clock.'

Told to me by Kenneth Williams, in the early 1970s.

—— 5 ——

Le Mesurier arranged for his own death notice to appear in *The Times* when appropriate. It duly appeared on 16 November 1983, in the form: 'John Le Mesurier wishes it to be known that he conked out on November 15th. He sadly misses family and friends.' His last words were, 'It's all been rather lovely.'

From a report in the same issue of *The Times*.

John LENNON

(1940–80) English singer and songwriter. Was given the middle name of 'Winston' at birth and acquired 'Ono' from his widow-to-be.

—— 6 ——

Appearing with The Beatles at the Royal Variety Performance in 1963, Lennon told the well-heeled audience: 'Those in the cheaper seats clap. The rest of you rattle your jewellery.'

The event took place on 15 November 1963.

—— 7 ——

In a newspaper interview, Lennon said, 'Christianity will go. It will vanish and shrink. I needn't argue about that. I'm right and I'll be proved right. We're more popular than Jesus now.' The remark lay dormant for several months but when The Beatles paid a visit to the USA, it was reprinted and caused an outcry. The Beatles were burned in effigy and their records banned by radio stations in the Bible Belt states.

The *Evening Standard* interview conducted by Maureen Cleave appeared in March 1966.

—— 1 ——

L ennon fairly quickly lost interest in Transcendental Meditation and certainly fell out with the Maharishi Mahesh Yogi whom he considered to be a dirty old man. Lennon wrote a song about him called 'Maharishi', but was persuaded to re-title it 'Sexy Sadie'.

Recounted in Peter Brown & Steven Gaines, *The Love You Make* (1983).

King LEOPOLD II

(1835–1909) Belgian monarch, who reigned from 1865.

—— 2 ——

O n learning that he must undergo a serious operation (which did indeed prove fatal), King Leopold, financially crooked, sexually depraved, but with a sense of humour, sent for his principal mistress (a 25-year-old ex-prostitute whom he had made a baroness) and married her. When the ceremony was over, he said to his best man – the prime minister – 'Let me introduce you to my widow.'

Told to me by Margaret B. of Brussels (1979).

—— 3 ——

T he parish priest of a village near one of King Leopold's country villas was sent by the outraged local population to remonstrate with him about his goings-on. 'Sir,' the unfortunate priest stammered, 'rumour has it that Your Majesty engages in the sin of fornication.' 'Well, well, well,' said the King, 'haven't people got vulgar minds? I was told the same story about you the other day, but I refused to believe it . . .'

Same source.

Alan Jay LERNER

(1918–86) American lyricist and playwright. With the composer Frederick Loewe, he wrote the musicals *My Fair Lady, Gigi, Camelot*, and others. Much-married.

—— 4 ——

L erner and Loewe were at the height of their powers and of their money-making capacity when one day in London they walked into a Mayfair motor-car showroom and both ordered Rolls-Royce convertibles. When Lerner reached for his cheque book, Loewe took out his and said, 'I'll get this – you paid for lunch!'

It is true that both men did once order Rolls-Royce convertibles from a showroom in London in a transaction that took a mere five minutes to complete. As Lerner describes in his memoir *The Street Where I Live* (1978): 'The story of the two Rolls-Royces made the rounds and, as usual, became distorted. One day I picked up a newspaper where it was reported that we had bought two Rolls-Royces in five minutes, and that when I reached for my chequebook, Fritz took out his and said, "I'll get this. You paid for lunch"!'
A more recent version of this anecdote appeared in *The Independent* (15 February 1992): 'One Lloyd's story tells how, after a particularly good lunch, [Bill] Brown and a brother found themselves outside a BMW car showroom. After his brother expressed admiration for a particular model, Mr Brown said, so the story goes: "I'll get that for you. You paid for lunch."'
Robert Lacey, the biographer, told an identical story about two Arabs and a Rolls-Royce on BBC Radio *Quote...Unquote* in February 1979.
Michael Grosvenor Myer of Cambridge notes: 'Can't give you chapter and verse, but distinctly remember in my youth, certainly no later than the 50s, a version as one of those page-foot fillers in *Reader's Digest*, concerning two Texas oilmen in a Cadillac showroom.' Sounds quite likely.

Oscar LEVANT

(1906–72) American pianist, writer and wit.

—— 5 ——

A lthough Levant was the foremost exponent of George Gershwin's music, a good deal of joshing went on between them. Gershwin once said, 'Oscar, if you had to do it all over, would you fall in love with yourself again?' Levant replied, 'George, why don't you sit down and play us a medley of your hit.'

Told by Benny Green on BBC Radio *Quote...Unquote* (1979). Edmund Fuller, *2500 Anecdotes for All Occasions* (1943) also gives Gershwin's remark to Levant.

Beatrice LILLIE

(1898–1989) Canadian-born actress, married to a Sir Robert Peel.

—— 1 ——

Miss Lillie, on tour in Chicago, was in a beauty salon with other members of her company. She overheard another client who had been kept waiting, complaining of 'All these theatricals . . .' Miss Lillie discovered that the complainer was Mrs Armour, wife of the Chicago meat-packing tycoon. On leaving the salon, she said to the receptionist in the hearing of Mrs Armour, 'You may tell the butcher's wife that Lady Peel has finished.'

Told in L. & M. Cowan, *The Wit of Women* (1969).

—— 2 ——

A squelch which *might* have been meant well-meaningly came from Bea Lillie when she dashed into a colleague's dressing room on a first night and exclaimed: 'Darling, I don't care what *anybody* says – I thought you were marvellous.'

In a letter from Tony Hepworth of Heaton, Bradford (1980).

LINGUISTS

—— 3 ——

Someone rather bold once said to Dr Samuel Johnson, 'You smell!' The eminent lexicographer, not taking offence, replied, 'No, *you* smell, *I* stink.'

Not exactly a 20th-century anecdote – on the other hand, perhaps it is. Michael Grosvenor Myer of Cambridge had this to say about the likely provenance of the exchange: 'Surely this is merely a folk tale about a pedant insisting on precise application of words, attributed to Dr Johnson because, as a lexicographer, he would be thought fastidious about usage. Compare the somewhat similar tale of Webster (another famous lexicographer, d. 1843) discovered by his wife as he embraced one of the maidservants: "Why, Noah, I am surprised!" "No, dear, you are astonished; it is I who am surprised."'

A version of the Noah Webster version appeared in *Pass the Port* (1976).

—— 4 ——

London has a large number of visiting Polish workers. Only some of them bother to speak English. I was having my house painted by two such Poles – one who spoke impeccable, idiomatic English, and one who didn't. At Saturday lunch time I had to tell the latter Pole that I was going out and would he please lock up when it was time for him to leave. I said, 'Goodbye' and he said, 'Night, night'.

From my memory of the incident, *c.* 1988.

LISTENERS

See RADIO LISTENERS

LIVERPUDLIANS

—— 5 ——

A Liverpool man went calling on his mate. His mate's wife answered the door. 'Hello, Mary,' he said, 'is George in?' She said he was, but had had a terrible accident that morning while having his breakfast. In fact, he had collapsed and died over the table. His mate was thoughtful for a moment. Then he said: 'Did he mention anything about a paintbrush?'

This was given as an example of Liverpool 'Scouse' humour in *The Liverpool Echo*, during the 1980s. However, in Kenneth Tynan's profile of Eric Morecambe in *The Observer* Magazine (9 September 1973), Morecambe tells it as a typical Tommy Cooper story (and he certainly wasn't a Scouser . . .)

Sir Andrew LLOYD WEBBER

(1948–) Swivel-eyed composer of hugely successful musicals. Would probably like to have been Puccini. His first two wives were called Sarah.

—— 1 ——

He is once said to have asked Alan Jay Lerner, 'Why do people take an instant dislike to me?' Lerner replied, 'Saves time.'

By the time it appeared in *The Independent on Sunday* (15 December 1991), this was an old story. Lerner (if it was really he who punched the line) died in 1986. However, the slur may simply have been imposed upon Lloyd Webber. The earliest newspaper mention I have found of the exchange is reported as involving a Sheffield Wednesday manager and player (*The Independent*, 12 January 1989). From June 1992, the joke was several times made against George Galloway, a Scottish Labour MP.

Frank LOESSER

(1910–69) American composer and lyricist.

—— 2 ——

The songwriter was married twice – first to Lynn Loesser, then to Jo Sullivan Loesser. One of these wives (it would be invidious to say which) was referred to as, 'the evil of two Loessers'.

In fact, it was Lynn. The person who made the remark was Harry Kurnitz, the screenwriter. He was having some sort of feud with her. Quoted in *The Observer* (31 March 1968).

LOVERS

—— 3 ——

A girl aged 16 had told her parents that she wanted to go on a fortnight's camping holiday with her boyfriend on his motorbike. When she was asked what her parents had thought of this plan, she replied, 'Oh, mummy says it's all right as long as I take a crash helmet.'

This supposedly overheard remark from Mark Miller of Buckfastleigh was included in my *Eavesdroppings* (1981). I subsequently received a letter from John Pinnell of London N2 claiming that this joke had originated in the offices of a life-assurance society where he worked 'some twenty years ago'. His version: 'The girl asked her manager for an extra week's leave of absence to tack on to her one week's holiday entitlement. She told him that her parents were not worried, "As both of us would wear crash helmets".'

—— 4 ——

Two girls were talking on the London Underground. One was overheard to say, 'I can't bear late nights. If I go out to dinner and am not in bed by 12, I go home.'

This appeared in *Pass the Port* (1976). Compare this from Mrs C. M. Brown of Cheltenham in my *Eavesdroppings* (1981): 'One teenage girl to another: "All of a sudden he said, 'I want to marry a virgin', so I got straight up out of that bed, got dressed and went home."'

—— 5 ——

Queen Mary was going round a hospital when she was struck by a fair-haired mother with a very dark baby. She commented on this and, indeed, returned to the woman's bedside after completing her rounds, saying: 'His father must have been very dark – wasn't he?' To which the woman breezily replied: 'Sure Ma'am, I don't know – he never took his hat off.'

From the entry for 18 August 1917 in *Lady Cynthia Asquith's Diaries* (1968).

—— 6 ——

Did you hear about the Irish girl who told her mother she was pregnant. To which the mother replied, 'Are you sure it's yours?'

A joke current in the 1980s.

—— 7 ——

A young and pretty typist was soon spotted by the office Romeo – a man of about forty. Adjusting his tie, he approached her and said, 'Hello, gorgeous, where have you been all my life?' To which she replied, 'Well, for most of it I wasn't born . . .'

Told to me by F. G. Seabrook of Whetstone (1985), but rather ancient even then, I suspect.

Heinrich LÜBKE

(1894–1972) President of West Germany.

—— 1 ——

In 1965, prior to a reception for Queen Elizabeth II outside Bonn, Lübke attempted an English translation of *'Gleich geht es los'* ('It will soon begin'). He came out with, 'Equal goes it loose.' Three years earlier, Lübke had greeted the president of India at an airport by asking, instead of 'How are you?' – *'Who* are you?' (To which his guest naturally replied, 'I am the president of India.')

Quoted in *Time* (30 March 1981).

Alfred LUNT

(1893–1977) American actor who formed a husband-and-wife partnership with Lynn Fontanne (1887–1983). They were always known as 'The Lunts'.

—— 2 ——

Fontanne, reporting back to Lunt, on the results of the famous couple's first-ever screen test, said, 'Alfred, it was absolutely remarkable! The camera does such wonderful things. You don't seem to have any lips. But the make-up and lighting were superb, and you looked absolutely marvellous! So handsome and striking, my darling, you have an entirely new career before you. I'd be so delighted with what they've done. Whereas, I – well, I'm absolutely appalling! Disaster! I look like some dreadful old shrew – a hag – I simply couldn't bear to look at myself another second!'

Alfred replied sadly, 'No lips, eh?'

There is a version of this in *Isaac Asimov's Treasury of Humor* (1971).

See also TRANSCRIBERS 183:2.

Sir Edwin LUTYENS

(1869–1944) English architect who designed the Viceroy's House, New Delhi, and the Cenotaph, London.

—— 3 ——

When Lutyens's son, Robert, was attempting to write a book about his father, they met for lunch at the Garrick Club in London so that Sir Edwin could make known his views on the project and its author. When the matter was broached, however, Sir Edwin, embarrassed, merely exclaimed, 'Oh, my!' Then, as the fish was served, he looked at his son over the *two* pairs of spectacles he was wearing and commented: 'The piece of cod passeth all understanding.'

Recounted in Robert Lutyens, *Sir Edwin Lutyens* (1942).

Humphrey LYTTELTON

(1921–) English Old Etonian jazz trumpeter, band leader and broadcaster.

—— 4 ——

When asked what title he would give to any further volume of his autobiography, Lyttelton said that his father had long ago chosen the right one for him: *My God, What Boots!* Wearing, as he does, size 13 shoes, Lyttelton would find these words in the hymn that begins 'My God, What Boots It To Repent'.

Told by him on BBC Radio *Quote...Unquote* (1985).

—— 5 ——

Question: what most famous Shakespeare quotation follows the line (said by Polonius to the King), 'I hear him coming; let's withdraw, my lord'? It is, of course, 'To be or not to be' in *Hamlet*. Lyttelton, appearing on *Quote...Unquote* (in 1985), suggested that it was, 'As the actress said to the bishop . . .'

—— 6 ——

Lyttelton's father, George, was a master at Eton and his later correspondence with a distinguished former pupil, Rupert Hart-Davis, was published in several volumes (from 1978 onwards). In that work, George Lyttelton recalled receiving a report on Humphrey's progress in the world from an examination paper that he had been marking. The subject of the paper was 'Jazz' and the essayist had stated: 'Humphrey Littleton [*sic*] is the leading English trumpeter, and – like many others – plays best when he is drunk.'

From a letter dated 18 August 1960 in *The Lyttelton Hart-Davis Letters* (Vol. 5, 1983).

M

Sir Ian McKELLEN

(1939–) English actor with imitable North
Country voice.

—— 1 ——

McKellen played Hamlet at the Cambridge
Theatre, London, in 1971. The production was
reviewed by Harold Hobson, theatre critic of *The
Sunday Times*, but it was on the radio rather than in
the newspaper that he delivered his cruellest judge-
ment. 'The best thing about Ian McKellen's Hamlet,'
he said, 'is the curtain call.'

> **Recalled by McKellen on BBC Radio
> *Quote...Unquote* (1979).**

—— 2 ——

In 1991 McKellen – just knighted – was invited to
No. 10 Downing Street by the prime minister, John
Major, to discuss gay rights. As it so happened, the
next visitor due to arrive was Edith Cresson, the
French prime minister, who had, not long before, let
fall a controversial word or two about the masculin-
ity of Englishmen.

On leaving Downing Street, McKellen said: 'I am
sorry it's raining and I won't be able to linger outside
to speak to Madame,' he said. 'But I am sure I would
only confirm her worst fears.'

> **Quoted in *The Independent* (28 September 1991).
> Cresson's comment on homosexuality among Eng-
> lishmen – 'Everyone knows it. It is in books and in
> history and it is a fact of civilization' – was quoted
> in *The Observer* (21 July 1991).**

Anew McMASTER

(1894–1962) Irish actor-manager.

—— 3 ——

McMaster was travelling with his company by
train one Sunday when it stopped at an isolated
rural station in Ireland. Lowering the window and

revealing his extravagant hat and other thespian
garb, McMaster inquired of a porter, 'What country,
friend, is this?' Being an educated Irish railway
employee, the porter recognized Viola's opening
line from *Twelfth Night* and promptly gave Shakespeare's own reply: 'This is Illyria – lady.'

> **Told by Ian McKellen on BBC Radio
> *Quote...Unquote* (1977).**

Harold MACMILLAN

(later 1st Earl of Stockton) (1894–1986) British
Conservative prime minister and paradigm of the
'elder statesman'.

—— 4 ——

In 1960, as British prime minister, Macmillan was
speaking about nuclear test bans before the United
Nations General Assembly. His speech was several
times interrupted by the Soviet leader, Nikita
Khrushchev, who shouted out remarks and at one
point angrily began banging his shoe on the desk.
Macmillan drolly asked if the shoe-banging could be
translated.

> **From a recording of the incident.**

—— 5 ——

It has become the custom for the Queen to gather
her ex-prime ministers together for a spot of
socializing from time to time. Macmillan once mused
on what the collective noun should be for such a
group. He came up with: 'A *lack* of principals'.

> **Source untraced. However, George Lyttelton in
> *The Lyttelton Hart-Davis Letters* (Vol. 3, 1981)
> (letter of 23 January 1959) has this as the collective
> noun for 'heads of colleges', which is more appo-
> site.**

See also <small>COLLINS</small> 59:5.

MADONNA

(Madonna Louise Ciccone) (1958–) Embarrassing
American singer who wears her sex on her sleeve
and her microphone on her head.

—— 1 ——

In an ad for Preparation H, Madonna was
described as sounding 'like Mickey Mouse on
helium.'

**Quoted in *Time* Magazine (1985). Also current in
1985 was the view that her singing sounded like 'a
sheep in pain'.**

John MAJOR

(1943–) British Conservative prime minister who
came from nowhere.

—— 2 ——

Major is alleged to have said when opening
his first Cabinet meeting: 'Well – who'd have
thought it?'

Source untraced.

Archbishop MAKARIOS

(1913–77) Cypriot priest and president.

—— 3 ——

After he had been reported dead during the
Cyprus coup of 1974, Makarios reappeared and
said, 'You should have known that it was not easy for
me to die – but tell me, were my obituaries good?'

Quoted in *The Observer* (29 December 1974).

MALAPROPS/
MALAPROPISTS

—— 4 ——

A law student (in a *viva voce* examination) was
asked what was necessary to render a marriage
valid in Scotland. He replied: 'For a marriage to be
valid in Scotland it is absolutely necessary that it
should be consummated in the presence of two
policemen.'

**From *Samuel Butler's Notebooks* (towards the end
of the period 1874–1902).**

—— 5 ——

A correspondent reported an overheard conversation: 'Did you see the ostriches on telly last
night?' 'What ostriches?' 'The ostriches that escaped.'
'I didn't know that any ostriches had escaped.' 'Of
course – you know – the American ostriches.'

**This was from Mrs S. Moore of Twickenham in
1981. However, Ned Sherrin in *Theatrical Anecdotes* (1991) pins it squarely upon Chrissie Kendall
– 'singer, dancer, actress . . . the champion
Malapropper of the British stage' – in 1979.**

—— 6 ——

Mrs Levi Zieglerheiter, American mother-in-law
of the 1st Marquis Curzon, declared on landing
in New York after a stormy crossing, 'At last I am
back on terracotta.'

Quoted by Kenneth Rose in *Superior Person* (1969).

—— 7 ——

There was the grandmother who was convinced
that the 'girl with kaleidoscope eyes' in the
Beatles' song 'Lucy in the Sky With Diamonds' was
in fact singing, 'The girl with colitis goes by'.

**Said to have been reported first by William Safire
of *The New York Times*.**

—— 8 ——

At a conference in 1954 in Berlin, France's foreign
minister, Georges Bidault, was introduced as,
'that fine little French tiger, Georges *Bidet* . . .'

Quoted in *Time* Magazine (30 March 1991).

Barry MANILOW

(1946–) American pop singer who has a substantial following among a particular type of female. Also a nose that is much remarked upon by the unkindly.

—— 1 ——

The British newspaper columnist Jean Rook once memorably described Manilow's voice as sounding like 'a bluebottle caught in the curtains'.

Quoted in Lynn Barber, *Mostly Men* (1991).

Herman J. MANKIEWICZ

(1897–1953) American screenwriter.

—— 2 ——

When a Hollywood agent who was famous for his rapacity told Mankiewicz how he had been swimming for two hours in shark-infested water and had got away with it, Mankiewicz commented: 'I think that's what they call professional courtesy.'

Told by Dick Vosburgh on BBC Radio *Quote...Unquote* (1979).

Princess MARGARET

(1930–) Sister of Queen Elizabeth II. Small in stature and has given up smoking.

—— 3 ——

On a visit to Chicago in 1979, the princess attended a private dinner party. A gossip columnist who talked to somebody who had sat adjacent to the mayor of Chicago at the party published the Princess's alleged remark that, 'The Irish are pigs.' In the aftermath, various explanations were offered as to what she *might* have said, including, 'I hate those Irish jigs.'

From various newspaper reports.

—— 4 ——

Princess Margaret has always been about the nearest the present royal family has got to the Bohemian. She used to smoke visibly, is photographed holding glasses of whisky and daringly wears dark glasses. The penalty she pays for this behaviour is not hard to find. In the early 1960s I recall seeing a headline in a French newspaper – I think it may have been *Paris Soir* – which read *'Margaret – Presque Aveugle'*. Accompanying it was a photograph of her wearing dark glasses. Hence the assumption that she was 'nearly blind'.

My memory.

10th Duke of MARLBOROUGH

(1897–1972) English aristocrat.

—— 5 ——

On returning from one of his several honeymoons in his later years, the duke was reported to have commented philosophically, 'I'm afraid Mr Mouse didn't come out to play.'

Reported in *Private Eye* at the time and repeated in the '300th Issue Quiz' in No. 299 (June 1983).

Arthur MARSHALL

(1910–89) English writer and entertainer who for many years combined his monologues as 'Nurse Dugdale' with sober teaching duties as a schoolmaster at Oundle. Then he became a script-reader for 'Binkie' Beaumont and a highly readable light journalist and columnist. Only towards the end of his life did he emerge as a well-known and much-loved public figure, guesting on panel games, his high-register voice swooping through cosy anecdotes, his shoulders heaving with convulsive laughter.

—— 6 ——

Once when coming out of the BBC TV Centre, Marshall was accosted by a woman seeking his autograph. The woman (inevitably) explained that she wanted it not for herself but for her daughter. However, when Marshall handed back the book, duly inscribed, she looked very disappointed. 'Oh,' she said with disappointment all over her face, 'I thought you were Arthur Negus.'

Recalled in *The Guardian* (28 January 1989).

—— 1 ——

Another story that Marshall liked to tell against himself was about the occasion he turned up for a recording of TV's *Call My Bluff* wearing an unusually prominent suit. Fellow panellist Frank Muir sized him up and down, ran his fingers along the lapels, and pronounced: 'Why pay more, Arthur, why pay more?'

Recalled by Marshall on BBC Radio *Quote...Unquote* (1980).

Christopher MARTIN-JENKINS

(1945–) English cricket journalist and commentator.

—— 2 ——

During the 1979 Cricket World Cup when England was playing Canada, Martin-Jenkins drew attention to the inclement conditions under which the match was being played, with these words: 'It is extremely cold here. The England fielders are keeping their hands in their pockets between balls.'

Recalled by him on BBC Radio *Quote...Unquote* (1983).

Chico MARX

(1886–1961) American film comedian (and noted womanizer).

—— 3 ——

When his wife caught Chico kissing a chorus girl, he explained, creatively: 'But, you see, I wasn't kissing her. I was whispering in her mouth.'

Quoted in Groucho Marx and Richard J. Anobile, *The Marx Brothers Scrapbook* (1974).

Groucho MARX

(1895–1977) American comedian.

—— 4 ——

Each member of the famous family of comedians used a name other than the one he was born with. According to Groucho, the nicknames were acquired at a poker game in about 1918: Leonard became Chico; Adolph became Harpo (he played the harp); Julius became Groucho; Milton became Gummo (though he left the act early on); and Herbert became Zeppo (though he also left in due course). Groucho once attempted to explain the nicknames. Chico was a 'chicken-chaser', he said; Zeppo was 'after the Zeppelin' which arrived in Lakehurst, New Jersey, at the time he was born (1901); and Gummo 'wore gumshoes'. As for Groucho, 'I never did understand . . .'

> On the record album *An Evening with Groucho Marx* (1972). In *The Marx Bros. Scrapbook* (1974), Groucho gave a slightly different account – the stage names were given by a 'monologist named Art Fisher . . . I think Fisher got the names from a cartoon that was appearing in the papers. *The Monk Family* or something like that.' And as for Groucho? 'He named me because I was stern and rather serious.'

—— 5 ——

Marx was told by the membership secretary of a beach club that he couldn't become a member because he was Jewish. Marx replied, 'My son's only half Jewish. Would it be all right if he went in the water up to his knees?'

Quoted in Arthur Marx, *Son of Groucho* (1973).

—— 6 ——

When *Confidential* magazine ran a muck-raking article, going over every area of Marx's life, Groucho dashed off one of his famous letters to the editor: 'Dear Sir, If you persist in publishing libellous articles about me, I will have to cancel my subscription.'

Quoted in Arthur Marx, *Son of Groucho* (1973).

—— 7 ——

Marx was going down in the lift from the sixth floor at the Hotel Danieli in Venice. At the fourth floor, four priests got in. One of them recognized Groucho and said, 'Excuse me, Mr Marx, my mother was a great fan of yours.' To which Groucho retorted: 'I didn't know you guys were allowed to have mothers.'

Told by Larry Adler (who was in the lift, too) on BBC Radio *Quote...Unquote* (1976).

—— 1 ——

Groucho declined an invitation to see Victor Mature and Hedy Lamarr in Cecil B. de Mille's film *Samson and Delilah* (1958), with the words: 'I never go to a movie where the hero's bust is bigger than the heroine's.'

Told by Gay Search (1981).

—— 2 ——

On the apparent absence of Eleanor Roosevelt at a White House reception, Groucho informed another guest: 'She's upstairs filing her teeth.'

Source untraced.

—— 3 ——

Groucho once drew a distinction between amateur and professional senses of humour. For an amateur, he said, the funniest thing would be the sight of a man dressed up as an old lady rolling down a steep hill in a wheelchair and crashing into a wall at the bottom of it. 'But to make a pro laugh,' he concluded, 'it would have to be a real old lady.'

Recounted by Kenneth Tynan in *Persona Grata* (1953).

Walter MATTHAU

(1920–) American film actor, real name Walter Matuschanskayasky, so now you know.

—— 4 ——

One night, Matthau was at a party with his wife, Carol. He wandered off and, in due course, she spotted him chatting to a woman who was somewhat 'mutton dressed as lamb'. Carol even heard him ask this apparition, 'How old are you?' At which point, Carol butted in and said, 'Why don't you saw off her legs and count the rings?'

Told by George Axelrod on BBC Radio *Quote...Unquote* (1979).

Francis MATTHEWS

(1931–) Smooth English actor who played Paul Temple on TV for a number of years.

—— 5 ——

As Matthews explains, 'Walter Plinge' is the name actors traditionally take in addition to their own when they are 'doubling', or playing two parts in a play. There was a lot of that in Matthews's early days in repertory theatre. But he remembers with mixed feelings a review he received in one local paper when he was playing two parts in a play: 'Francis Matthews was woefully inadequate in his part, but Walter Plinge gave a beautiful performance . . .'

Told by Matthews (1993).

Victor MATURE

(1915–) American film actor of romantic and he-man roles.

—— 6 ——

On being told that his clothes looked unusually rumpled on one occasion – 'as though he had slept in them' – Mature replied: 'Don't be ridiculous. I pay someone to do that for me.'

Told by William Franklyn on BBC Radio *Quote...Unquote* (1990).

—— 7 ——

On being turned down when he attempted to join an exclusive golf club – the grounds given were that he was an actor – Mature replied: 'I am not an actor – and I have 60 films to prove it.'

Recounted in Melvyn Bragg, *Rich: The Life of Richard Burton* (1988).

See also MARX 132:1.

W. Somerset MAUGHAM

(1874–1965) English novelist, playwright and writer.

—— 1 ——

Maugham paid a visit to the set of the 1941 remake of *Dr Jekyll and Mr Hyde* with Spencer Tracy in the title roles. He inquired at one point: 'Which is he playing now?'

Quoted in Leslie Halliwell, *The Filmgoer's Book of Quotes* **(1973).**

Robert MAXWELL

(1923–91) Czech-born British publisher, politician, tycoon and crook. According to someone I know who once penetrated his bathroom, he put boot blacking on his hair and eyebrows.

—— 2 ——

Maxwell was against smoking in the offices of most of his companies. Getting into a lift at one of them and encountering a man puffing at a cigarette, he immediately demanded how much the fellow earned. 'Seventy-five pounds a week,' came the reply. Maxwell took out his wallet, handed the man £300 – to cover a month's wages – and told him, 'You're fired.'

What Maxwell hadn't realized was that the man was not an employee, but merely a visitor.

Told variously since the late 1980s. A version appears in Peter Hay, *Business Anecdotes* **(1988).**

—— 3 ——

When the publishing wing of his empire moved into a London office block, it seemed perfectly natural to the tycoon that it should be renamed 'Maxwell House'. It was said that he did not understand the joke.

A memory from about 1983.

—— 4 ——

On one occasion, Maxwell received an unexpected invitation to a posh do in New York. He sent a courier back to London on Concorde to collect his tails.

Told in Tom Bower, *Maxwell, The Outsider* **(1988).**

George MELLY

(1926–) Portly English jazz singer and writer with an angelic smile. Always behatted and sartorially splendid.

—— 5 ——

'Melly's Law' – dating from the 1960s – was designed to help customers distinguish between male and female clothing shops. 'It's a male boutique,' Melly stated, 'if you go in to buy a tie and they measure your inside leg.'

Quoted by Ned Sherrin on BBC Radio *Quote...Unquote* **(1981).**

Sir Yehudi MENUHIN

(1916–) American-born British violinist. Child prodigy who lasted the course. Created a life peer in 1993.

—— 6 ——

When he was due to give a recital with the Russian-born cellist Rostropovich, Menuhin was annoyed to be informed by the Soviet authorities that Rostropovich was 'unwell' and would be unable to take part. Suspecting that this was unlikely to be the truth, he rang Rostropovich and confirmed that the authorities were merely being their customary obstructive selves. So he sent a telegram to the then Soviet president, Leonid Brezhnev, saying that if Rostropovich was not allowed to attend, he would call a news conference and announce that the Soviets had told a lie about Rostropovich's health and that he was perfectly capable of performing. Rostropovich was allowed to perform.

Told by Menuhin in May 1991.

Vivien MERCHANT

(1929–83) English actress.

—— 7 ——

When her husband, Harold Pinter, left her for Lady Antonia Fraser, Merchant was devastated. In a newspaper interview she came up with this classic example of the higher bitchery: 'He didn't need to take a change of shoes. He can always wear hers. She has very big feet, you know.'

Quoted in *The Observer* (21 December 1975).

Ethel MERMAN

(1909–84) American actress and singer, whose foghorn voice and forceful personality dominated shows such as *Annie Get Your Gun* and *Gipsy*.

—— 1 ——

When Irving Berlin was still fiddling with a song lyric just prior to the opening of a show in which Merman appeared, she refused to accept any more changes. 'Call me Miss Birds Eye,' she told Berlin, 'this show is frozen.'

Quoted in *The Times* (13 July 1985). The song may have been from *Annie Get Your Gun* or *Call Me Madam*.

—— 2 ——

Cole Porter once said of Merman that she reminded him of a brass band going by.

Quoted in *The Guardian* (16 February 1984).

William MERVYN

(1912–76) English actor, born to play bishops (which he did).

—— 3 ——

One of the first interviews I ever conducted on television was with William Mervyn, a bald, benign figure who suddenly had a great deal of success in late middle age before his rather early death. I think that in 1967, when I did the interview, he had two or three TV series running concurrently – or perhaps he had series running simultaneously on all the three channels that were then available. Anyway, already having a well-developed ear for cliché, I began by remarking, 'Well, Mr Mervyn, you seem to have struck oil.' Neatly seizing on the cliché, he replied, 'Yes, dear boy, but I've been drilling for thirty years . . .'

The 'dear boy' may be another clichéd interpolation by me. The interview was at Granada TV in Manchester on 10 April 1967.

Leonard MIALL

(1914–) English broadcaster and executive, latterly historian and obituarist.

—— 4 ——

A group from the BBC was in Italy years ago and its members were invited to a grand house for lunch. They were told that the house had a very wonderful garden but it turned out to be a bit of shambles. Miall said to his companion, 'This garden rather looks as if it was laid out by Incapability Bruno'.

Told by Sir Huw Wheldon on BBC Radio *Quote...Unquote* (1985).

Bette MIDLER

(1945–) American comedienne and actress. Charmingly vulgar and well-endowed.

—— 5 ——

Her first name is pronounced 'Bet' because her parents mistakenly thought that Bette Davis did likewise.

A fact.

Michael MILES

(1919–71) New Zealand-born TV presenter in Britain. He was 'your quiz inquisitor' on ITV's *Take Your Pick*, which ran for almost twenty years from 1955.

—— 6 ——

Take Your Pick contestants were given the option of opening a numbered box (which might contain anything from air tickets to Ena Sharples's hairnet) or of accepting a sum of money which might turn out to be worth more – or less – than what was in the box. The studio audience would chant its advice to the contestant – usually, 'Open the box!' So when Miles died, it was said that as his coffin was brought into the church, his funeral was interrupted by the congregation shouting, 'Open the box! Open the box!'

Source unknown, but included in my *Very Interesting...But Stupid!* (1980).

Edna St Vincent MILLAY

(1892–1950) American dramatist and poet.

—— 1 ——

Noël Coward, Beverly Nichols and Godfrey Winn were all invited to join Somerset Maugham at the Villa Mauresque in Cap Ferrat in order to have lunch with Millay. As she swept on to the terrace overlooking the blue Mediterranean, she exclaimed: 'Oh, Mr Maugham, but this is fairyland!'

Quoted in Ted Morgan, *Maugham* (1980). S. N. Behrman in *Tribulations and Laughter* (1972) has a version where the line-up is Coward, Cecil Beaton and Gerald Haxton.

Jonathan MILLER

(1934–) English doctor, opera director and polymath.

—— 2 ——

Someone said of Miller that he is 'too clever by three quarters'.

In my diary entry for 9 September 1975, I put, 'He is just "too clever by three quarters" yet he redeems it with a twinkle in his eye' – which would suggest it was an established view by that date.

Karl MILLER

(1931–) Scottish editor and academic.

—— 3 ——

When Miller was an undergraduate at Cambridge, he called on a friend whom he found *in flagrante*. So he left note saying, 'Called to see you but you were in.'

Quoted in a *Cosmopolitan* (UK) article (*c.* 1979).

Spike MILLIGAN

(1918–) Irish writer and entertainer, principally remembered for his scripts and performances for the radio *Goon Show*.

—— 4 ——

One day Milligan walked into an undertakers' shop in Camden Town, lay down on the floor and cried, 'Shop!'

Told by Harry Secombe or Peter Sellers on a BBC TV *Parkinson* chat show, 1970s.

See also WAUGH 191:4.

Liza MINELLI

(1946–) American singer and actress.

—— 5 ——

At the end of an interview on BBC TV *Nationwide*, the star was no doubt slightly put out when Hugh Scully, the interviewer, said, 'Thank you, Judy Garland.' But she rallied, and said, with aplomb: 'I'll tell Liza.'

Told by Ludovic Kennedy on BBC Radio *Quote...Unquote* (1983).

See also VREELAND 189:2.

Sese Seko MOBUTO

(1930–) Zaïrean president.

—— 1 ——

Mobuto once said, 'All journalists are spies – I know, I have been one.' He also said, 'The people of Zaïre are not thieves. It merely happens that they move things, or borrow them.'

Quoted in *The Sunday Times* (28 May 1978).

Monty MODLYN

(1921–94) English cockney personality and broadcaster. Like a rubber ball, he bounced through a series of radio and TV programmes in the 1960s and 70s. Once persuaded President Idi Amin to play the accordion, which was rather embarrassing.

—— 2 ——

Modlyn was once interviewing a doubly-titled peer for TV. It was Lord De L'Isle and Dudley, the owner of Penshurst Place in Kent. Throughout the interview, Modlyn addressed him as 'Lord De L'Isle . . . and Dudley' – rather as though 'Dudley' was the butler and standing just behind him . . .

This must have been for Thames TV's *Today* programme in the early 1970s.

V. M. MOLOTOV

(1890–1986) Russian politician. Soviet foreign minister at the outbreak of the Second World War.

—— 3 ——

A British diplomat once compared Molotov to 'a refrigerator when the light has gone out'.

Quoted in *Time* (24 November 1986). Winston Churchill said Molotov had 'a smile like the Siberian winter'.

Marilyn MONROE

(1926–62) American film actress and eternal sex symbol.

—— 4 ——

Addressing an audience of ten thousand US marines she said, 'I hear all you guys get all excited about sweater girls. I don't know why. I mean, take away their sweaters and what have they got?'

Told by Stefan Buczacki on BBC Radio *Quote...Unquote* (1988).

—— 5 ——

When asked if she had had anything on when being photographed for a calendar, she replied, 'Well, I had the radio on.'

Quoted in *Time* (11 August 1952).

—— 6 ——

When she was about to be married to Arthur Miller, she paid a visit to her prospective – Jewish – parents-in-law and was served matzo balls. After picking at them with a fork and obviously thinking very deeply about them, she turned to her loved one and asked, 'Arthur, isn't there another part of the matzo we could eat?'

Oral tradition. No doubt apocryphal.

—— 7 ——

Eve Arnold, the photographer, was summoned by Monroe to her suite at the Waldorf Hotel, New York, where the actress was also expecting a journalist. Monroe opened the door wearing a diaphanous black negligée and carrying a hairbrush. In due course, she asked if those present minded if she brushed her hair. 'Of course not,' said the journalist, and Monroe proceeded to brush her pubic hair.

Recounted by Eve Arnold in *The Independent on Sunday* (24 May 1992).

—— 8 ——

Monroe was asked if all the haggling over money and contracts in the movie business ever got her down. 'I'm not worried about the money,' she replied, 'I just want to be *wonderful* . . .'

Quoted in Peter Potter, *All About Money* (1988).

—— 1 ——

Monroe was chronically unpunctual. In May 1962, she was due to sing 'Happy Birthday, Mr President' at a birthday party for John F. Kennedy in Madison Square Garden, New York. She kept the audience of 22,000 people waiting so long that when she did eventually arrive, Peter Lawford introduced her as 'the late Marilyn Monroe'. She died three months later.

Source untraced.

1st Viscount MONTGOMERY of Alamein

(1887–1976) English soldier and the foremost self-publicist of his age.

—— 2 ——

Churchill said to King George VI, 'I'm worried about Monty – I think he's after my job.' And the king said, 'Thank God! I thought he was after mine.'

This version quoted in *The Observer*, 30 August 1992.

—— 3 ——

Montgomery once said, 'Consider what the Lord said to Moses – and I think he was right . . .'

For a long time, I was under the impression that this was something Montgomery – that blushing violet – had *actually* said. Then I came across the line in a sketch called 'Salvation Army' performed by Lance Percival as an army officer (albeit with a Montgomery accent) on BBC TV's *That Was the Week That Was* (1962/3). So that must have been the start of it, though it is totally in character.
Then I discovered in *The Lyttelton Hart-Davis Letters* (Vol. 4 – relating to 1959), exactly the same joke in the form, 'Did you hear of the parson who began his sermon, "As God said – and rightly..."?' No mention of Montgomery. Compare also a remark by Donald Coggan, Archbishop of Canterbury, on 7 June 1977, in a sermon for the Queen's Silver Jubilee service at St Paul's Cathedral: 'We listened to these words of Jesus [St Matthew 7:24] a few moments ago.' Then he exclaimed: 'How right he was!' One is reminded irresistibly of Lorenz Hart's stripper's song 'Zip' from *Pal Joey* (1940):

I was reading Schopenhauer last night,
And I think that Schopenhauer was right . . .

Compare also what William Jackson, Bishop of Oxford, once preached (according to *The Oxford Book of Oxford*, 1978): 'St Paul says in one of his Epistles — and I partly agree with him...'

—— 4 ——

In the 1960s, when moves were afoot to legalize homosexual activities between consenting adults, Montgomery was fundamentally opposed to what he termed a 'Buggers' Charter'. At the committee stage of the parliamentary bill, he suggested raising the age of consent from the age of 21 to 80. He then added, disarmingly, that he would himself be reaching his four-score years at his next birthday.

Recounted by Mervyn Stockwood in *Chanctonbury Ring* (1982).

Kenneth MORE

(1914–82) English stage and screen actor in chummy, back-slapping, 'Hello, old boy' parts.

—— 5 ——

During the Second World War, More found himself becalmed in a naval desk job at Liverpool. Wishing to see some action, he was told that the best way of bringing this about was to have his appendix out. A retired Petty Officer told him: 'Have an attack on duty. Suddenly grasp your side. Fall down in agony. Cry out with pain. You were an actor, weren't you? They'll have you off to hospital and whip your appendix out in no time. Then you'll go on sick leave. When you come back, you'll be posted somewhere else – to a ship, most likely.' More did exactly that, had his (extremely healthy) appendix taken out in a naval nursing home at Blundellsands, and in due course was posted as Watch Keeping Officer to a light cruiser, *Aurora*. This was in May 1942.

As recounted in his memoirs *Happy Go Lucky* (1959) and *More Or Less* (1978).

—— 6 ——

Angela Douglas, More's wife of his later years, once stunned their friends with the news that Kennie had landed a part in 'Chekhov's *The Three Seagulls*'.

As recounted by her on BBC Radio *Quote...Unquote* (1985).

Eric MORECAMBE

(1926–84) Likeable English comedian who was teamed with the excellent foil, Ernie Wise. The annual *Morecambe and Wise Christmas Show*, especially on BBC TV, was part of what people now think Christmas used to be like.

1

When Eric and Ernie appeared for the third time at the Glasgow Empire – notorious graveyard of English comic talent – they walked off stage to complete silence. The stage doorkeeper confided in them: 'Aye, lads, they're beginning to like you.'

Recalled in Roger Wilmut, *Kindly Leave the Stage* (1985).

2

When Eric had a heart attack in Leeds, it was 'like a Brian Rix farce', he said afterwards. He lay helpless in his Jensen in the deserted streets at about one o'clock in the morning, and the only living human being around was 'this man who'd been in the Territorial Army'. 'I asked him if he could drive,' Eric recalled, 'and he drove my £7000 motor car like a tank, for miles.' Then this man had to wake someone up at the hospital. Finally, as they wheeled Eric into intensive care, he heard the man whisper in his ear: 'Can I have your autograph before you go? . . .'

This version is largely as told to John Mortimer for *In Character* (1983). It had earlier appeared in a book called *Eric & Ernie* (1978).

3

On another occasion, Eric suffered heart trouble while he and Ernie were rehearsing a sketch for their Christmas show at Thames Television. They were deep in discussion of some difficult move when Eric succumbed. After a while spent lying on the studio floor, he was carried off by medical staff to an ambulance. Everyone turned to Ernie for his reaction. 'Well,' he said, 'I still think it would be better if I went through the door before speaking the line rather than after . . .'

Told to me by Barry Cryer in *c.* 1980. Compare the story from *Ego 3* (1938) by James Agate: one day in 1915 the woman partner of a bridge-fiend messed up a hand to such an extent that the old man made a considerable fuss about how the hand should have been played. A few days later, news arrived of the death of the old man's only son at the Front and naturally he did not play bridge for several weeks. When he did show up, the woman ex-

claimed, 'My dear Doctor F——, I am so sorry. I am so very sorry!' The old man gazed vindictively at her and said, 'That is all very well, madam, but it's too late. Had you led the King of Spades and followed it up with the Knave . . .'

John MORTIMER

(1923–) English playwright, novelist and QC, now stuck with his 'champagne socialist' tag.

4

Mortimer was in the crush bar at the Royal Opera House, Covent Garden, just before a production of *Don Carlo*, conducted by Giulini, directed by Visconti, and starring Placido Domingo. In came a 'Hunting Henry' character who asked loudly of his companion: 'What are they givin' us tonight, darlin'? Singin' or dancin'?'

As told by him on BBC Radio *Quote...Unquote* (1979).

5

On one occasion Mortimer was defending a 'lady singer' on drugs charges and heard himself going a trifle over the top in his final appeal to the Uxbridge magistrates. 'Give her justice,' he pleaded, 'for justice is what she has waited all these long weeks for – but let it be justice tempered with that mercy which is the hallmark of the Uxbridge and Hillingdon District Magistrates' Court . . .'

As recounted by him (1979). The singer was Julie Felix.

See also JUDGES 118:5.

MOTHERS-IN-LAW

—— 1 ——

Irvin S. Cobb in the foreword to *A Laugh a Day Keeps the Doctor Away* (1923), while asserting that there was only one mother-in-law joke in his collection, stated: 'The mother-in-law joke could not have originated with Adam, because Adam had no mother-in-law, but I have not the slightest doubt that Cain began using it shortly after his marriage.' Quite when the mother-in-law joke came to be recognized as a distinct species is impossible to tell, but Jerome K. Jerome in *Three Men In a Boat* (1889) has this in Chapter 3: 'Everything has its drawbacks, as the man said when his mother-in-law died, and they came down upon him for the funeral expenses.'

'Now that many years have passed since my delightful mother-in-law was called to that large mothers-in-law's meeting in the sky, I am often still to be found smiling at her remarks. She had a wonderful habit of getting expressions just slightly wrong. "Making money while the hay shines" was typical. And I remember once in church hearing her intoning, with very serious face, the words of the 23rd Psalm – "He maketh me to lie down in green waters".'

Told to me by Stanley Menzies of Church Stretton (1992).

Ted MOULT

(1926–86) English farmer with a thick Yorkshire accent who turned himself into a professional personality and – like a number of that band – eventually killed himself.

—— 2 ——

Moult appeared as a panellist on countless radio and TV quizzes and it was often said that he had once won BBC Radio's 'Brain of Britain' title. In fact, when he took part in the 1959 contest he was beaten in the first round.

His fame began rather with *What Do You Know?* and *Ask Me Another*. Information from Richard Edis, a later producer of *Brain of Britain*.

Sir James MURRAY

(1837–1915) Scottish philologist and lexicographer. Founding editor of *The Oxford English Dictionary*.

—— 3 ——

His favourite text was a saying of Charles Kingsley, which hung – rather curiously – in his bedroom: 'Have thy tools ready, God will find thee work.'

Quoted by K. M. Elizabeth Murray in *Caught in the Web of Words* (1977). This reminds me of the overheard remark (included in my *Eavesdroppings*, 1981): 'And, my dear, there was nothing in that room but a great double bed. And there was a framed text on the wall above it which said, "He is coming".'

Benito MUSSOLINI

(1883–1945) Italian dictator.

—— 4 ——

Mussolini is said to have styled his dress on that of Laurel and Hardy, his favourite film stars, whose 'sartorial distinctiveness he regarded as the embodiment of transatlantic chic'. He only changed his habit when told that Laurel and Hardy were more widely perceived as figures of fun, not as models of sophistication.

Thus according to A. N. Wilson, *Hilaire Belloc* (1984), who acknowledges D. Mack Smith, *Mussolini* (1981). However, Mack Smith merely says that Mussolini *stopped* dressing in this way because of Laurel and Hardy, not that he imitated their sartorial style.

N

NAME-DROPPERS

—— 1 ——

A colleague once remonstrated with William Clark, a one-time diplomatic correspondent and press secretary to Anthony Eden when prime minister: 'You are the most incorrigible name-dropper I have ever met.' To which he replied, 'Funny you should say that, old boy. The Queen Mother was saying the same thing only last week.'

> Recalled in *The Observer* (18 June 1989) and frequently put in the mouths of other folk. For example, from *The Daily Telegraph* (21 June 1979): 'Towards the end of his speech at the Museum of the Year Award lunch, Norman St John Stevas, Arts Minister, is reliably reported as saying: "But I mustn't go on singling out names... One must not be a name-dropper, as Her Majesty remarked to me yesterday."'

Fridtjof NANSEN

(1861–1930) Norwegian explorer in the Arctic and, from 1906 to 1908, his country's first ambassador in London.

—— 2 ——

Daniele Varè described how he met Nansen and tried to draw him out on the subject of his adventures. All Nansen would say was, 'The cold of the polar regions was nothing to the chill of an English bedroom.'

> Described by Varè in *The Laughing Diplomat* (1939).

Terry NATION

British TV scriptwriter and originator of *Dr Who* on BBC TV (from 1963).

—— 3 ——

Nation liked to explain how he named the Daleks, his most famous creation – menacing pepperpot-like machines which went around screeching, 'Exterminate! Exterminate!' He took the name, so he said, from the spine of an encyclopedia volume covering DAL to LEK. Later, however, he said this story had only been invented to satisfy journalists. In fact, the name 'simply rolled off the typewriter'.

> Sources: *Radio Times* (30 December 1971); *The Doctor Who Tenth Anniversary Special* (1973).

NEIGHBOURS

—— 4 ——

When asked to look after their house and pets by neighbours who were going away on holiday, the Joneses readily agreed. They duly looked after the dog but completely forgot about feeding the rabbit until one day the dog brought it in, dead and bloody. Full of remorse, the Joneses cleaned up the rabbit and put it in the cage, so that it would appear to have died a natural death. When the neighbours returned, the Joneses received a rather puzzled telephone call from them. This conveyed the information that the rabbit had died the day before they left for their holiday – 'and we buried him in the garden'.

> This was told to me by Gemma O'Connor in August 1989 and it was not until some time later that I began to appreciate that it was another of those 'urban legends' that go the rounds and are always related as though they had happened to a friend – or a friend of a friend – of the teller. It also gets told as a joke. In a BBC TV documentary about Jewish humour, screened in February 1990, a joke was told of a woman wanting to take a red cocker

spaniel with her on a plane going to Israel. She was told that this was not possible and that the dog would have to travel in the hold. On arrival, the baggage handlers had to find another red cocker spaniel to substitute for the one that had apparently died during the flight. But the woman had been taking her *dead* dog back to Israel to bury it.

NEWSREADERS

—— 1 ——

In these days of radio and TV 'all-news' stations broadcasting round the clock, it is salutary to be reminded that in the early days of British radio, if the view was taken that there was no news worthy of the name, an announcer would come on and say, simply, 'There is no news tonight. We will have some piano music instead.'

> Sources: The BBC's *Review of the Year 1930*, quoted in Asa Briggs, *The Golden Age of Wireless* (1965), and Ludovic Kennedy, 'The World Is Too Much With Us', The Standard Telephones and Cables Communication Lecture for 1982.

—— 2 ——

On 25 December 1950, Scottish nationalists removed the Stone of Scone from under the Coronation Chair in Westminster Abbey. It is said that Lionel Marson, a senior BBC newsreader gave the news and added that, 'The stone was first brought to England in 1297 by Edward Isst.' Summoned afterwards to tell the Head of Presentation what on earth he had meant by saying 'Edward Isst' he is supposed to have replied lamely, 'How was I supposed to know it was Edward Iced?'

> Told by Brian Matthew on BBC Radio *Quote...Unquote* (1980). The first part is probably true, the second part probably apocryphal. Jack de Manio in *To Auntie With Love* (1967) has a version related by John Snagge, who was the Head of Presentation in question.

—— 3 ——

In a BBC Radio 2 news bulletin, James Alexander Gordon intended to inform listeners that a certain Chancellor of the Exchequer had delivered his 'mini-Budget'. Instead, he referred to it as a 'bunny midget'.

> Told to me by James Alexander Gordon in 1983.

—— 4 ——

There is a definite art to reading out football results, not best demonstrated by the stand-in at ITN who began the list by saying, 'League Division One, Arsenal 2.' It thus appeared that a team called League Division had been beaten by The Gunners. He then proceeded to the end – only to find that he had one team left which had evidently not been playing anybody.

> Source: *Daily Star* (17 September 1985).

—— 5 ——

A BBC newsreader summarizing the weather forecast at the end of a bulletin spoke of 'a trough of low pleasure passing over Europe'.

> Recalled on BBC Radio *Quote...Unquote* (1979). Said to have been perpetrated by Robert Dougall.

—— 6 ——

In the mid-1970s there was a kidnapper and murderer in the English Midlands whom the popular press dubbed 'The Black Panther'. When he was eventually brought to book, a Radio 4 newsreader (who curiously continued to find employment for many years thereafter) told an astonished nation: 'At Oxford Crown Court today, the jury has been told that Donald Neilsen denied being the Pink Panther . . .'

> Well, he would, wouldn't he? The newsreader in question, as he readily admits, was Edward Cole and this must have been around 2 July 1976. Checked against a recording of the incident.

—— 7 ——

It has been said that it is all too easy for newsreaders to read whatever is put before them without allowing the material to be tasted beforehand by their brains. At lunch-time one day on Radio 4, a newsreader with this failing said that someone was 'unable to revive Mr X despite giving him the kiss of death'.

> Recorded in my diary on 7 July 1968. The newsreader, for whom this was an unusual lapse, was Robin Holmes.

—— 8 ——

A BBC foreign correspondent reporting the 1973 October War in the Middle East referred to the possibility of 'lesbian forces moving down from the north towards Israel'.

I think I have heard a recording of this. It is one of those jokes that is just waiting to happen again. In *The Kenneth Williams Diaries* (1993) – entry for 17 June 1969 – the comedian quotes his aged mother saying, 'Oh! they're opening a lesbian restaurant there!' He corrects her: 'It's Lebanese', and notes that she went on: 'Yes . . . they're all over the place now, aren't they?'

—— 1 ——

There was a marvellous slip by a rather po-faced newsreader belonging to the Rhodesian Broadcasting Corporation (prior, of couse, to it becoming the Zimbabwe Broadcasting Corporation). He referred to 'Aristotle Onassis, the Greek shitting tycoon'.

I heard this myself in Rhodesia and recorded it in my diary on 23 September 1977.

—— 2 ——

During the 1980 US presidential election, a newsreader on the BBC World Service told his startled audience: 'Mr Ronald Reagan has lost his head over President Carter . . . er . . . Mr Ronald Reagan has lost his *lead* over President Carter.'

The incident occurred on 20 September 1980 and I heard it.

—— 3 ——

A newsreader on BBC Radio 4 said: 'In response to complaints from the touring company of *Oh! Calcutta!*, the nude revue, that they were suffering from the cold, the theatre management has agreed to install fan heaters.'

The incident occurred on 12 December 1981.

Olivia NEWTON-JOHN

(1948–) British-born pop singer, raised in Australia. At the age of 30, to much amazement, she played a virgin schoolgirl in the film *Grease*.

—— 4 ——

It was once said of her: 'If white bread could sing, it would sound like Olivia Newton-John.'

Quoted in *The Telegraph Sunday Magazine* (September 1980).

Mike NICHOLS

(1931–) German-born American actor and director. Originally known for his witty sketches, written and performed with Elaine May.

—— 5 ——

The following exchange was overheard by someone sitting behind Nichols on a plane flying to London. The plane hit an air pocket and dropped precipitously about three hundred feet. A woman sitting next to Nichols turned on him furiously and said, 'What do we do *now*, Mr Success?'

Told by John Lahr on BBC Radio *Quote...Unquote* (1983).

—— 6 ——

During rehearsals for the Broadway production of Neil Simon's *The Odd Couple*, Nichols had a furious row with Walter Matthau, calling him every name under the sun and calling into question every possible characteristic the actor might have, and all this in front of the assembled cast and stage crew. When the row finally subsided, Matthau helped break the ice by calling out, in earshot of everyone, 'Hey, Mike, can I have my balls back, please?' Nichols called out, 'Props!'

Oral tradition.

David NIVEN

(1910–83) English film actor.

—— 7 ——

Although Noël Coward often recycled witticisms from his own conversation in his plays, there is one firm example of a borrowed witticism from Niven. A Coward diary note for 10 December 1954 states: 'Lunched and dined with Darryl Zanuck who, David Niven wickedly said, is the only man who can eat an apple through a tennis racquet!' This ended up as 'She could eat an apple through a tennis racquet' in Coward's play *Come Into the Garden, Maud* (1966).

—— 8 ——

Niven's first wife, Primmie, died tragically at Tyrone Power's house during a game of Sardines – in which everyone is squashed together in a closet, or similar place, and one person has to wander about in the dark trying to find them. Alas, Primmie opened a door in the dark and fell down a flight of stone steps. As she waited for the ambulance, she murmured the thought that was obviously troubling her most, 'We'll never be invited again . . .'

Recounted in Sheridan Morley, *The Other Side of the Moon* (1985).

Richard NIXON

(1913–94) 37th president of the US, who resigned under threat of impeachment in 1974.

—— 1 ——

When Nixon visited Britain as vice-president in 1958, he appeared on BBC TV's *Press Conference*. The production team was interested to be told in advance by an American security officer: 'If make-up is required, it will be applied by the vice-president's Military Aide.'

Told by Leonard Miall in *The Independent* (13 May 1991).

—— 2 ——

When Nixon lost to Kennedy in the 1960 presidential election, it was said that the TV debates had been an important factor in his defeat. He came over less well than Kennedy, who looked 'tanned, rested and fit', not least because Nixon visibly perspired, refused TV make-up, and allowed only minor treatment of his five o'clock shadow.

J. Leonard Reinsch, who masterminded Kennedy's success in these debates, also made things hard for Nixon by suggesting that the two candidates ought to stand during the first hour-long debate. He knew that Nixon had just injured his knee on a car door.

Sources: Richard Nixon, *Memoirs*, 1978; Leonard Miall in his obituary of Reinsch, *The Independent* (13 May 1991).

—— 3 ——

In 1962, Nixon was signing copies of his book *Six Crises* in a bookshop in California. When he asked one purchaser what dedicatee's name he should inscribe in the book, the customer said, 'You've just met your seventh crisis, Mr Nixon. My name is Stanislaus Wojechzlechki!'

Quoted in *Reader's Digest* (November 1962).

See also FROST 88:4.

Denis NORDEN

(1922–) English comedy scriptwriter, TV presenter and panellist.

—— 4 ——

In the 1950s, Norden had a hugely successful scriptwriting partnership with Frank Muir. They wrote *Breakfast with Braden*, *Take It From Here* and much else. On one occasion, the BBC bureaucracy paid them twice for the same script. When this was discovered, the BBC asked for the overpayment to be returned. Naturally reluctant to do any such thing, Muir and Norden concocted a reply which stated that 'Messrs Muir and Norden regret that they have no machinery for the return of cheques.' Apparently, this satisfied the BBC bureaucracy.

Untraced. As I discovered for myself when I was also paid twice by the BBC for a whole series of programmes, the bureaucracy has become a little wiser since then. Any overpayment is now merely deducted from future payments. I like the cheek of the Muir and Norden message, however. It is reminiscent of the way things are done in the army. If you break something, it is very important to retain the broken pieces. All the bureaucracy is interested in is that a mistake can be 'accounted for'.

Ivor NOVELLO

(1893–1951) Welsh actor, composer, songwriter and dramatist.

—— 5 ——

In 1944, the much-fêted Novello was imprisoned for two months (halved on appeal) for infringing wartime regulations which restricted the use of petrol for non-essential purposes. This should give pause for reflection to those who still campaign for a posthumous knighthood to be given to their hero.

Recounted in W. MacQueen Pope, *Ivor* (1951).

Lord NUFFIELD

(William Morris) (1877–1963) English motor
magnate and philanthropist.

—— 1 ——

Nuffield had been dining at an Oxford college. On
his departure, a porter produced his hat rather
quickly. Nuffield inquired, 'How d'you know it's
mine?' The porter replied: 'I don't, my Lord. But it's
the one you came with.'

> Recounted by James Morris in *Oxford* (1965). He
> was told it by the 'elderly servant' who adminis-
> tered the remark.

Trevor NUNN

(1940–) English stage director who, after much
serious work with the Royal Shakespeare
Company, became involved in money-making
musicals. Famous for 'Trevving' – i.e. embracing
and/or flattering people who are not entirely sure
what lies behind the gesture – though they
usually end up playing a part they had no
intention of accepting.

—— 2 ——

While he was running the Royal Shakespeare
Company, I once had to interview Nunn for
the BBC Radio arts programme *Kaleidoscope* and was
told in advance that he did not like 'microphone
interviews'. But when I went along to the Aldwych
Theatre, I was quite unprepared for him to throw up
his hands in horror at my first question – 'What did
you inherit from Peter Hall?' He clammed up and
asked to be allowed to walk round the stalls on his
own to think what to say. Eventually, he returned
and did an excellent interview.

> Recorded in my diary for 4 July 1974. I added: 'He
> all but embraced me for my patience . . . but it does
> seem remarkable that the head of a vast organiza-
> tion like the RSC – dealing in communication – has
> to go through all this to present a public image.'

—— 3 ——

Directing Nicol Williamson in *Richard III*, Nunn
was taking infinite trouble over how to kill off
the young princes in the tower. Williamson, exasperated at how long all this was taking, cried out: 'Why
don't you take them into the wings and bore them to
death?'

> Told by Sheila Hancock on BBC Radio
> *Quote...Unquote* (1989).

—— 4 ——

When Nunn was sole artistic director and chief
executive of the Royal Shakespeare Company,
he appeared to absent himself so frequently to work
in the commercial theatre (directing the musical *Cats*
and the like), that some RSC actors began to pine for
his presence. One of them even suggested that they
should write to *Jim'll Fix It* to see if the TV show could
arrange a meeting . . .

> Nunn is not very fond of this story. Indeed, he
> wrote at length to *The Independent* Magazine (26
> June 1993) trying to establish the correct facts. An
> actor 'friend' of his had, indeed, joked about
> making contact through the good offices of Jimmy
> Savile on an occasion when Nunn was absent from
> a company meeting. But, Nunn protested, this was
> during the period when he was joint artistic direc-
> tor of the RSC and entitled to work elsewhere for
> three months of each year.

NUNS

—— 5 ——

A young nun entered an order which operated a
strict vow of silence. She was told that the vow
could only be broken once every three years and
then only by the use of two words. So, after the first
three years, the girl goes to the Mother Superior and
says: 'Uncomfortable beds'. The Mother Superior,
'Right, my child, you have had your say and now
must return to your duties.'

Three more years pass and again the nun has the
opportunity to say two words to the Mother Superior. 'Bad food,' she says. 'Right,' says the Mother
Superior, 'you may return to your work.'

Another three years pass and the no-longer young
nun returns again to the Mother Superior and an-
nounces – in more than two words – 'I wish to go
home.'

'Thank goodness,' replies the Mother Superior,
'you've done nothing but bitch since you got
here . . .'

> This is a joke – told as an example of a joke – in John
> Osborne's play *Hotel in Amsterdam* (1968). In a
> version about a monastery, it is told by Lord Delfont
> in *Pass the Port* (1976).

Des O'CONNOR

(1932–) British entertainer, at one time chiefly famous through jokes about his singing style made by the comedians Morecambe and Wise.

—— 1 ——

The old Glasgow Empire theatre was a noted graveyard for aspiring comedians, especially those coming from south of the border. The audiences were famously hostile – ice-cream cones and shipyard rivets were said to have rained down on hapless comedians. The slow handclap, cries of 'Away and catch yer train', 'Och, go bile your heed', were among the methods used to wear down newcomers. On one occasion, the young O'Connor, who is nothing if not an all-round entertainer, was finding it extremely difficult to get any response from the audience. He sang, he danced, he told jokes, and then started working his way through a whole bandstand's worth of instruments. As he reached for a trumpet, a voice arose drily from the audience, and said, 'Och, is there no end to this man's talent?'

From Des O'Connor's own reminiscences, recorded for the BBC in 1985, and as recounted by Arnold Brown (1990).

David OGILVY

(1911–) British-born advertising executive, mostly working in the US.

—— 2 ——

Ogilvy said that the best advertising headline he had ever written contained *eighteen* words: 'At Sixty Miles an Hour the Loudest Noise in the New Rolls-Royce comes from the electric clock.' He recalled that when the chief engineer at the Rolls-Royce factory read this, he shook his head sadly and said,

'It is time we did something about that damned clock.'

From Ogilvy's *Confessions of an Advertising Man* (1963). The ad first appeared in 1958.

—— 3 ——

Raymond Rubicam's famous slogan for Squibb drug products, 'The priceless ingredient of every product is the honour and integrity of its maker', reminded Ogilvy of his father's advice: 'When a company boasts about its integrity, or a woman about her virtue, avoid the former and cultivate the latter.'

Quoted in ibid.

Sir Laurence OLIVIER

(1907–89) The supreme British actor of his age, also a theatre and film director, and first head of the National Theatre. Made a life peer 1970.

—— 4 ——

The physical appearance of Olivier's most famous creation on stage and screen – King Richard III – was based upon the American theatre director Jed Harris, whom Olivier also took the trouble to describe as 'the most loathsome man' he had ever met. The voice was based on imitations he had heard people do of Sir Henry Irving – 'I only used three notes.'

Sources: Laurence Olivier, *On Acting* (1986) and John Mortimer, *In Character* (1983).

—— 5 ——

In the famous production of Sophocles' *Oedipus Rex* at the New Theatre, London, in 1945, Olivier emitted a terrible scream when the tragic, blinded hero realizes the full horror of his sins. The particular nature of the scream was derived from a method of catching ermine that he had heard about. In the Arctic, they put down salt and the ermine comes to lick it and his tongue freezes to the ice. 'I thought about that when I screamed as Oedipus,' Olivier said.

As told to John Mortimer for a newspaper interview and collected in In Character *(1983). John Osborne in* Almost a Gentleman *(1991) rather oddly, or revealingly, seems to think that the ermine cry was used when Olivier was playing Shylock. See also Kenneth Tynan's review of the production incorporated in* A View of the English Stage *(1975).*

—— 1 ——

Olivier could be embarrassingly frank about his sexual performance. In particular, he worried about the smallness of his equipment. His second wife, Vivien Leigh, didn't help by being something of a nymphomaniac. After the first performance of *Uncle Vanya*, the Olivier production which opened the Chichester Festival Theatre in 1962, he was unhappy with the way it had gone. In his dressing room afterwards he confessed that it had gone off at 'half-cock'. 'Better half-cock,' rejoined Vivien Leigh, 'than no cock at all.'

I first heard this from an actor friend in 1983. If this really occurred at Chichester, Olivier and Leigh had already been divorced since 1960 and Olivier was now married to Joan Plowright (who was appearing with him in Uncle Vanya*).*

—— 2 ——

When Olivier undertook to play Shylock in a National Theatre production of *The Merchant of Venice* in 1970, the director was Jonathan Miller who had famously declared in *Beyond the Fringe*, 'I'm not really a Jew. Only Jew-*ish*. Not the whole hog, you know.' Miller was disconcerted to find that Olivier intended to give the part with all the subtlety of a Fagin played by Donald Wolfit. 'I do so love the Hebrew!' Olivier declared. Miller responded by suggesting that his love might be a little more appreciated if he did not wear false teeth and a larger-than-life false nose.

Recounted by Miller in a TV obituary for Olivier in 1989.

—— 3 ——

When he was making the film *Marathon Man* with Dustin Hoffman, Olivier was aghast at one of the techniques used by the young actor. In order to make himself look the way the script required, as though he had been two nights without sleep, Hoffman went for two nights without sleep. In consequence, he was in a terrible state. Olivier put it to him, 'Dear boy, why not try acting?'

A much-told story. Another version was published in The Times *(17 May 1982): 'Dear boy, you look absolutely awful. Why don't you try acting? It's so much easier.'* Marathon Man *was released in 1976.*

—— 4 ——

Olivier appeared by default in an overheard remark which was gathered from the immortal 'two ladies on a bus'. 'We went to Camber Sands on Saturday . . .', said one. 'Was it nice?' asked the other. 'Well, there's miles of sand. In fact, they filmed parts of that Lawrence of Olivier there.'

Told to me by Chris Knipe of Reading and included in Eavesdroppings *(1981).*

—— 5 ——

Olivier agreed to take part in a TV advertising campaign for Polaroid cameras. In it, he had to utter the lumpish slogan, 'You will feel like you are looking at the world for the first time.' No wonder he only did the commercials on condition that they would never be shown in Britain where he might have to watch them himself.

Source untraced.

—— 6 ——

Olivier was given a special Oscar at the Academy Awards in 1979. His acceptance speech had some of the audience weeping into their tuxedos, the rest wondering whether perhaps he would have done better to leave his scriptwriting to Shakespeare, or someone like that. His text went: 'Mr President and governors of the Academy, committee members, Fellows, my very noble and approved good masters [that bit *was* by Shakespeare], my friends, my fellow students . . . in the great wealth, the great firmament of your nation's generosities, this particular choice may perhaps be found by future generations as a trifle eccentric but the mere fact of it, the prodigal, pure, human kindness of it must be seen as a beautiful star in that firmament which shines upon me at this moment, dazzling me a little, but filling me with warmth and the extraordinary elation, the euphoria that happens to so many of us at the first breath of the majestic glow of the new tomorrow. From the top of this moment, in the solace, in the kindly emotion that is charging my soul and my heart at this moment, I thank you for this great gift which lends me such a very splendid part in this glorious occasion. Thank you.'

From a transcript of the speech.

OPERA SINGERS

—— 1 ——

When Stella Roman was playing Tosca in Puccini's opera, she was supposed to leap to her death from a prison parapet and land safely off-stage on a mattress. Roman, feeling insecure one night, demanded two extra mattresses to be placed to ease her fall. She leaped, and the mattresses bounced her back on stage. She had to kill herself all over again.

This version comes from Robert Merrill and Robert Saffron, *Between Acts* (1978). Hugo Vickers, *Great Operatic Disasters* (1979) claims the story originated with 'a large young American' at the City Center, New York in 1960, when a trampoline was placed instead of a mattress and the singer 'came up 15 times before the curtain fell'.

—— 2 ——

In a 1936 production of Wagner's *Lohengrin* at the Metropolitan Opera in New York, the tenor Lauritz Melchior awaited the arrival of the 'swan boat' on stage in the last act. Alas, when it came on, it departed before he had time to board. To the audience, he said: '*Wann geht der nächste Schwann?*' – 'When does the next swan go?'

According to Hugo Vickers, Melchior was in fact quoting what Leo Slezak, the Czech-born tenor, had said on a similar occasion thirty years before. (Leo's son Walter, who became an actor in Hollywood, actually entitled his 1962 memoirs, *What Time's the Next Swan?*)

Peter O'TOOLE

(1932–) Irish actor, born near Leeds.

—— 3 ——

What sort of job did O'Toole have before he achieved international fame playing Lawrence of Arabia in the 1962 film? Answer: a nose job.

A fact.

—— 4 ——

His playing of Macbeth at the Old Vic in September 1980 passed instantly into theatrical legend. It was terrible. Indeed, the whole production was atrocious, and was disowned by the then director of the Old Vic, Timothy West. The director of the play, Bryan Forbes, hit back on the night following the disastrous first night. In a curtain speech he said: 'Ladies and gentlemen, as you probably know, World War Three was announced today. We are bloodied but not yet bowed. I have always thought that Judas was one of the least attractive characters in human history.'

Newpaper reports of the time.

OVERHEARERS

—— 5 ——

A man well past his flirt-by date was attempting to flirt with a young slip of a thing. 'I've always wondered how old you are,' he said to her. 'My age and my bust measurement are exactly the same,' replied she. Said he, 'You can't be that young, surely? . . .'

Told by Sue Limb (1988).

—— 6 ——

Two drunks were arguing in a Glasgow pub. Finally, one got the other up against the wall and started banging his head against it, interspersing with the rhythm the words: 'I'm telling you . . . there are . . . FORTY-NINE ISLANDS IN THE JAPANESE ARCHIPELAGO . . . !'

Told by Jimmy Reid (1982).

—— 7 ——

Overheard remarks – or 'eavesdroppings' – bid fair to be considered a popular art form. Indeed, some writers make a point of elevating them to this plane by noting them down and using them in their works. The playwright Alan Bennett is a notable miner of this seam, especially when it is a case of one Yorkshire woman ear-wigging another. 'Who was it who painted that Sistine Chapel ceiling?' asked one. 'I don't know,' replied the other. 'It wasn't Underwoods of Bramley, was it?'

Told by Alan Bennett on BBC Radio *Quote... Unquote* (1981).

—— 1 ——

An old woman was in the chemist's shop and demanding of the man behind the counter if he knew of a good sweep. To much ribald laughter she said, 'I haven't had a brush up my flue for ages'.

Told to me by Nora Glynne-Jones. From my diary for 13 April 1968.

—— 2 ——

Peter Ustinov claims to have overheard this exchange between two charladies on the top of a London bus during the Second World War. One of them said, 'And do you know what he said to me? – "You bitch!" But I was ready for him. I'ad my answer prepared.' 'What did you say to 'im?' asked the other, eagerly. '"No I'm not", I said . . .'

Told by Ustinov on BBC Radio *Quote...Unquote* (1991) and, round about that time, in his show *An Evening With Peter Ustinov*.

OXFORD PEOPLE

—— 3 ——

In the late 1940s, Oxford University awarded an honorary degree to Edward Stettinius, the US secretary of state. Arriving in Oxford, Stettinius asked if he was expected to make a speech of thanks. To his horror, the university officials told him they were expecting a full-scale, formal address on America's postwar international policies.

The aides travelling with Stettinius worked all night on a speech and had it typed on 3×5 cards just in time to hand it to him as he joined the academic procession. Unfortunately, during the procession, Stettinius dropped the cards. He placed them back in his pocket, but not necessarily in the right order.

When he stood up to speak, he read from the cards well enough but it was clear to his aides that the cards were all out of sequence. Despite this, the Oxford audience gave Stettinius a standing ovation. One of the aides asked one of the dons what he though of the speech. 'Absolutely wonderful,' replied he. 'Statesmanlike and inspired. Churchill was never better. One of the finest speeches I have heard in my lifetime.'

'But,' said the aide, 'didn't you think the speech was organized in a very confusing manner?'

'Oh,' said the don, 'we're used to that sort of thing here at Oxford . . .'

Told to me by Charles G. Francis (1993).

—— 4 ——

There is an old Oxford joke, dating from the days when there were several all-female colleges, about a girl announcing loudly in the Junior Common Room that she had just met *a man*. At Somerville, the other girls asked, 'What is he reading?' At Lady Margaret Hall, 'Who is his father?' At St Hugh's they asked, 'What does he play?' And at St Hilda's they asked, 'Where is he?'

If this story is taken to show that St Hilda's undergraduates once had the reputation of being the most man-hungry, be it noted that of the colleges mentioned in the joke it is now the sole remaining all-female college. The joke was described as an 'old chestnut' in Dacre Balsdon's *Oxford Life* (1957).

—— 5 ——

Worcester College, Oxford, although very pleasant within and having a delightful garden with pond, is rather austere when viewed from Beaumont Street – not least because of the large clock over the entrance gate. 'Oh, I though that was the railway station,' a certain undergraduate is supposed to have remarked.

According to Dacre Balsdon's *Oxford Life* (1957), this remark was made by a 'bright young man' in a 'novel'. Which one, I know not. I first heard the remark in the more sophisticated form, '*C'est magnifique, mais ce n'est pas la gare*' in about 1961. Indeed, I remembered this jest in 1975 when I was devising what later became the radio programme *Quote...Unquote*. I knew that a quotations quiz required some kind of twist and so I put in the proposal that the participants would not only have to identify quotations but also invent them for specific situations. The example I gave was, 'What would Napoleon have said if he had arrived at Euston instead of Waterloo?' Suggested answer, '*C'est magnifique, mais. . . .*' The series was accepted by the then Controller of Radio 4 – Clare Lawson Dick – who thought it was a *very* witty idea. I then dropped the idea because, when it came to it, the participants were less inspired. When asked what Edward Heath might have said to Lord Nelson, one suggestion was 'Hello sailor!' . . .

P

PARENTS

—— 1 ——

Laurence Olivier recalled that a friend of his had a friend in the Welsh Guards whose father had said to him on his 21st birthday that he had three pieces of invaluable advice for him. They were: 'Never hunt south of the Thames, never drink port after champagne, and never have your wife in the morning lest something better should turn up during the day.'

Told by Laurence Olivier in *Confessions of an Actor* **(1982).**

—— 2 ——

In all innocence, I printed as original in my book *Say No More!* (1987) the unintentional put-down that had been sent to me by a *Quote...Unquote* listener: 'A mother was standing at the bus-stop with her three-year-old daughter, when the woman next to her commented: "Oh, what a pretty little girl! Is your husband very good-looking?"'

Compare this caption from the cartoon entitled 'A DOUBTFUL COMPLIMENT' that appeared in *Punch* **(3 August 1904). It showed a man walking with his children in a park being accosted by a woman:** *'Lady:* **"ARE THESE** *YOUR* **CHILDREN? WHAT DARLINGS! AND – ER – WHAT A VERY PRETTY WOMAN YOUR WIFE** *MUST* **BE!"'**

—— 3 ——

'Dear Miss, Sorry Jimmy is late but me and my husband rather overdone it this morning.'

From a note sent to Mrs C. M. Rowntree of London SW11 when she was a teacher. Broadcast on BBC Radio *Quote...Unquote* **(1980).**

—— 4 ——

'Dear Miss, Please excuse Mary from having a shower, being how she is. Being how you are yourself sometimes, you will understand how she is.'

Told in *Foot in Mouth* **(1982).**

—— 5 ——

'Dear Miss, Our Johnnie came home with a big hole in his trousers, will you please look into it?'

Told in ibid.

—— 6 ——

'Dear Miss Jones, Sorry Alan was away last week but with all the wet weather he's had diarrhoea through a hole in his shoe.'

Told in ibid.

—— 7 ——

'Dear Miss, I have not sent Johnny to school this morning because he hasn't been. I have given something to make him go, and when he's been he'll come.'

Told in ibid.

—— 8 ——

'Dear Miss, Please excuse Sandra being late. She was waiting for the bus at twenty to nine but came back to use the toilet and missed it.'

Told to me by Mrs. M. Rawes, married to an education welfare officer in Liverpool (1981).

—— 9 ——

'Dear Mr Walter, Susan was away from school yesterday as I took her to the herbalist about her nose and the tops of her legs.'

Told to me by Peter J. Walter of Tiverton (1981).

—— 10 ——

A man was driving along with a cargo of penguins when his lorry broke down. In due course, another lorry driver drew up and asked if he could be of any assistance. 'Yes,' said the first, 'I've got this load of penguins in the back. Could you take them to the zoo?' 'Certainly,' said the second and took them away.

A few hours later, the first driver managed to get into town and saw the second driver walking in the road with the penguins strung out behind him. 'I thought I told you to take those to the zoo?' 'Sure,' said the other driver, 'I did that. Now I'm taking them to the movies.'

Told by Jessica Mitford in *The Times* (9 October 1993). I hope I have put this in the right category...

Dorothy PARKER

(1893–1967) American writer and wit. The most quoted woman of the century? Some lesser-known anecdotes:

—— 1 ——

At the time she joined the *New Yorker*, money at the magazine was tight. So much so that when Harold Ross, the editor, asked Parker why she hadn't come in to write a piece, she replied, 'Someone else was using the pencil.'

Source untraced.

—— 2 ——

Some troublesome woman was being discussed and it was said, 'Anyhow she is very nice to her inferiors.' To which Parker replied, 'Where does she find them?'

This version is from *The Lyttelton Hart-Davis Letters* (1978) (for 22 January 1956).

—— 3 ——

When Parker married her second husband, Alan Campbell, they both received permission to take a week off work from the film studio for a honeymoon at Lake Arrowhead. Three weeks later, they had not returned, so the studio boss's secretary rang the couple and said, 'He wants to know why you haven't come back to work.' Parker replied: 'Tell him that I've been too f***** busy and vice versa.'

Quoted in John Keats, *You Might As Well Live* (1971). Context from a letter by Jason Lindsey in *The Independent* (27 July 1993).

—— 4 ——

Parker arrived at Southampton aboard the *Berengaria* and was met by the press who wanted to know what she would be doing in England. 'I came on the spur of the moment,' she answered, 'and

haven't worked out a schedule [pronounced *skedule*].' When one of the reporters pointed out that in England, the pronunciation was *shedule*, Parker exclaimed, 'Oh, skit.'

Context from ibid.

Luciano PAVAROTTI

(1935–) The leading Italian tenor of our times. Can fill opera houses the world over without padding.

—— 5 ——

During the 20-minute interval of an opera performance in Florence, the 25-stone man mountain partook of a light snack consisting of twenty meat and cheese sandwiches and three jugs of orange juice. Shortly afterwards, he explained why he takes Concorde on flights between Europe and New York: 'I cannot get in and out of aircraft toilets, but on three-and-a-half hour flights, I can hold out.'

Reported in *Today* (30 July 1987).

Anna PAVLOVA

(1885–1931) Russian ballerina.

—— 6 ——

When Pavlova made her last appearance in Edinburgh, the audience went mad with excitement at the end of the performance. They cheered, stamped, sobbed with emotion and flung flowers on the stage. Two ladies on the front row were clapping genteelly and one observed to the other: 'She's awfully like Mrs Wishart...'

Traditional, included in my *Eavesdroppings* (1981). Eric Maschwitz in *No Chip on My Shoulder* (1957) pinpoints the originator of the tale as Walford Hyden, a conductor who accompanied Pavlova on her world tours. His version: when she gave a performance of 'The Dying Swan' in *Glasgow* and finally sank to the floor in her feathered costume, Hyden heard a woman in the front row observe to her companion, 'Aye, she *is* awfu' like Mrs Wishart'.

—— 1 ——

Most famous for her 'Dying Swan' solo, Pavlova was touring the Netherlands right up to the end of her life. Her actual last words before she died were, 'Get my "Swan" costume ready!'

According to Barnaby Conrad, *Famous Last Words* **(1961).**

See also ENGLISH PERSONS 81:5.

Eva PERÓN

(1919–52) Actress and wife of Juan Perón, Argentine president. Eventually celebrated after a fashion in the musical *Evita* (1978).

—— 2 ——

Eva Perón once visited Europe but was not received as she thought appropriate for the powerful wife of the ruler of Argentina. She failed to get an invitation to tea at Buckingham Palace or the papal honour she hoped for in Rome. And in northern Italy she complained to her host that a voice in a crowd had called her a 'whore'. He replied, 'Quite so. But I have not been on a ship for fifteen years and they still call me admiral.'

Cited in the article 'The Power Behind the Glory', *Penthouse* **(UK) (August 1977). Tim Rice managed to squeeze the remark, just about, into his lyrics for** *Evita.*

Prince PHILIP

(1921–) Greek-born British Royal and consort of Queen Elizabeth II. Noted for saying 'bloody' rather a lot – e.g. 'The *Daily Express* is a bloody awful newspaper' (1962).

—— 3 ——

On a royal visit to New Zealand, the Queen and her husband (all three of them) were watching a demonstration of sheepshearing. Prince Philip, as always, had to ask a number of questions and do a lot of pointing. To the sheepshearer he said, 'How long will it take you to finish off these sheep?' Replied the sheepshearer, 'About half a bloody hour, I reckon.'

'Come, come,' said Prince Philip, conscious of the Queen's regal presence, 'that's putting it a bit strong, isn't it?'

'Oh, all right then,' said the sheepshearer, 'say *forty* bloody minutes.'

I probably heard this in the 1950s.

—— 4 ——

On a visit to a maternity hospital in the Solomon Islands in October 1982, Prince Philip was told that the population would double in twenty years – or at the rate of 5% a year. He burst out: '5%? 5%? You must be out of your minds . . . you're having far too many babies . . . you'll have a massive economic crisis in twenty years' time and blame everybody else.' Commentators rushed to point out that this was a bit rich coming from the father of four children.

Detail from *The Sunday Telegraph* **(October 1982).**

Pablo PICASSO

(1881–1973) Spanish painter.

—— 5 ——

An American GI told Picasso that he did not like modern art because it was 'not realistic'. Picasso then looked at a snapshot of the soldier's girlfriend and commented, 'My, is she really as *small* as that?'

Quoted in Bill Adler, *My Favourite Funny Story* **(1967).**

Mary PICKFORD

(1893–1979) Canadian-born American actress.

—— 6 ——

Pickford was one of the first Hollywood stars to appreciate her worth and capitalize upon it. With Charles Chaplin and Douglas Fairbanks Jr, she founded the United Artists film company – about which it was famously said that the 'lunatics were taking over the asylum'. For her fearsome business sense she was awarded the soubriquets 'Attila of

Sunnybrook Farm' and 'the Bank of America's Sweetheart'.

According to Dick Vosburgh on BBC Radio *Quote...Unquote* (1979).

Wilfred PICKLES

(1904–78) English North Country broadcaster whose folksy BBC radio show *Have a Go* ran for 21 years from 1946.

—— 1 ——

Pickles spent most of the 'quiz' programme chatting to the contestants. Faced with spinsters of any age from 19 to 90, he would ask, 'Are yer courtin'?' He would fish for laughs from all contestants with the question, 'Have you ever had any embarrassing moments?' One reply he received was from a woman who had been out with a very shy young man. Getting desperate for conversation with him she had said, 'If there's one thing I can't stand, it's people who sit on you and use you as a convenience.'

Probably from one of the Pickles books of reminiscence, such as *Wilfred Pickles Invites You To Have Another Go* (1978).

—— 2 ——

Pickles would end his programmes saying, 'This is your old pal, Wilfred Pickles, wishing you good luck and *good neet*!' He had first put this northern expression in the nation's ears during his brief and controversial stint as a BBC radio newsreader during the Second World War. Brendan Bracken, the wartime Minister of Information, had concluded that a voice such as that of Pickles would be less easy for German invaders to copy (should they succeed in taking over the BBC and wish to fool the nation). So Pickles was brought in and on one occasion ended the news (which till then had been read in God-like Oxbridge tones) with 'Goodnight everybody – and to all northerners wherever you may be, good neet!'

Source probably as above.

Sir Arthur Wing PINERO

(1855–1934) English playwright.

—— 3 ——

Pinero used to say that the only way to get anything across to an English theatre audience was for a character to say, 'I am going to hit this man on the head', then 'I'm hitting this man on the head' and finally 'I *have* hit this man on the head'. It might then just about realize what was going on.

Recounted in *The Lyttelton Hart-Davis Letters* (for 5 May 1957).

Harold PINTER

(1930–) English playwright, famous for the 'Pinteresque' quality of his work (when asked what his plays were about, he replied, 'The weasel under the cocktail cabinet'), and not least for the famous pauses he insists on in the stage directions for such plays as *The Caretaker* and *The Birthday Party*.

—— 4 ——

The playwright once reprimanded an actor for short-changing him over one of the famous pauses. 'You are playing two dots at the moment,' said Pinter, seriously, 'and I think if you check in the script you'll find it's three.'

Recounted in *The Observer* (12 September 1993). Similar attention to minutiae was shown when the text of his play *Moonlight* was published in 1993. An erratum slip drew attention to a mistake in the very first line of the play. It read 'I can't sleep. There's no moon. It's so dark, I' instead of 'I can't sleep. There's no moon. It's so dark. I'.

—— 5 ——

Pinter is a great cricket-lover (indeed, he once said cricket was greater than sex). More recently he wrote a 'poem' about the great batsman, Sir Len Hutton, which consisted in its entirety of three lines: 'I saw Hutton in his prime. / Another time, / Another time . . .' He circulated this work among his friends, but as reaction was slow in coming he asked one of them, his fellow playwright, Simon Gray, what he thought of it. Gray hedged, and then said, 'I'm afraid I haven't finished it yet.'

Quoted in *The Observer* (8 March 1992).

John PIPER

(1903–92) English painter.

—— 1 ——

Piper, though a painter of distinction, frowned upon honours. He declined a knighthood (his letter of rejection was drafted by Sir John Betjeman) but became a Companion of Honour in 1972, apparently on the grounds (as expressed by another of his friends, Adrian Stokes) that, 'It doesn't distort the nomenclature.'

From the obituary notice by Richard Ingrams in *The Independent* (30 June 1992).

Alan PLATER

(1935–) English playwright and TV adapter.

—— 2 ——

Understandably Plater is interested in the kind of stage directions that other writers give to actors. One he did *not* write himself but which he heard of in a screenplay was the instruction to an actor: 'He thinks about whistling "Danny Boy", but decides against it.'

Recounted by him on BBC Radio *Quote...Unquote* (1990).

Roy PLOMLEY

(1914–85) English broadcaster. He devised and presented the BBC radio programme *Desert Island Discs* from 1942 until his death. The simplest of ideas – which came to him while putting on his pyjamas in 1941 – was that a well-known castaway would select eight favourite gramophone records to take to a desert island. It is said that in the 43 years of his time with the programme, he never had a contract longer than six weeks.

—— 3 ——

Of all the thousands of guests on the show, several were unable to keep egotism at bay in their selection of records and books to take with them to the desert island. The entire choice of records by Moura Lympany, the pianist, was made up of eight she had recorded herself. Elizabeth Schwarzkopf came a close second with seven (plus an eighth on which she featured . . .). Birgit Nilsson chose six of her own recordings and Louis Armstrong five.

As recalled in *Desert Island Lists* by Roy Plomley (with Derek Drescher) (1984).

—— 4 ——

Plomley's worst hour came when he discovered over lunch before a recording that the Alistair Maclean he was talking to was not, as he had expected, Alistair Maclean, the world-famous author, but Alistair Maclean, the European director of tourism for Ontario. Plomley ploughed on with the recording, but it was never broadcast.

The intended Maclean never made it on to the programme either. Details from *The Observer* Magazine (19 January 1992).

POLICE PERSONS

—— 5 ——

A policeman had occasion to stop a car and speak to its driver. The driver did not take to being held up in this way and was rather abrupt and unhelpful to the officer. His wife, who was in the car with him, felt obliged to try and calm down the situation before her husband got himself into trouble. So she leaned over and said to the policeman: 'Please don't pay too much heed to him. He's always like this when he's had a few . . .'

Told to me by Alistair Edwards of Wilmslow (1982) who said he had heard it from the policeman himself.

—— 6 ——

There is the story of the man who had taken too much drink at lunch and was stopped by the police as he drove back to his office. 'The main thing,' he thought hazily to himself, 'is to be polite.' As the police officer bent down to look in the car, the driver flexed his muscles and said, 'Good consternoon, affable.'

Quoted in my *Foot in Mouth* (1982).

—— 1 ——

At the Ravenscraig picket line during the British miners' strike of 1984/5, protesters were being held back by mounted police. One miner called out to a policewoman, 'Hey, love, your horse is foaming at the mouth.' She gazed down at the miner and said, 'I'm not suprised. So would you be if you'd been between my legs for the last two hours.'

Recounted in *The Observer* (20 May 1984).

POLITICIANS

—— 2 ——

It is very important to know your element. There was once a Secretary of State for Air who was himself a qualified pilot. He went down to Southampton to see and try out a new flying boat. He went up in it and after a bit he asked the pilot if he might take over the controls. This, of course, was agreed. They approached an airfield and the Minister circled round it and lost height steadily until the young man could bear it no longer. He said, 'Sir, this is a flying boat, you know.' The Minister gave him a very old-fashioned look and circled the airfield again. He then moved off and brought the flying boat down carefully on Southampton Water. As he turned to go, the young man, feeling that he might have blotted his copybook, said, 'I hope, sir, you didn't mind my saying that: you know I thought you might have forgotten this was a flying boat.' The Minister looked at him and said, 'My boy, cabinet ministers don't make elementary mistakes like that.' He then turned, said goodbye, opened the door and stepped out into six feet of water.

Told by General Sir Brian Robertson, chairman of the British Transport Commission at the annual dinner of the Municipal Passenger Transport Association (Inc), Southend (1954).

Sandy POWELL

(1900–82) English North Country comedian.

—— 3 ——

Powell once told me the origins of his famous catchphrase, 'Can you hear me, mother?': 'I was doing an hour's show on the radio, live, from Broadcasting House in London. I was doing a sketch called "Sandy at the North Pole". I was supposed to be broadcasting home and wanting to speak to my mother. When I got to the line, "Can you hear me, mother?" I dropped my script on the studio floor. While I was picking up the sheets all I could do was repeat the phrase over and over. Well, that was on a Saturday night. The following week I was appearing at the Hippodrome, Coventry, and the manager came to me at the band rehearsal with a request: "You'll say that, tonight, won't you?" I said, "What?" He said, "'Can you hear me, mother?' Everybody's saying it. Say it and see." So I did and the whole audience joined in and I've been stuck with it ever since. Even abroad – New Zealand, South Africa, Rhodesia – they've all heard it. I'm not saying it was the first radio catchphrase – they were all trying them out – but it was the first to catch on.'

From a telephone interview (1979).

André PREVIN

(1929–) German-born American conductor,
pianist and composer.

—— 4 ——

When Previn was a very young pianist and a whizz-kid in Hollywood, there was a suggestion that he should give a performance of the Gershwin Piano Concerto with the Cleveland Symphony Orchestra conducted by the formidable Hungarian exile, George Szell. But Szell was not so sure. So Previn flew to Cleveland to convince him and was ushered into Szell's apartment. The conductor glowered at him across the table and said, 'Mr Previn would you be so kind as to play the solo part for me.' André Previn replied, 'Certainly . . . but where is the piano?' Szell said, 'There is no need for the piano – just play it here on the top of the table.' So Previn set to and fingered the entire solo part of the Gershwin piano concerto on the table while Szell watched fascinated. At the end there was a pause, and Szell said: 'No, no, very sorry, long journey, waste of time, very sad, no.' André Previn paused for a moment and then said, 'I can only tell you it sounds a lot better on my table at home.'

Told by Peter Wood on BBC Radio *Quote...Unquote* (1992).

PROFESSORS

—— 1 ——

'Walking one day in Oxford, I saw two elderly dons coming towards me engrossed apparently in some weighty discourse. As they passed me, I overheard just two words: "And ninthly . . ."'

In *Eavesdroppings* (1981) I gleefully printed this from S. H. Jarvis of Bristol. I am sure Mr Jarvis did indeed hear such a thing but I have subsequently discovered that the pedantic ninth point is a venerable institution. In Ronald Knox's *Juxta Salices* (1910), he includes a group of poems written while he was still at Eton. 'As no less than three of them wear the aspect of a positively last appearance [i.e. a promise not to write more], they have been called in the words of so many eminent preachers "ninthlies and lastlies".' Even before this, *The Oxford English Dictionary* (2nd edition) has Thomas B. Aldrich writing in *Prudence Palfrey* (1874/1885) of: 'The poor old parson's interminable ninthlies and finallies.'

Much the same, though marginally different: Benjamin Franklin, 1745, concluded his *Reasons for Preferring an Elderly Mistress* with: 'Eighth and lastly. They are so grateful!!' And the *OED2* takes such pedantry even further back, more loosely, finding its earliest citation for the word 'ninthly' on its own in 1579 and a 'fifthly and lastly' dated 1681.

Ultimately, the origin for all this sort of thing must be the kind of legal nonsense talk parodied by Shakespeare's Dogberry in *Much Ado About Nothing* (c. 1598): 'Marry, sir, they have committed false report; moreover, they have spoken untruths; secondarily, they are slanders; *sixthly and lastly*, they have belied a lady; thirdly, they have verified unjust things; and to conclude, they are lying knaves.'

My thanks to Michael Grosvenor Myer of Cambridge for this last point.

PUBLIC-RELATIONS PRACTITIONERS

—— 2 ——

When it came to Abraham Lincoln's turn to give his summation as the defence attorney, he said: 'My learned opponent has given you all the facts but has drawn all the wrong conclusions.' As it turned out he won the case. On the way out of court, the prosecutor stopped Lincoln and asked, 'How did you do it, Abe?'

'Well,' Abe said, 'During the recess I wandered into a café, sat with the jurors, and told them a story about a farmer who was mending a fence when his ten-year-old son came running, crying, "Dad, Sis is up in the hay loft with a hired hand and he is pulling down his pants and she is pulling up her skirts and I think they are going to pee over the hay."'

According to Lincoln, the farmer said to his son, 'You got all the facts straight, but you have drawn the wrong conclusion.'

Told to me by Charles G. Francis (December 1992) – as also all the others in this category.

—— 3 ——

A king once called three wise men together and proposed the same problem to each: 'Our island is about to be inundated by a huge tidal wave. How would you advise the people? The first man thought for a long time and then said, 'Sire, I would lead them to the highest spot on the island and then set up an all-night prayer vigil.' The second said, 'Master, I would advise the people to eat, drink and be merry for it would be their last opportunity to do so.'

The third wise man, said, 'Your majesty, if I were you, I would immediately advise the people to do their best to learn how to live under water.'

—— 4 ——

Brown was relaxing at his club. 'Say, do you think it'll rain?' he asked Gates, a public-relations man sitting next to him.

'I wouldn't say so,' said Gates.

The next day Brown received a bill for public-relations counsel.

A week later they met again at the club and Brown casually said, 'Think we're going to have a war again in the Middle East?'

'I doubt it,' replied the PR man.

The next day his bill arrived at Brown's home.

Brown took the second bill and rushed to the club. He found Gates relaxing in an armchair and stormed up to him, saying, 'Listen, you shyster, you're a crook,' he shouted. 'And, remember, I'm not asking. I'm telling . . .'

―――― 1 ――――

Biological laboratory technicians have stopped using rats for their experiments – they now use public-relations men. For one thing, the scientists don't become attached to them; furthermore, there are some things even a rat won't do.

―――― 2 ――――

A professional genealogist had accepted a very handsome fee from a wealthy client to research his family tree. In writing up his report, the genealogist was dismayed to learn that one of the client's ancestors had been executed in the electric chair.

Wanting to be tactful, he wrote up the relative as follows: 'Your Uncle Henry occupied the chair of Applied Electricity at a leading government institution. He was attached to his chair by the strongest of ties, and his sudden passing came as a great shock.'

―――― 3 ――――

A man was flying in a hot-air balloon, when the weather got suddenly darker. He decided to descend in order to find a landmark. All he could see was a man walking his dog across an open field. 'Hello, there!' bellowed the man in the balloon. 'Can you tell me where I am?'

'You are in a hot-air balloon, about 200 yards above the ground,' shouted the man below.

Said the man in the balloon, 'Are you by any chance a public-relations man?'

'Yes,' said the man on the ground, 'How did you guess?'

And the man in the balloon said, 'Because public-relations people are full of useless information.'

PUBLISHERS

―――― 4 ――――

Since the early 1980s, *The Bookseller* journal has reported annually on the Diagram Group Prize for the Oddest Title at the Frankfurt Book Fair. Publishers really do allow the most extraordinary things to go on title pages. Winners over the years have included: *The Joy of Chickens* by Dennis Nolan, *I Can Taste and Smell* by Peter Curry, *Entrepreneur: Career Management in House Prostitution*, *Proceedings of the Second International Workshop on Nude Mice, Eat*

Your House by Frederic Hobbs (an eco guide to self-sufficiency), and *Entertaining with Insects*.

I cannot remember now – from a lifetime's reading – whether books with the titles *Biggles Pulls It Off* and *Noddy's Magic Rubber* ever *really* were published. However, *Views of Gentlemen's Seats* is mentioned in Sir Walter Scott's Journals and *Men and Horses I Have Known* was glimpsed by me in a bookcase at Blenheim Palace. I have also been told about *Instructions for the Best Positions on the Pianoforte* by Col. Peter Hawker. *Twice Round the World with the Holy Ghost* is mentioned in the published edition of Evelyn Waugh's letters.

PUNSTERS

―――― 5 ――――

This was the caption to a cartoon in the edition of *Punch* dated 15 August 1900: 'By the way, Mrs Jocelyn, I hear you've taken a rippin' little place on the river this year.' 'Yes. I hope, when you're passing, that you'll – er – drop in!'

Which just goes to show that there's no joke like an old joke.

―――― 6 ――――

The Best of Myles reprints, as an overheard remark, this from Flann O'Brien's Dublin newspaper column (early 1940s): One person remarks, 'D'you know that my great-grandfather was killed at Waterloo,' and the other person asks: 'Which platform?'

A veritable old chestnut this one, even in the 1940s. Here is A. L. Rowse writing of Lord David Cecil in *Friends and Contemporaries* (1989): 'Anything for a laugh – simplest of jokes. I think of him now coming into my room [at Christ Church in the early 1920s], giggling and sputtering with fun. Someone had said, "My grandfather was killed at Waterloo" "I'm so sorry – which platform?"'

But I think there is a rock-solid first use – to be found as the caption to a cartoon by F. H. Townsend from *Punch* (Vol. 129, 1 November 1905). It shows a man and woman in evening dress at a party:

MR BINKS: 'ONE OF MY ANCESTORS FELL AT WATERLOO.'
LADY CLARE: 'AH? WHICH PLATFORM?'

This is the same Townsend who gave us 94:2. To the old joke is often added the further response, 'Ha, ha! As if it mattered which platform!'

J. Danforth QUAYLE

(1947–) American Republican vice-president,
noted for his gaffes.

—— 1 ——

During the 1988 election campaign in which Quayle was George Bush's curious choice as running mate, Quayle said various things: 'I didn't live in this century' was one; another was, 'The government shouldn't interfere in the bondage between parent and child.'

Recalled in *The Independent* (10 November 1988).

—— 2 ——

By March 1989, a British TV documentary was knee-deep in Danforthisms, the two most notable being: '[Of the Holocaust] It was an obscene period in our nation's history. No, not in our nation's but World War Two. We all lived in this century: I didn't live in this century but in this century's history' – eh? – and (as head of the Space Council) 'Space is almost infinite. As a matter of fact we think it is infinite.'

Quoted in *The Guardian* (8 March 1989).

—— 3 ——

In a speech to the Young Republicans National Federation in Nashville, Mr Quayle said that America was about to celebrate 'the 20th anniversary of Neil Armstrong and Buz Luken walking on the moon.' As every schoolchild knows, it was Buzz *Aldrin* who walked on the moon; Donald E. 'Buz' *Lukens* was a Republican congressman who had recently been convicted of sexual misconduct with a 16-year-old girl.

Reported in *The Independent* (17 July 1989).

QUOTERS

—— 4 ——

On the parade ground the sergeant was putting a squad of recruits through their paces. In a quiet moment, a cultured voice was heard to say, 'Come, sweet death!' The sergeant rounded on the squad, barking, 'Who said that?!', and the languid voice said from the ranks, 'Shelley, I believe it was, sergeant.'

> George L. Baurley of Dessau in Germany told me this in 1992, saying, 'It dates back to wartime or postwar days, when there was still conscription.' Paul Gregson subsequently came up with another version. According to him, the quoted line was 'They also serve who only stand and wait' and the languid voice said, 'Milton', whereupon the sergeant bawled, 'Milton, once pace forward, march!'

—— 5 ——

The American *National Inquirer* once produced a 27-page guide by its owner (Generoso Pope Jr) containing instructions to reporters. One was, 'Do not alter quotations. Don't think you can write them better than other people. For example, if someone says "Never in the field of human conflict was so much owed by so many to so few", don't change it to "The RAF did a grand job . . ."'

> **Told by Shelley Rohde on BBC Radio *Quote... Unquote* (1984).**

R

RADIO LISTENERS

—— 1 ——

A much-quoted view in British broadcasting circles – and one designed to promote the superior imaginative qualities of radio – apparently originated in a letter to *Radio Times* in the 1920s. It said, simply: 'The pictures are better'.

Oral tradition. Joyce Grenfell in a letter (dated 22 September 1962) and included in *An Invisible Friendship* (1981), wrote: 'Do you ever listen [to the radio]? I do. I like it best. As a child I know says: "I see it much better on radio than on TV."' Derek Parker in *Radio: The Great Years* (1977) has: '"I like the wireless better than the theatre," one London child wrote in a now legendary letter, "because the scenery is better."'

Michael RAMSEY

(1904–88) English Anglican Archbishop of Canterbury.

—— 2 ——

When Ramsey was archbishop, a jet-setting American clergyman arrived at Lambeth Palace to see him. 'Your Grace,' he declared breathlessly, 'Yesterday I saw His Holiness the Patriarch of Constantinople! This morning, I had an audience with his Holiness the Pope! And tonight I'm with you, the Archbishop of Canterbury!'

To which Michael Ramsey said: 'Prepare to meet thy God!'

Told by the Reverend Roger Royle on BBC Radio *Quote...Unquote* (1984).

'Roland RAT'

(*fl.* 1983–) British TV puppet.

—— 3 ——

When Roland Rat was brought in to help restore the ailing fortunes of TV-am, the breakfast TV franchise, in 1983, a spokesman for the station's rivals at the BBC commented: 'This must be the first time a rat has come to the aid of a sinking ship.'

From newspaper reports at the time.

Ted RAY

(1909–77) English comedian, whose actual name was Charles Olden – a surname he reversed to provide his first stage name 'Nedlo' ('the Gypsy Violinist'). He had a lightning wit and could produce jokes from his memory bank with computer-like speed.

—— 4 ——

Ray was being installed as King Rat, chief of the Water Rats, the variety performers' club. Part of his duties included saying grace before the meal – a task to which he was not accustomed and which he performed in an inaudible mumble. The toastmaster, in a typically stentorian tone, said to Ray, 'Speak up, sir, your guests can't hear you!' Quick as a flash, Ray replied, 'You mind your own business. I'm not talking to them.'

Recounted by Bernard Braden in *The Kindness of Strangers* (1990).

Ronald REAGAN

(1911–) American Republican president and film actor. In 1985, he was described as conducting 'government by anecdote', apparently feeling more at home in the showbusiness mode than in historical tradition. He certainly had the heat-seeking approach to anecdotes of the true chat-show host. The fact that, on occasions, these anecdotes proved to be devoid of any foundation in fact would hardly bother him. They were true as far as he was concerned. The following involve him and are, thus, presumably true.

—— 1 ——

In the 1930s, Reagan's first job on graduating was as a radio sports announcer. He would give live commentaries on boxing, football and baseball but sometimes did 'simulated' broadcasts of baseball games from the studio. He would improvise around the summaries of the progress of the game put out by Western Union telegraph. On one occasion, the ticker-tape machine went down on him and Reagan had to invent foul after foul of imaginary pitches until – six minutes later – the line came alive again and rescued him.

Recounted by *Newsweek* (21 July 1980) and *Esquire* (August 1980).

—— 2 ——

When it was announced that Reagan was going to stand for the governorship of California, Jack Warner, the film producer, exclaimed, 'All wrong, Jimmy Stewart for governor, Reagan for best friend.'

Quoted in Edmund G. & Bill Brown, *Reagan: The Political Chameleon* (1976).

—— 3 ——

Early in his first term as president, Reagan was the victim of an assassination attempt. A bullet missed his heart by inches, but the experience triggered off in him an almost manic series of jokes and quips. To surgeons as he entered the operating theatre, he said, 'Who's minding the store?' and 'Please tell me you're all Republicans.' Lying in intensive care with tubes in his mouth, he mumbled, 'Will I be fit for ranch work after this?' When aides told him, 'Sir, you'll be happy to know that the Government is running normally', he shot back, 'What makes you think I'd be happy about that?'

He also rattled off a series of quotations. To his wife, Nancy, he explained, 'Honey, I forgot to duck' – the explanation Jack Dempsey gave to *his* wife after losing the world heavyweight boxing championship to Gene Tunney in 1926. In a written note coming out of anaesthesia he paraphrased W. C. Fields with, 'All in all, I'd rather be in Philadelphia.' In another note he recalled Winston Churchill's observation, 'There's no more exhilarating feeling than being shot at without result.'

The written notes continued: 'Send me to L.A. where I can see the air I'm breathing' and 'If I had this much attention in Hollywood, I'd have stayed there'. Complimented by a doctor for being a good patient, he said, 'I have to be. My father-in-law is a doctor.' To an attentive nurse, he said, 'Does Nancy know about us?' and to another nurse who told him to 'keep up the good work' of his recovery, he said, 'You mean this may happen several more times?'

Reports in *The Daily Mail* (31 March, 1 April 1981) and *Time* (13 April 1981).

—— 4 ——

On a four-country tour of Latin America in 1982, the president became a little confused. Proposing a toast at a dinner in *Brazil*, he said, 'Now would you join me in a toast to President Figueiredo, to the people of *Bolivia* – no, that's where I'm *going* – to the people of *Brazil* and to the dream of democracy and peace here in the Western Hemisphere.'

In fact, he was headed next not for Bolivia but *Colombia*.

Reported in *Time* Magazine (13 December 1982).

—— 5 ——

Giving a piece of voice level prior to a radio broadcast on 13 August 1984, Reagan unwisely said: 'My fellow Americans, I am pleased to tell you that I have signed legislation to outlaw Russia for ever. We begin bombing in five minutes.' The test was surreptitiously recorded and soon made known to the world.

News reports of the time.

—— 6 ——

An example of optimism. On Christmas morning, a child finds a pile of manure in his room. His parents soon find him shovelling it away enthusiastically. As he explains to them, he is convinced, 'There must be a pony here somewhere.'

***Time* Magazine recorded this joke on 27 October 1986 as a particular favourite of Reagan's. That same year it gave rise to the oddest title for a movie (albeit the TV variety) I have come across for some**

time, namely, *There Must Be a Pony*. This had Elizabeth Taylor as a former child star pushed back into the limelight by a major soap-opera casting after a spell in a psychiatric hospital. The title is explained as an example of optimism in Robert Wagner's suicide note at the end of the film.

—— 1 ——

Reagan frequently used showbiz analogies in his political career. When asked whether he resented the popularity of Mikhail Gorbachev in 1987, he told students in Jacksonville, Florida, 'Good Lord, I co-starred with Errol Flynn once.'

Reported in *Time* (14 December 1987).

Sir Michael REDGRAVE

(1908–85) English classical actor who strayed into films occasionally. The patriarch of a theatrical dynasty and quite the most nervous public figure I have ever encountered. Towards the end of his life he was incapable of remembering his lines and in one play they were fed to him by radio into an earpiece.

—— 2 ——

At the end of a play, Redgrave was about to commit suicide and was left alone on stage with a retainer. He was supposed to utter the line, 'Bring me a pint of port and a pistol.' What came out was, 'Bring me a pint of piss and a portal.' The retainer bravely sought to undo the damage by inquiring, 'A pint of *piss*, my lord?' 'Aye,' replied Redgrave, curtly: '*And* a portal.'

Recounted in Melvyn Bragg, *Rich: The Life of Richard Burton* (1988).

William REES-MOGG

(1928–) English journalist. With his swottish looks and voice, Rees-Mogg was editor of *The Times* during the turbulent period of the 1960s and 70s prior to its rescue by Rupert Murdoch. He then became one of the Great and the Good, picking up a knighthood and a life peerage along the way.

—— 3 ——

When he relinquished the editorship of *The Times*, Rees-Mogg wrote an article in which he said, 'I have been sensible far too long, and now I need not be sensible, at least for the time being.' So saying, he became deputy chairman of the BBC and chairman of the Arts Council.

—— 4 ——

In 1988, Rees-Mogg added another string to his bow as chairman of the Broadcasting Standards Council. In a Channel 4 programme about TV obscenity he helpfully divided sex into 'Romeo and Juliet scenes', 'erotic scenes' and 'gropings which occur in the middle'. Earlier, in the House of Commons, Brian Wilson MP had argued that 'obscenity was in the groin of the beholder' and went on to describe Rees-Mogg as 'The Groin of the Nation'.

Reports in *The Guardian* and *The Independent* (17 May, 3 November 1988).

Lord REITH

(1889–1971) Scottish broadcasting executive. The first director-general of the BBC, Reith set lofty aims but also created an atmosphere of bureaucracy and pomposity which lasted until very recently.

—— 5 ——

One of Reith's tasks was to announce the most famous of all prewar broadcasts – the speech made after his abdication by the former King Edward VIII in 1936. 'This is Windsor Castle,' Reith announced. 'His Royal Highness the Prince Edward.' He was then heard by some listeners to leave the room and slam the door, thus indicating disapproval of what was to follow. In fact, all he had done as he slipped out of the chair to make way for the ex-king was to give 'an almighty kick to the table leg'.

Recounted by Reith in *Into the Wind* (1949).

—— 6 ——

The most famous Reith story concerns the young radio announcer who was caught *in flagrante* with a female employee. Quite what the extent of his misdemeanour was is not recorded, nor the precise location (was it Savoy Hill – the BBC's first base – or Broadcasting House?). Whatever the case, Reith was persuaded that the young man should not be sacked but retained because he had never done anything like it before and was, besides, a very good announcer. Reith only agreed to this on the understanding that, '*Never* in any circumstances must he introduce the Epilogue!'

Related in Malcolm Muggeridge, *Tread Softly for You Tread on My Jokes* (1966) and Jack de Manio, *To Auntie With Love* (1967).

Sir Ralph RICHARDSON

(1902–84) English actor, chiefly of classical roles on stage and screen, but latterly in more contemporary roles. A delightful eccentric, he travelled by motorbike well into his old age.

—— 1 ——

An actress rushed up to Sir Ralph at rehearsal one Monday morning and asked him if he'd had a good weekend. 'A terrible thing happened,' he replied sadly, 'my brother and his wife were burnt to death in a fire!' 'How terrible!' exclaimed the actress. 'No, no, I hardly knew my brother, hadn't seen him for fifty years . . .' 'But even so,' sympathized the actress, 'it's a terrible thing to happen'. 'Yes,' said Sir Ralph, ruminatively, 'But it won't happen again.'

Told to me by Jonathan Miller and recorded in my diary, 23 January 1976.

—— 2 ——

A play was in progress which was dying the death. Suddenly from the stalls a man stood up and asked, 'Is there a doctor in the house?' When a medical gentleman duly made his presence known, the first man said, 'Oh, doctor, isn't this a terrible play?'

A story told many times by Richardson – as in a TV interview, 1982 – and in *Pass the Port Again* (1980). It did not involve him, though Sheridan Morley has Richardson saying it himself to the audience of 'a truly terrible little thriller towards the end of his career' at the Savoy Theatre, London (*High Life*, September 1993).

Nicholas RIDLEY

(later Lord Ridley) (1929–93) English Conservative politician. An Old Etonian, a smoker, and insensitive to the media, he was ideologically close to Margaret Thatcher.

—— 3 ——

In March 1990, when two of Prime Minister Thatcher's ministers – Norman Fowler and Peter Walker – had withdrawn from the Cabinet, both giving as their reason for going that they wished to 'spend more time with their families', Gordon Brown, the Labour MP, suggested in the House of Commons that Ridley might care to follow suit. But the Secretary of State for Industry was having none of it. 'The last thing I want to do,' he said, 'is spend more time with my family.'

Quoted in *The Independent* (14 July 1990). Ridley was eventually eased out after making indiscreet remarks about Germany in a *Spectator* interview a few months later.

Angela RIPPON

(1944–) English TV presenter and former TV newsreader, who once impressed the nation by revealing that she had legs on *The Morecambe and Wise Show.*

—— 4 ——

In *Drive* magazine (September 1976), Ms Rippon wrote: 'For me the Motor Show ranks alongside Muhammad Ali, the Paris Winter Collection and the Eurovision Song Contest for over-rated ballyhoo that needs to be avoided at all costs.' The following spring she was invited to introduce the Eurovision Song Contest and had no hesitation in accepting.

Recounted on BBC Radio *Quote...Unquote* (1977).

Max ROBERTSON

(1915–) English radio and TV commentator, particularly on tennis.

—— 1 ——

During an outside broadcast, Robertson once described Princess Margaret as 'looking radiant in an off-the-hat face . . .'

Recounted by Wynford Vaughan-Thomas on BBC Radio *Quote...Unquote* (1980).

—— 2 ——

On another occasion, Robertson told listeners to Wimbledon: 'People behind Martina Navratilova, on the roller, have the best view of her receiving service.'

Quoted in my *Foot in Mouth* (1982).

Mickey ROONEY

(1920–) American film actor.

—— 3 ——

The diminutive Rooney is supposed to have approached a statuesque chorus girl with the suggestion that they might enjoy sex together. Replied she: 'All right, but if you do and I ever get to hear about it, I'll be very, very cross indeed.'

Told by Humphrey Lyttelton on BBC Radio *Quote...Unquote* (1988). However, I expect this may be an application of a general tall/short persons joke which had been current in Britain some time before: *The Observer* (11 March 1984) had a version between a male and a female journalist.

Lord ROSEBERY

(1847–1929) British Liberal prime minister.

—— 4 ——

Rosebery married Hannah Rothschild, one of the greatest heiresses in England. This did not, apparently, prevent him from saying on one occasion, 'I am leaving tonight; Hannah and the rest of the heavy baggage will follow later.'

Recounted in Robert Rhodes James, *Rosebery* (1963).

—— 5 ——

An Old Etonian, Rosebery told his servant to buy him a gramophone and, when death was imminent, to play upon it the Eton Boating Song. This was actually done, 'though perhaps he did not hear it', suggested Winston Churchill. 'Thus he wished the gay memories of boyhood to be around him at his end, and thus he set Death in its proper place as a necessary and unalarming process.'

Recounted by Winston Churchill in *Great Contemporaries* (1937). Rhodes James adds: 'It is doubtful if he heard the haunting music, redolent of hot summer afternoons, the quiet laughter of friends, and the golden days of his young manhood.'

RUMOURISTS

—— 6 ——

Within a month of war being declared in August 1914, there was an unfounded rumour that a million Russian troops had landed at Aberdeen in Scotland and passed through England on their way to the Western Front. The detail that they were seen to have had 'snow on their boots' was supposed to add credence to the report.

Arnold Bennett was one of several people who noted the rumour at the time. In his *Journals* (for 31 August 1914), he wrote: 'The girls came home with a positive statement from the camp that 160,000 Russians were being landed in Britain, to be taken to France . . . The statement was so positive that at first I almost believed it . . . In the end I dismissed it, and yet could not help hoping . . . The most curious embroidery on this rumour was from Mrs A. W., who told Mrs W. that the Russians were coming via us to France, where they would turn

treacherous to France and join Germans in taking Paris . . . This rumour I think took the cake.'

In Osbert Sitwell's *Great Morning* (1951), he records how his 'unusually wise and cautious' 16-year-old brother Sacheverell had written to tell him: 'They saw the Russians pass through the station last night . . . and Miss Vasalt telephoned to Mother this afternoon and said trains in great number had passed through Grantham Station all day with the blinds down. So there must, I think, be some truth in it, don't you?'

In *Falsehood in War-Time* (1928), Arthur Ponsonby said of 'Russians with snow on their boots', that 'nothing illustrates better the credulity of the public mind in wartime and what favourable soil it becomes for the cultivation of falsehood.' Several suggestions have been made as to how this false information caught hold: that the Secret Service had intercepted a telegram to the effect that '100,000 Russians are on their way from Aberdeen to London' (without realizing that this referred to a consignment of Russian eggs); that a tall, bearded fellow had declared in a train that he came from 'Ross-shire', and so on.

In fact, the British ambassador to Russia *had* requested the despatch of a complete army corps but the request was never acceded to. Ponsonby commented: 'As the rumour had undoubted military value, the authorities took no steps to deny it . . . [but] an official War Office denial of the rumour was noted by the *Daily News* on September 16, 1914.'

—— 1 ——

I recently saw in a book of 'amazing facts' a report to the effect that although the American Bill of Rights contains 463 words, the Ten Commandments, 297 words, and Lincoln's Gettysburg Address, a mere 266, an EEC directive on butter contained no less than 26,911 words . . .

At once, I knew this to be untrue. Not that I checked whether there was any such EEC directive. It is simply that this 'fact' is merely a colourful jibe at bureaucracy in general and has been around for a very long time. Max Hall in 'The Great Cabbage Hoax: A Case Study' (*Journal of Personality and*

Social Psychology, 1965, Vol. 2, No. 4) made a thorough survey of its origins. This was a follow-up to his original 1954 study. The origins seemed to lie with the US Office of Price Administration during the Second World War, though the joke really only began to spread wildly in 1951, during US involvement in the Korean War. Numerous examples were found in press and broadcasting of the rumour that the then Office of Price Stabilization had a 26,911-word cabbage order. This was compared with the brevity of the Gettysburg Address, the Ten Commandments and the Declaration of Independence. In another version, the cabbage order became a 12,962-word regulation on manually-operated foghorns.

As with rumours of a more inflammatory kind, is it not amazing that such a story can keep on turning up – even when the true facts have been established? There was never any cabbage order of any kind from the OPA or the OPS.

Bertrand RUSSELL

(1872–1970) British mathematician, philosopher and nuclear disarmament campaigner with a squeaky voice. He succeeded to an earldom in 1931.

—— 2 ——

A taxi driver said: 'I 'ad that Bertrand Russell in the back of my cab last week. And I asked him, "What's it all about, guv?" – and, d'you know, he couldn't tell me!'

Also told involving the philosopher, A. J. Ayer. The origin lies with T. S. Eliot, whose widow, Valerie, wrote a letter to *The Times* (7 February 1970) telling a tale that Eliot himself 'loved to recount'. This version begins with the taxi-driver saying, 'You're T. S. Eliot . . . I've got an eye for a celebrity. Only the other evening I picked up Bertrand Russell . . .' And so on.

S

SABRINA

(c. 1938–) English glamour figure.

—— 1 ——

Norma Sykes of Blackpool is one of the most fondly-remembered British TV appearers of the 1950s. At the age of 17, she appeared with Arthur Askey in *Before Your Very Eyes* and simply stood there, not saying anything, in a tight-fitting sequinned dress, showing off her 41-18-36 figure. She was called 'Sabrina' after the recent Hollywood film *Sabrina Fair*. Subsequently, she went to live in Hollywood and little more was heard of her. After the TV studio where she made her appearances, she earned the nickname 'the Hunchfront of Lime Grove'.

Detail from *The Sunday Express* (13 January 1985).

Mort SAHL

(1926–) American satirist.

—— 2 ——

The film *Exodus* (1960), based on the novel by Leon Uris about the early years of the state of Israel, lasts very nearly four hours. The story has it that Sahl was invited by Otto Preminger, the director, to a preview but after three hours had ground by, he stood up and implored, 'Otto – let my people go!'

No doubt apocryphal, but that is how Sahl tells it in a comedy routine on the LP *The New Frontier* (1961).

SAILORS

—— 3 ——

The shortest naval signal? When the liner *Queen Elizabeth* was passing the battleship *Queen Elizabeth* in mid-Atlantic, the battleship signalled 'SNAP'.

Source untraced.

3rd Marquis of SALISBURY

(1830–1903) British Conservative prime minister and the last one with a beard, to date.

—— 4 ——

After a hard day in Downing Street, dealing with various international issues, the prime minister changed into ceremonial dress and hurried to a levee at Buckingham Palace. King Edward VII took one look at Lord Salisbury and pointed out that whereas the upper part of his body was clothed correctly in diplomatic uniform, his trousers were those of the Hertfordshire Yeomanry. Lord Salisbury excused himself with what has become a classic diplomatic formula: he had left his home, Hatfield House, at an early hour that morning and since then his mind had been 'exclusively occupied *with less important matters . . .*'

Quoted in Leonard Miall, broadcast talk 'In at the Start' (No. 2), BBC Radio 3 (1982). Miall had it from Maurice Farquharson, the BBC's Head of Secretariat (1953–63).

—— 5 ——

The Marquis of Salisbury once sent a telegram to his heir, Viscount Cranborne, at the family seat in Dorset. It read simply: 'CRANBORNE.

CRANBORNE. ARRIVING 6.30 SALISBURY. SALISBURY.'

From a letter to *The Times* (15 April 1985).

Linley SAMBOURNE

(1844–1910) English cartoonist and illustrator, principally for *Punch*.

1

Sambourne had a wonderful way of saying things that were not malapropisms or spoonerisms but were a kind of lateral *un*thinking. Nobody knew whether his mistakes were intentional. The examples that I have most enjoyed are: 'He's so poor – he hasn't got a rag to stand on'; 'There was such a silence afterwards that you could have picked up a pin in it'; and, 'You're digging nails in your coffin with every stroke of your tongue.'

These are mentioned in literature on display at the 'Linley Sambourne House' in Kensington which is preserved by the Victorian Society and open to visitors.

2

Sambourne also once remarked, 'I don't care for Lady Macbeth in the street-walking scene.'

Quoted in R. G. C. Price, *A History of Punch* (1957).

Sir Malcolm SARGENT

(1895–1967) English orchestral conductor.

3

The nickname, 'Flash Harry', is said to have originated with a BBC announcer after Sargent had appeared on the radio *Brains Trust* and was also about to be heard in the following programme. The announcer informed listeners that they were to be taken over to a concert conducted by Sargent in Manchester. It sounded as if he had gone there straightaway, in a flash. However, the nickname also encapsulated his extremely debonair looks and manner – smoothed-back hair, buttonhole, gestures and all.

4

A frightful snob, Sargent warned the studio manager at the BBC's Maida Vale studio that he would be bringing with him a distinguished visitor, and that the visitor should be given a seat in the control room. The distinguished elderly man arrived and was welcomed by the studio manager. At the break, Sargent came in, shook hands with the visitor and said to the studio manager, 'I'd like you to meet my guest, the King of Sweden.' The distinguished visitor coughed quietly and corrected him: 'Norway . . .'

This version was told to me by Bernard Keeffe (1990).

5

Sargent used to remark that people in concert audiences did not seem to realize that although a conductor has his back to them he can still overhear conversations in the front rows. He once heard a lady say to her friend, 'I wish my backside was as flat as his.'

Recounted in my *Eavesdroppings* (1981), source untraced.

Albert SCHWEITZER

(1875–1965) Alsatian medical missionary and musician.

6

On a train journey in the American Mid-West, Schweitzer was spotted by two women who asked, 'Oh, Mr Einstein, may we have your autograph?' Schweitzer was not put out by this request and agreed that he and Albert Einstein did have the same sort of hair, so it was an understandable mistake. Then he said, 'Would you like me to give you Einstein's autograph?' The women nodded and so, taking out his pen, he wrote, 'Albert Einstein, by way of his friend, Albert Schweitzer.'

Told by Martin Jarvis on BBC Radio *Quote...Unquote* (1988).

SCOTS

—— 1 ——

Two Scotswomen had been rowed across the Sea of Galilee but complained of the high fare. Said one, 'You can cross Loch Lomond for one and ninepence . . .' The boatman quietly and reverentially replied, 'But this is the sea upon which Our Lord walked.' Voice from the bow, 'No wonder He walked . . .'

Told by Rosemary Anne Sisson (1981).

—— 2 ——

The Morningside accent is one of the glories of Edinburgh: it is what the posh people use. And yet there are many recollections of a Morningside lady whose tones you could cut with a knife, remarking, 'People talk of an Edinburgh accent, but I've never heard it.'

Recalled by Eric Anderson on BBC Radio *Quote...Unquote* (1986). Robert Stephens recalled (1991) how Maggie Smith had been complimented on her Edinburgh accent when playing the title role in the film *The Prime of Miss Jean Brodie*. A woman speaking in pure Morningside said, 'But there is no Edinburgh accent . . .'

Walter SELLAR

(1898–1951) English schoolmaster and co-author of the comedy classic *1066 and All That*.

—— 3 ——

When at Charterhouse, Sellar noted that one of his pupils had written at the top of his report: 'Height at beginning of term 4ft 4in. Height at the end of term 4ft 3½ins.' He simply commented: 'Seems to be settling down nicely . . .'

Told by Eric Anderson (1986).

Peter SELLERS

(1925–80) English comedy actor, latterly in films.

—— 4 ——

At the age of 22, confident of his ability to do convincing impressions but unable to get replies to his requests for work at the BBC, Sellers rang up the producer Roy Spears and pretended to be Kenneth Horne, then an established radio star. 'Dickie Murdoch and I were at a cabaret the other night,' he said, 'and we saw an amazing young fellow called Peter Sellers. And he was very good. Just thought I'd give you a little tip.' Shortly after this, Sellers revealed who he was. Spears was won over by his cheek and booked him for a programme called *Showtime.*

As told by Sellers in a *Parkinson* interview, BBC TV, in 1974, included in a tribute LP *Peter Sellers: The Parkinson Interview* (released *c.* 1981).

—— 5 ——

Sellers once received a fan letter which read: 'Dear Mr Sellers, I have been a keen follower of yours for many years now, and should be most grateful if you would kindly send me a singed photograph of yourself.' Unable to ignore this unfortunate spelling mistake, Sellers took a photograph and burned it round the edges using a cigarette lighter. A few weeks later, another letter arrived from the fan thanking him for the photograph, but adding, 'I wonder if I could trouble you for another as this one is signed all round the edge.'

As told many times by Sellers (see, for example, *The Listener*, 2 October 1969).

SEX OBJECTS

—— 6 ——

The man in uniform dancing with a girl told her – when she asked – that he was a Gurkha officer. 'But I thought all Gurkhas were black,' exclaimed the girl. 'No,' the officer corrected her, 'only our privates are black.' Said she: 'My dear, how fantastic!'

In *The Kenneth Williams Diaries* (1993) – entry for 28 July 1954, where Williams says he was told it by John Schlesinger.

1

Before the rise of the women's movement, some-one said, 'Treat every woman as if you have slept with her and you soon will.'

In a diary entry for 17 April 1966 I was already describing this as an 'old saying'.

2

An American broadcaster, Tex Antoine, said in 1975: 'With rape so predominant in the news lately, it is well to remember the words of Confucius: "If rape is inevitable, lie back and enjoy it."' ABC News suspended Antoine for this remark, then demoted him to working in the weather department and prohibited him from appearing on the air.

Quoted in Barbara Rowes, The Book of Quotes (1979). 'When rape is inevitable, lie back and enjoy it' is best described – as it is in Paul Scott's novel The Jewel in the Crown (1966) – as 'that old, disreputable saying'. Daphne Manners, upon whose 'rape' Scott's story hinges, adds: 'I can't say, Auntie, that I lay back and enjoyed mine.' 'A mock-Confucianism' is how Eric Partridge describes it in his Dictionary of Slang (1984 ed.), giving a date c. 1950 – and one is unlikely ever to learn when, or from whom, it first arose.

3

A notice outside a fried-fish shop proclaimed: 'CLEANLINESS, ECONOMY AND CIVILITY. ALWAYS HOT AND ALWAYS READY.' A passer-by remarked that this was the motto for a perfect wife.

The passer-by was possibly Edward Thomas and the remark was recorded by E. S. P. Haynes in his Lawyer's Notebook (1932).

George Bernard SHAW

(1856–1950) Irish playwright and 'publicist' (one who had something to say on almost every subject).

4

Sam Goldwyn attempted to buy from Shaw the film rights of his plays. There was a protracted haggle over what the rights would cost, which ended in Shaw's declining to sell. 'The trouble is, Mr Goldwyn,' said Shaw, 'you are interested only in art and I am interested only in money.'

Quoted in Alva Johnson, The Great Goldwyn (1937). Bennett Cerf, Try and Stop Me (1947), has it that Pygmalion was specifically at issue.

5

During the filming of Shaw's *Caesar and Cleopatra* in the early 1940s, Claude Rains became so exasperated by the author's frequent interruptions that he said, 'If you're not very careful, Mr Shaw, I shall play this part as you want it.'

Told by Kenneth Williams on BBC Radio Quote...Unquote (1979).

6

On the first night of his play *Arms and the Man* in 1894, the author took a curtain call and was greeted with cheers and a solitary hiss. Shaw bowed in the direction from which the hiss came and said, 'I quite agree with you, sir, but what can two do against so many?'

Told by St John Ervine in Bernard Shaw: His Life, Work and Friends (1956). Oddly, the identity of the perpetrator of the hiss is known – it was R. Goulding Bright, later to become a literary agent, who was under the misapprehension that, in the play, Shaw was satirizing the British army.

7

Shaw's contribution to the debate as to whether Shakespeare or Bacon wrote Shakespeare's plays was to suggest that Beerbohm Tree should play Hamlet. Then they should dig up both Shakespeare and Bacon and see which one had turned over.

Source untraced. Told on BBC Radio Quote...Unquote (1985). I fear this may be a misattribution: Alexander Woollcott wrote in While Rome Burns (1934) of a bad actor's performance of Hamlet: 'Scholars should have kept watch beside the graves of Shakespeare and Bacon to see which one of them turned over.'

8

To a hostess who had sent an invitation stating that on a certain day she would be 'At home', Shaw succinctly replied: 'So will G. Bernard Shaw'.

Apparently true, and recounted in Michael Holroyd, Bernard Shaw, Vol. 3 (1991).

See also CHURCHILL 53:4.

Norman SHELLEY

(1903–80) English actor, chiefly remembered for
his broadcasts on BBC radio *Children's Hour*.

—— 1 ——

In 1977, Shelley claimed that he had impersonated
Winston Churchill's voice on the radio during the
war. The BBC later confirmed that Shelley *did* record
the Dunkirk rallying speech in 1940 (which Churchill had delivered in the House of Commons) so that
it could be broadcast in the US. The prime minister
was too busy to do it himself but he approved
Shelley's impersonation and commented, 'Very good,
he's even got my teeth.'

> In its issue of 18 May 1991, *The New Scientist*
> published the findings of American speech re-
> searchers who had analysed twenty recordings of
> Churchill speeches released on gramophone
> records by Decca and suggested that *three* of them
> – the Dunkirk 'on the beaches', the 'blood, toil,
> tears and sweat' and 'finest hour' – were not actu-
> ally spoken by him. Earlier, Shelley's obituary in
> *The Times* (30 August 1980) had mentioned his 'on
> the beaches' recording 'which in 1940 the Ameri-
> cans believed to be delivered by Churchill himself'.

—— 2 ——

Shelley also claimed to have been the first actor to
have uttered the word 'f***' on the BBC. It was in
the early 1950s and in a Third Programme production of a Ben Jonson play. Unfortunately, he had
never encountered anyone who had heard the play
and the fact that the BBC received no complaints
about it would rather suggest that no one had.

> Recounted by Bernard Braden in *The Kindness of
> Strangers* (1990).

SHOPPERS

—— 3 ——

A pregnant girl was seen to be in distress, but
when the observer came close, she saw that the
girl was laughing rather than crying. The girl explained she had been on the way to the clinic and had
been told to take a urine sample. The only bottle she
had available was a whisky bottle and she put it in her
shopping basket. On the way to the clinic she popped
into a supermarket to do some shopping. When she
came out, she found someone had pinched it.

> Told to me by Nora Glynne-Jones. From my diary
> for 13 April 1968.

—— 4 ——

As every author and publisher knows, it is no easy
task getting people to buy books. Just what an
uphill task it is can best be illustrated by the overheard conversation between two old biddies in a
store in the run-up to Christmas. They were both
obviously on the look-out for Christmas presents for
their respective spouses. One said, 'What can I get
Harold for Christmas? I don't know what to get him.'
The other suggested, 'Why not get him a book?' 'No,'
replied the other, 'He's got a book.'

> Told to me by Miss E. Kissan of Bournemouth and
> included in my *Eavesdroppings* (1981).

—— 5 ——

Another problem for authors (and publishers and
booksellers) is that few potential purchasers of
books know what they are looking for. And even if
they do, they probably don't know the name of the
author, the title and the name of the publisher with
total accuracy. A bookseller in Leicester told me that
a woman once came into his shop and said, 'Have
you got a copy of Thomas Hardy's *Tess of the
Dormobiles*?'

> Source forgotten.

Walter SICKERT

(1860–1942) English painter.

—— 6 ——

As a young man, Denton Welch paid a visit to
Sickert and later wrote a description of the
oddities he had encountered. The great man perse-
cuted and terrified him and, during tea, danced in
front of him wearing boots 'such as deep sea divers
wear . . . to see how Denton would react to the
experience' (in Edith Sitwell's phrase). As Welch left
the house, Sickert said to him, 'Come again when
you can't stay so long'.

> Denton Welch's 'Sickert at St Peter's' appeared in
> *Horizon*, Vol. vi, No. 32 (1942). In *Taken Care of*
> (1965), Edith Sitwell comments on the article but
> gives the tag as, 'Come again – when you have a
> little less time.' Either way, this farewell was not
> originated by Sickert. Indeed, Welch ends his
> article by saying, 'And at these words a strange

pang went through me, for it was what my father had always said as he closed the book, when I had finished my bread and butter and milk, and it was time for bed.'

Georges SIMENON

(1903–89) Belgian-born French novelist and creator of the detective 'Maigret'.

—— 1 ——

In 1977, Simenon made an astonishing claim: 'I have made love to 10,000 women.' In an interview with the Zurich newspaper *Die Tat*, he explained: 'I contend that you know a woman only after you have slept with her. I wanted to know women – I wanted to learn the truth.' When he was asked if he was sure of the figure, Simenon said he had gone back and checked.

In 1983, Simenon's wife was quoted in Fenton Bresler's biography of the writer as saying, 'We've worked it out and the true figure is no more than twelve hundred.' Most of these were prostitutes. The original version of the claim appeared in an interview with Federico Fellini in *L'Express* (21 February 1977): 'I have made love to 10,000 women since I was 13½. It wasn't in any way a vice. I've no sexual vices. But I needed to communicate.'

Dame Edith SITWELL

(1887–1964) English poet and writer.

—— 2 ——

Of the popular lady novelist Ethel Mannin, Sitwell delivered this magisterial rebuke (and subsequently applied it to various other targets): 'I do not want Miss Mannin's feelings to be hurt by the fact that I have never heard of her ... At the moment I am debarred from the pleasure of putting her in her place by the fact that she has not got one.'

Quoted in John Pearson, *Façades* (1978) after a report in *The Yorkshire Evening News* (8 August 1930). By 13 March 1940, James Agate appears to have been reascribing this (in his *Ego 4*): 'About an American woman novelist [Mannin was English] who had been rude to her in print, Lady Oxford [i.e. Margot Asquith] is reported to have said, "I would put Miss B. in her place if she had a place."'

—— 3 ——

Noël Coward satirized Edith and her two brothers, Osbert and Sacheverell, in a revue sketch with the title 'The Swiss Family Whittlebot'. This did not go down at all well with the Sitwells and hostilities raged between the two camps for some time. Coward summed up his opponents as, 'Two wiseacres and a cow'.

Quoted by John Pearson in ibid.

F. E. SMITH

(1st Earl of Birkenhead) (1872–1930) English lawyer and politician about whom many tales are told – many of them clearly approved (and polished up for publication) by himself.

—— 4 ——

To a judge (Judge Willis) who had asked, after a long dispute over procedure, 'What do you suppose I am on the Bench for, Mr Smith?', Smith replied, 'It is not for me, your honour, to attempt to fathom the inscrutable workings of Providence'.

Quoted by Winston Churchill in *Great Contemporaries* (1937).

—— 5 ——

Gerald Gould, a book-reviewer in *The Week-end Review* had written something about Birkenhead that his lordship objected to. The Earl wrote a letter beginning, 'A Mr Gerald Gould has said . . .' In the next issue, Gould replied, and began his letter, 'An Earl of Birkenhead has said . . .'

Told to me by Matthew Norgate (1984).

—— 6 ——

Smith once found himself seated at dinner next to a woman who introduced herself as 'Mrs Porter-Porter, with a hyphen'. Smith quickly replied that he was 'Mr Whisky-Whisky, with a syphon'.

Quoted in John Campbell, *F. E. Smith, First Earl of Birkenhead* (1983).

—— 7 ——

The Labour MP, Jimmy Thomas, first entered the House of Commons in January 1910. One day he happened to ask Smith the way to the lavatory. 'Down the corridor, first right, first left and down the stairs,' Smith helpfuly advised him. 'Then you'll see a door marked "Gentlemen", but don't let that deter you.'

Also quoted by John Campbell.

—— 1 ——

When Thomas complained to Smith that he "'ad an 'eadache', Smith advised: 'Try taking a couple of aspirates.'

Some versions have Thomas saying he complained of 'an 'orrible 'eadache', rather. John Campbell quotes Thomas as saying, 'Ooh, Fred, I've got an 'ell of an 'eadache.'

Maggie SMITH

(1934–) English actress, in everything from revue to the classics. Made a Dame of the British Empire in 1990.

—— 2 ——

When playing Desdemona to Laurence Olivier's *Othello* at the National Theatre in 1963, Olivier made the mistake of criticizing her vowel sounds. She waited until he was blacked up for the role and carefully enunciated to him, 'How now, brown cow.'

Recounted in *The Independent on Sunday* (28 February 1993).

—— 3 ——

Smith was appearing with Edward Fox in Ronald Harwood's play *Interpreters* which was not going terribly well. Harwood, being a sociable cove, was nevertheless always popping in and out of the stars' dressing rooms, attempting to keep their spirits up. This did not go down well with Smith, so when she said, 'Oh, hello, and what are you doing?' and Harwood replied, 'Struggling with a new play, darling', she took the opportunity to comment, 'Aren't we all?'

Michael Coveney in *Maggie Smith: A Bright Particular Star* (1992), apart from retelling this version, also gives the exchange as, 'Trying to finish a new play, darling' and 'Try finishing this one first.'

—— 4 ——

When Smith was appearing in Peter Shaffer's *Lettice and Lovage* in New York, she soon found that her backstage calm was shattered when a musical show called *Queen Esther and her Gospel Singers*

moved into an adjoining theatre. As it happens, both theatres were owned by the Shubert organization, so it was arranged that thick black velour curtains would be hung at the back of each building, insulating Dame Maggie from the noise. The company manager broke the news to her: 'We've hung all the blacks.' 'Well,' replied she, 'I don't think there was any need to go that far.'

Told in Michael Coveney's book, as above.

John SNAGGE

(1904–) English radio announcer and commentator.

—— 5 ——

Commentating on the 1949 Oxford and Cambridge University Boat Race, Snagge allowed himself to observe at one point: 'I don't know who's ahead – it's either Oxford or Cambridge.'

How true. And he did – I have checked a recording of his commentary.

SPEECH-MAKERS

—— 6 ——

There is an old observation about speech-making (in my early days I used to begin speeches with it: about as original as saying 'Unaccustomed as I am to public speaking . . .') to the effect that you always end up making three speeches: the one you make to the bathroom mirror before setting out, the absolute drivel you say when you stand up to speak, and the magnificent oration you convince yourself you have made, as you drive home afterwards.

I first saw this in an advertisement in an issue of *The Times* dating from about 1928.

—— 7 ——

A female student at Bangor University was being courted by a man who was studying at Sheffield University. During term time, he frequently drove the two hundred miles or so to see her. Eventually they were married and the girl's father, making the traditional speech at the wedding, proclaimed: 'It must have been true love considering he drove two hundred miles to Bangor every weekend . . .'

Told to me by a correspondent, name forgotten, before 1987.

—— 1 ——

A man was assigned by his advertising and public-relations company to write speeches and articles for a self-made egomaniac, who not only underpaid the writer but subjected him to a continuous stream of abuse.

The ghostwriter finally had his revenge. He provided his employer with a long speech to read at a very important convention. The employer read the first eight pages of the speech which was typed in big printer's type. But when he turned to page nine in the middle of a sentence, he found only these words, printed in red: 'From here on, you pompous ass, you're on your own . . .'

Told by Charles G. Francis (1992).

The Reverend William SPOONER

(1844–1930) English clergyman and academic.
Warden of New College, Oxford (1903–24).

—— 2 ——

The word 'spoonerism' (to describe the accidental transposing of the beginnings of words) had been coined by 1900. Most of the classic examples from Spooner himself – if they are not apocryphal – had probably been spoken by that date. However, James Laver, the fashion historian, who had been an undergraduate at New College in the early 1920s, assured me that he had heard from Spooner's own lips the interesting biblical phrase, 'Through a dark glassly'.

From my diary for 5 December 1969. The phenomenon existed before Spooner gave his name to it, of course. Oonagh Lahr of Muswell Hill believes that the first ever was Shakespeare's choice of the name 'The Boar's Head' for the name of the tavern where the low-life scenes occur in *Henry IV*, parts 1 & 2. 'The Furness Variorum edition pointed out that this might be a spoonerism . . . though there is no way the intention could be proved' (letter from her, 1993).

—— 3 ——

Of a cat falling from a window, Spooner explained that it had 'popped on its little drawers'.

Quoted in Sir William Hayter, *Spooner* (1977).

—— 4 ——

Maurice Bowra recalled Spooner's sensitivity on the matter of spoonerisms. When a High Court judge speaking at a college celebration made a heavy joke about 'New College' and 'Kew knowledge', Spooner replied by comparing himself to Homer and Shakespeare – who also had works not their own attributed to them – and said, 'If I err, I do it in very good company.'

Bowra also told of an occasion after a college 'bump supper' (following a rowing victory), when undergraduates stood outside Spooner's window calling for a speech. He put his head out and said, 'You don't want a speech. You only want me to say *one of those things.*'

Recounted in Maurice Bowra, *Memories 1898–1939* (1966).

—— 5 ——

Coming across a stranger in New College quad, Spooner could only remember that the man was a newcomer to the college. 'Come to tea tomorrow,' he said. 'I'm giving a little welcome do to our new mathematics Fellow.'

'But, Warden, I *am* the new mathematics Fellow!' the man expostulated.

'Well, never mind,' said Spooner, 'come all the same.'

A much-told tale, original source untraced. Bowra, in the above book, has it happening to a Fellow called Stanley Casson.

—— 6 ——

'Poor soul – very sad, her late husband, you know, a very sad death – eaten by missionaries – poor soul.'

Quoted in the Hayter book, as cited above.

—— 7 ——

As will be apparent from the previous two stories, Spooner's real genius and charm was not for spoonerisms but for a kind of crazed logic which arose in the making of wrong associations. Julian Huxley recalled telling Spooner that a university expedition to Spitsbergen was going there because it was possible to go so far north without much difficulty on account of the Gulf Stream. He then heard Spooner explaining to his wife: 'My dear, Dr Huxley assures me that it's no further from the north coast of Spitsbergen to the North Pole than it is from Land's End to John of Gaunt.'

Recounted by Huxley in a BBC broadcast in 1942/ 3. In *Memories* (1970), Huxley did offer a regular spoonerism from the master: 'The Minx by spoonlight'.

—— 1 ——

Spooner reprimanded one of his congregation: 'Mr Coupland, you read the lesson very badly.' Replied Coupland: 'But, sir, I didn't read the lesson.' Spooner: 'Ah, I thought you didn't.'

Source untraced.

—— 2 ——

After spending some time on a Saturday night setting exam papers, Spooner finished the reading of the Ten Commandments in chapel next day with the words, 'Only six of these need be attempted'.

Source untraced.

—— 3 ——

The Warden met an undergraduate in Oxford who said, 'Good evening, Dr Spooner, I don't suppose you remember me?' To which Spooner replied: 'On the contrary, I remember your name perfectly, but I've completely forgotten your face.'

Attributed by Robin Hyman in *A Dictionary of Famous Quotations* (1973).

—— 4 ——

One of the first jokes I was told on arrival at New College, Oxford, in 1963 was that Warden Spooner had inquired of an undergraduate (*c.* 1918), 'Now, tell me, was it you or your brother who was killed in the war?'

Well, Frank Muir in *The Oxford Book of Humorous Prose* (1990) cites this from John Taylor's *Wit and Mirth*: 'A nobleman (as he was riding) met with a yeoman of the country, to whom he said, "My friend, I should know thee. I do remember I have often seen thee." "My good lord," said the countryman, "I am one of your honour's poor tenants, and my name is T. I." "I remember thee better now," (saith my lord). "There were two brothers but one is dead. I pray thee, which of you doth remain alive?"' And the date of this version? 1630.

—— 5 ——

It seems that Spooner's crazed logic could also take physical form. Once when he spilled salt on the table, he immediately poured claret on it.

Remark in a speech at a New College gaudy, 3 July 1992.

See also CLERGY 57:3.

Sir John SQUIRE

(1884–1958) English literary journalist, poet and critic.

—— 6 ——

In the spring of 1920, Squire set up an amateur cricket team called 'The Invalids'. Neville Cardus told of a match when an opposing batsman hit an easy catch high in the sky. Six of Squire's team ran to get it and jostled for position under the falling ball. Squire's voice boomed out the order, 'Leave it to Thompson!' As the ball thudded into the grass, they remembered that Thompson was not playing that week.

Recalled by Frank Muir in *The Oxford Book of Humorous Prose* (1990).

Norman St John STEVAS

(later Lord St John of Fawsley) (1929–) English Conservative politician.

—— 7 ——

When asked by the prime minister, Margaret Thatcher, why he needed to leave a Cabinet meeting ahead of her in order to dress for some official function they were both attending, St John Stevas said, 'Yes, Margaret, but it takes *me* much longer to change than it does you.'

Quoted on BBC Radio *Quote...Unquote* (1985).

Michael STEWART

(later Lord Stewart) (1906–90) English Labour politician.

—— 8 ——

While he was Foreign Secretary (1968–70), Stewart was interviewed by William Hardcastle for the radio programme *The World at One*. Curiously, at the end of each answer, he was seen to smile enigmatically over the interviewer's shoulder. When the recording was completed, the producer asked Stewart the reason for his odd behaviour. 'Well, this is for television, isn't it?' he replied.

Told in *Private Eye* at the time.

Christopher STONE

(1882–1965) English broadcaster.

—— 1 ——

Stone is sometimes described as the first 'disc-jockey' – though the term had not, of course, been coined. On the 1st (or was it the 7th?) July 1927, he introduced a programme of gramophone records for the BBC. Others – including Compton Mackenzie in 1924 – may actually have done the job before him, but Stone was the first person to be perceived as what later came to be dignified with the term 'record presenter'.

Extraordinary though it may seem, Stone's popularity was such that George Black, the impresario, actually presented him on stage at the London Palladium. And what was his act? He came on and said, 'I'm now going to play you a very nice record. I hope you enjoy it.' He would then put a record on and sit there, listening to it, along with the audience.

Recounted by Alfred Black in Roger Wilmut, *Kindly Leave the Stage!* (1985)

Tom STOPPARD

(1937–) Czech-born British playwright.

—— 2 ——

In answer to the journalists' clichéd question, 'Where do you get your ideas from?', Stoppard has replied, 'If I knew, I'd go there.'

Source? I think a *Guardian* interview. But compare what Joyce Grenfell says in *Joyce Grenfell Requests the Pleasure* (1976). She states that this was the reply to the question, 'Where do you get the ideas for your monologues?' The novelist Terry Pratchett was profiled in *The Observer* (8 November 1992): '"Where do you get your incredible ideas from?" asked a boy. (Someone always does.) "There's this warehouse called Ideas Are Us," Pratchett replied.'

Lytton STRACHEY

(1880–1932) English biographer.

—— 3 ——

In the First World War, Strachey appeared before a military tribunal to put his case as a conscientious objector. He was asked by the chairman what he would do if he saw a German soldier trying to violate his sister. He replied, 'I would try to get between them.'

Quoted in Robert Graves, *Goodbye To All That* (1929).

—— 4 ——

Strachey's last words are reported to have been: 'If this is dying, I don't think much of it.'

Quoted in Michael Holroyd, *Lytton Strachey: The Years of Achievement* (1968).

Barbra STREISAND

(1942–) American singer and actress.

—— 5 ——

The film critic Pauline Kael noted of Streisand's performance in *What's Up, Doc?* – 'She playing herself . . . and it's awfully soon for that.'

Source untraced.

—— 6 ——

Streisand told an interviewer: 'I am a nice person. I care about my driver having lunch, you know.'

Quoted in *The Sunday Times* 'Words of the Week' (1 April 1984).

Hunt STROMBERG

(1894–1968) American film producer.

—— 7 ——

Stromberg took over production of Robert Flaherty's documentary *White Shadows in the High Seas* in 1928. 'Boys, I've got a great idea,' he said. 'Let's fill the whole screen with tits.'

Quoted in *Halliwell's Filmgoer's Book of Quotes* (1978).

STUTTERERS

— 1 —

Two men – an Irishman and an Englishman – were sitting next to each other on an Aer Lingus flight from London to Dublin. The Irishman asked the Englishman what he was going to Ireland for. 'I-I-I'm going t-t-to audition for a j-j-job as a radio ann-ann- announcer,' stuttered the man with the English accent. 'Oh,' said the Irish man. 'And do you think you'll get the job?' 'N-n-no,' came the stuttered reply. 'Why not?' asked the Irishman. Replied the Englishman, 'B-B-Because I expect they'll g-g-give it to a bl-bl-bloody C-C- Catholic!'

Source untraced. First heard by me in about 1982.

Ed SULLIVAN

(1902–74) American journalist and TV impresario.

— 2 —

Sullivan introduced the British comedy act of Morecambe and Wise to American viewers as 'Morrecambey and Wise'.

Told by Eric Morecambe on BBC TV, *Parkinson*, c. 1975.

Edith SUMMERSKILL

(later Baroness Summerskill) (1901–80) English doctor and politician.

— 3 —

In the early 1960s, Summerskill took part in an Oxford Union debate on contraception or abortion (or possibly even boxing, which was her great *bête noire*). Her opening words were, 'Mr President, I cannot conceive . . .' She never got any further.

> **I think I was told this in about 1963, at the Oxford Union. (It wasn't true, of course – she had a lovely daughter.)**

Janet SUZMAN

(1939–) South African-born actress.

— 4 —

On tour at the Leeds Grand theatre in the title role of Ibsen's *Hedda Gabler*, Suzman was due at the very end of the play to go off into an inner room and there play the piano fantastically and wildly before shooting herself. However, the Grand did not have a piano and so it was arranged that – at this climactic point of the play – a tape recording of piano-playing would be put on. And so Suzman went behind a curtain to 'play' this wild tarantella and bring the play to its wonderful conclusion. Instead, there was a faint whirring sound and off the tape came the words: 'Ladies and gentlemen, will you please take your seats. The curtain will rise in five minutes.'

Told by her on BBC Radio *Quote...Unquote* (1981).

— 5 —

No mean Lady Macbeth herself, Suzman overheard this when sitting in the audience during a performance of Shakespeare's Scottish Play at the Chichester Festival Theatre. During one of the production's bloodiest moments a woman turned and whispered loudly to her companion: 'That reminds me, the blood donor people are coming on Thursday.'

Told by her on ibid.

Hannen SWAFFER

(1879–1962) English journalist.

— 6 —

A comedy by Kenneth Horne with the title *Yes and No* featuring Steve Geray and Magda Kun opened at the Ambassadors Theatre, London, in the autumn of 1938. It occasioned the shortest theatrical notice of all time. Swaffer wrote: '*Yes and No* (Ambassadors) – No!'

> **Based on a letter from Bill Galley of London WC1 in *The Sunday Telegraph* (24 March 1970). On *Quote...Unquote* (1993), Tony Hawks ascribed something similar to Dorothy Parker about the André Charlot musical show *Yes!* which was presented in London in 1923. Her one word crit. was 'No!' – but I suspect this has been foisted upon her.**

T

Elizabeth TAYLOR

(1932–) American film actress.

—— 1 ——

In 1966, Richard Burton elected to play the title role in Marlowe's play *Dr Faustus* at the Oxford Playhouse, supported by members of the Oxford University Dramatic Society. At the height of their joint fame, he was joined by his wife, Elizabeth Taylor, who played the non-speaking role of Helen of Troy. Even so, this was not good enough for one undergraduate member of the audience, who voiced the view that she was 'present more in body than in spirit'.

Personal recollection. (Alluding to 1 Corinthians 3:55.)

—— 2 ——

In October 1975, Taylor remarried Richard Burton and declared, 'There will be no more marriages or divorces. We are stuck like chicken feathers to tar – for lovely always.'

Quoted in *The Guardian*, 10 February 1976. In December 1976 she married Senator John Warner, divorced him in November 1982, and so on.

TEACHERS

—— 3 ——

Frank Carter, a classics master ar Winchester, when encouraging a pupil to attempt some unseen translation from the Greek, would say: '"Silence is golden", as the saying goes, 'but we should like a little small change.'

Told to me by Prof. Maurice Hugh-Jones (1987).

—— 4 ——

In a pupil's geography report, a teacher put, 'He does well to find his way home.'

Told by Arthur Marshall, BBC Radio *Quote...Unquote* (1987).

—— 5 ——

A physics master once, exasperatedly, told his class: 'I've taught you all I know – and now you know *nothing*!'

Told to me by Mrs B. J. Vines of St Annes-on-Sea (1987). The physics master was her husband.

—— 6 ——

Which schoolmaster was it who wrote of a pupil: 'With the dawn of legibility comes the horrendous revelation that he cannot spell'?

Told to me by Geoffrey J. Toye of Milton Keynes (1987). It may come from Ian Hay's *The Lighter Side of School Life* (1914).

Norman TEBBIT

(later Lord Tebbit) (1931–) English airline pilot and Conservative politician.

—— 7 ——

When the IRA attempted to blow up Prime Minister Thatcher and several members of her Cabinet in the Grand Hotel, Brighton, during the Conservative Party Conference in October 1984, two of the victims were Norman Tebbit and his wife, Margaret. She was permanently paralysed, but the Trade and Industry Secretary recovered from his injuries in due course. When he was about to be put under an anaesthetic for an exploratory operation he was asked if he was allergic to anything and replied: 'Yes – bombs'.

Report in *The Guardian* (13 October 1984).

TELEVISION VIEWERS

—— 1 ——

Two burly dockers were standing at a bus stop in Liverpool and swearing heavily because they were having to wait so long for a bus to come along. One turned to the other and said: 'If this f****** bus doesn't come soon, I'm going to miss *Blue Peter*.'

> Told to me by Mrs Wendy Freeman of Chessington (1981).

—— 2 ——

Two middle-aged women were discussing the merits or otherwise of colour television. One said to the other: 'Yes, we've looked at colour sets ourselves, but really, when it comes down to it, we prefer the "natural".'

> Told to me by Madeleine Howe of St David's, Exeter (1981).

Sir Denis THATCHER, Bt.

(1915–) English businessman and husband of Margaret Thatcher.

—— 3 ——

On the occasion when Mrs Thatcher was being photographed holding a baby calf during the 1979 General Election campaign and hordes of cameramen were pressing in, her husband commented, 'If we're not careful, we'll have a dead calf on her hands.'

> Press reports at the time.

—— 4 ——

Denis Thatcher once said: 'I like everything my beloved wife likes. If she wants to buy the top brick of St Paul's, then I would buy it.'

> This statement appeared in *The Observer* 'Sayings of the Week' column on 7 April 1985. I believe it was taken from an interview in *The Sunday Express*. Eric Partridge's *Dictionary of Slang &c.* (1984 ed.) suggests that the phrase 'to give someone the top brick *off the chimney'* means 'to be the acme of generosity, with the implication that foolish spoiling, or detriment to the donor, would result, as in

'his parents'd give that boy the . . .'' or ''she's that soft-hearted, she'd give you . . .'' Partridge's reviser, Paul Beale, inserted the entry and commented that he had heard this in the early 1980s but that it was probably in use much earlier.

Indeed, when Anthony Trollope was standing for parliament in 1868, he described a seat at Westminster as 'the highest object of ambition to every educated Englishman' and 'the top brick of the chimney'. In *Nanny Says*, Joyce Grenfell's and Sir Hugh Casson's collection of nanny sayings (1972), is included, 'Very particular we are – it's top brick off the chimney or nothing.' Presumably, Denis Thatcher was reworking this saying for his own ends. Unconsciously, he may have been conflating it with another kind of reference, such as is found in Charles Dickens, *Martin Chuzzlewit*, Chap. 38 (1844): 'He would as soon as thought of the cross upon the top of St Paul's Cathedral taking note of what he did . . . as of Nadgett's being engaged in such an occupation.'

—— 5 ——

Said Denis Thatcher on one occasion: 'I was at the 14th hole at Sandwich, looked at me watch and thought, "Bugger me, things are a bit tight." I then jumped in the car and went like a bat out of Hades up the A20. I got to Number 10, took the stairs three at a time, did me ablutions, changed into me Sunday best, and got to the bash only two minutes late. And *still* got a bloody bollocking!'

> Recounted in Peter Tory's Diary in *The Daily Star* (4 June 1985), giving the impression that he had been told the story by Thatcher himself.

—— 6 ——

Appearing on BBC Radio *Quote...Unquote* in 1984, Julian Critchley MP told a joke based on the unfortunate premise of Denis's demise. Someone who had been present on this sad occasion was asked whether Denis had uttered any memorable dying words. 'No,' said the witness, 'Margaret was with him till the end.'

> This was an old joke grafted on to the Thatchers. 'And wot were 'is last words, Mrs Jones?' . . . ''E didn't 'ave no last words. Oi was with 'im till *the end'* – this appeared in *Pass the Port* (1976), also in *Pass the Port Again* (1980) as told to an Irish priest by a woman who had just lost her father.

Margaret THATCHER

(later Baroness Thatcher) (1925–) British
Conservative prime minister.

— 1 —

When James Callaghan, the Labour prime minister, was compared by his son-in-law Peter Jay to Moses in 1977, Margaret Thatcher, then Leader of the Opposition, sought to make capital out of it by jesting in her speech to that year's Conservative Party Conference, 'My advice to Moses is: keep taking the tablets.'

This was, of course, a venerable jest even then. 'What Moses said to David Kossoff was "Continue taking the tablets as before"' was mentioned on BBC Radio *Quote...Unquote* (1976). Even so, according to an account given by Alan Watkins in *The Observer* (27 May 1988), the joke very nearly misfired. When Sir Ronald Millar, Mrs Thatcher's speech-writer, presented her with the effort, she 'pronounced the joke funny but capable of improvement. Would it not be more hilarious for her to say "Keep taking the pill"?' Sir Ronald and his colleagues were appalled at this apparent lack of understanding of their little joke and tactfully had to wean Mrs Thatcher off her version. 'Mentioning the pill would, they pretended to agree, naturally improve the joke no end. But did Margaret not think she would be taking a risk with the straiter-laced elements in the Party? Better on the whole to leave the tablets in the script.'

— 2 —

During her successful General Election campaign in 1979, Mrs Thatcher undertook various photo opportunities to emphasize how in touch she was with ordinary people. On one occasion, she was photographed standing on the back platform of a bus. As this was taking some time, she said, 'I'm beginning to feel like a clippie . . .' And then, observers recall, you could see the realization in her eyes that she might have said something patronizing, so she added: 'Who are all doing a *wonderful* job.'

Recounted by Graeme Garden on BBC Radio *Quote...Unquote* (1979).

— 3 —

From time to time, Mrs Thatcher displayed a curious blindness to innuendo. During the 1983 General Election she said of one of her aides, 'He couldn't organize pussy' – meaning, he couldn't put a saucer of milk before a cat. The following year she appeared on Michael Aspel's TV chat show. Asked if she ever had time to relax, she replied, 'No, I am always on the job.' (She appeared mystified by the studio audience's reaction.) Then during a speech at a Carlton Club dinner to mark Lord Whitelaw's retirement, she said, 'Every prime minister needs a Willie'.

Recalled by Michael Cockerell in *The Guardian* (8 April 1989).

— 4 —

When addressing guests at a reception in Jakarta, the capital of Indonesia, in 1985, Mrs Thatcher said, 'We are all impressed by the way that President Suharto and his Cabinet are handling the problems of Malaysia.' Her husband, Denis, whispered, 'Indonesia, dear, not Malaysia.' The Prime Minister corrected herself and then said a little frostily to her husband, 'Thank you, dear.'

Reported in *The Times* (11 April 1985).

— 5 —

For a period in the 1980s, Mrs Thatcher appeared to specialize in arriving at the scene of tragedies (fires, crashes, whatever) more speedily than members of the Royal Family. She would congratulate rescue workers on their efforts and then descend upon the injured in hospital. Labour MP Frank Doran started offering friends cards that looked as if they were for kidney donors in the event of an accident. In fact, they bore the words, 'In the event of serious injury, not to be visited by Margaret Thatcher.'

Reported in *The Observer* (12 March 1989).

— 6 —

When she was prime minister, Margaret Thatcher was dining in a London restaurant with the Chancellor of the Exchequer and a number of other Cabinet colleagues. The PM told the waiter that she would have steak and kidney pie. 'And the vegetables?' the waiter asked. 'Oh, they'll have the same,' Mrs Thatcher said.

Given in *The Guardian* in the week preceding 24 March 1985 as an example of Mrs Thatcher's (usually not very apparent) wit. But it was an old joke even then – having been applied to football managers dining with their players and other leaders-and-led situations.

THEATRE-GOERS

1

A popular critical formula for describing shows which put more effort into gadgetry and appearance than into the book, lyrics or performers apparently arose in connection with Irving Berlin's musical *Miss Liberty* (1949). Of that show it was first said that the 'audience came out whistling the set'.

Source untraced.

2

When the Russian ballerina Natalya Makarova gave up her career as a ballerina, she essayed a number of straight dramatic roles. In 1991, she appeared in a Chichester Festival Theatre production of the play *Tovarich*. Patrick Garland, who was the director, recalls the reaction of one Chichester regular who, presumably, was barely aware of Makarova's previous career. 'I'm sure that gel must have had ballet lessons,' he remarked. 'She moves like a dancer.'

Told by Patrick Garland in 1991.

3

One of the most bizarre audiences I have ever been a part of was during the London run of the stage-play *A Walk in the Woods*, starring Sir Alec Guinness. Even before the curtain went up, my wife pointed to a woman a few rows in front of us and said, 'She's got a baby with her'. After the initial reaction that, no, it couldn't be, it must be a doll, had moved on to, well, perhaps the baby sitter failed to show, it was time for the curtain to go up. And, lo, ten minutes into the play, the baby started yowling and, after a while, the mother had to take it out.

After the interval, we were in for more entertainment from fellow members of the audience. A couple of theatre-goers had been drinking well all evening up to this point and were now sat (wearing evening dress, let it be said) with a bottle of champagne between them. After a while, every time Sir Alec uttered one of the play's modestly distinguished lines, a voice would say out loud, 'Oh, wow, such poetry!' and sentiments of that type. The curious thing about this performance was that it was almost entertaining. The rest of us in the audience were stunned into wonderment at what would be said next. Either way, I don't expect Sir Alec regarded us as one of his best audiences.

Recalled in my book *Best Behaviour* (1992).

4

Surely it can't be true, but during the immensely long run of the musical *Les Misérables* in London, any number of stoic members of the audience were said to mutter, 'And when is Les going to make an appearance?'

Recalled by Mark Steyn (1989).

5

Long ago, during an interval half-way through a production of Shakespeare's *Antony and Cleopatra* at a London theatre, two well-dressed people went up to the manager and said, 'Tell us, is this, or is this not, *Bunty Pulls the String*?'

Told by Tom Stoppard on BBC Radio *Quote...Unquote* (1976). *Bunty Pulls the String* was a new comedy in c. 1912.

6

Although this anecdote dates from before the period covered by this book, it is too good to omit. Suzanne Lagier was a very stout actress and in one 19th-century melodrama she had to be carried offstage, in a fainting fit, by the diminutive actor, Taillade. He was unable to budge her. At which point, a voice cried out from the gallery, helpfully: 'Take what you can and come back for the rest!'

From *The Era Almanack* (1876). Another more ribald version of a similar occasion involving a dead body is that a voice from the gallery called out, 'Shag her while she's still warm!'

7

It is unforgivable, of course, to go on about what male ballet dancers carry about in their tights, but there was one reluctant ballet-goer who could never resist commenting: 'Ah, I see he's brought his sandwiches with him.'

Told to me by a *Quote...Unquote* listener, c. 1983.

8

An overheard remark from the Oberammergau Passion play (in 1934): in those days, the play lasted from 8 a.m. to 6 p.m., with a two-hour break for lunch. At about 4.30 p.m., an American member of the audience announced so that all could hear, 'Let's go, I've had enough!' Her companion replied: 'I'd like to stay and see how it finishes.'

Told to me by Peggy Gardner of Swansea (1980). Compare, however, the story about Oscar Wilde recounted by Joyce Hawkins for *The Oxford Book of Literary Anecdotes* (1975): in a *viva voce* exam-

ination at Oxford, Wilde was required to translate from a Greek version of the New Testament. When the examiners were satisfied, they told him he could stop but Wilde went on, explaining, 'I want to see how it ends.'

—— 1 ——

Once at the Edinburgh Festival, two very genteel elderly local ladies were present at a performance of Shakespeare's *Pericles*, which opened on a stage strewn with mirrored cushions and beaten brass tables. 'Where is it supposed to be?' whispered one. Said the other, reading from the programme, '"Egypt – a brothel in Alexandria"'. Declared the first, 'Och, it's *nothing like* a brothel in Alexandria.'

Told to me by Norman Bain of London SW18 (1981).

—— 2 ——

In New York, a prestige production of Ibsen's *Wild Duck* was under way. During the interval, a plump, well-heeled, middle-aged American couple began to discuss the play. The wife asked, 'Are you enjoying this dear?' The husband said, 'Oh, sure, honey, it's fine.' The wife persisted, 'Now, dear, I don't think you really like it, do you?' The husband gradually came out with, 'Well, honey, to be truthful, I was going by the name and I thought it was going to be a leg show.'

Told to me by Barbara Spry of East Hoathly (1977).

—— 3 ——

Patrick Garland, the theatre and TV director, says the most withering theatrical indictment he has ever heard was of a well-meant but rather pretentious play at Brighton. He saw it at a matinée and as the curtain came down to rather desultory applause, the woman in front of him turned to her neighbour and said, 'Well, Emily, all I can say is, I hope the dogs haven't been sick in the car.'

Told to me by Patrick Garland in 1979. This overheard remark has also been ascribed to the actor and director Sir John Clements at the Chichester Festival Theatre. Sheridan Morley always tells this story as though it was said after the Peter O'Toole *Macbeth*, which was not until 1980.

—— 4 ——

During a performance of Beethoven's opera *Fidelio* in Leeds, an enthusiastic female member of the audience was heard to say to her partner, 'Darling – I never knew Fellatio could be such fun!'

Source forgotten.

—— 5 ——

Two Edinburgh ladies (could they possibly be the same two as in 179:1?) were witnessing a fine histrionic performance of Lady Macbeth by an actress who was bringing out all the subtleties of the character. 'Does she not remind you of Mrs McAndrew?' commented one. 'She had something of the same problem.'

Told by Robert Stephens on BBC Radio *Quote...Unquote* (1991).

—— 6 ——

During a tense moment in Shakespeare's *Julius Caesar*, a voice was heard from the auditorium, saying: 'They've got a pair of sandals just like that at Dolcis . . .'

Told by Patrick Garland (1980). Christopher Matthew (1981) had it at a production of *Abelard and Héloïse*.

Ernest THESIGER

(1879–1961) English actor.

—— 7 ——

Thesiger was overcome by the usual embarrassment over what to say when going backstage after a performance to greet fellow thespians. He settled for, 'You *couldn't* have been better.'

Told by Paul Bailey (1983). Not to be confused with GIELGUD 93:2.

—— 8 ——

Thesiger went to Moscow on an Old Vic theatrical tour (with Paul Scofield as Hamlet and Mary Ure as Ophelia), several years after the newsworthy defection to the Soviet Union of two English spies. Not wishing to leave this event unnoticed, Thesiger went into one of the public conveniences of the Soviet capital and, finding himself alone, wrote on the wall, 'Burgess loves Maclean'.

This version is from Michael Pertwee, *Name Dropping* (1974). Burgess and Maclean defected in 1951. The Old Vic tour was in 1955. Rupert Hart-Davis in *The Lyttelton Hart-Davis Letters* (for 18 March 1956) has the tale told him by Gilbert Harding.

—— 1 ——

Thesiger kept on acting to a ripe old age and enjoyed telling the story of the person who had asked him, 'Excuse me, but weren't you Ernest Thesiger?' To which he replied: 'Madam, I was.'

Related in Derek Salberg, *My Love Affair With the Theatre* (1978) and Donald Sinden, *The Everyman Book of Theatrical Anecdotes* (1987). A similar story is told of Katharine Hepburn, see 104:6.

Dylan THOMAS

(1914–53) Bibulous Welsh poet.

—— 2 ——

'Llareggyb' is the name of the Welsh fishing village which is the setting for Thomas's much-loved radio play *Under Milk Wood* (1954). It was originally 'Llareggub' (and, indeed, that was the provisional title of the radio play) until somebody read the name backwards.

Subsequently, David Holbrook wrote a study of the poet entitled *Llareggub Revisited* (1962). Thomas had earlier used the place name in a story called 'The Orchards' (1936).

Daley THOMPSON

(1959–) English athlete.

—— 3 ——

After winning an Olympic gold medal in the decathlon at the Los Angeles games, Thompson was in a good mood, to put it mildly. Princess Anne came on to the track to congratulate him. Subsequently, he was asked by the press, 'What did you say to Princess Anne, and if you are going to have children, who is going to be the mother?' Thompson said, 'In answer to your second question, you have just mentioned the lady and I hope they are white.' Was it not unusual for Princess Anne to come on the track? 'Not when you are as close as we are.' Did Captain Mark Phillips know about this new romance? 'Who's he?'

Thompson concluded these celebratory remarks by adding, 'I haven't been so happy since my grand-mother caught her tit in a mangle.' This was bleeped out on TV.

Reported in *The Guardian* (11 August 1984).

William Hale THOMPSON

(1867–1944) American politician and Mayor of Chicago.

—— 4 ——

Anglophobia was the chief cause promoted by 'Big Bill' Thompson during a four-year period in the political wilderness before he successfully ran for his third term as Mayor in 1927. There are various versions of what this famous urban demagogue threatened to do if King George V ever had the temerity to set foot in the city (though no one had ever suggested he might). Either he would 'punch King George in the snoot' or he would 'bust King George in the snoot'. The usual American slang expression is 'to poke someone in the snoot' but, either way, Thompson did not get the chance. The King of England kept clear of the Windy City and protected his proboscis.

But did Thompson ever really use the words? William H. Stuart, in his Chicago 'diary', *The Twenty Incredible Years* (1935) noted: 'The writer never heard him say it. It does not occur in any written statement or speech ever given in the press by Thompson. Undoubtedly he did say it – many times – in discussing British propaganda in the public-school histories. Yes, he probably told many audiences that the king should stop sticking his nose into American school histories and should be "busted on the nose" if he didn't.'

On the other hand, Lloyd Wendt and Herman Kogan quote the following speech extracts in their 1953 biography *Big Bill of Chicago* – though perhaps they are their own creations: 'I wanta make the King of England keep his snoot out of America! That's what I want. I don't want the League of Nations! I don't want the World Court! America first, and last, and always! That's the issue of the campaign. That's what Big Bill wants ... I have no private war with the King of England, but I want him to keep his nose out of our schools.' Wendt and Kogan also quote Thompson's comment: 'What I said was, "King George has got to keep his snoot out of Chicago's schools" ... I say that the American people must not let King George lead us into another foreign war.'

Whatever the case, Thompson was re-elected

and pursued his campaign further by suspending a school board superintendent for introducing pro-British textbooks. In the subsequent trial, Thompson attracted nationwide ridicule. At the next election he was defeated.

'Tiny TIM'

(1930–) American entertainer. He played the ukelele and sang 'Tiptoe Through the Tulips' in a strange falsetto.

—— 1 ——

Tiny Tim's real name was Herbert Khaury, but earlier attempts at changing this had included 'Dary Dover', 'Emmett Swink' and 'Larry Love the Singing Canary'.

From my *Sixties Trivia* (1985).

—— 2 ——

Tiny Tim had long hair and was, shall we say, fey. But he was the original 'squeaky-clean' entertainer: 'I take my facials. I also cleanse my skin fifteen times a day (besides my momentary showers). Whenever nature calls I'm back in the shower again. Even when I go to bed, if I feel there's a stubble on my skin, I always shave it off again so my skin can be as smooth as a pillow. I also put my night creams on before I retire. Being clean spiritually and physically is very important in any society.'

In a BBC radio interview with me (25 October 1968).

—— 3 ——

Tiny Tim married a girl called 'Miss Vicki' – not in church but on the Johnny Carson *Tonight* show, in 1969. Curiously, the match did produce a child, but also ended in divorce. This, however, was not concluded on the Johnny Carson *Tonight* show.

From my *Sixties Trivia* (1985).

Sir Michael TIPPETT

(1905–) English composer.

—— 4 ——

Many years ago, Tippett used the fee paid to him by a television company for an interview, to buy a washing machine. According to Bernard Levin, Tippett felt it was only right to name the device after the benefactor who was, at least, indirectly responsible for his being able to afford it. 'Hence, the odd but pleasing fact – pleasing to me, anyway – that there is a washing machine in Wiltshire called Bernard Levin.'

In Levin's *Conducted Tour* (1981).

TOURISTS

—— 5 ——

'Definition: I am a traveller, you are a tourist, *they* are trippers.'

I was told this in about 1974 by John Julius Norwich. It may have originated in a *New Statesman* competition.

—— 6 ——

An elderly American visitor to an English stately home came across a sundial. When her companion explained that the sun caused a shadow to be cast from a metal blade across the face of the slab, thus allowing the time of day to be assessed, the old lady looked incredulous and said: 'Whatever will they think of next?'

Told to me by Mr J. Green of Rednal, Birmingham (1980).

—— 7 ——

Two American matrons were observing and admiring the well-endowed statue of Achilles on the edge of Hyde Park in London. One was overheard saying to the other: 'No, dear – Big Ben is a clock.'

This eavesdropping was told to me by Norman Mitchell of Weybridge in 1979. What I have discovered subsequently is the long history of amusement surrounding the 20-ft-high statue in dark, naked bronze. It was unveiled in 1822 after a subscription had been raised by the 'Country-women' of the first Duke of Wellington and his comrades in the victories that had culminated in the Battle of Waterloo, seven years before. So, even while he was alive, the Iron Duke was able to look out of his windows in Apsley House, a few score yards away, and see the superb monument. In 1826, William Cobbett wrote in *Rural Rides*, with customary venom: 'The English *ladies' naked* Achilles stands, having on the base of it, the word WELLINGTON in great staring letters, while all the other letters are *very, very small;* so that base tax-eaters and fund-gamblers from the country, when they go to crouch before this image, think it is the image of the *Great Captain himself!'*

Although 'The Ladies' Trophy' – as it was originally known – was provided with a fig-leaf, it provoked disquiet as being not the sort of thing respectable women ought to go around putting up. Indeed, it came to be nicknamed 'The Ladies' Fancy'. Lady Holland noted in her droll fashion that the female subscribers had had to take a *vote* on the fig-leaf question: 'It was carried for the leaf by a majority . . . The names of the *minority* have not transpired.' In fact, it seems it was the *gentlemen* co-opted to head the statue committee who had insisted on the cover-up. The fig-leaf was briefly removed by a prankster in 1961, revealing a situation which would have rendered our American tourist's remark redundant.

In his play *An Ideal Husband* (1895), Oscar Wilde has 'Mabel Chiltern' say: 'Then he proposed to me in broad daylight this morning, in front of that dreadful statue of Achilles. Really, the things that go on in front of that work of art are quite appalling. The police should interfere.'

The actor Donald Sinden says in *A Touch of the Memoirs* (1982): 'Looking one day at the enormous nude statue of Achilles at Hyde Park Corner I heard a Londoner say to a visitor . . .' But there you go.

In any case, Claire Rayner believes the remark to have been the caption to a *Punch* cartoon in the early years of the century, but this remains untraced.

—— 1 ——

A tourist visiting Windsor Castle was annoyed by the sound of aircraft taking off from Heathrow Airport near by and remarked, 'What a pity they built the castle so near to the airport.'

I included this in my *Eavesdroppings* (1981) and it had whiskers on even then. Even so, it is probably a reworking of the even more traditional remark about the monks having built Tintern Abbey too close to the road.

See also TRAVELLERS.

Sue TOWNSEND

(1946–) English novelist, author of the best-selling Adrian Mole books.

—— 2 ——

After years of poverty, Townsend had two books which were bestsellers, she had a play on in the West End, and she was wearing a new coat. But none of this seemed to count for very much when she was looking in at the window of a restaurant in St Martin's Lane, London, to see if her friends had arrived there yet. A 'bagman' came along, carrying about thirteen carrier bags, a bottle of sherry in his hand, slopping it all over the place, and stood by Townsend. She meanwhile continued peering into the restaurant window. Then the bagman sighed deeply and said, 'Ah, it's not for the likes of us . . .'

Told by her on BBC Radio *Quote...Unquote* (1985).

Philip TOYNBEE

(1916–81) English critic.

—— 3 ——

According to an oddly much-told tale, Toynbee was commissioned to write an article about the formidable novelist, Ivy Compton-Burnett, and was invited to have dinner with her. So apprehensive was he that he tanked up substantially before arrival and then accepted everything of an alcoholic nature that was offered to him. Up to the fish course, that is, when he passed out, face down on his half-finished plate.

When he finally awoke, many hours later, Toynbee's face was still in the fish, Miss Compton-Burnett and another guest had stolen away, and it was all too apparent that they had continued their substantial meal right to the end with Toynbee in this humiliating position.

Told by Paul Bailey (1983). A full-dress version can be found in Kingsley Amis, *Memoirs* (1991).

TRANSCRIBERS

—— 1 ——

Sometimes in broadcasting, when an interview or programme has been recorded, a transcript is prepared to make the producer's job easier during the editing. The transcribers do not have a very enviable task as they try to render in sensible prose the ravings of sundry show-offs, all speaking at once. But their partial hearings can give rise to some very intriguing scripts. On one occasion when I had Terry Wogan as a guest on BBC Radio *Quote...Unquote*, he used the idiom 'the Groves of Academe'. To my delight this emerged on the printed page as 'the Groves of *Aberdeen*'.

Quoted in my *Foot in Mouth* (1982).

—— 2 ——

On another show, when John Mortimer was telling an anecdote about Alfred Lunt and Lynn Fontanne (probably LUNT 127:2), the famous theatrical couple came out on paper as 'Alfred Lunt in Linford, Hants.'

The programme was in 1980.

TRANSLATORS

—— 3 ——

A favourite story of King George V's – which he never failed to want hearing re-told – concerned an English-born princess paying a visit to Uppsala Cathedral in Sweden. The Archbishop was keen to show off his knowledge of English and opened a chest of drawers in the sacristy with the words, 'I will now open these trousers and reveal some ever more precious treasures to Your Royal Highness.'

Quoted in Kenneth Rose, *George V* (1983).

—— 4 ——

The worldwide spread of the soft drinks Coca-Cola and Pepsi Cola has given rise to some difficulties in translating their slogans. It is said that 'Come alive with Pepsi' became, in German, 'Come alive out of the grave,' and, in Chinese, 'Pepsi brings your ancestors back from the dead.'

When Coca-Cola started advertising in Peking, 'Put a Smile on Your Face' came out as 'Let Your Teeth Rejoice'. Odder still, the famous slogan 'It's the Real Thing' came out as 'The Elephant Bites the Wax Duck.'

Source: J. C. Louis & Harvey Yazijian, *The Cola Wars* (1980) and *Time* (30 March 1981).

—— 5 ——

The English-language version of a car-rental firm's brochure in Tokyo exhorted hirers thus: 'When passenger of foot heave in sight, tootle the horn. Trumpet him melodiously at first, but if he still obstacles your passage, then tootle him with vigour.'

Quoted in *The Independent* (12 August 1993).

—— 6 ——

An Englishwoman found the bed in her French hotel extremely uncomfortable and put this down to the fact that the mattress was next to useless. Complaining at the reception desk, she unfortunately chose the word *matelot* for mattress. When this failed to produce the desired effect, she got very hot under the collar and shouted, '*Je demande un matelot sur mon lit!*'

When the hotel proprietor was told of this somewhat bizarre demand, she commented, '*Ah, les anglais! Quelle nation maritime!*'

Told by Eleanor Bron in 1986. I had earlier encountered a version told about an Afrikaans-speaking South African couple on their honeymoon in Amsterdam ...

TRAVELLERS

—— 7 ——

A Venetian gentleman was asked if he liked travelling. 'Why should I travel,' he exclaimed, 'when I am already here?'

Source untraced.

—— 8 ——

A traveller arriving at an Australian airport was confronted by an immigration officer requiring to know, 'Do you have a criminal record?' The traveller told him he hadn't – 'I didn't realize it was still compulsory.'

This – 'the oldest and hoariest Australian joke in existence' – has sometimes been credited to Henry Blofeld, the English cricket commentator, according to *The Times* diary (13 January 1990).

—— 1 ——

During the Second World War, an American GI found himself stationed in Bedford. He described it as 'a cemetery with traffic lights'.

Quoted in a letter to James Agate (and quoted by him in *Ego 8*, for 3 January 1945).

—— 2 ——

A child asked a stranger where he came from, whereupon his father rebuked him gently: 'Never do that, son. If a man's from Texas, he'll tell you. If he's not, why embarrass him by asking?'

From John Gunther, *Inside U.S.A.* (1947). He called it 'doubtless antique' even then, when he heard it told in San Antonio. I have heard it reworked about Yorkshiremen by Roy Hattersley (1984).

See also TOURISTS.

Sir Herbert Beerbohm
TREE

(1853–1917) English actor-manager.

—— 3 ——

Tree went to the Post Office and said he wanted to buy a stamp. When he was shown a whole sheet of them, he pointed at one in the middle and said, 'I'll have that one.'

Told in Hesketh Pearson, *Beerbohm Tree* (1956).

—— 4 ——

He saw a man in the street struggling under the weight of a grandfather clock. 'My poor fellow,' said Tree, 'why not carry a watch?'

Told in ibid. Coincidentally or not, there is a cartoon in *Punch* (27 March 1907) which shows a man struggling with a large clock (the sort, however, that would fit on a mantelpiece). A bystander, characterized in the caption as 'Funny Man', says to him: 'PARDON ME, SIR, BUT WOULDN'T YOU FIND IT MORE CONVENIENT TO CARRY A WATCH?'

Tommy TRINDER

(1909–89) English comedian. Big jaw, wore a hat.

—— 5 ——

One of his catchphrases was 'Trinder's the name'. He was using it in a London nightclub when Orson Welles and Rita Hayworth were present. So when Trinder said it to Welles, he replied: 'Why don't you change it?' As quick as a flash, Trinder said, 'Is that a suggestion or a proposal of marriage?'

In *Before Your Very Eyes* (1975), Arthur Askey puts this sometime just after July 1939 – a bit unlikely as Welles was not a name in London at that time. And although Askey does not mention Rita Hayworth in his version, she and Welles were not together until 1943, when they were married in the September.

Harry S TRUMAN

(1884–1972) American Democratic president.

—— 6 ——

Correctly speaking, there should be no full stop after the 'S' in Truman's name. It is not an abbreviation and is only there to provide a balancing sound between first name and surname. Honestly.

A fact. The same goes for David O Selznick (1902–65), the American film producer. In Rudy Behlmer's *Memo from David O. Selznick* (1973), Selznick described how he took a middle initial to distinguish himself from an uncle, also called David Selznick, whom he disliked. 'I . . . went through the alphabet to find [a letter] that seemed to give the best punctuation, and decided on "O".'

—— 7 ——

Truman had gone to the White House on the death of Franklin D. Roosevelt in 1945. In 1948, he sought election to the presidency in his own right but was not expected to win against the Republican challenger, Thomas E. Dewey. So confident was *The Chicago Daily Tribune* that Truman had lost that its issue for 2 November 1948 had the banner headline, 'DEWEY DEFEATS TRUMAN'. This enabled Truman to flourish a copy of the paper when he had convincingly won re-election.

From reports of the time.

—— 1 ——

In 1950, when Truman's daughter Margaret gave a singing recital in Washington she received a bad notice from critic Paul Hume writing in *The Washington Post*. 'She is flat a good deal of the time,' he said, 'she cannot sing with anything approaching professional finish . . . [and] she communicates almost nothing of the music she presents.'

The President immediately fired off a handwritten note to Hume: 'I have just read your lousy review buried in the back pages. You sound like a frustrated old man who never made a success, an eight-ulcer man on a four-ulcer job and all four ulcers working. Westbrook Pegler, a guttersnipe, is a gentleman compared to you. You can take that as more of an insult than a reflection on your ancestry.'

Subsequently, Truman asserted that he had really told Hume he would 'kick his balls in' but the published versions of the letter do not bear him out. Truman later said he worked on the assumption that 'every man in the United States that's got a daughter will be on my side' – and he was probably right.

Mark TWAIN

(1835–1910) American writer and humorist (real name Samuel Langhorne Clemens).

—— 2 ——

Twain said, the year before his death, 'I came in with Halley's comet in 1835. It is coming again next year and I expect to go out with it. It will be the greatest disappointment of my life if I don't go out with Halley's comet. The Almighty has said, no doubt: "Now, here are these two unaccountable freaks; they came in together, they must go out together."' And so it was. Twain died on 21 April 1910, the day after the comet reappeared.

Information from A. B. Paine (ed.), *The Autobiography of Mark Twain* (1912).

Kenneth TYNAN

(1927–80) English theatre critic and writer.

—— 3 ——

Even as a schoolboy in Birmingham, Tynan was a great ringmaster of events. In 1945, he invited James Agate, the leading drama critic of the day, to a conference at his school. Tynan went to meet the old man at the station. In the taxi, Agate put a hand on young Tynan's knee and asked, 'Are you a homosexual, my boy?' 'I'm af-f-fraid not,' stuttered Tynan. 'Ah, well,' sighed Agate, 'I thought we'd get that out of the way.'

Recounted in Kathleen Tynan, *The Life of Kenneth Tynan* (1987).

—— 4 ——

Tynan was initially an actor, though not a very good one. Beverley Baxter, reviewing 'The Worst Hamlet I Have Ever Seen' in a 1951 edition of *The Evening Standard*, said of Tynan's performance as the Player King: 'He would not get a chance in the village hall unless he were related to the vicar. His performance was quite dreadful.' However, Tynan very shortly afterwards replaced Baxter as the paper's drama critic.

Recounted in ibid.

—— 5 ——

In 1956, Tynan went to interview the aged theatre designer, Edward Gordon Craig, at his home in the south of France. Almost at once, Craig said, 'You have the right face for a critic. You have the look of a blooming martyr.'

In *The Observer* (29 July 1956). (Subsequently, Sir Alec Guinness admitted that he had drawn on Tynan's cadaverousness when creating the make-up for his part in the film *The Ladykillers*, 1955.)

—— 6 ——

There were four motions of protest in the House of Commons. There were outraged articles in the press. There were demands that the BBC should be prosecuted for obscenity. Nothing eventually happened. Somehow or other the nation managed to survive the shock. It was the first time the word 'f***' had been said on British TV.

Tynan said it in a discussion on theatre censorship on *Not So Much a Programme More a Way of Life* in November 1965.

U

Sir Stanley UNWIN

(1884–1968) English publisher and co-founder of
George Allen and Unwin.

—— 1 ——

Sir Stanley was dining with a foreign publisher who offered him a cigarette. Sir Stanley sharply rejected the offer, saying, 'I tried it once, but I didn't like it . . .' Later, towards the end of the meal, the foreign publisher suggested some brandy. Again, Sir Stanley rejected the offer, saying, 'Tried it once, didn't like it . . .' Next day, the two men happened to bump into Sir Stanley's son, Rayner. Sir Stanley made to introduce the boy, but, quick as a flash, the foreigner quipped, 'Your *only* son, I take it . . . ?'

Story told by Christina Foyle, September 1984. In fact, Unwin did have more than one son.

Sir Peter USTINOV

(1921–) English actor and playwright (of Russian
parentage).

—— 2 ——

Ustinov did a screen test for the part of Nero in the film *Quo Vadis* and then the filming was delayed for a year. The new producer of the film sent him a cable saying that he thought Ustinov was a little young for the part. Ustinov sent him a cable saying that if the film was delayed *another* year, he would be too old for it. MGM then sent him a cable saying, 'Historical research has proved you correct.'

Told by Ustinov in 1991.

Wynford VAUGHAN-THOMAS

(1908–87) Garrulous Welsh broadcaster – war reporter and commentator.

—— 1 ——

Arriving in Los Angeles after flying on an inaugural flight over the Pole, Wynford Vaughan-Thomas was – unusually – rendered speechless by an American broadcaster. V-T's description of the Greenland icecap apparently made the American broadcaster remember his sponsors who were makers of deodorants. Said he: 'It may be December outside, but it's always August under your armpits.'

Related in V-T's *Trust to Talk*, 1980. However, *News Review* (13 November 1947) had reproduced from the *Evening Standard*: 'He [John Snagge] had been against commercial broadcasting ever since he heard a Toscanini radio concert in New York interrupted by the sponsor's slogan "It may be December outside, ladies, but it is always August under your armpits".' See also BARNETT **23:10.**

—— 2 ——

Wynford was conducting a radio interview in the street with a passer-by during the Second World War when Eleanor Roosevelt had come over to Britain on a visit. Unfortunately, he also asked the man what he felt about Mrs Roosevelt. 'Oh,' he said, 'I wish I could have the chance of meeting her, but as far as I can understand from the press, it is only the American troops who are going to have intercourse with her.'

Told by V-T in 1981. Also related in Jack de Manio, *To Auntie With Love* (1967).

—— 3 ——

The Queen Mother was launching the *Ark Royal* and the TV producer said, 'See her in, cue her in, then keep your mouth shut as she pulls the lever, marvellous shots as the thing slides down, but I won't have time to cue you, so as soon as you see the hull hit the Mersey, come in and chuck the dictionary over the screen.' But when it came to the moment and the ship entered the water, the producer cut to a shot of the Queen Mother with a marvellous smile that filled the whole screen, as Vaughan-Thomas came in with: 'There she is, the whole vast bulk of her . . .'

Told by V-T in 1980. Also related in Jack de Manio, *To Auntie With Love* (1967).

—— 4 ——

Wynford used to enjoy telling the overheard remark from the girl who had told her friend of a dreadful happening: 'He put his hand *up my skirt* . . . you know, the Jaeger one with pleats . . .'

Told in 1980.

—— 5 ——

During the blackout in the Second World War, Wynford said that a voice was heard urging, 'Come on, Grandpa.' The old man explained that he could not find his teeth. To which the reply was: 'They're dropping bombs, not sandwiches.'

Told in 1980. The joke – which was fairly traditional, after all – made an appearance in the film *Reds* (1981).

VICTIMS

—— 6 ——

A distraught woman came rushing home, screaming: 'Help, help, I've been graped! I've been graped!' When she had been given the appropriate victim support, she was gently asked whether she hadn't meant to say 'I've been *raped*', rather than 'graped'. 'I know what I mean,' she replied, tartly, 'I was definitely graped. You see, there was a whole bunch of 'em.'

Not the most politically correct of jokes, I'm afraid. I remember it chiefly because it was used by David Frost (in conversation, *c.* 1986) to demonstrate how women were often poor joke-tellers. His own sainted wife, Lady Carina, had tried telling this one, but rather ruined the effect by giving as the punch line, 'You see, there was a whole *gang* of them.'

—— 1 ——

I went for an audition as a newsreader on Capital Radio before it started in 1973. There was a long wait during which I chatted to a secretary and to a girl who was also in for an audition. The latter told me a story of two friends of hers whose car was stolen one night but, rather oddly, returned to them the following morning. Inside the car was a note saying, very sorry, it had been needed in an emergency and here are two tickets for The Talk of the Town on Saturday.

So, off they trotted and, of course, when they returned home from the show they found their flat had been stripped from floor to ceiling.

From my diary entry for 6 August 1973 – another 'urban myth'. In Tom Burnam's *More Misinformation* (1980), he calls this 'The Repentant Car Thief' story and notes that it is well known in the US and that the tickets have also been for 'opera, ballet, rock concert, whatever'. He also mentions that the story has been reported from Grenoble in France.

—— 2 ——

There were a pair of brothers who became known as 'the fabulous Mizners'. They were American eccentrics. Addison Mizner was an architect and entrepreneur; Wilson Mizner was broke but bright and very witty. The latter was walking down the street when a robber came up to him and said, 'Can you *lend* me five dollars.' And Mizner said: 'Why – has it stopped getting dark?'

Told by William Franklyn on BBC Radio *Quote...Unquote* (1985).

Queen VICTORIA

(1819–1901) British sovereign.

—— 3 ——

'Why is Queen Victoria like a flower pot?'

I do not know the answer to this riddle. Answers on a postcard, please . . .

Gore VIDAL

(1925–) American novelist.

—— 4 ——

Vidal has had a number of outstanding feuds in his life. In 1968, he had an almighty spat with William F. Buckley who, he said, 'Looks and sounds not unlike Hitler, but without the charm'. Mutual lawsuits raged for a period.

Another feud was with the diminutive Truman Capote, of whom Vidal said, 'He should be heard, not read.' When Capote died, Vidal commented: 'Good career move'.

Quotes from *The Observer* (26 April 1981) and Ned Sherrin, *Theatrical Anecdotes* (1991). Capote died in 1984; in *Time* Magazine (8 April 1985), the graffito was reported, 'Elvis is dead', under which had been written, 'Good career move.'

Erich VON STROHEIM

(1885–1957) Austrian-born actor and film director in the US.

—— 5 ——

'The Man You Love to Hate' was the billing applied to him for the film *The Heart of Humanity* (1918) in which he played an obnoxious German officer who not only attempted to violate the leading lady but nonchalantly tossed a baby out of the window. At the film's premiere in Los Angeles, he was hooted and jeered at when he walked on stage. He had to explain that he was only an actor – and an Austrian, not a German.

Recalled in Thomas Quinn Curtiss, *Von Stroheim* (1971).

Harry VON ZELL

(1906–81) American broadcaster and actor who later appeared in the Burns and Allen television shows.

—— 1 ——

Introducing a radio broadcast by Herbert Hoover, he said: 'Ladies and gentleman – the president of the United States, Hoobert Herver!'

Confirmed by *Contemporary Biography* **(1944). Hoover was US president 1929–33.**

Diana VREELAND

(*c.* 1903–89) American fashion journalist, former editor of *Vogue*.

—— 2 ——

Lunching with Liza Minelli at the New York restaurant, La Grenouille, matters were not helped by the fact that Miss Minelli apparently mistook Vreeland for the PR woman of the Plaza Hotel. Accordingly, at the end of the meal, Minelli bade Vreeland farewell with the words, 'Please say hello to Ed, the piano player, for me' – the 'Ed' in question was in the Oak Room Bar of the Plaza Hotel. Vreeland was mystified by this but couldn't bring herself to accept that Minelli had failed to recognize her. So she went back to the *Vogue* office and upbraided her staff for not keeping her abreast of the latest slang. 'Say hello to Ed the piano player' subsequently appeared in several editions of *Vogue* as a trendy way to say 'goodbye'.

Recounted in *The Independent* **Magazine (2 September 1989) as having taken place 'about 20 years ago . . .'**

WAITERS

—— 1 ——

A classic eavesdropping was collected by Gilbert Harding when, having arrived at a restaurant well after last orders had been taken, he persuaded the staff to find him something to eat. Just as he was digesting the last morsel, he overheard one waiter say to another, incredulously, 'He's eaten it!'

The same story was told by Brigadier Sir Otho Prior-Palmer in *Pass the Port* (1976). The Harding version, as here, was told on BBC Radio *Quote...Unquote* (1979).

Sir Hereward WAKE

(1876–1963) English soldier.

—— 2 ——

A tribute in *The Times* that followed on from Sir Hereward's obituary, paid the major-general an unusual compliment: 'He loved shooting, hunting, horses, and above all dogs. The smell of a wet dog was delicious to him, and his devoted wife never let him know that, to her, it was abominable.'

From *The Times* (7 August 1963).

Ronald WALDMAN

(1914–78) English broadcasting executive.

—— 3 ——

The expression 'Did you spot this week's deliberate mistake?' – a way of covering up a mistake that was *not* deliberate – arose from a BBC radio series *Monday Night at Seven* (later *Eight*) in about 1938. Ronnie Waldman had taken over as deviser of the 'Puzzle Corner' part of the programme which was presented by Lionel Gamlin. 'Through my oversight, a mistake crept into "Puzzle Corner" one night,' Waldman recalled in 1954, 'and when Broadcasting House was besieged by telephone callers putting us right, Harry Pepper [the producer] concluded that such "listener participation" was worth exploiting as a regular thing. "Let's always put in a deliberate mistake," he suggested.'

Waldman revived the idea when he himself presented 'Puzzle Corner' as a part of *Kaleidoscope* on BBC Television in the early 1950s and the phrase 'this week's deliberate mistake' has continued to be used jokingly as a cover for ineptitude.

Max WALL

(1908–90) English comedian of incomparable voice and appearance.

—— 4 ——

L egend has it that Wall was banned for a while from BBC radio for interpolating the following unapproved gag in his routine: 'There was this tightrope walker who was walking along the wire when he encountered Marilyn Monroe. You see, he didn't know whether to toss her off or block her passage.'

Oral tradition, probably since the 1950s. Also attributed to Max Miller.

Raoul WALSH

(1887–1980) American film director.

—— 5 ——

W alsh's ex-wife used to attend all his films to make certain that he was still working and that, accordingly, his alimony payments would keep on coming. So Walsh always used to insert the same line of dialogue especially for her – 'I'm going to get out of here faster than I left my first wife' – even if it had no relevance to the plot.

Recounted in *The Independent* (12 January 1989).

Julie WALTERS

(1950–) English actress, as verbally-challenged off-screen as she is talented on.

—— 1 ——

Accepting an award from the British Academy of Film and Television Arts in about 1984, Walters gave a rambling acceptance speech, which can be more or less encapsulated in the words with which she ended: 'I don't know what to say.' Michael Aspel, the host, quipped, as she sat down, 'Well, you might have said "thank you".'

From my memory of the incident. It was probably when she received the Best Actress award for the film *Educating Rita*.

Dame Irene WARD

(1895–1980) English Conservative politician with a blue rinse, as I recall. Created a life peer – Lady Ward of North Tyneside.

—— 2 ——

In the House of Commons, during the Second World War, Irene Ward asked the Minister of Supply why Wrens were having to wait for their uniforms. The minister replied that there were problems in providing uniforms for the Navy and that sailors had been given priority over Wrens. To which Ward is supposed to have responded: 'How long is the minister prepared to hold up the skirts of Wrens for the convenience of His Majesty's sailors?'

Quoted in Richard Needham, *The Honourable Member* (1983).

Auberon WAUGH

(1939–) English journalist and ex-novelist.

—— 3 ——

Waugh received an invitation from a Senegalese journal to make a speech – in French – on the subject of breast-feeding. At the time, he had been writing a column in *British Medicine* and campaigning against compulsory breastfeeding in National Health hospitals – so it was not as unlikely as it might seem. He wrote the speech – in French – with considerable difficulty, only to discover, on arrival in Dakar, that his hosts were expecting a speech on press freedom.

Recounted by him in *Will This Do?* (1991).

Evelyn WAUGH

(1903–66) English novelist.

—— 4 ——

The comic Spike Milligan had great admiration for Evelyn Waugh. Whether this was reciprocated in any way must be in doubt. Once when passing White's Club in St James's, Milligan saw Waugh coming out and hastened over to ask for his autograph. Waugh duly scribbled on a bit of paper and handed the result to Milligan who duly thanked him and went home. When he looked at what Waugh had written on the paper, it said, 'Go away'.

Told by Milligan on BBC Radio *Quote...Unquote* (1977).

WEATHER FORECASTERS

—— 5 ——

A few hours before a devastating storm broke over south-eastern England in October 1987, Michael Fish reassured BBC TV viewers: 'A woman rang to say she'd heard there was a hurricane on the way. Well, don't worry. There isn't.' Technically he was right – it wasn't a hurricane – but few noticed the difference.

Quoted in *The Observer* (19 October 1987).

—— 1 ——

Another legendary weather forecaster – not Fish – was distracted by a letter falling off the map, in the days when weather maps were actually in front of the camera rather than electronically generated. The first letter of the word 'FOG' had disappeared, and the forecaster duly apologized for the 'F in Fog'.

Oral tradition.

Laurence WELK

(1903–92) American conductor and accordionist whose old-fashioned TV show was popular in the mid-century. He retained a Middle European accent and even entitled his autobiography *Wunnerful, Wunnerful* (1971).

—— 2 ——

Welk was another great TV performer who had problems with idiot boards. On one occasion, he announced that he was going to play a selection of music made famous during the years 1939–45 – or, as he put it, 'During the years of World War Aye-Aye'.

Told to me by David Frost, *c*. 1984.

Orson WELLES

(1915–85) American film actor and director.

—— 3 ——

Welles obtained his first professional stage engagement in Dublin by sending a note to Micheál MacLiammoir and Hilton Edwards at the Gate Theatre. It stated, 'Orson Welles, star of the New York Theater Guild, would consider appearing in one of your productions and hopes you will see him for an appointment.' He was 16 years old at the time.

Recalled in Frank Brady, *Citizen Welles* (1989).

—— 4 ——

In a New York stage production of *Julius Caesar* in 1937, Welles, playing Brutus, kept trying to reproduce a moment that had occurred accidentally in one performance. Because there were not enough rubber knives for the assassination scene, Welles had had to use a real knife. On one occasion, he fumbled and dropped it, and the knife stuck in the stage and quivered. Later in the run, Welles lost his balance and actually plunged the real knife in the chest of Joseph Holland who was playing Caesar and severed an artery near the heart. As he fell, Holland whispered, 'Christ, I've been stabbed!' (He was rushed to hospital and could not act for two months.)

Recalled in ibid.

—— 5 ——

The Welles film *Mr Arkadin* (1962) was based on his own novel (1956). Early on in the film, the eponymous character holds a party in his castle and tells a fable: 'A scorpion, who could not swim, begged a frog to carry him to the other side. The frog complained that the scorpion would sting him. This was impossible, said the scorpion, because he would then drown with the frog. So the pair set forth. Halfway over, the scorpion stung the frog. "Is that logical?" asked the frog. "No, it's not," answered the scorpion, as they both sunk to the bottom, "but I can't help it, it's my nature."'

> **Quoted in ibid. In *The Time of My Life* (1989), Denis Healey recalls how he once 'delighted the sheikhs in the mountains surrounding Aden' with the same story. His version ended with the frog asking, 'Why did you do it? You know you'll drown.' And the scorpion replies, 'Yes, I know, but after all, this is the Middle East.' The story is also told (twice) in the film *The Crying Game* (1992).**

—— 6 ——

For a while, Welles was married to Rita Hayworth. After it was all over, she said: 'Oh, Orson was clever all right . . . The morning after we were married, I woke up, and I could tell by the expression on his face that he was just waiting for the applause . . .'

> **Told in *The Kenneth Williams Diaries* (1993) – entry for 18 June 1955.**

See also TRINDER 184:5.

WELL-MANNERED PEOPLE (and others)

1

A litter lout, driving through Bury St Edmunds, chucked a cigarette packet out of her car window. An elderly female resident picked up the packet and handed it back. 'I think this belongs to you,' she added. 'I just threw that away,' said the litter lout. 'Finished with it. Don't want that.' The elderly female resident said: 'And neither does Bury St Edmunds . . .'

A familiar story. In *The Kenneth Williams Diaries* (1993), he has a version on 1 January 1969.

2

After leaving Johannesburg on a flight to London, a rather smug and self-opinionated woman travelling in the first-class section beckoned the stewardess to come to her. 'Tell me,' she said, grandly, 'What's the domestic situation in England these days?' Replied the stewardess: 'I don't think you will have any trouble finding a job, madam.'

Source untraced, but current before 1980.

H. G. WELLS

(1866–1946) English novelist and writer.

3

When Dame Rebecca West, the writer, died in March 1983, mention was made of her affair seventy years before with Wells. One obituarist said she had been attracted to him 'because he smelt of walnuts' (he, whether true or not, had been attracted by her 'hard mind').

No source was given for the 'walnuts' assertion, but it chimes with another mention of H. G. Wells given in Ted Morgan's biography of W. Somerset Maugham. When Maugham asked Moura Budberg (another lover of H. G. Wells) what she saw in the paunchy, played-out writer, she replied, 'He smells of *honey*.'

Whatever Wells smelt of, it seems to have been effective and surely ought to have been bottled and put on the market.

Discussed in *The Guardian* (16 March 1983). The honey reference is also mentioned in *The Lyttelton Hart-Davis Letters* (for 16 January 1957).

The WELSH

4

'A Welshman is a man who prays on his knees on Sundays and preys on his neighbours all the rest of the week' – Anon.

Source untraced.

5

'Welshmen prize their women so highly that they put a picture of their mother-in-law on the national flag' – Anon.

Told by Canon Don Lewis of Swansea (1983).

Timberlake WERTENBAKER

(1928–) Anglo-French-American playwright.

6

The critic Sheridan Morley was having lunch with an elderly American and running through the London theatre scene when he happened to mention the name of this playwright. 'Timberlake Wertenbaker?' The elderly American rolled the name round his tongue a few times and then said, 'My daughter was at school with a girl called Timberlake Wertenbaker. Any chance they might be the same person?'

Told by Sheridan Morley in *The London Magazine* (February 1993).

Loelia, Duchess of WESTMINSTER

(1902–93) Loelia Lindsay was an English socialite and the third wife of the 2nd Duke of Westminster from 1930 to 1947. She wrote a book entitled *Grace and Favour* (1961).

—— 1 ——

She once said: 'Anybody seen in a bus after the age of thirty has been a failure in life.'

Quoted in *The Daily Telegraph* (*c.* 1980).

Sir Huw WHELDON

(1916–86) Welsh broadcaster and TV executive.

—— 2 ——

Even as an old man, Wheldon said he still cringed at a review of his schoolboy rugby playing that once appeared in *The North Wales Chronicle*: 'He lacks on the field the abounding confidence he has off.'

Told by Sir Huw in 1985.

—— 3 ——

When requested by a newspaper to supply his own epitaph, Wheldon volunteered: 'He never used a sentence where a paragraph would do.'

In *The Daily Mail* (9 June 1976). He reacted a little uneasily when I reminded him of this a few years later. The actual headstone on his grave in St Peris churchyard, Nant Peris, Snowdonia, simply states that he was a 'Soldier, Broadcaster, Administrator'.

—— 4 ——

Wheldon was at a University of London convocation in the early 1980s, resplendent in a crimson robe topped by a huge black velvet hat. Asked what it was, he replied: 'Doctor of Music at the University of Lausanne. I borrowed it from the BBC's costume department.'

Recounted in Paul Ferris, *Sir Huge* (1990).

—— 5 ——

When Ned Sherrin was working on the BBC TV satire shows in the mid-1960s, there was a palace revolution and one of his bosses was replaced by another (Donald Baverstock by Huw Wheldon, as Controller of Programmes, 1965). It all took place over a weekend and when Sherrin arrived on Monday morning the new man – Wheldon – was already totally installed in his predecessor's office, except that everything representing the old man had been taken out. The office was absolutely naked and bare. Sherrin greeted Wheldon with the words, 'Oh, Huw, I see you've put your stamp on the office already.'

Told by Sherrin on BBC Radio *Quote...Unquote* (1980), not mentioning Wheldon's name. Later, he revealed all in *Theatrical Anecdotes* (1991).

Wilfrid Hyde WHITE

(1903–91) English actor, specializing in pinstripe gents and conmen. He also played Colonel Pickering in the film of *My Fair Lady* (1964).

—— 6 ——

A keen student of racing form, but inept at handling his financial affairs, Hyde White was declared bankrupt in 1979. At the bankruptcy hearing, he was asked by the official receiver, 'If you cannot tell us how you spent such a large sum in so short a time, perhaps you can tell us what will win the Gold Cup at Ascot this afternoon?' Hyde White obliged, but added: 'Only have a small bet, otherwise we might find ourselves changing places.'

From Hyde White's obituary in *The Independent* (8 May 1991).

William WHITELAW

(later Viscount Whitelaw) (1918–) English Conservative politician.

—— 7 ——

Whitelaw is famous for his informal sayings. The essence of these 'Whitelawisms' or 'Willieisms' is a touching naivety which may conceal a certain truth. The most notable is his description of the then prime minister, Harold Wilson, during the 1970 general election going 'around the country stirring up apathy'. On the face of it, a nonsensical remark, but conveying, oddly, just what Wilson was doing.

> In *The Independent* (14 July 1992), Whitelaw told Hunter Davies: 'It's a strange thing. I did say those words, but the real meaning has been lost. For a start, I meant to say "spreading apathy" not "stirring it up" ... Wilson was so sure of victory that he was going round the country calming people down, telling everyone not to worry, leave it all to him. I was really attacking him for encouraging people not to want a change, not saying people were apathetic to him.'

—— 1 ——

There are many others, collected by journalists over the years, and there is no reason to doubt that Whitelaw actually said them – if not in these words, then, we may be sure, in something like them. For example, on arriving in Ulster as secretary of state (25 March 1972) he said: 'One must be careful not to prejudge the past.'

—— 2 ——

When both Whitelaw and Margaret Thatcher were candidates for the Conservative leadership in 1975, they both arrived in Eastbourne to attend the National Young Conservatives' conference. He met her and he kissed her. This called for explanation, and he duly gave it: 'I have over a period of time, when I have met her – as indeed one does – I have kissed her often before. We have not done it on a pavement outside a hotel in Eastbourne before. But we have done it in various rooms in one way and another at various functions – it is perfectly genuine and normal – and normal and right – so to do.'

> Reported in *The Observer* (9 February 1975).

—— 3 ——

In the House of Commons (on 1 December 1981), he said: 'We are examining alternative anomalies.'

> Reported in *Hansard*.

—— 4 ——

Asked in 1984 whether he thought Mrs Thatcher would fall over any more banana skins, Whitelaw said: 'I think there will be banana skins as long as there are bananas.'

> Quoted in *The Observer* (22 April 1984).

—— 5 ——

Less remarked upon have been Lord Whitelaw's characteristic speech rhythms and his use of inversion and parentheses in longer utterances. A modest example – commenting on the lifting of the siege at the Iranian embassy in London, May 1980, he said: 'The operation, and I think the people of this country and many in the world will think so too, was an outstanding success, and it showed we in Britain are not prepared to tolerate terrorism in our capital city.'

> From the *Daily Telegraph* report of the incident.

Richard WHITELEY

(1943–) English broadcaster. Associated with Yorkshire Television's local *Calendar* programmes since 1968, the first face to appear on Channel 4 in 1982, and host of the 'words and numbers game' *Countdown* ever since.

—— 6 ——

Hosting a live afternoon chat show called *Calendar Tuesday* in October 1977, Whiteley was interviewing a man called Brian Plummer, who had written a couple of books about ferreting. Plummer was holding two ferrets and Whiteley one. Whiteley's (probably because it was nervous) sank its teeth right into his finger and did not leave off for half a minute. Plummer said, 'Don't worry, she's only playing with you!' – and, indeed, if the ferret had meant business it could have gone right through to the bone. Even so, Whiteley's pain was excruciating and only ended when Plummer unloaded the two ferrets he was holding and applied appropriate pressure to the tender parts of the errant ferret.

The tape of the incident having now been seen by almost everybody in the television-watching world has meant that wherever he goes Whiteley is known as 'the Ferret Man' and people call out 'Where's your ferret?' As he ruefully concedes, when he dies, the newspaper placards will not say, 'Perceptive TV Interviewer Dies' or 'First Man on Channel 4 Dies'; they will say, simply, 'Ferret Man Dies'.

> Recounted to me by Richard Whiteley in August 1993.

Billy WILDER

(1906–) Austrian-born American film director.

1

Visiting Paris just after the Second World War, Wilder was asked by his wife to bring back a bidet. Unsuccessful, he sent her a telegram, 'Unable to obtain bidet. Suggest headstand in shower.'

This version of a much-told tale comes from Leslie Halliwell, *The Filmgoer's Book of Quotes* (1973).

2

Towards the end of his distinguished Hollywood career, Billy Wilder was summoned to a studio by the 'movie brat' who was now its head. 'Great to meet you at last, Billy. Hope you'll come on the team. Believe we can make you some *very* interesting offers . . . Now, Billy, tell me – what have you *done*?' Wilder paused a second and then said, with the utmost politeness: 'After you . . .'

Told to me by Alexander Walker (1985).

Kenneth WILLIAMS

(1926–88) English comedy actor.

3

For a while, he was billed as 'Kenneth C. Williams' but desisted when he started being mistaken for the writer of *A Streetcar Named Desire*.

Told to me by Kenneth Williams in the early 1970s.

4

My diary for 14 May 1968 records: 'To Pinewood [to cover the filming of *Carry on Up the Khyber* for BBC Radio *Movie-Go-Round*]. Talked first to Kenneth Williams [who] told one story which, alas, is not transmittable. He was playing a love scene with Joan Sims and broke wind. When shooting was stopped, he protested that Rudolph Valentino had done just the same thing in his time, so what was the matter? Gerald Thomas, the director, pointed out that in those days films were silent . . .'

Williams had recorded the story in his own diary on 3 May 1968 (presumably the day it had happened), as was revealed on publication of *The Kenneth Williams Diaries* (1993). It can only have been untransmittable on dear old *Movie-Go-Round*, as it soon became a familiar part of his TV chat-show patter.

5

Kennie was mean as hell (except when he was being quietly and spontaneously generous). I remember him urging me to buy a season ticket for the deck chairs in Regent's Park – 'It'll save you 50p,' he said. He also told (with how much self-awareness, I know not) of going into Burtons, the tailors, to complain about a jacket he had bought there and which was now threadbare at the elbows ('It's a disgrace!', he added). 'How long have you had it?' they asked him. 'It must be ten years now,' he replied.

Personal recollections.

6

And then there is the story of him going into the bank in Great Portland Street to draw out some cash. The employee gushed all over him and said he had seen all his films, heard all his broadcasts, was a great fan. 'So, what can I do for you, Mr Williams?' 'I want to draw £50.' 'Oh, yes,' said the bank clerk, 'and have you any identification . . .'

Of course this was preposterous, but K.W. created a great scene rather than simply saying, 'Fancy that.'

7

On one occasion, Williams claimed to have heard two men outside a London club. One said: 'I've just been to *Evita*.' The other replied: 'You don't look very brown.'

Told by him on BBC Radio *Quote...Unquote* (1979).

See also EVANS 82:5.

Nicol WILLIAMSON

(1939–) Scottish actor on stage and screen.
Increasingly reclusive.

8

Williamson soon lost patience with a group of noisy young Americans in the audience at a performance of *Macbeth*. He got off his throne, walked down to the footlights and calmly said, in iambic pentameters:

> If you don't shut your mouths a friend of mine
> Will pass amongst you with a baseball bat.

Whereupon he adjusted his crown and continued in complete silence.

Told by Sheila Hancock in *Ramblings of an Actress* (1987).

—— 1 ——

In 1969, Williamson was playing Hamlet in Boston when, suddenly, in the middle of a scene, he announced that he was giving up his acting career and walked off stage. After calming down, he then returned and carried on to general applause.

Recounted in Peter Hay, *Broadway Anecdotes* (1989).

—— 2 ——

In 1991, Williamson was playing in a play called *I Hate Hamlet* on Broadway. He clouted his co-star, Evan Handler, so hard with the flat blade of his sword that the man fled the stage. Earlier, Williamson had interrupted a scene between Handler and Jane Adams, telling them, 'Put some life into it! Use your head! Give it more life!'

Now, after the sword incident, Handler stormed out of the theatre, handing in his notice on the way. While the audience waited for the play to resume, Williamson turned to them and said, 'Well, should I sing?'

Reported in *The Independent on Sunday* (5 May 1991).

Gary WILMOT

(1956–) English entertainer.

—— 3 ——

Being interviewed by David Frost on TV-am, Wilmot was asked which comedian had influenced him most. 'Norman Wisdom,' he replied. 'Why him?' asked Frost. 'I think it must be because he's black,' replied Wilmot.

I noted this (4 January 1987), as I was also appearing on the programme.

Sir Harold WILSON

(1916–) Pipe-smoking (only in public) British Labour prime minister. Also wore glasses (not in public). Later created a life peer – Lord Wilson of Rievaulx – in 1983.

—— 4 ——

Throughout his years in public life, Wilson came out with a stream of homely sayings, in keeping with his pipe-smoking image. He advised people not to do their shopping when they were hungry. He described his Cabinet tactics thus: 'I see myself as a deep-lying half-back feeding the ball forward to the chaps who score the goals'. He also said, 'I'm an optimist, but I'm an optimist who takes his raincoat.'

Shopping remark untraced; football remark quoted in *The Observer* (29 December 1974); optimist remark quoted in *The Observer* (18 January 1976).

—— 5 ——

Making a speech, Wilson once asked rhetorically, 'Why do I emphasize the importance of the Royal Navy?' A voice from the crowd called out, 'Because you're in Chatham!'

Quoted in Allen Andrews, *Quotations for Speakers and Writers* (1969).

—— 6 ——

Interviewed around midnight on election night in 1964, Wilson was asked, 'Do you feel like a prime minister now?' He replied, 'Quite frankly, I feel like a drink.'

Quoted in *The Observer* Magazine (5 April 1992).

WILSON KEPPEL & BETTY

The fondly-remembered 'international comedy dance act', made up of Jack Wilson (1894–1970), Joe Keppel (1895–?) and several 'Bettys' after the original Betty Fox. Wilson and Keppel teamed up in the US in 1910 and made their first British appearance at the London Palladium in 1932. The two men wore fezzes and moustaches and the trio performed a comic Egyptian sand dance called 'Cleopatra's Nightmare'.

—— 1 ——

When they were to appear in Las Vegas they arrived at customs in New York. 'Where are you going?' they were asked. 'Las Vegas.' 'In the Nevada desert?' 'That's right.' 'What have you got in the bag?' And they said, 'Sand.' They were actually taking their own sand to Las Vegas.

> **As told by Ernie Wise on *Parkinson*, BBC TV, before 1975.**

Robb WILTON

(1881–1957) English comedian.

—— 2 ——

Towards the end of his life, Wilton was attending a funeral and declared: 'There's not much point going home really, is there?'

> **Told on BBC Radio *Quote...Unquote* (1991). Ned Sherrin, *Theatrical Anecdotes* (1991) has Lorenz Hart saying something similar about his Uncle Willie at his (Hart's) mother's funeral in 1943. As it happens, Hart himself died first.**

Godfrey WINN

(1908–71) English journalist.

—— 3 ——

Winn went to interview Bernard Braden and his wife, Barbara Kelly, in the early 1950s. He arrived bearing pencil and pad, and a square cardboard box which the Bradens' children suspected might contain something for them. They were to be disappointed. When the interview was over, Winn summoned a photographer and a make-up girl. The latter did her stuff and then opened the cardboard box, lifting out a toupee which she then placed on Winn's head.

> **Related by Bernard Braden in *The Kindness of Strangers* (1990). I can vouch for the likelihood of this story. In 1967, as researcher on a Granada TV programme called *X Plus Ten*, I entered a TV make-up room just as Winn's portable hairpiece (merely a quiff at the front by this time) was being delicately lowered into position.**

Bernie WINTERS

(1932–91) English comedian who was originally the funny half of a double act with his brother, Mike. Latterly, he appeared with a St Bernard dog called Schnorbitz.

—— 4 ——

Bernie and Mike were once playing the Glasgow Empire, in front of its awesome Scots audiences. Mike began by playing the clarinet and then was joined by Bernie. A voice in the audience exclaimed: 'My God, there's two of them!'

> **Re-told by Ernie Wise in *The Independent* (6 May 1991).**

Sir Donald WOLFIT

(1902–68) English actor-manager.

—— 5 ——

A gun did not go off or a sword was forgotten, so Wolfit got an actor to kick him to death, expiring with the cry, 'The boot was poisoned!'

> **Ned Sherrin, *Theatrical Anecdotes* (1991) describes this quite rightly as probably apocryphal. In fact, Gyles Brandreth in *Great Theatrical Disasters* (1982) (whence the story originates), admits he made the whole thing up. But compare the story about Osgood Perkins 10:7.**

Wee Georgie WOOD

(1895–1979) English music-hall comedian.

—— 6 ——

Wood, who was of boyish proportions, lived to a ripe old age. On one occasion, towards the end of his life, he hailed a taxi and said to the driver, 'Take me to the British Museum.' The driver looked alarmed at this and said, 'You're taking a bloody chance, aren't you?'

> **Told by Peter Jones on BBC Radio *Quote...Unquote* (1981). Joe Ging, who was curator of the National Museum Hall in Sunderland told me in a letter (8 May 1984) that Wood performed his museum's**

opening ceremony in July 1975. During his speech, Wood said, 'I was picked up at the Post House Hotel, Washington, by a taxi-driver from Sunderland. "Where are you going to, Mr Wood?" asked the taxi-driver. "I'm going to open a museum," I replied, proudly. To which he replied, "You're taking a bloody chance, aren't you?"' Joe Ging concedes that this was too good a story for Wood only to have used on one occasion.

Thomas WOODROOFFE

(1899–1978) English radio outside-broadcast commentator who committed the most famous broadcasting boob of all on the night of 20 May 1937 by appearing to be drunk and repeating the famous phrase 'The Fleet's lit up'.

—— 1 ——

The BBC took a kindly view of Woodrooffe's boob and, after a short suspension, it was clear that the incident had not put paid to Woodrooffe's broadcasting career. In 1938–9 he was the BBC's sole commentator for the FA Cup Final, the Grand National and the Derby. Commentating on the Cup Final, he declared in the closing minutes: 'If there's a goal scored now, I'll eat my hat.' There was, and he did.

Recounted in Asa Briggs, *History of Broadcasting in the United Kingdom* (Vol. 2, 1965). When war broke out, Woodrooffe returned to the Navy and did little broadcasting after 1939.

Peter WOODS

(1930–) English TV newsreader and reporter.

—— 2 ——

On one occasion, Woods appeared to be having considerable difficulty reading a news bulletin early in the evening on BBC2. It wasn't so much that his voice was going up and down but he was saying things like, 'And the latest trade figures show *an awfully big* trade gap . . .' After a while, he was replaced on the screen by Robin Day, who was about to do an interview and announced, 'We leave the newsroom . . . ah . . . earlier than expected.' Later, Woods was interviewed in the BBC bar and put it all down to 'trouble with his sinuses'.

From a sound recording of the incident, probably in the mid-1970s.

WRITERS

—— 3 ——

William Lisle Bowles (1762–1850) was the Vicar of Bremhill. 'The Vicar-poet was a thorough eccentric. Tuning his sheep bells in to thirds and fifths, he dressed as a druid and appeared at Stonehenge on the fourth of June. His absent-mindedness exceeded even [Thomas] Moore's; he engraved his own poems on the tombstones of parishioners, and on one occasion presented a friend with the Bible inscribed "with the author's compliments".'

From Terence de Vere White, *Tom Moore* (1977). Also in S. C. Hall's *A Book of Memories* (1871). Outside the time-scale of this book, but never mind.

—— 4 ——

A bright young thing met an author and said, 'I liked your book. Who wrote it for you?' The woman writer in question replied, 'I'm glad you enjoyed it. Who read it to you?'

Very anon. Told on BBC Radio *Quote...Unquote* (1979).

—— 5 ——

The 1929 film of *The Taming of the Shrew* with Douglas Fairbanks and Mary Pickford is traditionally supposed to have the on-screen credit: 'With additional dialogue by William Shakespeare'. Not quite, what it does say is 'with additional dialogue by Sam Taylor'.

See *Halliwell's Film Guide* (1987) for the inaccurate version. Compare the film *My Own Private Idaho* (1992) which *does* have the credit 'With additional dialogue by William Shakespeare' – legitimately, as it is a re-telling of the Prince Hal/Falstaff story using some of the dialogue from *Henry IV*.

Z

Pia ZADORA

(1956–) American film actress.

—— 1 ——

This diminutive, well-husbanded actress is said to have once played the title role in *The Diary of Anne Frank* – the stage dramatization of the actual plight of a Dutch Jewish family hiding from the Germans in the Second World War. So unimpressed with her performance was one audience that when the Nazi stormtroopers arrived to search for Anna, a cry was heard from the auditorium: 'She's in the attic . . . !'

Told, for example, by Irene Thomas on BBC Radio *Quote...Unquote* (1986). Ned Sherrin, *Theatrical Anecdotes* (1991) says: 'I asked Ms Zadora about this on breakfast television and she said she was happy to put the record straight. She had never acted off-Broadway and never played Anne Frank.'

INDEX

This index is to prominent names occurring in the anecdotes and in the background notes. It also provides a general guide to subjects and themes dealt with in the anecdotes. Names and key-words are listed strictly in letter-by-letter order. '55:7' indicates that the relevant anecdote is number 7 on page 55; '**9:1**', given in bold, indicates a main entry.

F

G

Y

Z

'I SAID IT MY WAY'

The Guinness Dictionary of
Humorous Misquotations

Colin Jarman

From the compiler of the bestselling *Guinness Dictionary of Poisonous Quotes* comes a unique collection of intentional and often witty reworkings of hundreds of well-known sayings, proverbs, catchphrases and quotations.

I Said it My Way provides a useful source for unusual and rarely anthologised quotations for speechwriters, broadcasters and journalists. It will appeal to everyone interested in the history and development of some of the world's most famous sayings and to anyone who revels in verbal dexterity and playful use of language.

The Guinness Dictionary of
Quotations for All Occasions

Gareth Sharpe

A quick and practical reference guide to useful quotations appropriate to a wider range of contexts, *The Guinness Dictionary of Quotations for All Occasions* is arranged thematically according to the purposes for which quotations can be used: from important family celebrations and festivals such as weddings, birthdays, Christmas and New Year, to messages of congratulations, good luck and consolation.

The quotations are drawn from a broad range of sources, including the utterances of statesmen and women past and present, writers, actors and musicians. They range from the light-hearted and humorous to the more profound and reflective. Here are words of wisdom from scholars and philosophers, messages of goodwill for the Christmas season, quips to enliven a wedding speech, one-liners to raise the spirits of those who are in hospital, words of sympathy, support and consolation, as well as words of welcome, apology and excuse. Whatever the words you are looking for, you will be sure to find them in *The Guinness Dictionary of Quotations for All Occasions*.

The Guinness Dictionary of
Yet More Poisonous Quotes
Colin Jarman

Hard on the heels of its forerunners *The Guinness Book of Poisonous Quotes* and *More Poisonous Quotes* comes *The Guinness Book of Yet More Poisonous Quotes*, in which compiler Colin Jarman presents a further collection of hard-hitting barbs.

Culled from ancient history to the present day and hurled at all manner of individuals and institutions, the insults in this anthology of absolute acrimony will amuse, entertain and equip you for disputatious discourse! The rattling retorts are gathered under subject matter for ease of reference and no mercy is shown – filmstars, authors, politicians, artists, sports personalities and royalty stand side by side in the firing line of wicked wit.

Praise for *Poisonous Quotes* and *More Poisonous Quotes*:
'A joy for cynical browsers.' *Yorkshire Post*
'All the best, and worst, put downs are here. Delicious!' *Mail on Sunday*
'It never fails to raise a chuckle.' *Manchester Evening News*

The Guinness Dictionary of
More Poisonous Quotes
Colin Jarman

Following the runaway success of *The Guinness Dictionary of Poisonous Quotes*,
Colin Jarman has compiled *More Poisonous Quotes* – a jarring journey through
still further verbal venom covering a myriad of subjects ranging from . . .

. . . ACTING TO ART . . .
'I got so sick of starry-eyed close-ups of Elizabeth Taylor that I could have gagged.'
Raymond Chandler

'Rossetti, dear Rossetti, I love your work
But you really were a bit of a jerk'
George MacBeth

. . . POP TO POLITICS . . .
'Bananarama are living proof that make-up works.'
Chesney Hawkes

'The US Presidency is a Tudor monarchy with telephones.'
Anthony Burgess

Bursting with barbed ballyhoo, cutting comments and acidic asides, *More
Poisonous Quotes* dishes the dirt on all the victims of vitriol, including the
politicians who battled it out in the 1992 UK General Election.

Read for reference or simply for entertainment, the cynical sniping is
guaranteed to offend.

The Guinness Dictionary of
Poisonous Quotes

Colin Jarman

Who did Thomas Carlyle refer to as 'a hoary-headed and toothless baboon'?
What does Joan Rivers think of Madonna's armpits? Who advised Prince
Philip to 'find an ordinary wife'?

The Guinness Dictionary of Poisonous Quotes is an anthology of over 1500
cocksure criticisms, waggish witticisms and verbal vulgarities unleashed on
unsuspecting victims over the years.

Gore Vidal: 'Capote should be heard, not read'
Peter Fleming on the Shakespeare Memorial Theatre: 'A courageous attempt
to disguise a gasworks as a racquets court'
Mel Brooks: 'If Hollywood keeps gearing movie after movie to teenagers, next
year's Oscars will develop acne'
Victor Hugo: 'Waterloo was a battle of the first rank won by a captain of the
second'
Woody Allen: 'In California they don't throw their garbage away – they make
it into TV shows'

Actors, politicians, newspaper magnates, architects, writers and singers . . .
no-one is safe from the venom of the poisonous quote.